GLOBAL COMMUNICATION

THOMAS L. MCPHAIL

GLOBAL COMMUNICATION

THEORIES, STAKEHOLDERS, AND TRENDS

Fourth Edition

WILEY Blackwell

This fourth edition first published 2014
© 2014 John Wiley & Sons, Inc

Edition History: Allyn & Bacon (1e, 2002); Blackwell Publishing Ltd
(2e, 2006 and 3e, 2010)

Registered Office
John Wiley & Sons Ltd, The Atrium, Southern Gate, Chichester, West Sussex,
PO19 8SQ, UK

Editorial Offices
350 Main Street, Malden, MA 02148–5020, USA
9600 Garsington Road, Oxford, OX4 2DQ, UK
The Atrium, Southern Gate, Chichester, West Sussex, PO19 8SQ, UK

For details of our global editorial offices, for customer services, and for information
about how to apply for permission to reuse the copyright material in this book
please see our website at www.wiley.com/wiley-blackwell.

The right of Thomas L. McPhail to be identified as the author of this work has been
asserted in accordance with the UK Copyright, Designs and Patents Act 1988.

Wiley also publishes its books in a variety of electronic formats. Some content that
appears in print may not be available in electronic books.

Designations used by companies to distinguish their products are often claimed as
trademarks. All brand names and product names used in this book are trade names,
service marks, trademarks or registered trademarks of their respective owners. The
publisher is not associated with any product or vendor mentioned in this book.

Limit of Liability/Disclaimer of Warranty: While the publisher and author(s) have
used their best efforts in preparing this book, they make no representations or
warranties with respect to the accuracy or completeness of the contents of this book
and specifically disclaim any implied warranties of merchantability or fitness for a
particular purpose. It is sold on the understanding that the publisher is not engaged
in rendering professional services and neither the publisher nor the author shall be
liable for damages arising herefrom. If professional advice or other expert assistance
is required, the services of a competent professional should be sought.

Library of Congress Cataloging-in-Publication data is available for this book.

9781118622025 (paperback)

A catalogue record for this book is available from the British Library.

Cover design by Cyan Design

Set in 10/12pt Minion by SPi Publisher Services, Pondicherry, India
Printed in Singapore by C.O.S. Printers Pte Ltd

4   2015

Contents

Contributors

Junhao Hong received a PhD in communication from University of Texas at Austin in 1995. He is a professor at the Department of Communication, State University of New York at Buffalo. He is also an associate in research at the Fairbank Center for Chinese Studies, Harvard University, and a senior fellow at the Communication for Sustainable Social Change Center at the University of Massachusetts Amherst. He has served as president of the Chinese Communication Association (CCA) and president of the United Societies of Chinese Studies (USCS). His research areas include international communication, media and society, and the impact of new communication/information technology, with a focus on China and Asia. He has published and edited several books, and has published more than 120 research articles in various journals and book volumes.

Lawrence Pintak is Founding Dean of the Edward R. Murrow College of Communication at Washington State University. Previously, he was Director of the Kamal Adham Center for Journalism Training and Research at The American University in Cairo and publisher and co-editor of the online journal *Arab Media and Society*. He is the author of *The New Arab Journalist: Mission and Identity in a Time of Change* (I. B. Tauris, 2010), and several other books about the media and international affairs. A former CBS News Middle East correspondent, he has contributed to many of the world's leading news organizations in his 30-year career in journalism on four continents. His work regularly appears in in the *New York Times*, the *International Herald Tribune*, *Columbia Journalism Review* online, *Daily Star* (Beirut), *Arab News*, and a variety of publications around the world.

Alexa Robertson is Associate Professor at the Department of Media Studies (IMS), Stockholm University, Sweden. A historian by training, she moved to IMS after many years at the Department of Political Science, where she earned her PhD. Robertson does research and teaches on the political role of the media under globalization, and the role of culture in politics. She recently completed a book entitled *Media and Politics in a Globalized World* which, like her 2010 book *Mediated Cosmopolitanism: The World of Television News*, will be published by Polity. In *Global News: Reporting Conflicts and Cosmopolitanism* (Peter Lang, forthcoming), she compares reporting on three channels often referred to as "counter-hegemonic" (Al Jazeera English, Russia Today, and Chinese CCTV) with four "Western" channels (CNN International, BBC World, Deutsche Welle, and Euronews) to see whether they do indeed report the world differently. The thread running throughout is the question of how media representation is conceived and effected in a world of diversity and transborder flows. Her studies of media coverage of the Arab uprisings have been published in the *International Journal of Press/Politics* and *New Global Studies*.

Nancy Snow is Professor of Communications at California State University, Fullerton and Adjunct Professor of Public Diplomacy in the Annenberg School at the University of Southern California. She is the author or co-editor of eight books, including the *Routledge Handbook of Public Diplomacy*, *Propaganda, Inc.*, and *Information War*. She has taught public diplomacy at Tsinghua University in Beijing, Sophia University in Tokyo, and the Interdisciplinary Center's Lauder School of Government, Diplomacy and Strategy in Herzliya, Israel. A two-time Fulbright recipient (Germany, Japan) and Abe Fellow with the Social Science Research Council, she holds lifetime memberships with the Public Diplomacy Alumni Association, the Public Diplomacy Council at George Washington University, and the Fulbright Association.

Preface

After September 11, 2001 the peaceful satisfaction of many nations that began with the end of the Cold War and the demise of communism came to an early and abrupt end, foreshadowing the rise of a new enemy – global terrorism. Along with this new elusive enemy came new wars and an increase in global communication, primarily war coverage. From embedded journalists with videophones covering the wars, to new media outlets, such as Al Jazeera, Al-Arabiyya, and Al-Hurra, to photos being sent home and around the world on the Internet, the role and scope of international media shifted dramatically. This fourth edition captures the major aspects of this new and in many cases disturbing era, updates the materials contained in earlier editions, and contains updated information on the importance of global public diplomacy (Chapter 4), the European scene (Chapter 9), the volatile Arabic media scene (Chapter 13), and China/Asia (Chapter 14).

This book portrays international communication from differing perspectives – it examines a number of major trends, stakeholders, and global activities, while promoting no particular philosophical or ideological school, whether of the left or the right. Rather, it seeks to provide information about major international trends of a theoretical, cultural, economic, public policy, or foreign relations nature. Moreover, in order to provide a framework for understanding the interconnection between the international communication environment and the global economy, *Global Communication* documents major historical events that connect the two. It also highlights communication industry mergers and acquisitions which now frequently transcend national boundaries.

Just as the printing press and the assembly line were necessary events for the industrial revolution, so also the Internet and modern communication technologies are essential for the international communication revolution. This book traces the influence and roles of major global communication technologies such as satellites, videophones, mobile devices, and personal computers. Collectively, these and other technologies have transformed the international communication environment, making possible the advent of global media systems such as CNN (Cable News Network), MTV (Music Television), the BBC (British Broadcasting Corporation), and the Internet itself.

As part of the background needed to examine global media and related sectors, it is important to understand the history of the international communication debate, which developed initially within the halls of the United Nations Educational, Scientific and Cultural Organization (UNESCO). This debate about the New World Information and Communication Order (NWICO) is important because it identified two significantly different philosophies, each supported by a different set of scholars and nations. Because the debate reflects much of the concern about the philosophical, cultural, and artistic threats that are of paramount concern to many nation-states, the phenomenon of "electronic colonialism" – the impact and influence of music, Hollywood feature films, and syndicated television series, plus other media from industrial nations – is also detailed. One large and vocal group supports a free press perspective without regard to its economic and cultural consequences; the other group supports a more interventionist approach, calling on governments and other organizations to be concerned with essentially non-commercial dimensions of the international communication environment. Because of the roles each group played, the policy positions, agencies, and leaders on both sides of the debate are examined extensively. Several new major global stakeholders, including the significant role of the global advertising industry, are also detailed.

A second major theme of the book concerns the economic implications of international communication. Although the economies of the international communications industries cannot be separated from governmental and cultural policy debates, it is important to recognize that most communication organizations are independent, active, commercial, and aggressive players in the international communication arena. They have global influence and they affect the communication environment both at home and abroad. As such, attention is also given to communication enterprises such as the Hollywood feature film industry; media giants such as Disney, Time Warner, Viacom, Bertelsmann, Sony, and News Corporation; as well as the Internet, international wire services such as the Associated Press and Thomson Reuters, and several multinational advertising agencies. As will be demonstrated, some of these organizations appear to be oblivious to the global policy debate and are willing to let the marketplace alone determine the winners and losers, whereas others are very concerned about the non-economic aspects of "trade" emerging in the international communication sector.

All major global multimedia conglomerates are based in the United States, Europe, and Japan. Most of the concern about cultural issues emanates from nations in Latin America, Africa, and Asia. Therefore, a world system theory (WST) perspective is outlined in Chapter 1 to decipher some of the structural cleavages in the international communication field. It approaches the nations of the world through an economic lens. In Chapter 1 electronic colonialism theory (ECT) is outlined and it basically views the world through a cultural lens. These two theories, WST and ECT, help unify the various stakeholders as well as identify their collective impact on globalization.

Any book about international communication would be deficient if it examined only one of these two major themes. A review focused solely on NWICO without mention of CNN or the BBC, for example, would ignore the contemporary reality and economic aspects of global communication. Similarly, a book that emphasized the Internet and other new communication options and opportunities to the exclusion of the philosophical debate would fail to provide the necessary historical and cultural background and perspectives. To a surprising extent, the end of the Cold War and the collapse of the Soviet Union have shifted the debate in favor of the trade-focused parties. Only by detailing major themes and examining their interrelationships can a student of international communication come to understand the complexities of the global communication scene and the implications of the rapid change in the global communication landscape that continues on a daily basis worldwide.

We should not underestimate the nature and depth of the transformation taking place in global communication. The era of the Enlightenment (c.1600–1800) contributed to the intellectual transformation of Western societies, and so today we are going through a similarly profound alteration in our societies, fueled by the major structural changes in global communication, primarily the Internet. Just as the major contributors to the Enlightenment era were Francis Bacon, John Locke, Adam Smith, Jean-Jacques Rousseau, Isaac Newton, Catherine the Great, and others, so also today we have a critical mass of change agents who are forming the intellectual nucleus to create a new type of society with their profound insights and innovations. People such as Marshall McLuhan, Bill Gates, Steve Jobs, Charles Saatchi, Tim Berners-Lee, Margaret Whitman, Carol Bartz, Mark Zuckerberg, Larry Page and Sergey Brin of Google, and others are collectively providing the intellectual architecture and means to transform and create a new information era. Hundreds more working in their homes, laboratories, or universities in various nations around the world have contributed to the ongoing revolution in international communication. Yet few of these individuals responsible for creating a new media framework or paradigm have truly understood the long-run ramifications of their contributions on the type of society we will have in 50 years' time. In all likelihood, our future society will be dramatically different from the industrial society of even a mere 70 years ago at the end of World War II.

It is important to keep in mind that this intellectual transformation is not limited to economics, politics, trade, or education; rather, it will affect all of these areas as well as transform our concept of self, community, and nation-state. Yet one major problem with this transformation is appearing already: this new society changed by the media is located only in select parts of the globe, primarily in those core nations that have already benefited from the previous industrial era. This overall intellectual transformation is occurring at the same time as a large number of poor nations are still attempting to come to grips with enormous social problems ranging from illiteracy, poverty, subjugation, famine, civil wars, and poor health, particularly HIV/AIDS. As we move forward into a new era transformed by global media, we might also consider dichotomies created by the reality of a relatively small cluster of nations with full access to the Internet, digital television, and wireless telephony, and at the other extreme billions of people on the other side of the "digital divide" who have yet to make a phone call, read a newspaper, or use a PC mouse. One cannot be certain how parts of a world so intrinsically linked to media will interact with the vast numbers of individuals who so far have lived without it; but we will be watching closely.

Acknowledgments

I would like to thank my friends who tested the materials and provided useful feedback and suggestions. I also want to thank Brenda McPhail for her assistance, patience, and feedback; and Rebecca and Ryan McPhail for keeping me abreast of the significance of new media, blogging, YouTube, MTV, and the latest in technologies, like the iPod and tablets. Jason Fisher undertook several duties in excellent fashion relating to this new edition. Finally, I want to thank my students, who survived earlier drafts of the new material.

1

Global Communication

Background

Introduction

The world of international communication has changed rapidly in recent years. Following World War II, global communication was dominated by the tensions arising from the Cold War, pitting the old Soviet Union against the United States and its allies. Much of the rhetoric, news space, face time, and concern dealt with some aspect of government control of mass communication, or the impact of governments and other entities on free speech, or the free flow of information or data across international borders. Likewise, much of international coverage on both sides of the Atlantic had an East/West tone, reflecting a communism versus democracy wedge. With the demise of the former Soviet Union and communism as a major global force, the factors underpinning international communication shifted dramatically. No longer did crises around the globe create major confrontations between two superpowers. What's more, the end of communism spelled the demise of the Soviets as enemies of the free press and the free flow of information. In many editors' and producers' opinions, it also spelled the end, ignoring, or at least downgrading the importance of foreign news coverage. That clearly changed for a while after September 11, 2001.

Today, the United States stands alone as the world's only superpower. While other economic entities, such as the European Union and parts of Asia, compete daily with the United States in the global marketplace, there is no large-scale foreign military threat to the United States. But today there are new enemies and threats out there. The Taliban, al-Qaeda, the Islamic jihad, suicide bombers, extremists, and a vast array of terrorist cells around the world have taken up new weapons to confront the Western nations. The new weapons are primarily low-tech: smartphones, netbooks, the Internet, social networking sites, video cameras, Twitter, Facebook, and other means. Improvised explosive devices (IEDs) have replaced the nuclear bomb scare of the Cold War era. This widespread terrorist phenomenon has again seen a modest editorial shift to greater coverage of international

Global Communication: Theories, Stakeholders, and Trends, Fourth Edition. Thomas L. McPhail.
© 2014 John Wiley & Sons, Inc. Published 2014 by John Wiley & Sons, Inc.

affairs. The "good guys versus bad guys" mentality has returned. Terrorists of many stripes are replacing communism as the evil force. The Middle East and other nations harboring and training extremists are the new Evil Empire.

International News

Why is international news important? Essentially we are experiencing an expanding global economy where events in foreign lands impact us on a daily basis. Examples are everywhere. A volcano in a Nordic country spreads choking ash over most of Europe; a revolution in the Middle East impacts the price of gas around the globe; a banking disaster in the United States or Greece shakes the stock markets around the world.

Yet the problem is that though we know the global economy is expanding, the amount of international news coverage overall, particularly in the United States, is declining. Consider that the United States still exerts substantial influence around the world via both hard and soft power. This in turn should translate into a citizenry that is well informed about both foreign events and foreign policy decisions.

This decline is significant when viewed through the prism of how the media contribute to the promotion and expansion of the democratic process both here and abroad. Given this metric the overall decline seems to be accompanied by a parallel decline in support for both foreign aid as well as the promotion of transparent and open democracies around the globe. For example, the Nordic countries have a more internationally focused press and give the highest amount of foreign aid while the United States now ranks eighteenth in terms of per capita giving. Foreign aid for humanitarian efforts is not a major policy issue for the average American, and with decreasing foreign news coverage this downward trend is likely to continue.

Looking back, the golden age of international news coverage lasted from the 1940s to the end of the 1980s. A major boost during this era was the introduction of satellite broadcasting. The three main reasons for the decline are: first, the end of the Cold War and the implosion of the old Soviet Union (editors lost their "good guys versus bad guys" frame); second, the decline of newspaper circulation and revenues (part of this was the result of alternative Internet-based information sources of all types, and the expensive costs of running foreign bureaus); and, third, the global economic crisis of the last decade. Collectively they forced almost all for-profit media outlets to lose enthusiasm for foreign stories, and foreign bureaus were reduced.

Yet despite all of the compelling reasons for more, not less, international news, this coverage continues to decline: the reality is that the proportion of international news across the media is at an all-time low, down from 30 percent 30 or 40 years ago to about 14 percent today. It is as if the global interconnectivity has been cut in half, where the reality is that it has doubled. The interconnectivity has been driven by factors such as the expansion of the global economy, the spread of cable and satellites, along with growing access to the Internet.

A paper presented at the 2012 annual conference of the Association for Education in Journalism and Mass Communication by Katherine Bradshaw, James Foust, Joseph Bernt, and Brian Krol entitled "Domestic, International, and Foreign News Content on ABC, CBS, and NBC Network News from 1971 to 2007" makes the point that "viewers saw far fewer stories about the rest of the world in the three most recent years sampled 1995, 2001, 2007."[1] All three years are in the post-Cold War era. But in their study, which included 1989 (the last year of the Cold War), there were 342 foreign stories on the three major networks compared to only 68 in 2007.[2] Clearly editors and producers across the media spectrum are showing less interest in foreign news. They see foreign news as expensive in an era of cutbacks. In a lecture, Alisa Miller, head of Public Radio International, explained how in today's media environment, international stories and news have declined: "From a decrease in foreign news bureaus to the prevalence of recycled stories, the news map of our current landscape is both dangerously one-sided and scandalously negligent in its management of the global village."[3] Miller documents the startling statistics about the state of international news coverage in the United States and the same is true in several other places.

Part of the larger problem is the turmoil and uncertainty created by the online phenomena and opportunity for others to provide information, formally or informally. Consider a report in October 2012 by the Reuters Institute for the Study of Journalism:

> even after more than a decade of often dramatic turmoil in the media sector, we are only at the beginning of a longer transitional period. Today, inherited forms of media, especially linear television, still dominate media use, attract a large proportion of advertising, and support the majority of content creation-especially when it comes to news. All of this is likely to change, with profound implications for media as we know them.[4]

During the 1990s, *Time* magazine, the *New York Times*, and network newscasts had been replacing their foreign bureaus and international coverage with a parochial domestic agenda. The terrorism and its followers have put international news back in prime time. In addition to the various government investigations into issues like weapons of mass destruction (WMD), the 9/11 Commission, the Abu Ghraib and Guantanamo Bay prison scandals, war crimes, and public safety have led to a new global agenda and media focus.

International communication refers to the cultural, economic, political, social, and technical analysis of communication and media patterns and effects across and between nation-states. International communication focuses more on global aspects of media and communication systems and technologies and, as a result, less on local or even national aspects or issues. Since the 1990s, this global focus or prism through which interactions are viewed or analyzed has been altered substantially by two related events. The first is the end of the Cold War and the sweeping changes this has brought; this includes political realignments across Europe. The second is increasing global interdependence, which is a fixture of the expanding global economy. The global economic recession demonstrated the interdependence of economies big (like the United States), and small (like Iceland). But this interdependence has more than an economic orientation; it also has a cultural dimension. This cultural dimension, in turn, has three important traits:

1 How much foreign content is contained, absorbed, or assimilated within the cultural domain?
2 How is this foreign content being transmitted (e.g., by books, movies, music, DVDs, television, commercials, mobile appliances, or the Internet)?
3 How are domestic or indigenous cultures, including language, being impacted by this foreign content?

These aspects, issues, and questions are what this book is about. *Global Communication* highlights an international or global approach to the broad range of components that collectively make up the discipline of international communication. Because "we live in an era of new cultural conditions that are characterized by faster adoption and assimilation of foreign cultural products than ever before,"[5] this book investigates in some detail who and where these cultural products are coming from and why, and addresses issues and concerns about their impact in foreign lands and on foreign minds.

Historically, the US government has orchestrated international communication policy and the many activities relating to transborder communication activities. During the 1950s and 1960s, the US State Department, the Central Intelligence Agency (CIA), the National Security Council, and the Pentagon played central roles within international organizations to promote policies to suit Cold War agendas and objectives. This behavior was evident at a number of international conferences, but it was particularly clear in the US position regarding the New World Information and Communication Order (NWICO). Ultimately, the hostile rhetoric became so intense that the United States (under President Reagan) withdrew from the United Nations Educational, Scientific and Cultural Organization (UNESCO) in the 1980s. The United States remained outside UNESCO until 2004 and left again in 2012. The United Kingdom withdrew as well and has since returned.

When the Soviet Union disintegrated in the early 1990s, the counterpoint to much of the US rhetoric and foreign policy, whether overt or covert, disappeared. The old rationales – Cold War rhetoric, concern about communism, and fear of nuclear destruction – became less prominent in the new environment of openness and cooperation with Eastern Europe, as well as Russia. Foreign trade replaced concern about foreign media initiatives.

Latin American Media

Latin American media are significantly different from media markets in America and Europe. Several countries in Latin America, such as Argentina, Brazil, Chile, Colombia, and Peru have experienced political, economic, and social turmoil since the end of World War II. Some other nations continue to be controlled by dictators with military backing. Given this environment, the radio and television industries in these nations tend to be either government-owned and government-controlled or heavily regulated. In a few cases powerful domestic media conglomerates are controlled by wealthy families, such as Televisa in Mexico or Grupo Globo in Brazil. In other Latin American nations, the independent print press frequently is allied with the political and religious elites. There is little investigative journalism since both the state-owned or commercial media do not favor it and several investigative reporters have wound up dead. Although Latin American markets are substantial in terms of population and growing consumer base, they are still relatively underdeveloped compared to their North American and European counterparts, but that is changing. Sallie Hughes and Chappell Lawson discuss the obstacles which Latin American media confront on a frequent basis. They identify

> five general barriers to the creation of independent, pluralistic, and assertive media systems in the region: (a) violence against journalists encouraged by a generalized weakness in the rule of law; (b) holdover authoritarian laws and policies that chill assertive reporting; (c) oligarchic ownership of television, the region's dominant medium; (d) the spottiness of professional journalistic norms; (e) the limited reach of print media, community-based broadcasters, and new communication technologies.[6]

Despite these structural issues, the Latin American environment is changing in terms of governments and mass communication. Many governments moved to a more open and democratic way of attempting to improve overall social and economic conditions for the populace. In telecommunications and mass media systems, there was a noticeable liberalization, deregulation, and privatization as reform legislation was passed in many Latin American nations. The growing increases in literacy, access to the Internet, and cheaper satellite dishes have collectively moved the debate over media's role in society. Several Latin American countries are clearly at a crossroads; they must decide whether they will follow this new neoliberal path, including broader ownership of the media, or revert to the historical tendency of military coups, government control and ownership, favoritism to elite families, and heavy censorship.

Despite the uneasy balance between old and new, the Latin American market is characterized by two significant phenomena. First, by virtue of the domination of the Spanish language (with the exception of Brazil, where Portuguese is spoken), Latin America has not been as readily inundated with US television shows or films, which carry English-language soundtracks. In contrast, English-speaking nations such as Canada, Australia, and the United Kingdom were easy international markets for, first, Hollywood feature films, and then US television programs, followed by music. This language difference led to a second important Latin American media phenomenon. Because these countries were forced to produce their own programming, they created an interesting and successful genre known as the telenovela. Telenovelas are Spanish soap operas that are extremely popular from Mexico to the tip of South America. They have been successful enough to be exported to Spain, Russia, Cuba, Puerto Rico, and many other non-English-speaking European countries, as well as Florida, Texas, and California. Many of the leading telenovela actors and actresses are national celebrities, like soccer stars, in the various regions of Latin America. The export market for telenovelas is expanding rapidly because they cost much less to produce than their Hollywood and New York counterparts.

On the feature film front, the scene is not as encouraging. Over 60 percent of the theater screens across Latin America regularly show Hollywood films. In Latin America there are few film houses or even nations that can mount and finance blockbuster films to rival Hollywood.

Another difference between North America and Latin America is the role and success of newspapers. In North America, many newspapers have folded over the last decade, and single-newspaper cities are the norm rather than the exception. By contrast, Latin American newspapers are still a substantially growing market, with over 1,000 newspapers in circulation and readership, on a daily basis, in excess of 100 million. Because of the high circulation figures, newspaper advertising is competitive with radio and television, making it a challenge for start-up private stations to succeed. Finally, because newspapers are privately owned, the publishers and editors generally support the movement toward greater democratization as well as government reforms to privatize the communication sector.

Left-Wing Connection: Latin America

In the postwar era, Latin America displayed a unique joint interest in labor unions, priests and nuns pursuing liberation theology as they sought Marxist or left-wing solutions to deal with corrupt regimes, many of which had military connections. Ideological fervor and rhetoric spread across Latin America as unions, clergy, and academics sought to tap the discontent of the peasants to mobilize support for economic and political change. For the most part, their efforts failed, the prime exceptions being Cuba, now Venezuela, and likely El Salvador and Chile. There were occasional major confrontations, such as the uprising in Chiapas, Mexico. In this revolt, the rebels went so far as to exclude the major Mexican broadcaster, Televisa, from their various press conferences. Latin American academics were particularly critical of North American models, such as open markets, free enterprise, private ownership, and advertising-supported media. They frequently attacked the violence of Hollywood feature films or the wasteland of television shows ranging from *The Simpsons*, to *Baywatch*, to reality shows, to MTV videos. They regarded American junk culture with the same disdain as they did American junk food.

With the demise of Marxism and the end of the Cold War, these same Latin American groups have lost steam and credibility. Labor unions are becoming isolated as democratization begins to take hold in several nations, along with greater economic prosperity. Leftist academics are finding fewer opportunities to promote anti-US media criticism as liberalization, privatization, and deregulation take hold across the communication sectors. Latin American academics tend to write flourishing and lengthy essays critical of American culture with little, if any, empirical data to support their assertions. Today, change is bringing greater media choice, more advertising, less government ownership, and reduced regulatory control of electronic media across Latin America.

The roles of media and culture, together with their impact on economic growth in Latin America, have been demonstrated in the literature. Cultural change and economic change are linked, but as David Holman points out, "the 'McDonaldisation' of all societies is possibly inevitable, but it is possible to eat McDonald burgers, and to wear jeans, without losing any of the most cherished aspects of the national culture."[7] Yet historically Latin American communication scholars have been among the most critical of the United States, even anti-United States, in their writings. The vast majority work from a Marxist platform, which is now stale and suspect with the end of the Cold War. Yet some continue their diatribes, not appreciating how substantially the global communication scene has changed.

What follows is a dramatic example of how the Cold War atmosphere framed media activities in relation to Washington and a Latin American nation, in this case Chile.

Chile–US Government Media Interaction

The 1973 military coup in Chile during the Cold War provides an example of the US government's concern, influence, and backstage role in the US media in dealing with foreign events. In this case, as in others, it is important to realize that frequently the US press corps has little background knowledge, local information or sources, cultural awareness, or even native language skills in preparation for breaking foreign stories. In the past, this weakness was frequently addressed by willing and well-trained US embassy staffers who provided background briefings to visiting US journalists in order to furnish them with "off the record" information and to help them establish meetings and interviews. The information generally was selected to frame, support, and promote US position and foreign policy objectives abroad. Although there is nothing intrinsically wrong with this practice, problems develop when journalists write their stories or file their video clips without acknowledging the substantial influence or assistance of US embassy personnel.

From 1970 to 1973, the US government sought to assist in the overthrow of Chile's democratically elected leftist government. The United States was hostile to Chilean president Salvador Allende, whom US President Richard Nixon had labeled a communist threat. According to the US State Department, Allende had to be removed or he might set an example, and communism spread across South America. When the Chilean military seized power in September 1973, the US government supported General Augusto Pinochet, despite the fact that he had been associated with many nefarious crimes, including supporting Chilean death squads. Pinochet subsequently ruled Chile for 17 years.

The specific role of the CIA cannot be detailed, but it is instructive to examine its relationship with the US media in Chile. Prior to and during the revolution, the CIA directed its Chilean station chief to engage in propaganda. He was to spread misinformation when it suited US objectives. According to the *New York Times*:

> The CIA's propaganda efforts included special intelligence and "inside" briefings given to the US journalist … Particularly noteworthy in this connection is the *Time* cover story which owed a great deal to written materials provided by the CIA. [Moreover,] CIA briefings in Washington changed the basic thrust of the story in the final stages, according to another *Time* correspondent.[8]

The result of this cosy relationship between US foreign affairs officials and foreign correspondents was a *Time* magazine cover story openly calling for an invasion of Chile to thwart the Marxist president and to stop the spread of communism throughout South America. During this era *Time* was a cheerleader for stopping leftists by any means.

The point of this example is not to debate the role of the CIA in ultimately assisting in the overthrow of a democratically elected leader, but rather to focus on the role of foreign correspondents during the height of the Cold War. The US State Department, Department of Defense, and CIA all actively courted US foreign correspondents. The foreign correspondents in turn were to varying degrees willing to accept advice, leads, and in some cases copy from US embassies around the world. This situation was particularly true in countries where English-speaking US journalists did not speak the native language. In these cases, embassy staff and CIA operatives had enormous clout and access. They knew which locals spoke English and were sympathetic to the US position. American embassies set up media interviews and assisted journalists with logistics and acquisition of compatible equipment and other necessities for gathering pro-United States news in foreign venues.

For over a decade, without the *raison d'être* of the Cold War and the anti-communist fervor that once dominated the agenda and mindset at the US State Department and its network of foreign embassies, CIA operatives have been marginalized and replaced by trade representatives. US ambassadors and their staffs courted economists, investors, and the business community. Journalists no longer received priority access or assistance. Indeed, unless journalists are reporting on successful business ventures by US investors or corporations, they have difficulty getting their phone calls returned.

In the post-Cold War era, US embassies focused on trade and the provision of the organizational and logistical work necessary for US corporations to expand exports in these countries or regions. Senior embassy personnel spent the majority of their time seeking out investment opportunities, organizing trade fairs, or identifying new export markets while nurturing existing ones. Within the new reality of US embassy culture and foreign policy there is now a shared emphasis. The business press now shares media attention with security, terror, or war issues. Some US journalists abroad deal with foreign policy and terrorism while others still look at foreign profits, mergers, and acquisitions in the post-Cold War environment.

This book looks at global media; global communication technologies such as the Internet; global advertising; multimedia organizations; European, Middle Eastern, and Asian media; and global events from post-Cold War and 9/11 vantage points. But some historical themes of concern continue to shape the scope and impact of global communication. These themes are best understood by examining where, why, and in what context NWICO emerged. But before we discuss NWICO, we need to note that, from a historical perspective, the role and invention of the telegraph in the mid-nineteenth century had profound consequences for international communication. This new technology resulted in a paradigm shift from national to international communication.[9] It resulted in information becoming a commodity, particularly for the expanding print press and telegraph traffic. Finally, it also fostered a new breed of journalists – the war correspondent.

History of the War Correspondent

Prior to the Crimean War (1853–6) there had been many wars. What separates the Crimean War from the others is the impressive fact that it was the first to be covered by a foreign correspondent. For example an earlier war of 1812, fought by Canada and Great Britain against the United States, ended in 1815 with the Treaty of Ghent, with Canada and Great Britain as the victors. The treaty was signed in Europe in December 1814, but this agreement did not reach North America until February 1815. During the Crimean War, however, with the newly invented telegraph, it was possible for reporters to send daily dispatches. The new technology of the telegraph had been patented in Europe by Charles Wheatstone in 1838.

The background to the war was a dispute between Russia and France, under Napoleon, over control of the Middle East. The British also had a vested interest in the conflict since they controlled the seas and trade routes, and aspired to continue their colonial expansion in the Middle East. The Russians lost the Crimean War under the Treaty of Paris. Following this, they pulled back from their global expansionist goals. They soon sold Alaska in 1867 to the United States for $7.2 million.

William Harold Russell was the first foreign war correspondent for the London-based *Times*, which was founded in 1785 and is now controlled by News Corp. Three interesting factors emerged from his coverage. First, Florence Nightingale, the legendary nursing pioneer, complained to the British press about how poorly British war casualties were being treated, and about the horrific medical conditions compared to the excellent French facilities. The coverage in the *Times* eventually led to the dismissal of the cabinet minister responsible for the conduct of the war. Second, Queen Victoria of Britain called for a Royal Commission on Health and War (1856–7), but Nightingale was not appointed to the commission because only males were eligible. Third, the impact of the *Times* coverage was so important and explosive that the number of journalists assigned to cover the US Civil War (1861–5) skyrocketed. The London *Times* circulation nearly doubled. In the United States, with over half a million deaths, the pictures and accounts were major copy for the infant print press across both North and South. Several foreign correspondents from Europe also covered the Civil War. For example, British reporters supported the slavery-afflicted South to protect the cheap source of cotton for British factories. Finally, the massive circulation increases also fueled the demand for greater literacy so that many more people could read the war coverage in the newspapers.

New World Information and Communication Order (NWICO)

The foregoing examples are indicative of some of the major issues in international communication. In the past, much of this debate focused on the New World Information and Communication Order. NWICO dominated the international communication agenda for decades. It represents:

1 an evolutionary process seeking a more just and equitable balance in the flow and content of information;

2 a right to national self-determination of domestic communication policies; and

3 at the international level, a two-way information flow reflecting more accurately the aspirations and activities of less developed countries (LDCs).[10]

Despite the fact that some proponents still champion this vision, many believe that NWICO can no longer be taken seriously. Even UNESCO, where much of the debate took place, has abandoned it. Yet NWICO may be born again because of the deep divisions which emerged from the World Summit on the Information Society (WSIS). WSIS is covered in more detail later in this book.

An appreciation of its basic premises and of the issues that divided nations remains an important and relevant element in a full understanding of the different views about international communication. Not everyone views the global media flows and control over aspects of the communication scene the same way.

NWICO's ultimate goal was a restructured system of media and telecommunication priorities in order for LDCs to obtain greater influence over their media, information, economic, cultural, and political systems. For LDCs, or peripheral nations, the current world communication system is an outgrowth of prior colonial patterns reflecting commercial and market imperatives.[11] NWICO was promoted as a way to remove this vestige of colonial control. However, Western governments and news organizations vigorously opposed any such plan, fearing it would bring increased government interference with the press, thus ultimately reducing market share and profitability.

In seeking to gain a more balanced flow of information, peripheral regions postulate potential mechanisms that clash with strongly held journalistic traditions and practices in the West. From time to time they called for government control of the media, limited reporter access to events, journalistic codes of ethics, licensing of reporters, and taxation of the broadcast spectrum – all ideas that Western journalists, media owners, and policymakers abhor. Even the call for a "balanced flow" of information, which was approved by UNESCO in the 1970s, was criticized as interference with free press, free flow, and free market mechanisms. Only an open and free flow of information is viewed as being fully consistent with the goals of a truly free press. Yet the critics maintain that the free flow is really a one-way flow – from core nations to other regions of the world, with little or no reciprocity.

Many critics attack the Western press as if it were a monolithic, rational system. They fail to realize that what eventually winds up in Western newspapers, on radio, or on television is determined by a complex, and not entirely consistent, process of decision-making. As Mort Rosenblum explains:

> Correspondents play an important part in selection by determining what to cover in the first place. But most of the process is in the hands of editors at different stages. These are the gatekeepers. Each medium and each type of correspondent operates in a different fashion, but the principle is the same. A correspondent's dispatch first goes to one gatekeeper and then what emerges – if anything – goes on to others. All along the way; the original dispatch may be shortened, lengthened, rewritten, or thrown away entirely. This series of editors determines what is to be eventually shared with the public; and they decide what the American people may never know.[12]

This is an important point. What people in Western or core societies learn about peripheral regions is meager and the result of several gatekeepers. What makes this successive diminution of information about poor nations so paradoxical is that, both technically and theoretically, there is more international information available today than ever before. The Internet, satellites, fax machines, video discs, portable computers, radio, smartphones, and direct long-distance dialing have collectively replaced the slow and cumbersome dispatches of the past.

But practically, the story is quite different. There are several contributing factors. The major one is simply the high cost of international reporting. The estimated cost to place and equip a single foreign correspondent abroad for one year is $300,000. This has led to a net reduction in the number of reporters that wire services, networks, or individual papers that are willing to post abroad. Second, restrictions ranging from censorship and outright bans to withholding critical interviews past filing time, threats of physical abuse unless proper slants are evident, jailing, or even death all serve to reduce or limit the amount of available copy. Third, the high turnover of foreign correspondents and the pack journalism phenomenon make editors and publishers reluctant to spend time and money to significantly increase foreign coverage. Fourth, the trend toward "parachute journalism," in which large numbers of foreign correspondents, assorted paparazzi, and belligerent camera crews descend by the planeload on international scenes of conflict or natural disasters, tends to trivialize or sensationalize events that are far more complex than a 30-second clip or a few paragraphs can capture. Finally, the lack of public concern, as reflected in the trend toward light, fluffy, gossipy, and trendy journalism, focusing on celebrities or trivia, reduces the incentive for editors to provide in-depth and continuous coverage of a broad range of foreign issues and conflicts. On the print side, in the United States the *New Yorker* magazine, the *New York Times*, the *Wall Street Journal*, the *Economist*, and the *Washington Post* are clear exceptions.

The reason for this shift in newspapers has been a mix of accounting and fiscal concerns related directly to declining circulation numbers, a movement toward local community journalism, and the Internet taking away readers and advertisers as well. The policies of the media are increasingly governed by marketing experts, who make news decisions to reflect focus-group results, rather than by editors. Clearly, the exceptional and unusual still dominate what is reported. In-depth front-page pieces on population, education, health care, environment, and other development successes are still rare. Rosenblum, in talking about "the System," makes this point:

> Foreign correspondents do often seem to be mad as loons, waiting on some source for hours in the rain so they can write a dispatch which might well end up blotting spilled coffee on an editorial desk back home. Editors seem madder still, suffering hypertension over whether their own man reached some obscure capital in time to duplicate stories available to them by other means. And their combined effort, when it reaches breakfast tables and living rooms across the United States, often appears to be supercilious and sloppy.[13]

This system is geared as much to amuse and divert as it is to inform, and it responds inadequately when it is suddenly called upon to explain something as complex and menacing as a dollar collapse or a war in Asia. Yet it is the American citizen's only alternative to ignorance about the world.

> Because of the system – and in spite of it – most Americans are out of touch with events that directly affect their lives. When crisis impends, they are not warned. When it strikes, they are not prepared. They know little about decisions taken on their behalf which lessen their earnings, restrict their freedoms and threaten their security.[14]

Why is this the case? What are the implications? In an era of so much information, why is there so little useful information? As this book describes in detail, international news coverage is going to change. The question is whether it will improve in accuracy, quantity, and quality, or whether gatekeepers will restrict or heavily censor news. That is why awareness of global media issues and positions is central to understanding international communication. That is also why this book has specific chapters on the Middle East and China, since they are important players in what Marshall McLuhan labeled the "global village."

Two major theoretical outlooks or theories will assist in organizing and understanding the events, trends, and major stakeholders in the rapidly changing field of international communication. They are electronic colonialism and world system theories. Both are described in the following section, and then their interrelationships are outlined. In addition, throughout *Global Communication* certain examples of the media scene or global operations as they reflect and apply to these underlying two theories are commented on.

Electronic Colonialism Theory

Traditionally, mass media research looks either at select micro issues, such as agenda-setting, ownership, or violence, or at a specific medium, such as print, radio, television, or the Internet. Only occasionally do scholars examine the macro aspects of the overall mass communication system. Harold Innis, Marshall McLuhan, Armand Mattelart, Jacques Ellul, Ben Bagdikian, and George Barnett are representative of the macro research school. Electronic colonialism theory reflects much of the current global concerns, particularly with reference to culture, and is a good theoretical concept with which to begin. It provides a theoretical frame for examining the stakeholders and transnational issues.

Global Colonialism

Over the course of history, there have been only a few major successful trends in empire-building. The first era was characterized by military conquests. These occurred during the Greco-Roman period and witnessed the expansion of the Roman Empire throughout most of what is modern Europe, including North Africa. This early era is labeled military colonialism.

The militant Christianity of the Crusades during the Middle Ages represented the second era. The Crusades, with the Catholic pope as patron, sought to control territory from Europe, across northern Africa, to the Middle East. Beginning around 1095, a series of crusades over 200 years resulted in eastern expansion and the establishment of new European colonies promoting Christianity in the Middle East and across Africa. The territories were seized from Muslims, as Western civilization became the dominant international force or hegemony. Relics and treasures from various nations, as well as the Greek Orthodox Church, were plundered and returned to the Vatican as gifts. For example, in 1204 the Crusaders sacked and desecrated Constantinople's holiest cathedrals and shrines. To this day much of the history and treasures of the eastern Greek Orthodox Church are locked in the Vatican's basement. In 2004 Pope John Paul II made a token gesture and returned the bones of two early Greek theologians, but many Greeks are still waiting for the plundered gold, silver, and artworks from this era. This era is labeled Christian colonialism.

Beginning with the invention of significant mechanical advances in the seventeenth century, the third era – of mercantile colonialism – continued until the mid-twentieth century. Spawned by a desire for cheap labor, the importation of raw materials, and ready export markets – created by the colonies – for finished products, the industrial revolution created mercantile colonialism. Asia, Africa, the Caribbean, and the Americas became objects of conquest by European powers. France, Great Britain, Spain, Portugal, the Netherlands, Belgium, Italy, and the Nordic nations systematically set about extending their commercial and political influence. These expanding empires of Europe sought markets, raw materials, and other goods unavailable at home. In return, they sent administrators, immigrants, a foreign language (usually English), and their educational system, religion, philosophy, high culture, laws, and lifestyle which were frequently inappropriate for the invaded country. None of this concerned the conquerors, such as the vast British Commonwealth, who thought they were doing the conquered a favor. In the 1700s and 1800s international status was a function of the number and location of one's foreign colonies.

During the latter part of this era, industrialized nations sought to extend their influence through transnational corporations that supplemented and extended more traditional means of control. But the common denominator remained a desire for economic advantage – plentiful raw materials, cheap labor, and expanding markets. Mercantile colonialism also included other commercial imperatives such as advertising, government regulation, and laws, including contract and intellectual property rights, which better suited the larger and more powerful industrialized nations than the weaker foreign colonies or regions. These collective actions began the global economy which the United States would master and dominate following World War II.

A key element in the success of mercantile colonialism was the invention of the printing press by Johannes Gutenberg. In the early 1450s Gutenberg produced 200 copies of the Bible. Despite their high cost, the Bibles completely sold out, ushering in a new era of communication. Although he was forced into bankruptcy and eventually died a poor man, Gutenberg provided the means for others to amass incredible wealth and power. Initially, the presses were used to mass-produce religious materials in the vernacular, but soon "penny press" newspapers appeared. Over time the printing press undermined the absolute authority and control of the Roman Catholic Church and European monarchies alike. Also, the demand grew for a literate workforce capable of operating the increasingly sophisticated technology of factory production. The demand for public education and the evolution of mass societies created nations with greater literacy and some disposable factory wages. These phenomena permitted the purchase of newspapers, movie tickets, telegrams, books, and eventually radios.

World Wars I and II brought an end to major military expansion and positioned the industrialized nations of the West in command of international organizations, vital trade routes, and global commercial practices. During the 1950s, the business and economic climate encouraged transnational corporations to grow and to consolidate domestic and foreign markets based on the production of mass-produced goods, from breakfast cereals to cars. As the industrial revolution ran its course, two major changes occurred during the late 1950s and early 1960s that set the stage for the fourth and current era of empire expansion.

The two major changes were the rise of nationalism and decolonization, centered mainly in developing nations, and the shift to a service-based information economy among core nations. The service economy relies substantially on satellites, telecommunications, and computer technology to analyze, transfer, and communicate information. It renders obsolete traditional national borders and technological barriers to communication. This

Table 1.1 The four eras of global colonialism

Military colonialism	1000 BCE–1000 CE
Christian colonialism	1000–1600
Mercantile colonialism	1600–1950
Electronic colonialism	1950–Present

fact has significant implications for industrial and non-industrial nations alike as the military, religious, and mercantile colonialism of the past was replaced by the "electronic colonialism" of today and tomorrow (see Table 1.1).

Electronic colonialism represents the dependent relationship of poorer regions on the post-industrial nations which is caused and established by the importation of communication hardware and foreign-produced software, along with engineers, technicians, and related information protocols. These establish a set of foreign norms, values, and expectations that, to varying degrees, alter domestic cultures, languages, habits, values, and the socialization process itself. From comic books to satellites; computers to fax machines; CDs, DVDs, and smartphones to the Internet, a wide range of information technologies make it easy to send and thus receive information.

The issue of how much imported material the receiver retains is critical. The concern is that this new foreign information, frequently favoring the English language, will cause the displacement, rejection, alteration, or forgetting of native or indigenous customs, domestic messages, or cultural history. Now poorer regions fear electronic colonialism as much as, perhaps even more than, they feared the mercantile colonialism of the eighteenth and nineteenth centuries. Whereas mercantile colonialism sought to control cheap labor and the hands of laborers, electronic colonialism seeks to influence and control the mind. It is aimed at influencing attitudes, desires, beliefs, lifestyles, and consumer behavior. As the citizens of peripheral nations are increasingly viewed through the prism of consumerism, influencing and controlling their values, habits, and purchasing patterns becomes increasingly important to multinational firms.[15]

When viewers watch the television show *Baywatch*, they learn about Western society and mores vicariously. *Baywatch*, which began in 1989, hit a peak in the mid-1990s when more than one billion people a week in nearly 150 countries viewed it. With shows like this, along with *Dallas*, *The Cosby Show*, *All in the Family*, *Friends*, and *Fresh Prince of Bel-Air*, foreign viewers began to develop a different mental set and impression of the United States. Another example is *The Simpsons*, the longest-running prime-time animated cartoon ever developed. The show has now surpassed 300 episodes and is widely distributed around the globe. It has a leading cartoon character, Homer Simpson, who generally behaves as a moron and places his family and friends in bizarre situations. The show and characters thrive on portraying distasteful aspects of US life, culture, education, and community. Yet the program has been so successful that not only does it continue, but it has also spawned other weekly animation shows such as *South Park*. Likewise, movies such as *Basic Instinct*, *Rambo*, *Scarface*, *Silence of the Lambs*, *Natural Born Killers*, and *Texas Chainsaw Massacre* deliver the trappings of an alternative lifestyle, culture, language, economy, or political system that go far beyond the momentary images flickering on the screen. Electronic colonialism theory details the possible long-term consequences of exposure to these media images and messages to extend the powerful multinational media empires' markets, power, and influence.

Not surprisingly, the recent rise of nationalism in many areas of the world seeks to counter these neocolonialist effects. Many of these newer nations are former colonies of European powers. Their goal is to maintain political, economic, and cultural control of their own history, images, and national destiny. It is within these cultural issues that students of journalism, cultural studies, communication, and telecommunications find theoretical, policy, and research interest. For example, issues that concern both developing nations and the industrial ones, and frequently find them on opposing sides, are the performance and role of international wire services, global television networks, advertising agencies, and the Internet.[16]

History of Electronic Colonialism Theory

Prior to World War I, when international communication consisted primarily of mail, some newspapers were crossing national borders, as was limited electronic communication, which was a mixture of wireless and telegraph systems using Morse code. There was no international communication theory.[17] Also, the feature film industry was in its infancy, but there were examples of movies created in one nation being shown in another nation. For example, Hollywood exported to both Canada and Mexico some of its major films, even at this early stage. Likewise some European films were exhibited in movie houses in other nations.

This early communication era was dominated by the systematic exploitation by powerful European nations of foreign colonies that were to be a source of cheap labor and raw materials. In turn, these resources were manufactured into finished goods and sent back to the various colonies. Many of the onsite colonial leaders were either government officials or wealthy European families who dispatched many locals to rural or remote areas. Examples of this phenomenon are the Maori tribes in Australia and New Zealand, Native Indians across North America, Zapatistas in Mexico, French Canadians in Quebec, and many tribes across Africa. Given the pervasiveness of Great Britain's colonial empire, the non-commercial British Broadcasting Corporation (BBC), which was founded in 1922, was also exported as the operating model for many new radio systems that were being started across the globe. Reuters, then a British wire service, covered British expeditions for English-language newspapers.

During the late 1920s and 1930s, there did emerge an alternative workers' culture which promoted a grassroots orientation to art, culture, and some local media. Labor organizations sought to promote folk art, decentralize the bourgeoisie orientation of the elite cultural industries, like opera, and promote local media with a non-commercial orientation. During this phase there emerged a European group of critical scholars, now referred to in the literature as the Frankfurt School. A group of philosophers which included Herbert Marcuse, Jürgen Habermas, Max Horkheimer, and Theodor Adorno developed a body of theory critical of power elites. To some extent they planted the seeds of electronic colonialism theory by focusing academic attention on ownership and power issues.

Many labor-based and critical initiatives became mute for two major structural reasons: the Great Depression and World War II. It was only after the end of World War II in 1945 that there were substantial international expansion of the mass media and transborder activities involving communication as well as cultural products. Global advertising also became a growth area. In addition, many of the academics associated with the Frankfurt School relocated to North American universities and some American critical scholars would take up the cultural imperialism track or viewpoint over time.

On December 10, 1948 the United Nations recognized the growing importance of the interaction of culture and the arts within the Universal Declaration of Human Rights. Article 27 of the 30-article proclamation states:

1   Everyone has the right freely to participate in the cultural life of the community, to enjoy the arts and to share in scientific advancement and its benefits.
2   Everyone has the right to the protection of the moral and material interests resulting from any scientific, literary or artistic production of which he is author.[18]

National government media services, such as the BBC, the United States' Voice of America, and Canada's Radio Canada International, along with many others, began to expand their activities to multiple languages, with a strong desire to promote the fundamental concepts of free speech, free press, and democracy, particularly in light of a campaign to thwart, counter, or indeed stop the growing global threat and rise of communism. Most short-wave, government-backed radio services promoted a Cold War agenda in their broadcasts.

In the late 1960s and throughout the 1970s, the debate about international communication moved to the halls of UNESCO in Paris, France. Certain constituencies, such as the old Soviet Union countries, academics in Nordic and Latin America countries, and some social democratic party forces across Europe, began to express early concern about the negative impact of Western culture and the global economy. Although there was significant support for non-commercial media systems, there was also concern expressed about the global syndication of Hollywood films and television shows, along with the impact of music, particularly that emanating from the United Kingdom and the United States, under the banner of rock and roll. This debate about the importation of junk culture, much like junk food, hit a responsive chord at UNESCO.

During the 1980s, under the philosophical mantra of US President Ronald Reagan, a new era of privatization, liberalization, and deregulation not only took hold in North America, but also across Europe, strongly promoted by Prime Minister Margaret Thatcher in the United Kingdom. There was a significant emphasis on market forces, free enterprise, and entrepreneurship, and a strong reversal of any type of sympathy or support for non-commercial media, government regulation, or public ownership of telecommunication systems. Market forces also led to a flurry of mergers and acquisitions across the communication sector. Consolidation created global giants and this trend continues. In 2004 WPP, a British-based advertising firm, purchased the US-based Grey Global and Sony of Japan bought MGM. One new global player deserves to be singled out – Ted Turner created a satellite-delivered all news network, Cable News Network (CNN), in 1980, which would come to alter global news, as well as other broadcasting practices, significantly.

Finally, during this period, there were three seminal documents that formed the basis for a school of cultural imperialism. To some extent these were forerunners to the eventual development of electronic colonialism theory. In particular, Herbert Schiller's 1969 work entitled *Mass Communication and American Empire*, Tapio Varis's work for UNESCO and his 1974 article entitled "Global Traffic in Television," and Jeremy Tunstall's 1977 book, *The Media Are American*, served as a new catalyst and basis for promoting critical research in terms of analyzing international communication flows, impact, and imbalances.[19] Critical scholars such as Dan Schiller and Bob McChesney, along with others, are still carrying on some of the research. Yet it was not until the 1990s that a major new group finally emerged as a global non-governmental organization (NGO).

The International Network for Cultural Development (INCD) was established in 1998 to defend cultural expression and cultural diversity, and to promote national and multilingual cultural expression. It sought to promote genuine authentic media rather than, or indeed to counter the impact of, the dominance of English-language mass media which controlled the flow of cultural products across national boundaries. INCD took up the debate on international communication with new vigor and sought out new global participants, including senior government officials. They were opposed to multinational communication corporations promoting a homogenized global culture. INCD, along with UNESCO and several academics, sought to align itself with government officials to promote an alternative to the market-based, free enterprise capitalist system, which was clearly dominating global communication and served the interests of mainly American, Japanese, and European media conglomerates. A major goal of INCD is to promote through the auspices of UNESCO an international convention that now defines and aims to protect cultural and linguistic diversity along with support for open artistic expression.

Much of the dominance that occurred since the middle of the twentieth century has been documented in my 1981 work entitled *Electronic Colonialism: The Future of International Broadcasting and Communication*.[20] This early work, along with the first edition of *Global Communication*, documented and expanded the literature about international communication. Collectively these works laid the groundwork and further amplified the theory of electronic colonialism. It is this theory to which we now turn and add additional details.

What is Electronic Colonialism Theory?

Just as mercantile colonialism focused on empires seeking the toil and soil of others, frequently as colonies, so now electronic colonialism theory (ECT) looks at how to capture the minds and, to some extent, the consumer habits of others. ECT focuses on how global media, including advertising, influence how people look, think, and act. The aim of ECT is to account for how the mass media influence the mind. Just as the era of the industrial revolution focused on manual labor, raw materials, and then finished products, so also the information revolution now seeks to focus on the role and consequences concerning the mind and global consumer behavior.

Consider how culture is conveyed in a multimedia world. Historically grandparents and tribal elders played a central role in recreating, transmitting, and transferring culture. They relied on oral communication along with family, community, or tribal connections. Culture is basically an attitude; it is also learned. It is the learning of shared language and perceptions that are incorporated in the mind through education, repetition, ritual, history, media, or mimicking. The media's expanding role becomes a shared media culture which influences perceptions and values. Examples of media systems that attract heavy users are Hollywood movies, MTV, ESPN, soap operas, CNN, the Internet, and video games. These systems tend to be the output of global communication giants, such as Time Warner, Disney, Viacom, Sony, and News Corp. Collectively they have the real potential to displace or alter previous cultural values, language, lifestyles or habits, activities, and family rituals. This is particularly true for heavy users of one or two external media. Over time, ECT states that these changes can and usually do impact friends, family, and community ties. A virtual community or new friends who replace former community ties share two things: first, a preoccupation with identical media, such as MTV, talk radio, Facebook, or Al Jazeera; and, second, the embedded media culture that involves new or different messages, perception, learning, and habits. An example of this is the new subculture of black slang. It is at the core of the new media-induced culture for this group. Rap music, movies, concerts, dress, and playgrounds repeat and reinforce this niche linguistic trend.

A way to look at ECT is to think about it as though we go through life wearing various masks. We learn how to play out the appropriate roles, such as child, parent, spouse, student, immigrant, minority, athlete, or boss.[21] But with ECT the masks become somewhat invisible because we begin to think and feel differently, as we become what we watch, do, or listen to. The media become a veil of collective new images, which we absorb into our minds and eventually, even if subtly, we begin to act out, dress, or speak differently as we consume input from the mass media rather than from family, community, or former friends. The socialization process is hijacked by the media empires rather than the colonial empires of days gone by. It is as if we have moved with modernization from a tribal state where culture was located in a fixed territory, region, or nation to a mediated state of mind where we might have more in common with someone or some group halfway around the world via social media or MTV rather than in our own house, school, or neighborhood.

Now with ECT a new culture has emerged that is a global phenomenon driven primarily by large multimedia conglomerates. They control, reproduce, and spread the global flow of words, images, and sounds. They seek to impact the audiences' minds without regard to geography.[22] Their audiovisual products become sold and standardized without regard to time or space. They are marketed to international consumers who come to view their world outlook and buying habits as the logical outcome of a new media culture, as outlined and identified by ECT. For example, many Hollywood films and DVD sales now make more revenue outside the United States than at home, while MTV, Disney, Apple, Microsoft, and Google have more aggressive expansion plans outside the United States than within it. IBM is a good example. Over 70 percent of all IBM employees work and live outside the United States. For many conglomerates the US domestic market is saturated, and thus off-shore sales, audiences, consumers – that is, expansion – is a logical trend that is enabled and explained by the phenomenon of ECT. The leading American communication giants describe themselves as global companies and not US companies. Their corporate strategic plans all focus on expanding global markets and on developing products and services for international consumption. They position themselves as stakeholders, beneficiaries, and advocates of the global economy. They are the foot-soldiers of electronic colonialism.

Another example of the growing focus on international trends and consumers who cannot seem to get enough of audiovisual, mainly American, material is to be found in the movie industry. It is interesting that the international audiences for American movies continue to grow at a rapid rate while domestic movie-goers are declining slightly. This phenomenon appears to apply even to movies which are duds at home but are attractive abroad. Consider two examples. In 2012 the movie *Battleship* made only $65 million in the United States but $238 million globally, and in the same year *John Carter* took in $73 million domestically but $210 million off-shore. This trend also applies to domestic hits that become huge successes internationally. Two prime examples are *Pirates of the Caribbean*, which grossed $241 at home but a staggering $803 million overseas, and *The Croods*, which grossed $143 million at home and $243 overseas. Clearly major American movies companies are aware of this growing trend and it will likely influence what does get produced in the future. Finally, it is additional evidence that the electronic colonizing of the minds abroad will continue unabated.

World System Theory

World system theory (WST) provides the concepts, ideas, and language for structuring international communication. It was proposed and developed by Immanuel Wallerstein.[23] The theory has also been linked to dependency theory[24] in that some of the criticisms are similar to the rhetoric and writings of the critical school of media scholars. Others have applied world system theory to specific sectors, as Thomas Clayton did to comparative education, and George Barnett and Young Choi did to telecommunications.[25] This chapter develops world system theory as it applies to international communication. The previously explained theory of electronic colonialism applies directly to the actions and reactions in the semiperipheral and peripheral zones, as developed by Wallerstein and others. These zones constitute prime export markets for multimedia firms.

World system theory states that global economic expansion takes place from a relatively small group of core-zone nation-states out to two other zones of nation-states, these being in the semiperipheral and peripheral zones. These three groupings or sectors of nation-states have varying degrees of interaction on economic, political, cultural, media, technical, labor, capital, and social levels. The contemporary world structure follows the logic of economic determinism in which market forces rule in order to place as well as determine the winners and losers, whether they are individuals, corporations, or nation-states.[26] It is assumed that the zones exhibit unequal and uneven economic relations, with the core nations being the dominant and controlling economic entity. The core nations have the power and are essentially the major Western industrialized nations. The semiperipheral and peripheral nations are in a subordinate position when interacting with core nations. Core nations exert control to their benefit and define the nature and extent of interactions with the other two zones. Core nations define the relations between the core and the semiperiphery as well as between the core and the periphery. The core provides technology, software, capital, knowledge, finished goods, and services to the other zones, which function as consumers and markets. The core nations also force a neoliberal approach concerning free markets and deregulation with the two weaker zones. The semiperipheral and peripheral zones engage in the relationship with core nations primarily through providing low-cost labor, raw materials, mass markets, or low-cost venues for feature films. Mass media technology (hardware) or products (software) represent the finished goods or services that reinforce and frequently dominate relations between the three sectors. World system theory is useful in examining the cultural industries, mass media systems, audiovisual industries, technology transfer, knowledge, regulatory regimes, and activities of the biggest global stakeholders, which pursue interrelated strategies to maximize corporate growth, market share, revenues, and profits.

Thomas Shannon describes the economic, labor, technology, and other processes among the three zones, as shown in Figure 1.1.[27] Central to these relationships is the learning of appropriate economic values that facilitate modernization. Some of these values are conveyed through advertising as well as in the content of Western core-produced mass media exports. Also central to the relationships among the sectors is a mass communication system that allows the transfer of media materials to create either a broadly based popular culture for a mass market or audience, or alternative cultures for a niche market large enough to encourage imports of select media products or services. The essential point is that, despite criticisms of modernization theory and goals, there are nevertheless clear stages and goals that peripheral nations need to learn, pass through, adopt, or clear as a precondition for advancing to the next zone, the semiperiphery. The nations in the semiperiphery engage in both core-like and periphery-like

Figure 1.1 Relationships in the capitalist world economy
Source: Thomas Shannon, *An Introduction to the World-System Perspective*, Boulder, CO: Westview Press, 1989, p. 29 © 1989, 1996 by Westview Press. Reprinted by permission of Westview Press.

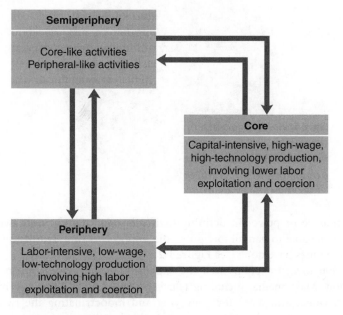

economic and media behavior. They strive to emulate core values over peripheral values in order to become a core nation over time.

The core nations are generally considered to be the United States of America, the European Union, without the most recent 10 entrants which are considered to still be semiperipheral nations, Canada, Japan, Norway, Israel, Australia, New Zealand, South Korea, Switzerland, and South Africa.

The semiperipheral nations are China, Brazil, India, Chile, Turkey, Mexico, Venezuela, Argentina, Russia, Saudi Arabia, Egypt, Oman, Pakistan, Croatia, Iceland, Philippines, and the 10 new members of the European Union (Cyprus, Czech Republic, Estonia, Hungary, Latvia, Lithuania, Malta, Poland, Slovak Republic, and Slovenia), which are on the fast track to become core nations. The European Union provides the necessary leadership and access to capital and consumer markets to rapidly improve their economies compared to their former status of being small, marginal nations on the world's stage. Over the next few decades China, Brazil, and India are also likely to become core nations and to rival both the United States and the European Union as world economic powers.

The peripheral nations – that is, most of Africa, Latin America, and large parts of Asia – are the least developed nations, frequently referred to as the "Third World" or as developing countries. This zone has the least trade, the weakest economies, high rates of corruption and health problems, and the fewest news stories written or broadcast about them, plus the worst Internet connectivity on the planet. The news stories that do appear about these countries are negative, focusing on coups, civil wars, or natural disasters. Industrialization, which is central to the rise of capitalism and capitalists, has yet to reach this peripheral zone. Literacy – the ability to read newspapers, books, or magazines – is also lacking in this zone. A defining characteristic of the peripheral zone is the agrarian nature of their economies.

Figure 1.2 Breakdown of the three world-system zones, 2013

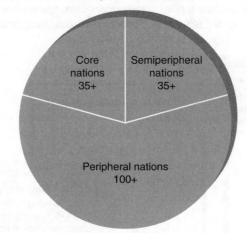

They lack influence or power in defining their relations with the core, with the major exception of being able to ban all foreign media imports, as Iran, North Korea, and other authoritarian regimes have done (see Figure 1.2).

World system theory explains well the expansion being played out in international communication. Mass media, including television and feature films, are major vehicles (sound, print, video, and data) for conveying and indoctrinating the two subordinate zones. The dominant capitalist ideology is embedded within the transactional structure, marketing, and strategic plans of the major core cultural industries. The major multinational media conglomerates come from core nations, particularly the United States and the European Union. They seek to influence, expand, and promote their range of cultural products, including books, magazines, movies, music, and so forth, into the two subordinate zones for profit. The software and hardware of international communication are constructed and marketed by core industries and enterprises. They are then sold directly or indirectly (through co-productions, minority ownership, licensing agreements, etc.) to semiperipheral and peripheral nations as quickly as these markets can absorb and pay for them. Just as the general world system theory explains that capitalist ideologies are necessary for the working and expansion of the global economy, so also the major multimedia conglomerates have a parallel goal of directly enhancing their performance, both at home and abroad, by promoting and endorsing core capitalist mechanisms and values within the two subordinate zones. Jim Collins, for example, describes Walt Disney as a visionary who used his company's products "to shape society and its values": "From Israel to Brazil, Sweden to Australia, children grow up with the guiding hand of Walt Disney partly shaping their imaginations and world outlook."[28] This is a classic example of what electronic colonialism is all about. The business leaders of core multinational media firms seek to convert and capture the attitudes, minds, and purchasing behavior of global customers in such a fashion that their products or services are purchased first and frequently.

If the economic, social, and cultural values of core nations are not accepted and internalized by the subordinate zones, then the necessary attitudes and required behavior to purchase core-produced CDs, movies, videos and DVDs, iPods, and books will not develop. Consumer spending is ultimately required in all zones. Core-based cultural industries and ideologies require the successful sale of core goods and services across the other two zones in order to increase market share as well as to join with other core industries such as automobiles, fast food, equipment, airplanes, computers, and so on, so as to reap the benefits of an expanding global economy The utilization of advertising campaigns for cultural products, which are in many instances customized for the other zones, is also part of the overall capitalist movement.

Advertising itself represents a mini "case study" of world system theory and is covered in Chapter 15. Without going into excessive detail here, it is worth noting that almost all new media outlets worldwide are commercial stations or networks which rely solely on advertising revenue for their income and profits. This gives advertising enormous influence and a central role in the ultimate success of new ventures. Further compounding this dependency is the fact that all of the advertising agencies are multinational corporations from core nations. These core-headquartered agencies bring with them everything from accounting practices, research, graphics, and artwork to placement strategies that are imposed on media customers in the subordinate zones, as part of their comprehensive full-service contracts. Whether the enterprises are in print, radio, television, outdoor billboard, or the Internet, multinational advertising agencies frequently rule in the crucial component of the communication enterprise.

World system theory carries an implied belief that prosperity will accrue to the two subordinate zones as they become more pro-capitalist and expand their markets to include the core nations. But a major part of the prosperity problem is that as core nations expand their cultural artifacts and products to the other zones, these economic transactions often do two things. First, they require foreign customers to purchase core products, with the eventual profits returning to the multimedia conglomerates, most of which are based in Europe or the United States. Second, communication products manufactured in core nations usually displace or replace indigenous cultural products with foreign alternatives and values. Local films, music, books, and so forth in the two subordinate zones must now compete with major advertising and promotion campaigns affiliated with the core products that local firms are simply not able to afford. So in discussing prosperity, one needs to ask – prosperity for whom? Who is being rewarded – a local person or a foreign firm? As core enterprises expand into the subordinate zones, it is the multimedia firms that reap the prosperity in a measure not commensurate with their impact on or assistance in the subordinate zones.

One argument in favor of this imbalance of influence makes the case that labor, central to world system research, does benefit in the two subordinate zones. For example, when movies or television series are produced in the subordinate zones, extras, drivers, local restaurants, and merchants of all trades are involved, or when newspapers, magazines, or records are sold, a commission is paid to the local shopkeeper. Many other examples also illustrate that the subordinate zones do profit by being part of core nation transactions. In fact, core nations actively court other core nations' media firms to undertake business in their countries. Consider the following example, which deals with the filming industry and Canada–United States relations, both of which are core nations.

Many Canadian nationalists are worried about US media and cultural influences. Since the early introduction of radio in Canada, there has been a constant concern about US media spillover into Canadian homes, theaters, and minds. Yet as media giants become more concerned with and focused on global markets and profitability, Canada has increasingly welcomed film-making by Hollywood movie studios and US television networks. Montreal, Toronto, and Vancouver are prime locations for US companies producing movies and television series. These productions create thousands of jobs annually and contribute millions of dollars to the Canadian economy. Canada, as the core nation physically closest to the leading core nation, the United States, has to accept the growing role that US, particularly Hollywood, studios play in its economy, employment, and culture. As media costs escalate, particularly for leading stars, Canada begins to look like Hollywood North. A special report by *Maclean's* (Canada's weekly news magazine) entitled "Northern Exposure" sums up the situation: "Stars want good roles, studios want to save money and create good entertainment. By filming in the Great White North, they can have it all."[29]

Finally, although there is not much specific empirical media research[30] with a world system theory focus, one notable exception is a study by Kyungmo Kim and George Barnett. Their article, "The Determinants of International News Flow: A Network Analysis,"[31] is a good example of the utility of world system theory. They apply both world system and dependency theories. Following a detailed examination of international news flow across 132 nations, they conclude: "the findings of this research reveal the inequality in international news flow between the core and periphery. The Western industrialized countries are at the center, dominating international news flow. Most African, Asian, Latin American, and Oceania countries are at the periphery."[32] Based on a regression analysis of their data, they further conclude:

> This center–periphery structure of the international news flow network has two implications for communication dependency. First, Western industrialized countries are at the position in which they produce and sell international news. In contrast, the peripheral countries consume and depend on their information from the core countries. One way this happens is through the maintenance of historical colonial relationships.[33]

The authors point out that not much truly global research on international news flow has been undertaken for a variety of structural reasons; this study is a major exception. In 2008 Barnett and others produced another empirical piece with a world system framework entitled "The Structure of International Aid Flows and Global News." After examining Agence France Presse (AFP), Associated Press (AP), CNN, and Reuters in terms of coverage, countries mentioned, and the flow of aid, they concluded: "The results indicate that global news coverage is significantly related to aid allocations and relations. Recipient countries with a high level of news coverage receive more aid and have more international relations than those with less coverage."[34]

A similar twist is reported by Clifford Bob in his book *The Marketing of Rebellion: Insurgents, Media, and International Activism*.[35] After examining 45 activists and NGO leaders he concludes that aid goes to those with the most media skills and not necessarily the neediest or most worthy. Getting face time on CNN or the BBC is priceless for an NGO spokesperson during a crisis. Coverage does count. Bob claims that there is a Darwinian struggle for scarce resources among NGOs. Those needed resources could be money, media exposure, or relief aid.

In conclusion, the three zones of WST reflect a world where the living standards are extremely broad. Modernization and globalization have failed to produce the economic and social change that many academics and policy experts predicted. Wallerstein recognizes this:

> The whole discussion from 1945 to today has been one long effort to take seriously the reality that world-system is not only polarized but polarizing, and that this reality is both morally and politically intolerable. For countries at the bottom, there seemed nothing more urgent than figuring out how to improve their situation, and first of all economically. After all, all these people had to do was to see a movie and they would know that there were other people in the world that were better off than they were. As for the countries

at the top, they realized, however dimly, that the "huddled masses yearning to breathe free" represented a permanent danger to world order and their own prosperity, and that therefore something, somehow had to be done to dampen the tinderbox.[36]

The tinderbox is now loaded with terrorists who have two dominant traits: religious extremism and anti-Western ideologies. The Western or core nations have yet to come to grips collectively to solve this global phenomenon.

The Connection between Electronic Colonialism and World System Theories

There is a substantial and important link between electronic colonialism theory and world system theory. ECT posits that mass media when exported carry with them a broad range of values. These values are economic, social, cultural, and sometimes political or religious in nature. Increasingly they carry with them the English language, in terms of music, movies, or the Internet. WST theory elaborates and extends ECT by dividing the nations of the globe into three categories; it then expands on how the core category works to influence the two subordinate categories. Some core nations are concerned about the impact and penetration of ECT as well. Canada, France, the United Kingdom, Israel, New Zealand, and Australia are prime core nations that continually worry about the Americanization of their domestic cultural industries and consumer behavior. They realize that with each additional commercial media outlet more will be spent on foreign syndicated shows, leaving even less money for indigenous productions of all genres.

Nations in the subordinate categories, mainly the semiperiphery and periphery, have a multitude of reasons, whether they be economic, social, cultural, or moral, to be concerned about the implications of ECT. Dependency theory, in relation to attitudinal shifts brought about by repetitive interactions with core businesses, is an example of ECT. For example, since the 1980s there has been a steady stream of research from Latin America on the structural impact, mostly negative, of relations with core nations, particularly the United States, but also with former colonial powers in Europe, particularly Spain. Although much of this research failed to utilize or identify either electronic colonialism and world system theories as being relevant, in retrospect both theoretical constructs have much to offer in terms of organizing and explaining Latin American research and theory.

Just as WST applies to all three zones, so also ECT has different applications in each zone. Utilizing appropriate aspects of both theories will significantly enhance future research in international communication. ECT, with its cultural lens, and WST, with an economic lens, are well suited to examining the global activities of multinational cultural industries jointly.

Communication Forces among Nations

International communication as a commercial sector is an ideal case study of the application of world system theory. Multinational communication conglomerates, major wire services, as well as major advertising agencies are all based in the core zone. When operating in other core nations, or in semiperipheral and peripheral nations, they do so with a well-refined and strategically set agenda drawn from the capitalist economic system. The semiperipheral and peripheral zones are viewed as prime potential markets for core-based multimedia corporations, which define the relations between the semiperipheral and peripheral nations. Part of the corporate goal is to influence the attitudes and values of potential customers as explained by the theory of electronic colonialism. There is no threat of force (such as military conquest), yet marketing strategies, research, advertising, and economic savvy permit core-zone businesses to influence consumer behavior by creating global mindsets that favor their cultural products and services. Core nations thrive on market-based activities since they make the rules.

To understand the post-Cold War global communication environment, it is necessary to understand the evolution of the two quite different views of the core industrialized nations, and that the peripheral regions are, after decades of modernization efforts, still locked into the peripheral zone. Indeed, some peripheral nations are now worse off than they were under European colonial masters. Their situation – in terms of economy, health, education, indigenous media, and technology – has only deteriorated over time.

Also, during the 1990s, the movements toward liberalization and privatization saw many nations' state-controlled and state-owned media monopolies coming under siege. The siege was not from an armed military intruder, but rather a mix of three new strong hegemonic communication forces. These forces were:

1 the expansion of cable and satellite broadcasting systems;
2 an avalanche of Western, primarily American, television and movie programs; and
3 the collective rules of the World Trade Organization, the World Bank, and the International Monetary Fund.

These three forces, together with hardware, software, and free market rules, radically altered the media environment and balance in a vast number of core and semiperipheral nations between 1980 and today. Whereas only one or two public television channels were the norm for years, suddenly dozens of new channels and choices have appeared on television sets as cable or satellite services became available around the globe. The effect was to create electronic colonies, built mostly around US shows or music, out of a new generation of viewers and listeners around the world.

For years, public broadcasting systems, particularly in Europe, had attempted to enlighten and to inform their audiences. But with new channels came new opportunities to promote entertainment, advertising, market forces, and the clear goal of making a profit. Commercial channels sought out popular programming ranging from *Big Brother, Millionaire, The Weakest Link, Survivor, The Simpsons*, to soap operas and reality shows, to *Baywatch*. In their wake, they left smaller audiences for the public broadcasters, which in turn were coming under increasing pressure from politicians and regulatory authorities to do something about their shrinking audiences. At the same time, many commercial broadcasters were seeking increased revenue from public sources. Every new commercial channel that is introduced steals away a portion, even if it is small, of the audience from the public channels. The public networks find themselves seriously challenged by financial, technological, and regulatory forces which are in many cases beyond their control. The new forces all emanate from the core nations to the semiperipheral and peripheral zones. In the latter, the consumption of media from local, sometimes bland, monopolies is frequently being replaced by Western media and foreign values that have had considerable cultural, economic, regulatory, and political repercussions over time.

Breadth of the Problem

The range of global communication activities is extensive indeed. At one end of the spectrum is the large group of developing, or peripheral, nations concerned with basic communication infrastructures, such as the introduction of radio or telephone services. At the other end are the core nations, some of which have been industrialized for over a century while others are concerned with their own survival in the rapidly evolving information age and do not want to become information colonies of other nations. Communication issues related to mergers, transnational data flows, computers, censorship, privacy, and employment in cultural industries are central policy concerns for several industrialized nations, particularly across Europe. This is highlighted by the fact that today more than 50 percent of the US gross national product (GNP) depends on information-based services and industries. This means that future highly skilled employment will be directly related to the ability to supply all aspects of the information chain – hardware, software, and research and development – that are necessary to participate and to be a net winner in the information age.

Clearly, for Western core nations such as Canada, France, Switzerland, Australia, the Nordic countries, and others the fear is that they may become electronic colonies of the United States. This represents a serious threat and challenge to their culture and identity, and to their employment opportunities in the communication sector. It is forcing these countries to rethink their national media philosophies and public support, including subsidies to the arts. Issues related to national sovereignty, culture, language, and electronic colonialism are once again raising questions about the appropriate role of government intervention, fiscal assistance to cultural industries, and media ownership regulations. The emergence of the electronic newspaper, interactive cable services, the Internet, smartphones, and direct satellite broadcasting is raising questions about the role of regulation and the concept of national borders or boundaries Although the specific questions may differ, the basic issues are not far removed from the scope of concerns of peripheral nations in relation to their communication disparities and problems.

Another issue for industrialized countries relates to the growing conflict between economic and national security imperatives. From the beginning, competitive and commercial pressures have affected information flows as media outlets tried to silence the voices of their competitors. Today, the major supporters of the free-flow philosophy are governments responding to pressures from multinational corporate interests – from American Express to Microsoft, IBM, and Time Warner – that are seeking to protect or to extend their corporate (and not necessarily US national) interests. What is good for IBM in selling computer systems to Iran, Cuba, China, or Venezuela, for example, may not necessarily be good for the national, or indeed international, interests of the United States. Yet these corporations and their advertising agencies rely on open borders and open markets, backed by the World Trade Organization, in order to compete effectively in the global economy.

Finally, it should be recognized that much of the pressure and support for the free-flow philosophy is coming from print media, both daily newspapers and major weekly magazines. Their concern is intense and historically genuine. But technology is quickly moving them toward government involvement in the dissemination of their messages. Although print and electronic media are still running on separate legal and regulatory tracks, their paths are expected to converge as print media increasingly rely on electronic information systems such as the Internet to take their messages to consumers. The current wave of newspapers in distress or going out of business will continue. Their fate was predicted as early as 1980.[37] Although the print media have always been regulated to some degree,[38] they will find themselves increasingly restrained by legislative, regulatory, or court actions that are clearly inconsistent with the spirit of a free press or the United States' First Amendment rights.

What is significant, then, is that international communication is no longer solely focused on the role of the print press and the newsgathering habits of the international news agencies, such as AP and Reuters. It is growing to encompass a broad range of issues that arise from the emergence of the Internet, global broadcasting, global advertising, and the global economy. The further economic decline of LDCs, the pervasiveness of satellite-delivered television programming, and the ability of the Internet to defy traditional means of control are all reigniting the debate about the appropriate environment for international communication, along with the appropriate role of government in global communication policy.[39] Good examples of the transnational problems that have arisen are the WikiLeaks controversy and an online community calling itself Anonymous. In 2010 the WikiLeaks founder and director Julian Assange released 251,287 pages of US embassies' cables, several of which contained embarrassing information. Anonymous is a group of Internet "hacktivists" who expose attempts at Internet censorship or surveillance, and who have hacked into various government websites to expose embarrassing information, for example:

> The hacktivist group Anonymous hijacked the U.S. federal sentencing website early Saturday, using the page to make a brazen and boisterous declaration of 'war' on the US government. The group claims mysterious code-based 'warheads,' named for each of the Supreme Court Justices, are about to be deployed … The statement opens with a lament for Aaron Swartz, the Reddit programmer and Internet activist who committed suicide earlier this month. Promising revenge for his treatment at the hands of a federal prosecutor, the screed veers into some of the most inflammatory – dare we say hyperbolic – language we've seen on a simple front page hack.[40]

The Impact of Social Media

During the Cold War era the three major American national broadcasting networks – ABC, CBS, and NBC – dominated the US airwaves and priority was given to foreign news. But with the introduction of cable systems and broadcast satellites in the 1970s, these telecommunication advances changed news programs forever. Viewers suddenly had many more channels to choose from. One side effect of this explosion of choice is fragmentation of the networks' audiences and a decline in advertising for news broadcasting. Other industrialized Western nations are facing similar problems, but their situation is different from that of the United States. For decades public broadcasters like the BBC had a monopoly on radio and then television broadcasting. But after the end of World War II all public broadcasters faced a plethora of new and aggressive commercial competitors.

A recent report, entitled "One Third of the World's Population is Now Online," shows the movement online and the expansion of information and communication technologies (ICTs) across the globe. The report documents the growing use of information and communication technologies, particularly mobile phone and social media usage in developing countries, and shows that a third of the world's population is now online.[41]

Collectively the online phenomena, the introduction of citizen journalists and professionals online, the continuing fragmentation of the audience, new stakeholders, and other factors paint a bleak picture for the future of international news. The shift to Internet-based information has tended to cater to rather parochial issues and matters rather than more cosmopolitan and international items. Digital technologies have created perplexing challenges for legacy media outlets as they, and a range of new tech-savvy providers, seek a new business model which reflects the new environment and captures a sufficient audience as well.

Format for the Balance of the Book

The foregoing highlights the general themes of this book. It examines broadcasting, mass media, and news services ranging from MSNBC, MTV, and CNN to television sitcoms and Hollywood export markets. It investigates the roles of the major players, whether they be News Corp, Sony, the BBC, Disney, Bertelsmann, Viacom, or Time Warner. It probes the role of advertising and the influences, as well as future, of the Internet and their ability to transcend national boundaries and beliefs.

The growing importance and significance of other major regions is reflected in new chapters in the fourth edition, which deal with the media in the Middle East, particularly Al Jazeera, in Europe, and in Asia. There is also a new chapter on public diplomacy. It focuses on the important issue of US public diplomacy in a global world of ideas and ideologies.

Global communication of all types is undergoing major re-examination. In order to understand the various factors influencing the processes of international communication, we need to know who the major stakeholders are and how certain economic and technical forces are changing the global media landscape. This book details the changes in the nature, flow, and control of all types of international communication, including news, in the future. In order to accomplish this, the remainder of *Global Communication* outlines the major institutions, individuals, corporations, technologies, and issues that are altering the international information, telecommunication, and broadcasting order. This includes all types of media activities – wire services, Internet, fax, electronic data, satellite broadcasting, journalism, film, radio, television, mobile phone use, and advertising. Traditional assumptions about media flows and priorities are being challenged and altered daily. What follows is a descriptive and analytical portrayal of how certain events, some very recent, are affecting the domestic and foreign information environments of today and tomorrow. Central to the discussion are the collapse of communism, the importance of global media and communication organizations, global wars and their coverage, the influence of global advertisers, and, finally, the substantial and somewhat unanticipated impact of personal computers, mobile devices, and the Internet.

These issues are explained and interpreted through three major movements or theories: NWICO, electronic colonialism, and world system theory. Collectively, they help organize or frame the trends, economics, technologies, and stakeholders involved in the dynamic, globally significant, and expanding role of international communication. Part of the dynamic is the pace of mergers and acquisitions affecting several of the global communication stakeholders. As the global economy evolves and increases in influence, international communication moves in unison with it. The other part is the rapid pace of innovation of technologies which support global communication, and to a large extent make it easier. International communication will have a greater impact on the future of the planet than exploration and transportation combined.

Notes

1. Katherine Bradshaw, James Foust, Joseph Bernt, and Brian Krol, "Domestic, International, and Foreign News Content on ABC, CBS, and NBC Network News from 1971 to 2007", paper presented at the Annual AEJMC Conference, Chicago, 2012, 3.

2. Bradshaw et al., "Domestic, International, and Foreign News Content," 3.

3. Alisa Miller, "The News about the News," at http://www.ted.com/talks/lang/en/alisa_miller_shares_the_news_about_the_news.html, accessed September 5, 2013.

4. Rasmus Kleis Nielsen, *Ten Years that Shook the Media World*, Reuters Institute for the Study of Journalism, at http://reutersinstitute.politics.ox.ac.uk/fileadmin/documents/Publications/Working_Papers/Nielsen_-_Ten_Years_that_Shook_the_Media.pdf, accessed August 8, 2013.

5. Hong-Won Park, "A Gramscian Approach to Interpreting International Communication," *Journal of Communication* 48(4) (1998), 79.

6. Sallie Hughes and Chappell Lawson, "The Barriers to Media Opening in Latin America, *Political Communication* 22 (2005), 9–10.

7. David Holman, "Economic Policy and Latin America Culture: Is a Virtuous Circle Possible?" *Journal of Latin American Studies* 31 (February 1999), 176.

8. *New York Times* (September 13, 1998), WK 7.

9. Jill Hills, *The Struggle for Control of Global Communication: The Formative Century*, Urbana, IL: University of Illinois Press, 2002.

10. There are several ways of defining and categorizing the nations of the world. Frequent dichotomies include North/South, East/West, developed/underdeveloped, socialist/capitalist, industrialized/developing. Another system categorizes according to core, semiperipheral, and peripheral. Although the system is far from perfect, this book will use the following categories. Western nations include the industrialized nations, which according to the World Bank are Australia, the United Kingdom Canada, Finland, France, Italy, Japan, the Netherlands, Sweden, Switzerland, United States, and Germany. Most of these are situated in the North and are core nations. The peripheral nations are located mainly in Asia, Africa, and Latin America – generally to the South.

    It should also be noted that nations are continually obtaining independence or moving back and forth on both the political and the economic continua. Examples include Russia, Indonesia, Iran, Iraq, Mexico, Brazil, the former Yugoslavia, Venezuela, and Poland. No definition will fit accurately over time. Therefore, the terms are used for the sake of convenience, because they reflect the major global parties involved in the NWICO debate. These categories also apply to the theories of electronic colonialism and world system which will be detailed later.

11. Ha-Joon Chang, *Bad Samaritans: The Myth of Free Trade and the Secret History of Capitalism*, New York: Bloomsbury, 2008.

12. Morton Rosenblum, *Coups and Earthquake*, New York: Harper & Row, 1979, pp. 1–2.

13. Rosenblum, *Coups and Earthquake*, pp. 1–2.

14. Rosenblum, *Coups and Earthquake*, pp. 1–2.

15. Cultural reproduction theorists view international media initiatives as a means of reproducing and socializing students in peripheral nations into knowledge systems that make them more compatible with Western ideals and, equally important, Western consumer values. Cultural reproduction theorists see foreign mass media as reproducing and socializing the populace of other nations into a knowledge system or frame of mind that will make them more compatible with or sympathetic to foreign ideas and consumer values. See Alan Hedley, "Technological Diffusion or Cultural Imperialism? Measuring the Information Revolution," *International Journal of Comparative Sociology* 39(2) (June 1998), 198–213. Hedley states: "Also flowing from this analysis is the potential for cultural dominance that the information revolution may foster. However, unlike previous technological revolutions, what are at stake are the very minds and thought processes of those dominated. Only powerful nations currently have the ability to choose the type of information society most compatible with their cultural institutions" (p. 210). Edward Goldsmith focuses on the role of transnational corporations and their expanding development of the global economy: "The new corporate colonialism is thus likely to be far more cynical and more ruthless than anything we have seen so far. It is likely to dispossess, impoverish and marginalize more people, destroy more cultures and cause more environmental devastation than either the colonialism of old or the development of the last 50 years. The only question is. How long can it last?" ("Development as Colonialism," *Ecologist*, 27(2) (March–April 1997), 69-78, p. 76).

16. The major global stakeholders for all these sectors are detailed in later chapters. Some readers may want to refer to these chapters now.

17. Jill Hills, *The Struggle for Control of Global Communication*, Chicago: University of Illinois Press, 2002.

18. United Nations, *Universal Declaration of Human Rights*, 1948.

19. Herbert I. Schiller, *Mass Communication and American Empire*, New York: A. M. Kelley, 1969; Tapio Varis, "Global Traffic in Television," *Journal of Communication* 24(1) (1974), 102–9; Jeremy Tunstall, *The Media Are American*, New York: Columbia University Press, 1977.

20. Thomas McPhail, *Electronic Colonialism: The Future of International Broadcasting and Communication*, rev. 2nd edn, Newbury, CA: Sage, 1986.

21. David Napier, *Righting the Passage: Perceptions of Change After Modernity*, Philadelphia: University of Pennsylvania Press, 2004.

22. Al Reis and Jack Trout, *Positioning: The Battle for Your Mind*, New York: McGraw-Hill, 2001.

23. Immanuel Wallerstein, *The Modern World System*, New York: Academic Press, 1974; *The Modern World System III*, San Diego, CA: Academic Press, 1989; and "National Development and the World System at the End of the Cold War," in A. Inkeles and M. Sasaki (eds.), *Comparing Nations and Cultures: Readings in a Cross-Disciplinary Perspective*, Englewood Cliffs, NJ: Prentice Hall, 1996, pp. 484–97. A definition of world system theory, along with a fine review of research trends, is contained in Thomas Hall's "The World-System Perspective a Small Sample from a Large Universe," *Sociological Inquiry* 66(4) (November 1996), 440–54.

24. André Frank, *Capitalism and Underdevelopment in Latin America*, New York: Monthly Review Press, 1969; Barnett Singer and John Langdon, "France's Imperial Legacy," *Contemporary Review*, 27(2) (May 1998), 231–8; Alvin So, *Social Change and Development: Modernization, Dependency, and World System Theory*, Newbury Park, CA: Sage, 1990.

25. Thomas Clayton, "Beyond Mystification: Reconnecting World System Theory for Comparative Education," *Comparative Education Review* 42 (November 1998), 479–94; George Barnett and Young Choi, "Physical Distance and Language as Determinants of the International Telecommunications Network," *International Political Science Review* 16(3) (1995), 249–65.

26. Or groups of nation-states such as those in NAFTA, the European Union, ASEAN, or MERCOSUR.

27. Thomas Shannon, *An Introduction to the World-System Perspective*, Boulder, CO: Westview Press, 1989.

28. Jim Collins, "Shaping Society," *USA Today* (September 23, 1999), 19A.

29. "Northern Exposure," *Maclean's* (October 11, 1999), 71.

30. John Comer, Philip Schlesinger, and Roger Silverstone (eds.), *International Media Research: A Critical Survey*, London: Routledge, 1997.

31. Kyungmo Kim and George Barnett, "The Determinants of International News Flow: A Network Analysis," *Communication Research*, 23 (June 1996), 323–52. See also G. Barnett, T. Jacobson, and S. Sun-Millar, "An Examination of the International Communication Network, *Journal of International Communication* 3(3) (1996), 19–43; G. Barnett, "A Longitudinal Analysis of the International Telecommunications Network: 1978–1996," *American Behavioral Scientist* 44(10) (June 2001), 1638–55; G. Barnett, B. S. Chon, and D. Rosen, "The Structure of International Internet Flows in Cyberspace," *NETCOM (Network and Communication Studies)* 15(1–2) (September 2001), 61–80.

32. Yon Soo Lim, George Barnett, and Jang Hyun Kim, "The Structure of International Aid Flows and Global News," *Journal of International Communication* 14(2) (2008), 139.

33. Kim and Barnett, "The Determinants of International News Flow," 344.

34. Lim, Barnett, and Kim, "The Structure of International Aid Flows and Global News," 134.

35. Clifford Bob, *The Marketing of Rebellion: Insurgents, Media, and International Activism*, New York: Cambridge University Press, 2005.

36. Immanuel Wallerstein, "After Developmentalism and Globalization, What?" *Social Forces* 83(3) (March 2005), 1265–6.

37. In 1980, after examining a series of emerging videotext systems across North America, I realized that the newspaper industry was a prime target for eventual competition from a coalescing of electronic inventions. For example, in chapter 1 of a public policy study, entitled "The Electronic Newspaper," I predicted in prescient fashion basically what is unfolding today.

What does all this mean, or what should it mean, for daily newspapers? Basically, it means the door-to-door newspaper as we know it today is on the skids. While it is difficult, if not impossible, to determine the rate of transition to the electronically disseminated newspaper, it is reasonable to believe that a major part of this transition will occur within the twenty-first century. Clearly, it will not be an overnight change. Certain newspaper services will slowly be transferred to a computerized videotext system. As more and more of these services leave the prototype stage and begin operating as subscription services, the financial viability of the print newspaper will become increasingly challenged. At the same time, the financial ability of information providers to develop and to encourage additional information services will increase (T. L. McPhail, *The Future of the Daily Newspaper: Public Policy Issues*, Montreal: Institute for Research on Public Policy, 1980, pp. 5–6).

38. This refers to journalistic limitations. Most agree that there should be no limitations on the political, economic, or social consequences of investigative journalism, but clearly there are legal limitations. These include the laws related to libel, slander, defamation, obscenity, and so forth that do constrain what is printed or aired. For example, in 2004 US Federal officials used the Intelligence Identities Protection Act of 1982 to charge journalists from major media outlets with illegal activities.

39. Another forum of nations is the International Network for Cultural Diversity (INCD), which began with a meeting in Canada in 1998, followed by meetings in Mexico, Greece, Switzerland, South Africa, and Croatia, plus a growing number of regional meetings. These meetings focus on cultural identity, cultural policy, and the impact of cultural globalization. A growing concern of the member nations is the treatment of cultural industries, particularly television, film, and magazines by the World Trade Organization (WTO). The INCD group, which does not include the United States, views the WTO's policies as favoring the one-way flow of Hollywood and New York products around the globe to the detriment of local cultures. One policy option being floated at INCD meetings is the removal of cultural goods and services from WTO agreements. This initiative has major implications concerning global trade for the major stakeholders detailed in later chapters.

Finally, Canada is providing leadership for the INCD group for the obvious reason that it is on the cutting edge of becoming an electronic colony of the United States to a very large extent. It has become a branch plant of US media empires. The foreign content of Canada's mass media is staggering: 98 percent of theater revenues are for foreign, mainly Hollywood, films; 83 percent of magazines sold are foreign, for example *Time*, *People*, and *Sports Illustrated*; 80 percent of music sales in all formats are foreign; and more than 60 percent of television programming on the three national networks comes from other nations, despite decades of electronic media content regulations, along with handsome financial subsidies, from the Canadian federal government.

40. Chris Taylor, "Anonymous Hacks US Government Site, Threatens Supreme 'Warheads,'" *Mashable* (January 26, 2013), at http://mashable.com/2013/01/26/anony-mous-hack-government-website-declares-war/, accessed August 7, 2013.

41. *The World in 2011 – ICT Facts and Figures*, Geneva: ICT Data and Statistics Division, 2011, at http://www.itu.int/ITU-D/ict/facts/2011/material/ICTFacts Figures2011.pdf, accessed August 7, 2013.

2

Development Research Traditions and Global Communication

Introduction

This chapter looks at the changing area of development communication. This area has focused on peripheral nations, the problems they face, and how modernization has essentially failed to deliver change in these regions. Illiteracy, the lack of a telephone service and of connectivity to the Internet, the general failure to produce indigenous content, and the few indigenous media successes all come into play. After six decades of development, the peripheral nations still lack access to modern telecommunications and mass media. This chapter addresses the history and major approaches to and theories of development communication, the role of non-governmental organizations (NGOs), the competition for scarce resources, the "CNN effect," and the paradigm shift now underway. This shift will be the focus of the chapter. The key aspect is that for decades the old paradigm of modernization had an economic focus or lens, whereas the new focus is on policy matters with a social and cultural lens. One of the emerging roles in the new paradigm is how media and telecom systems are promoting democracy as well as a broader quality of life and environmental issues. Part of the change is a bottom-up grassroots approach rather than the top-down bureaucratic practices that have dominated the field since the end of World War II. Much of the early emphasis, projects, and funding was motivated by a desire to thwart the growth of communism around the globe, particularly in underdeveloped nations.[1]

Over the past decade some objections to globalization have emerged. Not all see the same benefits, if they see any at all. Nor are the benefits of globalization equally shared by all. Compounding this criticism is the post-Cold War fear of the United States becoming a hegemonic power and defining aid and international policies to suit its own goals, rather than the receiving nation's needs and goals. Family planning and the role of women are a particularly sensitive area. There has been a significant increase in feminist scholarship dealing with the media within a development context during this time. Other factors include what is now being referred to as coercive democracy where the United States is combining its post-Cold War

Global Communication: Theories, Stakeholders, and Trends, Fourth Edition. Thomas L. McPhail.
© 2014 John Wiley & Sons, Inc. Published 2014 by John Wiley & Sons, Inc.

military power with its hegemonic economic power to set conditions on foreign aid or international treaties that cripple weaker nations or regions. The bulk of the benefits from aid and treaties tend to go to Western nations, while those in peripheral regions see little improvement.

During the 1980s, several factors came together to further the movement questioning Western aid, globalization, free market values, liberalization, and the impact of foreign media. Among them was the failure and subsequent rejection of the theory of modernization promulgated by major industrialized core nations and aid agencies, along with a cadre of academics since the end of World War II. Implementation of that model had failed to produce positive economic results in the eyes of peripheral nations as well as a growing body of critics. In reality, after decades of core-based modernization attempts, some peripheral nations are now worse off while others have made little progress. Within the overall theoretical framework, the mass communication system was a substantial component in the mix of factors that should have moved peripheral nations to at least semiperipheral status and then to industrialization and modernization. Herein lies the connection between modernization theory and development communication. In theory, development communication should work in concert with other growth factors to lead poorer nations to modernization or, at least, to move them from the peripheral zone to the semiperipheral zone. In practice, those peripheral nations that did invest in media infrastructures realized too late that these systems were bringing in more foreign, not local, content. For example, where cable or satellite media were introduced, affluent locals watched CNN, the BBC, or MTV rather than domestic broadcasts.[2]

In retrospect, just as educational television in the West failed to bring about the projected revolution in the classroom, the prediction that broadcasting was the means by which poor nations could rapidly transform into industrialized nations was similarly misguided. Indeed, during the last decade, some peripheral nations moved in the opposite direction with regard to housing, the environment, currency, literacy, and health care, particularly in relation to the spread of HIV/AIDS.

Some poor nations, for example, assumed that the introduction of color television would be the appropriate medium to foster economic and cultural development. But color television is expensive and has limited uses and applications. In peripheral nations where color television broadcasting is available, few households even have access to black-and-white television sets. Digital television, which is now the standard in core nations, raises a new issue and barrier. This new technology will render existing analog broadcasting systems and their receivers obsolete. In their eagerness to "measure up," many peripheral nations are likely to aspire toward the digital format and related new technology, but its costly introduction is likely to set back, rather than promote, development. New core-manufactured hardware will consume vast sums of money.

This chapter traces the various streams of the major theories of communication, both American and European, as well as major research trends that underpin the knowledge base for students of international communication. Beginning with development theory, the review highlights major contributions to the theoretical and applied international media research literature. The chapter concludes with a discussion of the application and implications of the theories of electronic colonialism and world system theory.

Development Journalism/Communication

Development journalism and communication are attempts to counterbalance the thrust toward electronic colonialism. They acknowledge that the demands of an infant press differ from those of a mature press. To impose the legal, economic, or regulatory models of one on the other results in a failure to appreciate the underlying fundamental differences that are a result of a combination of historical and cultural factors. Development journalism is the concept that attempts to deal with the needs, strengths, and aspirations of journalistic endeavors in the emerging developing nation-states.[3] It is a media theory that encourages an engineered press – a press committed to government-set priorities and objectives. It assumes that everyone, including the local media, needs to work in unison to support national goals. Totalitarian and military regimes in a substantial number of peripheral nations follow and enforce this media theory and approach.

Consequently, development journalism serves essentially to promote the needs of developing countries. It encourages indigenous media and discourages reproduction of Western media models, which debase, challenge, or marginalize local and traditional cultures. Most peripheral media systems are underdeveloped, with few newspapers, some radio outlets, and usually one television system at most. Access to the Internet is very limited. Under these conditions, administrators, editors, and reporters in peripheral regions find little relevance in Western media values and systems which do not serve the needs of peripheral nations or highlight their interests or concerns. Except for the occasional political coups, civil wars, pirating, or natural disaster, all of which focus on bad news, few of their stories are told in the mainstream media, or from the peripheral nations' own perspective. In fact, research indicates that the vast majority of international media offerings emanate from a few core nations as sources. Consider the following:

1   Major Western news agencies such as the Associated Press, Bloomberg, Reuters, Getty Images, and Agence France Presse provide about 90 percent of the entire world's wire service information. They are all based in core nations.
2   Major Western newspapers, magazines, and journals are virtually all published in the United States or Europe. In Europe, most of these are located in the countries of foreign colonial powers and still enjoy significant sales in current or former colonies.
3   International radio programming such as Voice of America (United States), the BBC (United Kingdom), Deutsche Welle (Germany), and other Western short-wave services transmit programming specifically designed for international audiences. The perspective is invariably that of the Western core industrial nations, but the majority of the global audience are located in non-core nations.
4   Global television news, newsreels, photos supplied by firms such as CNN, BBC, AP, Getty, and Reuters have established worldwide markets for their products using material produced or designed for initial use in the United States, Europe, or other Western media and communication systems.
5   Television programming and feature films are almost exclusively the province of Western nations. Over two-thirds of available global video programming comes from the United States alone, and its share of the international market is growing.
6   All major global advertising agencies are based in the United States, Europe, or Japan. If there is any physical presence of agencies at all in semiperipheral or peripheral nations, it is only in the form of small branch offices of the leading global agencies.
7   Getty Images, which moved the fragmented stock photography industry into the digital age, is now another major provider of photographs and imagery, along with the wire services, so visual imagery worldwide has a clear Western bias.

Although the seeds of a theory of development journalism were sown shortly after World War II, it was decades before the debate about the role of the mass media reached the West. Originally, the dominant paradigm for development communication reflected a mainstream consensus of opinion among all stakeholders that encouraged both economic and industrial growth. It was assumed that as the gross domestic product (GDP) increased so too would communication activities of all types, including the development of telecommunication as well as mass media systems. This economic-based "growth is good" model or mantra was the underpinning for modernization theory. It ignored the fact that enormous capital investment was required to finance sustainable communication development. Without adequate domestic professional and fiscal resources, peripheral nations found themselves even more dependent on external foreign aid, which invariably had strings attached. Also, many of the aid projects came with associated cultural baggage, such as the abandoning of certain cultural traditions, but this was ignored or downplayed as the price of "progress."

Over time, piecemeal programs evolved to encourage development. However, it soon became clear that foreign aid turned out to be little more than a weapon on the Cold War battlefield. The Soviet Union supported communist-oriented nations and regions, while the United States assisted fledgling democracies ostensibly committed to free enterprise and free press models. Moreover, uncounted sums of this aid were skimmed off by corrupt regimes or military officials, or were wasted by inept, untrained bureaucrats with family connections but little experience of working on large-scale development projects. This blatant failure to improve the conditions in developing countries led to a rethinking of development communication.

The immediate result of such rethinking was manifest in sensitivity to the structural and cultural constraints on the impact of communication, in addition to a conscious awareness that the mass media were just a part of the total communication infrastructure. It became evident that successful and effective use of communication in any community requires adequate knowledge of the availability, accessibility, relations between, and utilization of communication infrastructure and software in that community.[4]

The problems were not limited to the lack of communication progress in developing nations. Some critics found fault with Western researchers who ignored indigenous media and failed to stress the importance of sustaining local cultures. African scholar Kwasi Ansu-Kyeremeh observes that "the paltry literature regarding various interpretations of indigenous communication systems elsewhere and in Africa"[5] is a problem in itself. And this lack of relevant models is only part of the problem in peripheral nations. Ank Linden points out that "Governmental authorities in Third World countries often seem to be more interested in maintaining the status quo than in strengthening the communication capacity of the people."[6] Many peripheral leaders did not want external help, which could jeopardize their control of the people along with the opportunity for them to skim off much of the foreign aid. When this happened, American and other officials were willing to look the other way as long as the regimes were anti-communist. Concern about the sociology and culture of communication, whether in the form of orally transmitted folklore or of color television transmitted live via satellite, heightened the need for a revised vision of cultural development and the role of communication in it. Whereas the Western media valued freedom of the press, free speech, and the free flow of information, most peripheral nations began to reject these and related values as luxuries they could not afford. They had no multitude of competing views and media systems. Most of these countries were fortunate to have a single electronic medium, usually radio. Finally, of course, virtually all peripheral regions lack the necessary telecommunications infrastructure required for modern media systems, including mobile phones and access to the Internet.

Moreover, the position of peripheral nations on the role of government control conflicted with that of the core and democratic nations. In some cases, development media initiatives sought the support of local governments, and in others, the governments imposed rigid controls. In both situations, the media had little choice but to accept and repeat the messages those in control wished to disseminate. The result was two diametrically opposed journalistic philosophies about the relationship between the media and government. Western journalists favored a free press, and journalists in less-developed countries followed a development journalism approach.

Development journalism/communication is a pivotal concept in this new environment. Its proponents are newly emerging nations, all in the periphery, primarily in Africa, Latin America, and Asia, with low income, high illiteracy rates, and virtually no modern media systems except for the ruling elites and the military. The infrastructure and finances to support a broad-based advanced telecommunications system simply do not exist. Where they do exist, they are controlled by the ruling elites or by foreign corporations, such as Walmart. As the poor countries see it, in order to rapidly improve the economic and social position of peripheral nations, a concerted effort by both government and media is required. The luxury of competing and critical views on government policies and programs within the national media is viewed as detrimental to the colossal task of "catching up."

In order to correct the imbalances and mistaken impressions created by the Western press, peripheral nations continue to promote their media theory of development journalism. At a practical level, they reject neutrality and objectivity in favor of active roles as promoters of government objectives. They engage in advocacy journalism. Their reporting reflects the stated objectives of their governments, and they see no conflict between this and their journalistic objectives. In some instances, countries may attempt to limit any positive reporting of Western activities. In some cases only negative stories of the West are disseminated in order to reinforce the view of it as the "Great Satan." Unfortunately, by acting in this way, development journalism commits the same grievous crime it so readily attributes to the Western press.

Finally, many media corporations based in Europe and North America have reduced their numbers of reporters in Africa, Asia, and Latin America, in particular, for three significant reasons:

1 the cost of stationing full-time reporters in foreign bureaus;
2 the perception of a lack of interest among editors and management in routine events in distant lands;
3 the ease of air travel and the relative portability of equipment.

The cost of stationing full-time reporters in foreign bureaus has increased dramatically. These media corporations are profit-driven and are always seeking ways to reduce costs, so they close foreign bureaus. Second, with the end of Cold War tension, there is at least a perception of a lack of interest on the part of editors and management in events in distant lands. Less space and time are allotted to foreign news. Third, core-based editors realize that when a usually negative major news story breaks somewhere in a peripheral nation, they can dispatch a crew and reporters to the location in a relatively short period of time owing to the ease of airline travel and the portability of equipment. This is known as "parachute journalism." This phenomenon further fuels the criticism and antagonizes the critics of Western media because it contributes to the largely negative coverage of peripheral nations and regions. A tsunami, coup, earthquake, kidnapping, or riots where Americans are involved is what get covered.

Historically, the notion of development and progress was intertwined with economic issues and measurements; so now we turn to a consideration of economic models of growth and modernization.

The Economic Growth Model

Perhaps the best-known categorization of stages of development is the one advanced in 1960 by US economist Walter Rostow in *The Stages of Economic Growth: A Non-Communist Manifesto*. This was one of the central early works which set modernization theory on an economic trajectory. Others were *The Passing of Traditional Society* by Daniel Lerner, *Diffusion of Innovations* by Everett Rogers, and *Mass Media and National Development* by Wilbur Schramm.

Walter Rostow asserted that the development process can be divided into five clearly defined stages, as shown in Table 2.1. In most versions of this scheme, traditional and modern societies are placed at opposite ends of an evolutionary economic scale. Development is viewed as evolution beyond or out of traditional structures and ways that supposedly cannot accommodate rapid social change or produce sufficient economic growth. The new attitudes, values, and social relationships that support social change and industrialization are frequently conveyed through mass media as well as educational systems.

The economic growth model assumes development to be irreversible, like biological evolution. Modernization occurred when the necessary conditions for change were established, and the process continued inexorably. Societies absorbed the stress and change as they adapted themselves and their institutions to the new order and ways of doing things in order to prosper. In reality, however, this dominant paradigm of development following a modernization track did not produce the success stories that governments, foundations, universities, and aid agencies had promised. The complex processes and depth of traditional customs and behaviors rendered most development efforts futile. Corrupt regimes did little to help the situation as well. Criticism of the model mounted and continues today.

To understand the role that mass media were thought to play in development under the dominant paradigm, it is important to note that one of its most prominent features was the assumption that development could be equated with economic growth, the type of rapid growth that core nations experienced through capital-intensive, technology-driven industrialization. As Everett Rogers points out, "economists were firmly in the driver's seat of development programs. They defined the problem of underdevelopment largely in economic terms, and in turn this perception of the problem as predominantly economic in nature helped to put and to keep economists in charge."[7] Despite criticisms, theorists and aid practitioners continued to be preoccupied with the economic determinism of Western models of modernization, in large part because they produced measurable phenomena. Non-economic factors, such as culture, language, customs, and the role of women, were largely ignored.

Yet, as nations struggled to move from the peripheral to the semiperipheral zone and finally to elite core status, the nations and their citizens needed to adopt the trappings and values of a modernized state. Embedded in the modernization process is the ever pervasive and influential role of mass media and communication technologies. Anthony Giddens states:

Table 2.1 Rostow's stages of economic growth (from Walter Rostow, *The Stages of Economic Growth*, New York: Cambridge University Press, 1960 © Cambridge University Press 1960, 1971, 1990)

1	Traditional society
2	Establishment of preconditions to take off
3	Take-off into sustained growth
4	Drive to maturity
5	The age of high mass consumption

The media, printed and electronic, obviously play a central role in this respect. Mediated experience, since the first experience of writing, has long influenced both self-identity and the basic organization of social relations. With the development of mass communication, particularly electronic communication, the interpenetration of self-development and social systems up to and including global systems becomes even more pronounced.[8]

To some extent, Giddens is speculating that modernization will ultimately lead to Marshall McLuhan's "global village," where communication systems are capable of importing images, data, and sounds from around the corner or around the globe, with similar technologies and similar effects. One of the most profound effects will be that the language of the "global village" will be English.[9]

In summary, development has been viewed as "a type of social change in which new ideas are introduced into a social system in order to produce higher per capita incomes and levels of living through modern product methods and improved social organization."[10] But after decades, a growing chorus of critics began to make themselves heard.

The Inadequacy of the Economic Growth Model

For the most part, attempts at direct social and economic change in peripheral regions never materialized, and the effort of core nations to engineer social change in poorer regions of the world have been largely unsuccessful. In fact, a *World Development Report* for 1998–9 published by the World Bank[11] points out that developing countries are still relatively worse off, vis-à-vis the core nations, in terms of growth. One only has to look at the relative penetration of information technologies or at Internet access per capita to see how far behind peripheral nations are in the information revolution and global economy. Some critics go so far as to claim that the World Bank and the International Monetary Fund (IMF) have been counterproductive in terms of global development.[12] Critics, such as those opposing trade agreements, point out that the economies of developing nations simply have not improved through World Bank intervention and that local private enterprises are frequently squeezed out by large IMF projects or multinational conglomerates entering peripheral regions in cooperation with the IMF or other aid agencies.[13]

Another major problem is illiteracy. Along with economic stagnation, many peripheral nations have growing illiteracy rates. Poor regions are defined in part by their high illiteracy rates. Illiteracy makes access to the consumption of certain mass media such as newspapers, magazines, books, and much of the content on the Internet irrelevant to a large proportion of the population in peripheral areas. Nations with high birth rates see themselves moving downward in terms of both literacy and overall economic status.

Many peripheral-based critics began questioning the entire functional school of media theory. In general, the functional theorists uncritically accepted the position of media elites and the reinforcement of the status quo as legitimate and rational behavior for the media systems. But today, the relevant questions about constructing communication systems in peripheral nations are: What is their purpose and for whom are they being developed?

Imported economic practices, technologies, and media often create confusion because traditional systems are unable to support the required change. In turn, some analysts have shifted to non-economic explanations of development, identifying variables such as mass media exposure; telecommunications, political, and social structural changes; social mobility; population control; along with individual psychology and commitment as preconditions for positive development and eventual modernization.

The development of mass communication was portrayed under the dominant paradigm as part of a universal, inevitable sequence of changes that traditional societies undergo in the transition to modernity. Mass communication was thought to function best in the service of centralized government development agencies when it was geared toward raising the public's aspirations and facilitating the acceptance of new ideas, values, and inventions for the purpose of overall growth and higher gross national product (GNP). Critical questions about the impact on traditions, tastes, values, language, history, role models, or cultures inherent in foreign mass media were simply not addressed. As Ilan Kapoor states, "the field of international development struggles harder and harder to escape its reputation as a Trojan horse."[14]

The Research Traditions

When communication researchers turned their attention to development and modernity, they had a dual heritage. First, they were influenced strongly by the body of theory on the development process that had been built up in other fields, particularly economics, political science, and sociology. But equally strong influences on development communication research were the well-established traditions and orientation of social science research in the communication field. The following sections briefly review the major research traditions in the discipline of communication: functionalism, structuralism, and professionalism. Almost the entire body of literature dealing with international communication since World War II has been guided and influenced by these schools of thought. (Critical theory, which looked at power and other variables, and which had its roots in the Frankfurt School, did not seriously challenge the dominant paradigms.)

Functionalism

The traditions of functionalism began to take shape with the commercially oriented, early mass communication research of the 1930s and 1940s in the United States. Functionalism reflected the marketing concerns of a consumer society. Lazarsfeld, one of the pioneers of mass communication research, described this type of work as "administrative research."[15]

Historically, US mass communication research isolated specific media purposes, messages, or effects from the overall social process. It did not attempt to relate communication to the social, ideological, political, cultural, and economic systems in which it operated. Explanations about the specific communication data were seldom discussed in terms of the larger communication system, or from a macro theoretical perspective. A linear, one-time analysis was typical of the early stages of research and still afflicts the discipline today.

US mass communication researchers concentrated on collecting and classifying data in order to illuminate new forms of social control, persuasion, or attitude change. They did not see it as their function to interpret these facts or to build grand theories about structural and systemic determinants of the communication process. This early trend continues, with a focus on quantitative, empirical, behavioral science methods as opposed to highly conceptual, qualitative, speculative, theoretical, semiotic, or philosophically discursive approaches to mass communication research. European academics favored this type of approach, though there were a few noticeable exceptions.[16]

This emphasis on quantitative, empirical methodology at the micro level is not surprising considering that most early mass communication research studies were commissioned by broadcast networks, government agencies, foundations, or large advertising organizations. Their aim was to deal primarily with specifically defined concerns about message effectiveness. These sponsors or agencies wanted to know what kind of political propaganda or persuasion technique would produce the desired effect. They were interested in the influence of such things as votes, purchases, attitudes, or behavior change of individuals. In terms of studies in less-developed regions of the world, the subjects were mostly male farmers. Sponsoring organizations wanted hard data about the impact of particular messages. They had no interest in how these findings fit into a greater social, ideological, or cultural scheme. Melvin Defleur and Sandra Ball-Rokeach note that as a result, the study of audiences to discover effects almost monopolized mass communication research.[17] Following the functionalism approach, US researchers have tended to accept the system as a given and to implicitly endorse it by failing to examine how their understanding of communication could be enriched by questioning other basic characteristics of the system, such as ownership, power, or the role of women.

A final note: Much of the data gathering was undertaken by disparate groups of graduate students under the supervision of major American academics, but once the field data were collected the teams of researchers would return to their universities, leaving subjects across the peripheral regions with almost nothing.

Structuralism

Some critics, such as Herbert Schiller, Dan Schiller, Dallas Smythe, Bob McChesney, and Howard Frederick, probed more deeply into the question of who communicates with whom and for what purposes. They found that the real shaper of peripheral nations' communication systems and the messages they produce is media from core nations. Most peripheral regimes do not have the expertise or resources to establish domestic communication systems that genuinely reflect their history, needs, concerns, values, and culture. Consequently, they rely on the transfer (usually through foreign aid programs or United Nations agencies) of core nation communication technology and software. Imported TV series, sitcoms, feature films, and wire service copy are far cheaper to acquire than the equivalent domestically produced media programs.

In addition, it is important to note that most of the international communication industry is owned and controlled by giant core nations, mainly in the form of European, US, or Japanese transnational communication conglomerates. Good examples are Time Warner, Disney, Viacom, Comcast (NBC), News Corporation (which owns Fox and the *Wall Street Journal*), Apple, Google, Amazon, Microsoft, Sony, and Bertelsmann. These corporations are tied closely into a subtle and invisible network of core-based political, ideological, and economic elites, and they use the communication industry to perpetuate certain "needs," tastes, values, and attitudes so as to increase profits. Sales and market share are the defining matrices. When a peripheral nation imports, either through purchase, loan, or donation, communication technologies (from simple short-wave radio equipment, to printing presses, to ground stations for color television by means of satellite or the Internet), together with their software, it imports an alternative way of life. Herbert Schiller and others on the left described this as cultural imperialism, while advocates claim that it is becoming steadily more important in the exercise of global power:

> The marketing system developed to sell industry's outpouring of (largely inauthentic) consumer goods is now applied as well to globally selling ideas, tastes, preferences, and beliefs. In fact, in advanced capitalism's present stage, the production and dissemination of what it likes to term "information" become major and indispensable activities, by any measure, in the overall system. Made-in-America messages, imagery, lifestyles, and information techniques are being internationally circulated and, equally important, globally imitated. Multinational media corporations are major players in the world economy. Information and communications are vital components in the system of administration and control. Communication, it needs to be said, includes much more than messages and the recognizable circuits through which the messages flow. It defines social reality and thus influences the organization of work, the character of technology, the curriculum of the educational system, formal and informal, and the use of "free" time – actually, the basic social arrangements of living.[18]

A substantial body of literature deals with the central concept of cultural imperialism,[19] which usually applies either to specific peripheral nations or to specific communication industries such as filmmaking, advertising, television sitcoms, or mass circulation magazines. The central finding of the research is that exporting corporations establish ground rules in such a way that the peripheral nations are at a structural disadvantage from the start. Yet this is considered a crucial process in world system theory. Somehow, this imbalance is supposed to exist in order for core nations to grow and succeed even more.

A good example of this process is reflected in the activities of the US retailer Blockbuster, which rents and sells videos, DVDs, and video games. In addition to its US stores, Blockbuster has more than 1,295 stores in 23 other countries. Many of these are in semiperipheral and peripheral nations. One can easily imagine what happens to a small, local family-owned and family-operated video store in peripheral nations such as Thailand, Argentina, Brazil, Mexico, or Chile when a Blockbuster store opens in the same community. Finally, as it and others seek to become the leading global player in the rental market, Blockbuster also brings with it a vast library of Hollywood feature films, American music, and US marketing and advertising expertise, with little room or interest for low-quantity video or DVD rentals of foreign indigenous productions.

Another example is Walmart, which has over 6,000 stores internationally, 1,200 in Mexico alone. In 2012 these foreign venues greeted 200 million customers per week and produced close to $125 billion in annual revenue. The stores have over two million associates and a home entertainment section which sells consumers electronics of all types, DVDs, video games, and e-books. Walmart is one of the largest sellers of video and music in the world. The company has come out strongly in support of the United Nation's eight Millennium Development Goals (MDG). The MDGs have both direct and indirect applications to development communication.

Professionalism

An integral but seldom discussed instrument of cultural imperialism is the technocratic baggage – including technicians, engineers, producers, directors, behind-the-scenes personnel, and writers – that is required for the technical maintenance and operation of an imported communication infrastructure. These technocrats and engineers, along with their manuals, are usually on loan from the industrialized nations or are trained and educated in core nations. They bring to peripheral countries value systems and attitudes associated with Western professionalism about how communication systems should be "properly" run and how they should work. This socialization frequently adds another layer to the software that itself portrays a foreign culture. Moreover, technological personnel are frequently in the employ of various core-nation aid agencies – governmental, educational, or religious organizations – that are also heavily value-laden enterprises with a proselytizing agenda.

These realities may help to explain why the introduction of mass media in many peripheral nations has failed to produce substantial results. Although there were some efforts to promote cultural sovereignty and indigenous productions, in the final analysis, these efforts produced little of substance on a national level. A noted authority in the field, Robert Stevenson, states: "Development journalism – very much a part of the New World Information Order debate at the United Nations Educational, Scientific and Cultural Organization (UNESCO) in the 1970s – now has a record, and it is not impressive."[20]

Given its preoccupation with audience research, US communication studies has not investigated the ties that bind media institutions to other sources and structures of power, whether domestic or international. In essence, communication experts have taken for granted that more modern technology, including communication hardware and software, will be beneficial and will promote more economic growth. In fact, the policies they support do not necessarily advance development, or improve their quality of life, but tend to foster a neocolonial-like dependence on organizations from core nations. Increasing amounts of media and information technologies often contribute to the already unbalanced distribution of benefits by concentrating additional communication power in the hands of ruling elites. These elites may be political, religious, or military in nature. This creates tension and frustration in peripheral regions by promoting inappropriate and inaccessible consumer products and values, further expanding the economic gap between core and peripheral nations.

Professionalism, as a body of research, did not have a parallel counterpart in European communication studies. The European tradition differs in two dramatic ways. First, many of the studies undertaken by European communication scholars deal with either critical theory emerging from the Frankfurt School of the 1930s, or with cultural studies which examine issues from a very different perspective from the North American traditions. Furthermore, practicing media professionals in Europe have distinctly different training than their US counterparts. Whereas most US professionals are required to have a university degree, preferably from one of the leading schools of journalism, European media outlets prefer to train their personnel through apprenticeships at regional media outlets, particularly provincial newspapers. Thus, European media professionals learn their craft by doing rather than by studying.

Despite the substantial difference between European and US socialization of media professionals and technicians, it is important to note that the critical school frequently examines ownership by media elites or economic aspects of the industry. These European researchers often reach conclusions similar to those of US scholars. Basically they have found dysfunctional elements in the exportation of considerable amounts of communication hardware, software, and related cultural products.

Western Research Failings

More exhaustive approaches focusing on structural, contextual, and procedural determinants of communication have been low-priority research concerns in the United States. US students of communication have never sought a conceptual inventory that would provide a complete basis for explaining communication in the context of an overall social system. This failure to recognize communication as inextricably tied to social structure and power has hampered the field. Even the diffusion of innovation research tradition has flawed assumptions. Luis Beltran writes:

> One basic assumption of the diffusion approach is that communication by itself can generate development, regardless of socioeconomic and political conditions. Another assumption is that increased production and consumption of goods and services constitute the essence of development, and that a fair distribution of income and opportunities will necessarily derive in due time. A third assumption is that the key to increased productivity is technological innovation, regardless of whom it may benefit and whom it may harm.[21]

The dominant research tools of diffusion studies – interview, sample survey, and content analysis – are another obstacle to the exploration of social structure as a key factor in the communication process. A preoccupation with methodological precision and small samples has taken precedence over macro theoretical formulations.

This brings us to another feature of communication research that militates against the adoption of a macro social approach that encompasses the roles of structural and organizational variables. Most theoretical models of development tend to locate internal sources of problems in developing countries and seldom look at external agencies or practices, such as the World Bank or World Trade Organization, or at the foreign ownership of media, advertising agencies, and telecommunication systems. Many of the peripheral nations have simply been glad to be the recipients of foreign aid or to have a global corporation build a plant or office in their country and create new employment opportunities.

It was suggested earlier that the lack of an adequate focus on structure in development communication research in particular, and US communication studies in general, is related to researchers' acceptance of the premise that the system is in sync. Basically, researchers did not question the system since they viewed it as working for everyone's benefit. This acceptance makes it difficult for researchers to question the structure and organization of that system, instead encouraging them to concentrate their attention on how mass communication could act on audiences in a way that promotes conformity, purchases, and adjustment to a larger consumption-driven social order.

One could argue that the lack of a structural focus stems also from the empirical, quantitative slant of US communication research and a corresponding reluctance to theorize at the macro level, as Marshall McLuhan did. The influences of communication on ideological and value systems, patterns of social organization, or subtle, difficult-to-measure matrices of power and social interaction are much harder to handle with empirical precision. These variables are less subject to rigorous measurements than the effects of specific messages on specific audiences. Study of those influences necessarily involves some theorizing, hypothesizing, and a speculative thinking not always firmly rooted in hard data. But such modes of understanding run against the grain of the exactness of the behavioral science tradition of US communication research as promoted and reinforced at universities.

A decade ago, the claim of scientific neutrality and objectivity was being challenged by a growing number of critics in the communication and journalism fields. Some comparative research is also appearing. In his Foreword to *Images of the US around the World: A Multicultural Perspective*, Majid Tehranian makes the following point concerning the image of the United States in a global context:

The image of the United States thus gradually deteriorated from a friend to a foe. In the meantime, however, the flow of American soft power in the spread of its cultural influence around the world through its cultural exports (English language, books, films, music, radio and TV programs, blue jeans, Coca-Cola, Madonna, and Michael Jackson) has seduced the younger generation nearly everywhere into emulating the American ways. The repugnance against Americanization has led some critics of US cultural influences to call it westoxification. Just like intoxication, the afflicted not only fall victim to its influence but revel in it. [22]

New Departures

Current students of the discipline have found development communication theory and research methodology wanting in several respects, and they are undergoing a re-examination. To overcome these limitations, efforts are underway to find more sophisticated tools for measuring the influence of social structure; for example, the non-economic variables of social life and culture, at both macro and micro levels.

In addition, Marxist theories of communication and development gained attention during the 1960s and 1970s. In these models, the causes of underdevelopment are traced back to international imbalances caused by the dominance of capitalist systems and the imperialist control they exercise over peripheral regions, first through colonization and now by commercialization. There is a growing consciousness of the role that multinationals play in perpetuating colonial dependence both culturally and ideologically through their economic and political control of the international communication industry. This understanding is reflected in many new models that consider the influence of global political and economic power structures on development in their attempts to describe the causes of and solutions to underdevelopment. But in the early 1990s, with the demise of communism and its champion, the Soviet Union, much of the interest in and research with a Marxist underpinning quickly lost advocates and viability. Marxist communication literature lost its credibility. Still, the predominately European-based critical school of cultural studies is gaining broader attention. Although it offers a significant alternative, the problems of operationalizing its premises make large-scale research projects difficult and very costly.

For decades, communication scholars such as Schiller and Rogers pointed out the centrality of communication in the development process, but their research and scholarship had little impact outside the discipline of communication. Most of the aid agencies, foundations, and government organizations responsible for implementing development policies are controlled and dominated by economists or political scientists, and these academics failed to understand the crucial role of communication in the development cycle. They bring a silo mentality to the tasks at hand. If they had incorporated the role of communication, they might have been more successful, and the voices of criticism might have been fewer and less vociferous.

The good news is that there is evidence of a growing movement for change. The World Bank provides a good example. Long focused on the more easily measured economic indices of development such as miles of asphalt or tons of concrete, the World Bank is reconsidering its focus. It has discovered the centrality of communication within the overall development process. Each year the World Bank publishes its *World Development Report*, which identifies factors that promote sustainable development. It also reflects the thinking of the bank's senior staff. Historically, the reports have focused on large-scale projects, some of which relate to transportation and agrarian infrastructures. The 1998 report, however, marks a dramatic shift by regarding communication as central to future development. The report suggests three lessons that are particularly important to the welfare of the billions of people in developing countries:

1   Developing countries must institute policies that enable them to narrow the knowledge gaps separating poor countries from rich.
2   Developing country governments, multilateral institutions, nongovernmental organizations, and the private sector must work together to strengthen the institutions needed to address the information problems that cause markets and governments to fail.
3   No matter how effective these endeavors are, problems with knowledge will persist. But recognizing that knowledge is at the core of all development efforts will allow us to discover unexpected solutions to seemingly intractable problems.[23]

In the face of its critics, the World Bank is attempting to reposition itself as an institution that understands and fosters the central role of information, knowledge, and communication in its expanding global mandate.

Finally, a new movement under the umbrella of participatory communication has emerged. It seeks to use communication as a tool at the grassroots level. A goal is to bring about social change by using non-formal education methods. NGOs, in particular, attempt to work with local people in peripheral regions to share efforts and goals. This approach seeks to promote ownership at the community level. Participatory communication is not top-down but aims at being sensitive to local traditions, culture, and language by engaging locals at every stage of both planning and implementation[24]: it seeks to be a bottom-up process. The regions of Africa, Latin America, and Asia have attempted with varying degrees of success to implement social change along the lines of participatory communication strategies.

Yet even participatory development (PD) or communication approaches have critics. Ilan Kapoor writes: "The argument, in other words, is that complicity and desire are written into PD, making it prone to an exclusionary, Western-centric and egalitarian politics … Critics point out that, far from being inclusive and bottom-up, it reconfigures power and value systems which may end up being exclusionary, if not tyrannical."[25]

Postscript

As noted earlier, the criticisms identified here created widespread cause for concern among academics, professionals, and policymakers. Some are calling for a new definition of development journalism/communication in light of the failure of dominant models.[26] The many nations in the peripheral zone are still stuck in that most marginal, least desirable zone, with little if any power. In Chapter 3, we will examine the role of UNESCO in bringing communication concerns to the forefront of the international arena. UNESCO represents some practical and theoretical alternatives for media flows, indigenous practices, and cultural sovereignty. These issues deserve the attention of students of development and the media, as well as professionals actively involved in the collection, observation, and reporting of foreign news, cultures, projects, and viewpoints.

When UNESCO championed the cause for a re-examination of international communication flows, the debates about media flows took on a life of their own. By introducing communication issues into global political discourse, UNESCO simultaneously found both supporters and detractors. Whereas some nations recognized the validity of the arguments and concerns, others interpreted them in terms of Cold War rhetoric and divisions. More is said about the significance of the UNESCO in Chapter 3.

Communication research with an international focus is changing, complex, and in some cases controversial. Previous theories and approaches appear limited, which is why the application of world system theory, as well as the theory of electronic colonialism, to global communication trends is a welcome addition to the discipline. Electronic colonialism theory examines the cultural forces influencing individuals' attitudes and behavior in foreign countries, whereas world system theory attempts to explain and separate the different nations or regions of the world into a three-stage platform or construct emphasizing economic variables or conditions.

We now turn to major global stakeholders, including US and foreign multimedia conglomerates. An important point to keep in mind is that new digital technologies are blurring the old boundaries between software and hardware, between broadcasting and telecommunication. Old divisions and distinctions are becoming meaningless as giant communication firms morph into digital providers of a broad array of products and services to end users – customers – around the globe without regard for national boundaries. The convergence of delivery systems in a broadband or wireless environment is forcing regulators and multimedia conglomerates to rethink their global strategies. Convergence, involving the interlocking of digital technologies, computing, telephony, and global networks, is rapidly changing the commercial environments, with new stakeholders entering the arena on an almost daily basis. Think Apple, Google, Twitter, Facebook, or YouTube and the pace of change involved becomes obvious.

Notes

1. A landmark speech which established the framework, concerns, vision, and mandate for what would become the extensive involvement of the United States in both development communication projects and a plethora of anti-communism activities was President Harry Truman's inaugural address of January 20, 1949. The address expressed a mix of concern for the less fortunate of the world, particularly following World War II, and an early fear of the potential spread of communism which would eventually lead to the Cold War. Truman called for a new program aimed at spreading the economic and scientific benefits of the United States to underdeveloped countries. This would soon translate into a massive amount of talent and monetary aid for projects with a modernization focus, several of which had a communication- or media-related dimension. For a more detailed discussion, see Thomas McPhail, *Development Communication: Reframing the Role of the Media*, Oxford: Wiley-Blackwell, 2009.

2. Normandy Madden, "Cable, Satellite Media Lure Influential Viewers," *Advertising Age International* (October 1999), 36.

3. The history of development journalism may be traced to the Department of Development Communication at the College of Agriculture, University of the Philippines. It was established in 1973 for the purpose of training students to assist in the communication process of transmitting, by way of the media, the government's policies on agricultural development.

4. Andrew Moemeka, "Development Communication: A Historical and Conceptual Overview," in Andrew Moemeka (ed.), *Communication for Development*, Albany: State University of New York Press, 1994, p. 7.

5. Kwasi Ansu-Kyeremeh, "Indigenous Communication in Africa: A Conceptual Framework," in Kwasi Ansu-Kyeremeh (ed.), *Perspective on Indigenous Communication in Africa*, Legon, Ghana: School of Communication Studies Printing Press, 1998, p. 1.

6. Ank Linden, "Overt Intentions and Covert Agendas," Gazette 61(2) (1999), 153.

7. Everett Rogers, "Communication and Development: The Passing of the Dominant Paradigm," *Communication Research* 3 (1976), 215. Rogers wrote the "Introduction" to the first edition of *Electronic Colonialism*.

8. Anthony Giddens, *Modernity and Self-Identity*, Stanford, CA: Stanford University Press, 1991, p. 4.

9. David Crystal, *English as a Global Language*, Cambridge: Cambridge University Press, 1997.

10. Everett Rogers, *Modernization among Peasants: The Impact of Communication*, New York: Holt, Rinehart and Winston, 1969, pp. 8–9.

11. *World Development Report 1998–99: Knowledge for Development*, New York: World Bank and Oxford University Press, 1998.

12. Kevin Danaher, *10 Reasons to Abolish the IMF and World Bank*. New York: Seven Stories Press, 2001.

13. See, e.g., Doug Bandow and Ian Vasques (eds.), *Perpetuating Poverty: The World Bank, the IMF, and the Developing World*, Washington, DC: Cato Institute, 1994, which dissects the role of the World Bank and the International Monetary Fund in promoting the politicization of economic life, inhibiting private enterprise, and delaying the emergence from poverty. The contributors argue that because of the nature of their structure, the World Bank and the IMF cannot change pro-market policies (p. 362). See also Danaher, *10 Reasons to Abolish the IMF and World Bank.*

14. Ilan Kapoor, "Participatory Development, Complicity and Desire," *Third World Quarterly* 26 (2005), 1203. Kapoor also expands on his criticism in *The Postcolonial Politics of Development*, New York: Routledge, 2008.

15. Paul Lazarsfeld, "Remarks on Administrative and Critical Communication Research," *Studies in Philosophy and Social Science* 9 (1941), 2–16.

16. Two of the most notable exceptions are Kyungmo Kim and George Barnett, "The Determinants of International News Flows: A Network Analysis," *Communication Research* 23(3) (June 1996), 323–52, and Jianguo Zhu, "Comparing the Effects of Mass Media and Telecommunications on Economic Development: A Pooling Time Series Analysis," *Gazette* 57 (1996), 17–28.

17. Melvin Defleur and Sandra Ball-Rokeach, *Theories of Mass Communication*, New York: Longman, 1975.

18. Herbert Schiller, *Communication and Cultural Domination*, White Plains, NY: International Arts and Sciences Press, 1976, p. 3.

19. Some scholars see this substantial body of literature as being overly representative of the body of knowledge in international communication. One critic refers to this aspect in the following way: "The root of the problem is that the research paradigm of the field of international communication is dominantly critical" (Michael G. Elasmar, "Opportunities and Challenges of Using Meta-Analysis in the Field of International Communication," *Critical Studies in Mass Communication* 16(3) (September 1999), 382). After applying a meta-analysis, the author claimed that the majority of writers used polemics rather than empirical evidence to support their conclusions. Many of the pieces are authored by academics in the semiperipheral and peripheral regions. In the same article, Elasmar also called for the utilization of more meta-analysis in order to move the field of international communication to a higher plane.

20. Robert Stevenson, *Global Communication in the Twenty-First Century*, New York: Longman, 1994, p. 13.

21. Luis Beltran, "Alien Premises, Objects and Methods in Latin American Communication Research," *Communication Research* 3 (1976), 107–34.

22. Majid Tehranian, "Foreword," in Y. Kamalipour (ed.), *Images of the US around the World: A Multicultural Perspective*, Albany: State University of New York Press, 1999, pp. xvi–xvii.

23. *World Development Report 1998–99*, p. 1.

24. Hermant Shah, "Modernization, Marginalization, and Emancipation: Toward a Normative Model of Journalism and National Development," *Communication Theory* 6(2) (May 1998), 143–67.

25. Kapoor, "Participatory Development, Complicity and Desire," pp. 1203–4.

26. For further details see J. Servaes, T. Jacobson, and S. White (eds.), *Participatory Communication for Social Change*, London: Sage, 1996, and T. Jacobson and J. Servaes (eds.), *Theoretical Approaches to Participatory Communication*, Cresskill, NJ: Hampton Press, 1999.

3

The Message

The Role of International Organizations

Introduction

Historically, the United Nations Educational, Scientific and Cultural Organization (UNESCO) has tried to avoid controversy. Yet its role, profile, and focus in the international information and communication debate are unmistakable. UNESCO, a specialized agency of the United Nations based in Paris, sponsored crucial international conferences that focused on the global communication debate and also directed its research program toward promoting new policy initiatives, such as the New World International and Communication Order (NWICO). Initially UNESCO invested much, backstage as well as publicly, in NWICO. This eventually led to major problems for the agency, the greatest of which was the withdrawal during the 1980s of the United States and the United Kingdom from UNESCO membership. When they left, they also took their crucial financial support, which had been about one-third of UNESCO's total annual budget. UNESCO put its efforts and credibility into supporting a call for NWICO, but with the demise of the Cold War, UNESCO was found wanting. It had made a strategic mistake in relying extensively on strong Soviet support for NWICO.

Before describing the critical historical meetings and stakeholders in the global debate, it is important to note that the global media have two rather distinct origins. In the United States, their origins are strongly rooted in commercial media systems in which advertising and market forces play crucial roles. Initially with newspapers, radio, and now with television, telecommunications, and the Internet, the US model is one of corporate influence with private ownership and control. The US model treats media and culture as economic commodities. By contrast, in Europe and in most countries of the world, the historical model is one of government ownership or government control of the mass media. The BBC is a good example of a non-commercial radio and television network subsidized by both the government and listeners or viewers, who pay an annual license fee. In most of the world (in particular former colonies of European countries), radio evolved as a

Global Communication: Theories, Stakeholders, and Trends, Fourth Edition. Thomas L. McPhail.
© 2014 John Wiley & Sons, Inc. Published 2014 by John Wiley & Sons, Inc.

government medium without commercials or the influence of marketplace competition. The role of electronic media was to inform, educate, and "entertain", not to make money from advertisers. Broadcasting monopolies were the early pervasive global model. When television technology emerged, these same government-approved outlets took responsibility for television broadcasting. For several decades they limited the number of national television networks to only one or two, much as they did with radio. They viewed the media as cultural partners that were necessary to promote a nation's history, culture, education, and the arts. When commercial television emerged, a mixed model was accepted in Europe and in many other countries. The commercial model of the United States was frowned upon until vast audiences began viewing the shows presented by new alternative commercial radio and television stations. With deregulation and the advancement of cable and satellite technologies, several competing commercial broadcasting systems were born. These new stations, systems, or networks frequently are foreign media giants, such as Disney, MTV, ESPN, or Fox, and frequently reach larger audiences than the original domestic government-controlled networks.

It is important to keep this duality of approach in mind when considering the following the global debates. The debates themselves tended to move along two different tracks, the one track being more commercial, market-driven, and oriented to free enterprise, the other being non-commercial, publicly funded, and government-controlled and government-regulated in the public interest. The following sections review the history of the international communication debates, illustrating the global fundamental differences in the origins, philosophies, roles, and environments in which global communication stakeholders have operated and, in some monopolistic, government-regulated environments, continue to operate.

More than half of the nations in the world – those in the peripheral regions – still place some restrictions on journalists or media outlets. Even though the commercial, advertiser-supported networks have attracted by far the largest audiences internationally, there is still a dedicated and loyal niche audience supporting public broadcasting, led by outlets such as the BBC. Many non-Americans view the international communication debate from a very different perspective: "Decolonization in itself has not made the world more just and peaceful. The evidence shows more news and images come from the Western world and the access to non-Western culture in terms of information, knowledge, entertainment and images becomes more scarce."

UNESCO: Backdrop to the NWICO Debates

UNESCO, originating in Great Britain in 1945, acknowledges in its constitution that "since wars begin in the minds of men, it is in the minds of men that the defenses of peace must be constructed." On the basis of this lofty ideal, it has transformed itself from a passive force into an active force in international affairs. It views its mission as that of a catalyst for and supporter of development:

> Both on the theoretical and the practical levels, UNESCO has a vital role to play. The current economic relations between industrialized and developing countries certainly must be transformed, but on their own they cannot change the political and socio-cultural factors that shape integrated developments. Thus UNESCO has the task of helping: to enlarge the scientific and technological bases which permit each country to use its natural resources better;... to increase and improve communications and

information systems;... to promote the progress of social sciences so that each society can undertake its own studies and utilize the instruments of change without losing its own identity.[1]

Formally established as a specialized agency of the United Nations in 1946, UNESCO entered the international arena with 20 member states, the vast majority being core nations. Its budget is drawn from a levy imposed on each member state. Although based in Paris, the Secretariat draws its personnel from all member states.[2] In the early years, all members were core or semiperipheral nations. Peripheral nations began joining UNESCO after World War II. Many were former colonies of European core nations – this created a tense working environment. Today, delegates from several peripheral nations hold senior positions in UNESCO. To a large extent most peripheral nations view UNESCO as the one specialized agency of the United Nations which understands them and promotes their needs and agenda with its focus on a broad range of development initiatives.

UNESCO's mandate is broad, covering educational, scientific, cultural, and communication programs and research projects around the globe. The convening and sponsoring of international ministerial and research conferences to discuss various aspects of this broad mandate is one of UNESCO's most important and time-consuming tasks. In fact, it is through this role that UNESCO became a major player in the international communication debates that led to NWICO.

Originally, the Western nations, particularly Britain, France, and the United States, dominated UNESCO. However, beginning in the 1950s and continuing today, power and influence shifted as a result of the continual addition of former colonies. The one country one vote procedures that govern the agency have provided the peripheral nations with a voice and power. During the 1960s, the shared ideological and economic conditions of several of these peripheral nations led to the development of a power bloc or lobby known as the Group of 77. Although this bloc has grown to include well over 100 nations, its role and that of these newly emerged nations within UNESCO is fraught with contradictions. As UNESCO expert Richard Hoggart explains:

> The new nations, who were, in general, creations of the early sixties, tend to take the UN seriously though ambiguously. Since the UN was set up by the victorious allied powers, it has the stamp of Western ways of thinking. On the other hand, its record in anticolonialism is good and it has made a considerable contribution to the emergence of some new states. Their relationship to the UN is therefore rich in ambiguities.[3]

This ambiguity is no better illustrated than in their attitudes toward global communication. On the one hand, many of these nations want - some desperately - to become modern industrialized countries with all the media trappings that money and technology permit, such as color digital television, personal computers, cellular phones, and satellites. Yet, as noted earlier, most lack even the basic telecommunication infrastructures for telephone, let alone sophisticated ground terminals for satellite television transmission, or broadband cable or fiber optics for Internet access. Some of their populations cannot even read. At the same time, many of these nations reject Western culture – Hollywood films, Madison Avenue commercials, and core nation or foreign-produced television programming. Many in the peripheral zone will accept only indigenous domestic media products. The dilemma, of course, is that core nation technology and shows are easily accessible and cheaper than the production or creation of high-quality indigenous systems or software.

Throughout its existence, UNESCO has had its critics. Part of that criticism is a result of the periodic negative assessment of its parent, the United Nations. Another flash point, during the mid-1970s, was a decision that excluded Israel from the European regional grouping, creating a barrage of criticism from the Western press, and leading the United States to temporarily withhold its contribution to UNESCO, an amount equal to about 25 percent of the agency's total budget. Recently the United States again withdrew following a pro-Palestine vote.

Paradoxically, another cause for criticism was the consistent demand of peripheral countries for better development initiatives. UNESCO's initial response to critics was to focus on education, which culminated in the publication of the 1972 Faure Commission report, *Learning to Be*.[4] But with the completion of that major effort, a substantive policy vacuum developed that permitted the introduction of a series of resolutions by republics of the Soviet Union concerning the development of national media and communication policies. UNESCO, core governments, and multinational media corporations largely ignored the issues and questions being raised because they underestimated the strength, determination, voting power, and depth of animosity felt by both the Soviet Union and peripheral nations. These peripheral nations had a long list of grievances about international media flows. The lack of substantive policy permitted the Soviet Union and several peripheral nations to hijack UNESCO's planning agenda in the late 1970s. The result was the eruption of the global communication debates which dominated the activities of UNESCO for more than two decades. This chapter highlights the major forums in which the media and communication debates crystallized. Even today, many nations around the world are concerned about and critical of the impact of foreign software on their domestic values, attitudes, and beliefs. A good example is the concern of the American-dominated Internet Corporation for Assigned Names and Numbers (ICANN). It is based in California and its main task is to manage the allocation of Internet domain names and addresses globally. Several critics want to turn ICANN over to a new UN agency and to remove it from the hegemonic control of the US government.

Identifying the Issues and Taking Sides

The debate officially began in 1970[5] when UNESCO's General Assembly outlined the need to articulate national communication policies and a series of publications dealing with this issue began to emerge. This examination, by the peripheral nations in particular, led to increased documentation and greater awareness of the one-way flow of media messages from core to peripheral nations. It also became apparent that national communication development policies for semiperipheral and peripheral nations could not be produced when so much of their media were produced or controlled by foreign firms based in London, Paris, Toronto, New York, or Los Angeles.

Subsequently, three significant resolutions were introduced that increased the visibility and divisiveness of the global media issue. The first related to the rapid development of direct broadcast satellite (DBS) technology. DBS allowed media outlets to transmit their messages directly to receiving sets throughout the world. Whereas traditional ground station broadcasting signals could be controlled or blocked to prevent the widespread transmission of alien messages, DBS signals could easily circumvent these restrictions and procedures. In response, UNESCO passed a resolution – by a vote of 100 to 1, with the United States as the only dissenter – to require satellite broadcasters to obtain the prior consent of national governments and their regulators before transmitting messages to a foreign territory. Even though there was no technical way to enforce the resolution, its passage represented a bold rejection of US communication policy, along with the "free press" and "free flow" rhetoric and business practices.

The second resolution called for regional meetings of experts to discuss national communication policies. This resolution received the unanimous support of the General Assembly, but dissension arose when it was decided to hold these meetings in peripheral regions and not in the core industrialized nations, as had been UNESCO's tradition. A few of the key early meetings were held in Latin America.

The third contentious resolution, which was introduced by the USSR, sought to acknowledge both the right and the responsibility of national governments to control the media messages available to their citizenry. Although the resolution failed, it was attractive to many peripheral nations, which were heartened to have the support of at least one of the superpowers. Although the peripheral nations had achieved a significant presence in UNESCO, this Soviet "sharing of the minds" with respect to communication policy lent strength to their votes, opinions, and influence. For their part, the Soviets had no journalistic qualms or ethical dilemmas about extending international government control of media; clearly, their major objective was to aggravate the United States, Europe, and other core nations.

The Non-Aligned Movement

As the process of decolonization continued and previous colonial powers no longer had control over the foreign policy of their former colonies, many developing nations feared becoming satellites or pawns of one of the two superpowers, the United States and the Soviet Union. Consequently, a new political pressure group emerged. In 1973 a summit meeting of foreign ministers of non-aligned countries met in Algiers. During this meeting, participating nations acknowledged their desire to develop a unique foreign policy stance independent of both the United States and the USSR. They wanted to create a "third option" to reflect their independence. Many of the policy positions postulated sought to overcome the consequences of past colonization. Among these was a demand for the decolonization of information and an end to the one-way flow of media.

A series of non-aligned conferences followed in Peru, Tunisia, Mexico, India, and Sri Lanka. At each successive meeting, the rhetoric and action progressed from attacking transnational communication corporations to developing an action plan for the establishment of a wire service, Inter Press Services, which would begin as a pool of contributing government information services. Additional issues included debate about the New International Economic Order (NIEO) and awareness of the growing power of a nucleus of oil-rich, non-aligned countries in the Middle East, known as the Organization of Petroleum Exporting Countries (OPEC).

In addition to the non-aligned summit meetings, a crucial seminar was held at the University of Tampere in Finland. Finland's President Urho Kekkonen, in addressing the issue of cultural imperialism, asserted that the theory of the "free" flow of information was really a rationale for a "one-way" flow. Not coincidentally, a major research study was also presented at the conference that documented the pervasive influence of US and British television program sales internationally.[6] As research increasingly revealed evidence of the one-way flow of media products, particularly wire services, the anti-Western rhetoric escalated.

Meetings in Latin America

While the non-aligned countries proceeded to articulate their complaints and to develop communication strategies, several UNESCO-sponsored meetings were convened to investigate the disparities in international information flows and participation in national communication policy development. The major issues quickly became the relationship between communication policies and economic, social, and cultural development, and the role of governments in promoting the latter by controlling the former. A major conference to examine these questions was set for July 1976 in San José, Costa Rica, but two background meetings were held: in Bogota, Colombia, July 4–13, 1974, and Quito, Ecuador, June 24–30, 1975. Background papers, data, and research documents, which attacked AP and Reuters in particular, were presented outlining several grievances about a broad range of international communication issues. Foreign wire services, particularly those headquartered in New York, London, and Paris, came in for considerable criticism for their focus on "bad news" and their coverage of Latin America.

It should be emphasized that all parties to the debate understood that these regional conferences were creating a momentum for a major international conference focusing on media and information flow issues. Global information flows and media policies dominated the debate at UNESCO just as education had done in the 1960s. However, while there had been a general consensus about the positive role and impact of education, a strong and highly divisive polarity of opinion (free press versus government control) was developing on global information policies. To some extent the United States failed to take these meetings and findings seriously.

The 19th UNESCO General Assembly, Nairobi, 1976

The vital role of information and the debate about how to promote development through information policies were the focus of the 19th UNESCO General Assembly. By this time, most peripheral countries had abandoned the desire for and their rhetoric about a free press in favor of a development press, one that would assist in the positive development of their poor nation-states. They wanted a cultural stamp of their own making and not one imported from core nations or "made in the United States." The director-general of UNESCO, Amadou-Mahtar M'Bow from Senegal, Africa, could not have agreed more.

The major document placed before delegates at the Nairobi conference was a resolution similar to the one that had been introduced by the Soviet Union in 1971. It was entitled "Draft Declaration of Fundamental Principles Governing the Use of the Mass Media in Strengthening Peace and International Understanding and in Combating War, Propaganda, Racialism and Apartheid." This declaration, specifically Article 12, which required that national governments take responsibility for all media systems, guaranteed extensive attention from the Western press. Once again, the Western media coverage of UNESCO was very negative. One thorny issue was the call for the licensing of journalists.

Before outlining the major events in Nairobi, I think it is important we remember a situation from the early 1970s that again cemented Western, particularly US, faith in the value of a free press, in which two junior reporters for the *Washington Post*, Carl Bernstein and Bob Woodward, pursued a lead that ultimately led to the resignation of Richard Nixon as president of the United States. The Watergate scandal reinvigorated a latent distrust of government regulations and demonstrated to the people of the United States and other core nations the need for a press free from government control. Even the mere suggestion of increased government control of the media was anathema to the US public and Western journalists. In a similar fashion, British control of the national press during the Falkland Islands invasion in 1982 irritated many British reporters and publishers as well as the British public. Consequently, the Western model of the press as the "fourth estate" had been strongly reinforced in advance of the Nairobi conference.

Leaving aside other issues, it was Article 12, calling for state responsibility for media activities, that dominated the conference. In the "spirit of Nairobi," a compromise was reached, mainly behind the scenes, to shelve the draft declaration and to reduce pressure among the peripheral nations and non-aligned militants by forming a new group to study the issue further. UNESCO created the International Commission for the Study of Communication Problems, headed by Senator Sean MacBride of Ireland.

Having accurately analyzed the strong Western objection to development journalism and government oversight or control of press activities, Director-General M'Bow wanted to avoid an outright showdown, as well as save his career. Although he was able to delay the debate and critical vote until UNESCO's next General Assembly, to be held in Paris in 1978, he also exacerbated the problem by linking the debate over a new international information order to the proposed new international economic order.

New International Economic Order

In order to provide a complete picture of the rise of the non-aligned movement, it is necessary to describe the development of the NIEO. During the early 1970s, the United Nations and its member agencies became major vehicles for change, offering hope to emerging peripheral nations. Many observers were surprised by the extent to which the resolve and the magnitude of change adopted by the United Nations was misanalyzed not only in terms of NWICO, but also with respect to the underlying NIEO. It took Western economists several years to come to grips with NIEO, and only a few understood its link to international communication.

Just what was the NIEO that the United Nations, and therefore UNESCO, was supporting? In effect, it represented a major change for the West, which traditionally controlled the United Nations and its organizations. This was clearly no longer the case. When 146 nations met in Paris for five weeks of UNESCO meetings in the fall of 1978, the largest group, 106 member states, were developing countries, and many were also part of the so-called non-aligned nations. They were originally labelled the "Group of 77," and this term is still used of them despite their increased size and influence.[7]

Given the shift, it should not be surprising that the pressure for changes to enhance the development opportunities of peripheral nations became a pressing issue on the agendas of the United Nations and its specialized agencies. In response, on May 1, 1974 the United Nations General Assembly passed a resolution to adopt a major program of action establishing a new international economic order. The declaration encouraged member states to:

work urgently for the establishment of a New International Economic Order based on "equity, sovereign equality, interdependence, common interest and cooperation among all states," irrespective of their economic and social systems which shall correct inequalities and redress existing injustices, make it possible to eliminate the widening gap between the developed and the developing countries and ensure steadily accelerating economic and social development and peace and justice for future generations.[8]

The result was a flurry of research and conferences conducted to clarify the issues and develop strategies for achieving the goal.[9]

Despite all the activity, enhanced economic development for peripheral nations failed to occur. However, the peripheral nations found an unexpected opportunity for change when OPEC, originally founded in Baghdad in 1960, was able to force a substantial increase in the price of oil, a basic commodity throughout the world.[10] During the 1970s, OPEC quickly became a model for peripheral nations to emulate in hope of obtaining the economic concessions and achieving the financial growth that had eluded them over decades of foreign control and occupation.

The changes in economic orientation and philosophy brought about by NIEO influenced all aspects of the United Nations and UNESCO. Everything from the influence of transnational corporations to the role of the major wire services and the impact of popular culture was examined in light of either NIEO or NWICO. The anti-colonial rhetoric of the new order was harsh. Colonial domination, neocolonialism, racial discrimination, apartheid, media images, cultural imperialism, chronic imbalances, Western hegemony, and violations of human rights were all subject to severe criticism. Although the goals of the new order were lofty, its real objective was to shift international power from Western core nations to a loose coalition of peripheral regions, Arab OPEC regions, non-aligned nations, and socialist countries (namely, the USSR). The next goal was to effect a change in sociocultural priorities under the protection or guidance of NWICO.

The Debate Begins in Earnest

As UNESCO prepared for the next general meeting, the future of Director-General M'Bow rested on how he handled the contentious Draft Declaration on the Mass Media. He realized that the "spirit of Nairobi" had been built on acrimony and distrust. The agreement to establish the MacBride International Commission as a means of buying time and reducing the growing pressure had been worked out backstage at the last moment to avoid a walk-out by Western delegations. That compromise was no longer sufficient to withstand the mounting strain.

M'Bow also had to do something to restore UNESCO's image, which had become severely tarnished. UNESCO's Secretariat perceived the problem as one created by the Western press, which emphasized the negative aspects of UNESCO's leadership, initiatives, and programs. In reality, however, UNESCO's public image was more negatively affected by its shift from a passive, pro-Western agency to an activist, pro-development, periphery-oriented agency. Its ideological commitment to fundamental change, through NIEO, for example, was little understood and was perceived as a threat to the free markets and economic security that core nations had taken for granted since UNESCO's inception in the 1940s. But newly independent peripheral nations looked to this specialized agency of the United Nations to understand and to deal with their international grievances.

As for the plight of peripheral nations, "it was as though they had moved from military colonialism to technological neo-colonialism without a thought beyond the purely practical and profitable."[11] Many peripheral nations had rushed to accept Western technology and software designed for other cultures and other needs, and now conceded that Western-controlled aid was not the answer to their problems. They had seen aspects of electronic colonialism and they did not like what they were seeing. They did not want to be consumers of a foreign and alien culture. As a result, peripheral nations approached the media and culture debate with a call for greater distributive justice bolstered by years of discussions.

They had flexed their muscles, voted, received attention, and won; now they were prepared to go after the Western mass media.

In his opening address to the 1978 General Assembly, M'Bow set the framework for UNESCO's future agenda. Noting that "the establishment of a new international economic order constitutes … one of the major contexts, and no doubt the largest, within which the activities of the Organization will take place," M'Bow continued by asserting that the imbalances between the West and the peripheral nations were not limited to "solely the production and exchange of information and knowledge."[12] In this way, M'Bow insured that NWICO would become further intertwined with the NIEO. After reviewing several other UNESCO activities including human rights, education, disarmament, and science and technology, M'Bow turned to communication. He acknowledged "the task awaiting the international community in this field over the next few years represents a real challenge, since it is a task which is at one and the same time immense, complex, essential and urgent."[13] Then M'Bow proceeded to review the MacBride Commission, highlighting specific areas that required further research and clarification, including disparities in global communication. In closing, M'Bow criticized his opponents and urged them to adopt NWICO:

> I believe very sincerely that the draft now before you could meet with a large measure of agreement, provided that it is read objectively and dispassionately, and that form of words are patiently sought which dispel the ambiguities of hidden motives that some people still read into it. In this way, the large measure of agreement that the General Conference considers necessary could be achieved.[14]

M'Bow lost ground quickly as Western nations, in response to his address, spoke up against the submitted draft declaration. In plenary sessions, in corridors, and in media briefings UNESCO was divided along East/West lines, with the East (socialist) receiving support from many peripheral and OPEC nations. It was clear that the controversial draft declaration on the role of the mass media would have significant implications. It represented a distinct change from the free flow of information policy established by the United Nations and formally supported by the United States since the 1940s.

Moreover, peripheral nations clung to their objections to the Western media. Their criticisms reflected three primary issues. The first argument was a straightforward anti-capitalist approach that criticized the commercial orientation of the press, radio, television, and film industries. The second line of attack focused on the one-way flow of information from the United States, through wire services, television programming, music, and Hollywood productions, to other nations, with little if any reciprocal trade. Fear of electronic colonialism motivated the third argument, which featured a dislike of the history, norms, morals, language, lifestyles, and cultural aspects conveyed through the content of core nations' press, radio, television, advertising, music, and film productions.

For many Western delegates, the issue boiled down to one of state control over the mass media. Secretary of State for Canada John Roberts delivered one of the strongest speeches during the entire assembly. In explaining Canada's reservations about the declaration, Roberts stated:

> I am making no secret of my disquiet, and that of the Government of which I am a member, concerning the Draft Declaration on the Mass Media … On every continent there are some people who think that governments should regulate journalists, should tell them, in the public interest, what to write, or should pass judgment on their accuracy.

Canadians do not believe that either politicians or public servants should have anything to say in the management, direction or correction of the media. Quite the contrary. In their view, only a free press can guarantee that the decisions of the state power are in harmony with the wishes of the people. Governments have no means of knowing what the needs of society are for its own well-being, unless they are told by an informed public.[15]

The address was well received, and because Canada had a standing in UNESCO, the Western wire services gave coverage to Robert's remarks. In response, Dr. Phillip Muscat from Malta summed up the major peripheral nations' grievances:

The service that emanates from the big international press and news agencies sometimes tends to be slanted against the developing countries of the Third World and their leaders. Great prominence is given to certain news items of minor importance, while national achievements in vital sectors are barely mentioned or wrongly reported. Moreover, in certain instances the international press is used as a destabilizing factor against the governments whose only crime is generally that of standing up for their rights, their sovereignty and independence.[16]

Following the plenary session, M'Bow began, as he always did, by criticizing Western press coverage of the issue. He then called for the development of a universal journalistic code of ethics to govern the actions of media and journalists. Many feared that such a code would lead to a system that could ultimately be used to restrict journalists' freedom. The Soviet Union and authoritarian nations thought they had an ally in M'Bow and an issue, NWICO, with which to restrict the Western media.

Ultimately, UNESCO's 20th General Assembly approved a compromise draft declaration on the mass media that endorsed freedom of the press. This represented a significant diplomatic reversal in favor of the West and moderate developing nations and a temporary reprieve for Director-General M'Bow. Although it was M'Bow who had initially presented, endorsed, and pushed the first controversial draft declaration, the Western press unanimously and rightly blamed the Soviet bloc for the attack on their free press philosophy. One suspects that M'Bow, with his back to the wall and his career on the line, abandoned what he had cherished in October to pacify the Western nations and thereby retain their substantial funding. Of course, it is likely that M'Bow also recognized that the forthcoming final MacBride International Commission Report and the next UNESCO General Assembly provided opportunities for him to regroup and to present his NWICO proposal once again.

UNESCO in the 1980s

zAs described in the previous section, it took a reluctantly accepted eleventh-hour compromise to pull the 20th General Assembly's session on mass communication out of the fire in 1978. Yet the delegates to UNESCO general assemblies continued to put on at least the face of consensus and unanimity at international communication discussions which invariably tottered on the brink of open warfare and collapse. In Belgrade in 1980, the General Assembly adopted a mass media resolution by consensus when nobody called for a vote on it. Unbelievable as it may seem, that resolution actually won approval because it advocated proposals based on the principles of both sides of the debate. The result was an uneven and inconsistent declaration.

Despite its equivocal language, reciprocal concessions, and unanimous approval, the resolution was "one of the most bitterly fought over in UNESCO's history."[17] It revealed the extent to which the Western and developing world positions were irreconcilable. Even though concessions were made by both sides, the peripheral nations, acting with the support of the Soviet bloc, seemed to get the better of the West. According to several observers, their advantage appeared to turn on the inclusion of some principles that could be interpreted as anti-free press.

The launch of the International Programme for the Development of Communication (IPDC) at the 21st General Assembly also created a great deal of controversy and suspicion. A 39-member intergovernmental council was established to administer the program and set out its priorities and policies. IPDC continues today with the goal of aiding communication projects and training in peripheral nations.

In retrospect, the 21st General Assembly was remarkable for the decisions made. It not only approved a version of the NWICO, but also accepted the MacBride Commission report, which clearly endorsed activities that would promote development journalism and communication, and it created the IPDC to implement some of those policies. What was unclear at the time was the degree to which the hostility brewing against Director-General M'Bow would, by mid-decade, reach sufficient intensity to justify the withdrawal of both the United Kingdom and the United States from UNESCO.

The 22nd General Assembly of UNESCO convened in Paris on October 25, 1983. One hundred and sixty-one countries participated in the five-week conference, which turned out to be one of the most critical in the history of UNESCO. Just a few weeks after the meetings were adjourned, US State Department's dissatisfaction with UNESCO's stance on a number of issues led to an announcement of the United States' intention to withdraw from UNESCO at the end of 1984 unless its demands for substantial change were met. The United States did withdraw.

The meetings began with the presentation of "The Draft Programme and Budget for 1984–1985," which was prepared by the UNESCO Secretariat on the basis of the consensus reached by the delegates. Of most relevance to this discussion is "Major Programme III: Communication in the Service of Man," outlined below:

Programme III.1 Studies on Communication:

(a) to simulate the development of research, especially concerning the sociocultural impact of new communication technologies, the democratization of communication and the future of books and reading;

(b) to further elaborate the concepts of "the right to communicate" and access to and participation in communication, and to continue to study the idea of the responsibility in communicators;

(c) to continue the study of methods for planning, programming and financing of communication, with special reference to the communication industries.[18]

The program continued by encouraging the reduction of current international communication imbalances through the development of a plurality of information sources and through cooperation and collaboration. It acknowledged that the activities listed in the program would "facilitate a detailed examination of a new information and communication order, with a view to promoting its establishment."[19] It had been hoped that the freedom of the press issue and NWICO, which had divided UNESCO for over a decade, might be only a minor topic at this meeting. On the first day of debate, however, two serious and contentious issues arose. The first was the substantial increase in the budget for communications. The second was a Soviet Union proposal calling for curbs on press freedom as part of NWICO.

The Soviet delegation realized that the First Amendment was sacred to the US press, and its intention was to aggravate the United States and other Western delegations. The Soviet draft urged UNESCO to draw up a list of "mass media organs" whose reporting had violated the guidelines that the organization had enunciated earlier. These were the same guidelines that most Western governments had criticized as being hostile to the freedom of the press. The Soviets were forced to withdraw their contentious resolution, but its introduction had heightened distrust of NWICO by providing a concrete illustration of its threats to press freedom.

Although the media debate was a key issue, the size of the budget increase created another serious problem for the United States. The United States was the only one of the 161 nations to vote against the $374.4 million budget. At the final vote, 10 other countries abstained after asking for a budgetary freeze. The final budget adopted was about $12 million less than that first proposed, but the cuts did not go deep enough for the United States, which had been seeking "zero growth" in all UN agencies.

Although the United States failed to achieve as much as it had hoped, it was certainly more successful than it had been in the past decade. It had curbed the development of NWICO, and there was an emerging shift toward the Western perspective on press matters. Although the final budget did not represent zero growth, it was only 2.5 percent higher than the previous one. So what prompted the United States decision to pull out of UNESCO less than a month later?

Shortly after the close of the 22nd General Assembly, stories began appearing in the US press about the possible withdrawal of the United States from UNESCO. According to a *New York Times* report, the proposal was being considered in the State Department and a decision was expected soon.[20] Gregory J. Newell, Assistant Secretary of State for International Organization Affairs, said that his office had conducted a study of the performance of some 19 organizations and noted that in addition to mismanagement and lack of budgetary restraint, there were problems of politicization within many UN agencies. He asserted that internal studies had shown what the Reagan administration viewed as improvements in many UN multilateral agencies, but that UNESCO had responded inadequately. Newell then ordered a complete review of UNESCO, which would later justify the US withdrawal.

Opponents of the withdrawal pointed to the improvements made at the 22nd General Assembly. They feared that withdrawal would leave the organization vulnerable to those who opposed US interests. Moreover, the United States Commission for UNESCO, while acknowledging there were problems, voted by an overwhelming majority to continue membership and to fight for change from within. But Newell recognized the vulnerability of UNESCO and used it to condemn and threaten the entire UN system.

Following the reviews, the US State Department recommended, on December 21, 1983, that the United States file notice of its intention to withdraw from UNESCO on January 1, 1985. The decision had to be made by December 31, but the United States would have one year in which to reassess the situation. President Ronald Reagan sent a formal letter of withdrawal to Director-General M'Bow on December 29, making it clear that the departure was temporary and that the United States retained the right to rejoin. According to a State Department spokesperson, the decision was taken because "UNESCO has extraneously politicized virtually every subject it deals with, has exhibited hostility toward the basic institutions of a free society, especially a free market and a free press, and has demonstrated unrestrained budgetary expansion."[21] Under President Reagan the White House and the Department of State had ignored the United Nations and UNESCO and now they were trying to punish the United Nations for promoting policies that questioned the United States' role as a global commercial power.

Officially, the State Department's recommendation to withdraw from UNESCO was based on what it identified as three major problems:

1 the politicization of issues;
2 the promulgation of statist concepts; and
3 mismanagement and fiscal irresponsibility.

The United States officially withdrew from UNESCO in January 1985. (It returned under President Bush in 2002 and now has left again.)

New Era, Leaders, and Strategy

M'Bow stepped down as director-general at UNESCO in 1986, leaving it politically weakened and fiscally poor. His successor, Federico Mayor, from Barcelona, Spain, was elected as the new director-general in 1987 and held office until 1999. During his tenure, Mayor altered the agency's role and did not support NWICO. Mayor assumed the leadership of UNESCO at arguably the lowest point in its history. Its budget had been slashed as a result of the withdrawal of the United States and the United Kingdom, and negative media coverage by Western newspapers and magazines had tarnished its reputation.

Mayor issued a new communication strategy, stressing the Western principles of freedom of press and freedom of expression, and the development of an independent and pluralistic media. This philosophical and ideological shift was not only more attractive to the West, but it also coincided with the fall of the Berlin Wall in November 1989, which raised expectations of an independent press throughout central and eastern Europe.

In order to implement the new communication proposals, Mayor announced that a series of UNESCO meetings would be convened in Namibia, Kazakhstan, Chile, and Yemen. At each of these regional meetings, UNESCO's free press communication proposal was to be enunciated, and ideas to promote press freedom and media pluralism in the regions would be explored. For example, the Windhoek Resolution, which emerged from the 1991 Namibia conference to promote a pluralistic and free African press, declared that:

1 Consistent with article 19 of the Universal Declaration of Human Rights, the establishment, maintenance and fostering of an independent, pluralistic and free press is essential to the development and maintenance of democracy in a nation, and for economic development.
2 By an independent press, we mean a press independent from governmental, political or economic control or from control of materials and infrastructure essential for the production and dissemination of newspapers, magazines and periodicals.
3 By a pluralistic press, we mean the end of monopolies of any kind and the existence of the greatest possible number of newspapers, magazines and periodicals reflecting the widest possible range of opinion within the community.

4   The welcome changes that an increasing number of African States are now undergoing towards multiparty democracies provide the climate in which an independent pluralistic press can emerge.

5   The worldwide trend towards democracy and freedom of information and expression is a fundamental contribution to the fulfilment of human aspirations.[22]

Wherever Mayor went he promoted the new UNESCO communication strategy, primarily to two audiences: the current UNESCO membership and the United States. Not only did he advocate resolutions supporting new free and pluralistic press initiatives throughout the regions of the world, but he also sought to convince the United States that UNESCO's communication policy was very much in line with American free press traditions and that the United States should return to UNESCO. Support for NWICO also fell with the Berlin Wall.

This revised communication policy at UNESCO paved the way for the return of the United Kingdom, but the United States was not persuaded. In fact, UNESCO's critics in Congress, the State Department, and outside of government remained adamant that the United States stay out of UNESCO.

UNESCO in the 1990s and Beyond

In the early 1990s, as a result of dramatic but peaceful political revolutions, the former Soviet Union and its client states rapidly abandoned totalitarian structures, including their press systems. Consequently, many journalists and editors from the newly independent states of eastern and central Europe began to participate in the new communication strategy debate within UNESCO. The general conferences produced several resolutions supporting the goals of the new strategy. In particular, there was considerable support for independent and free media along the lines of the Western model. In addition, the IPDC encouraged proposals that facilitated the founding of free and open press activities in peripheral nations.

In the late 1990s UNESCO produced a major document titled *World Information Report* which began to detail the information resources in almost 200 countries around the globe. Its publication marked a change in emphasis within UNESCO in the study of the global information highway, including the Internet. The *World Information Report* provided extensive documentation of computer-based information-processing, including the shift toward multimedia, telecommunications, and electronic databases.

The report is divided into three parts. The first section describes the information services in individual countries or regions. The second section details the infrastructures for information industries and focuses on technical issues including multimedia and telecommunications. The final section discusses issues and trends, such as the emergence of the information society, information highways, economic implications, copyright matters, and other social or legal questions. The report concludes with a chapter outlining the necessity for international cooperation in order to insure access for all through the interconnection of global information technologies.

In October 1999 two important events occurred in UNESCO. First, a new director-general was elected after major candidates had emerged from Australia, Saudi Arabia, Egypt, and Japan. The Japanese ambassador to France, Koichiro Matsuura, began his six-year term as director-general of UNESCO immediately, presiding over an annual budget of $300 million, and was re-elected to a second term. Since the last two directors-general had come from the core nations of Spain and Japan, the next director-general was elected from a semiperipheral nation – Irina Bokova from Bulgaria. In 2011 she issued a statement about the exit of the United States:

> In this time of economic crisis and social transformation, I believe that UNESCO's vital work to promote global stability and democratic values is in America's core interests.
>
> The United States is a critical partner in UNESCO's work. The withholding of US dues and other financial contributions – required by U.S. law – will weaken UNESCO's effectiveness and undermine its ability to build free and open societies.
>
> US funding helps UNESCO to develop and sustain free and competitive media in Iraq, Tunisia and Egypt. UNESCO literacy programmes in areas of conflict give people the critical thinking skills and confidence they need to fight violent extremism. To sustain the democratic spirit of the Arab Spring, UNESCO is training journalists to cover elections objectively."[23]

The second event concerned allegations of cronyism and mismanagement, specifically that the French government had used the Paris-based UNESCO to place former government aides on UNESCO's payroll throughout the 1990s. The British newspaper the *Guardian* ran extensive stories documenting the administrative problems, going so far as to report that almost half of UNESCO's appointments in the 1990s failed to meet the administrative criteria for credentials and for fair and open competition for senior appointments.[24]

In 2004 Matsuura organized a meeting to draft a global convention on the protection of cultural diversity and artistic expression. This followed an earlier 2004 meeting with over 600 delegates from 132 UNESCO member states, and numerous NGOs, at which the protection of cultural goods and services (including, for many of the participating nations, the mass media) was discussed. This Convention on the Protection and Promotion of the Diversity of Cultural Expressions put UNESCO on a likely collision course with the World Trade Organization (WTO).

The convention was approved by UNESCO in 2005, with only the United States and Israel voting against it. The convention seeks to affirm the rights of nations to determine their own cultural policies, and to recognize that culture is linked to identity, values, and concept of self. The convention does not regard culture as a commercial good to be bought and sold, like cars or wheat, but as a distinct and in many cases unique entity which thus needs to be protected from electronic colonialism. The convention covers the five related activities of creation, production, distribution, access to, and enjoyment of cultural expressions and activities. Finally, it also seeks to protect languages, particularly diverse or indigenous languages.

The WTO is seeking to expand its mandate by including cultural industries in its remit in such a way as to reduce all protectionist measures, such as quotas, grants, subsidies, license fees, and a host of other protectionist tariffs. This matter has the potential to become a major global public policy issue, with the United States on one side and the cultural nationalists from many nations on the other.

Finally, UNESCO is also heavily involved in the World Summit on the Information Society (WSIS; see Chapter 5). UNESCO is providing assistance for many of the WSIS action plan areas under the umbrella of its major initiative "Knowledge Societies." Some critics of the WSIS claim that it seeks to promote governments having a role in media oversight, and to them it sounds like a resurrection of the discredited NWICO. Given that the second meeting of WSIS was in anti-free-press and authoritarian Tunisia, the outlook was dim for all agencies, including the International Telecommunication Union (ITU) and UNESCO, which sponsored WSIS and supported the bizarre selection of Tunisia for a major international conference dealing with the media and communication.

Conclusions

Although the UNESCO General Assembly has always addressed 13 major programs, beginning with the 1976 meeting in Nairobi, its conferences have been dominated by the single communication program, NWICO, and its fallout. Like a lightning rod, NWICO attracted all the media attention. Not only was it an issue of distinct interest to the media, but it also polarized the delegates to the point that the United States and the United Kingdom withdrew from membership of UNESCO. It also created significant public image problems for the agency and threatened its internal operations and financial stability. Today, UNESCO still has major fiscal and image problems. Historically, the debate was about aspects of electronic colonialism that the core nations did not want to hear about, deal with, or come to terms with. Peripheral nations were concerned that their cultures, values, languages, and influence were being displaced by slick, heavily advertised sounds and images from a few core nations.

Although there is little doubt among those familiar with UNESCO that the organization does sound work in several areas ranging from literacy and environmental concerns to scientific and educational topics, these efforts receive scant attention at the general assemblies and in the global media. This imbalance is clear when one realizes that UNESCO's communication sector receives less than 10 percent of the agency's budget, but well over 90 percent of its media coverage. The problem is further complicated because that coverage, particularly in Western nations, is overwhelmingly negative. It is difficult, therefore, for concerned individuals and governments to be supportive of UNESCO when the public at large is not favorably impressed, and when the uninitiated believe that all UNESCO does is debate communication and promote anti-free-press policies.

The historical role of the former Soviet Union is also clear. It was obvious to many that the Soviet Union was promoting an anti-free-press agenda and that it had considerable rein within the halls of UNESCO. A second challenge related to internal leadership. After 11 years as director-general, M'Bow had failed to respond to the growing negative perception of UNESCO, even within the UN system. His term came to an abrupt end in 1987. Finally, and perhaps most surprising, was the implosion of the Soviet Union, which spelled the end of its role as the great benefactor, champion, and savior of UNESCO and NWICO.

Despite the problems NWICO created, the overall debate in UNESCO has been informative. It not only forced a reanalysis and reaffirmation of its values, but also accentuated the need for hard data and the planning of practical strategies in order to enhance communication development throughout the world. NWICO continues to evolve in its search for practical and applied measures aimed at redressing media imbalances and promoting greater concern for cultural sensitivity and indigenous software. The peripheral nations still cling to NWICO in the face of greater core nation media pressure to adopt Western philosophies, products, and practices. Finally, a small group of academics and journalists from around the globe continue to promote the aims of NWICO. Under the banner of the MacBride Round Table, they meet every two years to examine the state of affairs in peripheral nations.[25] This is an advocacy group created in 1989 to examine the global communication imbalances identified in the 1980 MacBride Report, titled *Many Voices, One World*, commissioned by UNESCO.[26] It is expanding the research agenda to include Internet issues as part of the NWICO legacy. Yet for the most part NWICO is a dead issue. As Ulla Carlsson sums it up: "The only concrete political result of the work on a NWICO within UNESCO was a focus on the development of national media in the third world through, among other things, increased development assistance."[27]

Finally, UNESCO is moving into an area loaded with contention: the Convention on Cultural Diversity.[28] This hot issue could once again see major donor nations re-examine their commitment to UNESCO and its programs.[29]

Notes

1. UNESCO, *What is UNESCO*, Paris: UNESCO, 1977.
2. For an excellent look at the internal workings and problems of UNESCO's Secretariat, see former Assistant Director-General Richard Hoggart's *An Idea and Its Servants: UNESCO from Within*, London: Chatto & Windus, 1978.
3. Hoggart, *An Idea and Its Servants*, p. 64.
4. Edgar Faure et al., *Learning to Be*, Paris: UNESCO, 1972.
5. Some analysts date the beginning of the NWICO debate to 1968, when the Declaration on Human Rights was amended to include the notion of a balanced and free flow of information. Given the subsequent differences in interpretation, policy decisions, and political maneuvering related to this phrase, it is interesting to note that it was the United States that first introduced the amendment.
6. Kaarle Nordenstreng and Tapio Varis, *Television Traffic: A One Way Street? A Survey and Analysis of the International Flow of Television*, Paris: UNESCO, 1974.
7. Brenda Pavlic and Cees Hamelink, *The New International Economic Order: Links between Economies and Communications*, Reports and Papers on Mass Communication 98, Paris: UNESCO, 1985.
8. United Nations, *Declaration on the Establishment of a New International Economic Order*, G.A. Res. 3201, Sixth Special Session, UN Supp. (No. 1), UN Doc. A/9559.
9. See, e.g., UNESCO, *Moving Towards Change: Some Thoughts on the New International Economic Order*, Paris: UNESCO, 1976.
10. The history of OPEC is also viewed by communication scholars as a classic case study of initial Western media inattention, and then biased reporting, once OPEC was able to establish itself as a major instrument of political and commercial power – extending to the gas pump.
11. Hoggart, *An Idea and Its Servants*, p. 193.
12. UNESCO 20C/Inf. 9, October 28, Paris: UNESCO, 1978, p. 4.
13. UNESCO 20C/Inf. 9, p. 14.
14. UNESCO 20C/Inf. 9, p. 15.
15. John Roberts, UNESCO document 20C/vr (prov), November 6, 1978, press release.
16. Phillip Muscat, UNESCO document 20C/vr (prov), November 4, 1978, press release.
17. *New York Times* (October 25, 1980), p. 14.
18. UNESCO, *Draft Programme and Budget for 1984–1985*, "III: "Communication in the Service of Man," 22C/5, Paris: UNESCO, 1983, p. 2.
19. UNESCO, *Draft Programme and Budget for 1984–1985*, p. 3.
20. *New York Times* (December 15, 1983), D1.
21. *New York Times* (December 30, 1983), D4.
22. UNESCO, *Declarations on Promoting Independent and Pluralist Media: Declaration of Windhoek*, Paris: UNESCO, May 3, 1991, mimeographed, p. 4.
23. Director-General Irina Bokova, press release, February 11, 2011.
24. Jon Henley, *Guardian*, October 18, 19, 21, 1999.
25. This group seeks to examine issues of access, ownership, equality, and trends in global communication in the tradition of the MacBride Report. See, e.g., Richard Vincent, Kaarle Nordenstreng, and Michael Traber (eds.), *Towards Equity in Global Communication*, Crosskill, NJ: Hampton Press, 1999.
26. Sean MacBride, *Many Voices, One World*, New York: Unipub, 1980.
27. Ulla Carlsson, "From NWICO to Global Governance of the Information Society," in Oscar Hemer & Thomas Tufte (eds.), *Media and Glocal Change*, Gothenburg, Sweden: Nordicom, p. 208.
28. The background, related activities, and future plans/meetings of the convention are available at http://www.unesco.org/culture/en/diversity/convention (accessed August 13, 2013).
29. Events at UNESCO are a lot like history on the run. To keep up with matters discussed in this chapter, including the agenda of the new Director-General, Irina Bokova, see www.unesco.org/

4

Public Diplomacy

New Dimensions and Implications

Nancy Snow

Introduction

In global communications, ideas matter. But ideas alone can't make any measurable difference if they are not properly marketed to an audience, be they consumers or citizens. Consider one relatively unknown junior senator from Chicago, Illinois, who used outstanding marketing and persuasion skills, along with Internet savvy, to package his ideas effectively enough to win the American presidency in 2008. In many respects, Barack Obama is the ultimate public diplomat. He is the new gold standard. He used his powerful oratorical skills to convey his beliefs and ideals to the American people. In the process, he became an international celebrity who illustrated a new globally minded US president, not only sensitive to what others think about the US nation and its people, but also committed to changing unpopular foreign policies like pledging a "new beginning" with the Muslim world in his June 2009 speech in Cairo and ending the post-September 11 slogan, the "war on terror," on which the wars in Afghanistan and Iraq were predicated.

The Personal is Political in Public Diplomacy

Public diplomacy (PD), with its emphasis on political power relations, has a strong tie to national security and foreign policy outcomes. This translates into distinct public diplomacy agendas driven by specific administrations and their leaders in power. While President Obama may emphasize a more collaborative public diplomacy style that brings together global partners in mutual endeavors, his predecessor, President George W. Bush, brought attention to a unilateral style of public diplomacy through his administration's emphasis on winning the US-led "war on terror." Bush asked the nation, "Why do they hate us?"[1] and

Global Communication: Theories, Stakeholders, and Trends, Fourth Edition. Thomas L. McPhail.
© 2014 John Wiley & Sons, Inc. Published 2014 by John Wiley & Sons, Inc.

instituted international communication campaigns that would attempt to overcome the animus that had led to the terrorist attacks in 2001.

James Glassman was the final and only male under-secretary of state for public diplomacy and public affairs for President Bush. His predecessor, Karen Hughes, was President George W. Bush's communications director and a member of the White House Iraq Group (WHIG), the marketing arm of the White House set up to sell the 2003 invasion of Iraq to the American people. She was described by the *Dallas Morning News* as "the most powerful woman ever to serve in the White House."[2] Margaret Tutwiler, former ambassador to Morocco and protégée of Secretary of State James Baker, though she served a short five months in the position, offered a memorable statement that echoed the frustrations associated with being a nation's image czar: "There is not one magic bullet, magic program or magic solution. As much as we would like to think Washington knows best, we have to be honest and admit we do not necessarily always have all the answers."[3]

Tutwiler emphasized active listening on the part of the US government – including listening to its diplomats serving on the front lines – and expanding the discussion of American values and policies to public venues outside of traditional elites in diplomacy and government: "We only have to look at the activities of US corporations overseas to see the value of being present and engaged in neighborhoods that we in government have for too long neglected."[4] She also announced a slight increase in educational exchanges, particularly youth exchanges, focused primarily on the Middle East. When Tutwiler suddenly announced her switch from government public relations to the New York Stock Exchange executive suites, one could not help but notice that the move occurred during the week that the first brutal images of abused Iraqi prisoners in Abu Ghraib were released worldwide, rendering her youth exchange program from the Middle East – Partnerships for Learning, with fewer than 200 participants – a minute drop of hope in an ocean of anger and resentment.[5]

Glassman, Hughes, Tutwiler, and the most noted under-secretary, Charlotte Beers, were tasked with carrying out a public mission to communicate with global publics in the service of national security and foreign policy objectives of the United States. Charlotte Beers, who once headed J. Walter Thompson and Ogilvy & Mather, is considered a legend in the advertising world. Known as the "Queen of Branding" and the "Steel Magnolia of Advertising," the Texas-born Beers convinced then Secretary of State Colin Powell that America needed a rebranding campaign on US foreign policy in the post-9/11 environment. As Powell explained his decision to the Senate Foreign Relations Committee, "Well guess what? She got me to buy Uncle Ben's rice and so there is nothing wrong with getting somebody who knows how to sell something."[6]

From Uncle Ben to Uncle Sam

The suggestion that selling Uncle Sam was as seamless a sales job as packaging instant rice did not sit well with many observers in the press and public. Andrew Alexander of the British *Daily Mail* wrote, "One shouldn't laugh, really, but I must confess to a short guffaw on reading that Washington's new war propaganda chief is a woman head of an advertising agency whose personal triumphs included Uncle Ben's rice and Head and Shoulders shampoo." Columnist Frank Rich of the *New York Times* cracked: "The Bush appointee in charge of the propaganda effort is a CEO (from Madison Avenue) chosen not for her expertise in policy or politics but for her salesmanship on behalf of domestic products like Head and Shoulders shampoo. If we can't effectively fight anthrax, I guess it's reassuring to know we can always win the war on dandruff." Steve Lopez of the *Los Angeles Times* joked that the White House decision to choose Beers as chief propaganda queen led to his "second out-of-body experience" since the onset of the war in Afghanistan on October 7, 2001. (His first out-of-body experience was the White House decision to choose the project title Operation Infinite Justice, which was quickly dumped for the more modest Operation Enduring Freedom.) At first befuddled that the White House would put an ad executive in charge of America's image war, Lopez sarcastically snipped: "Who knows? Maybe they're onto something. Just the other day I took a sip of Coke and began singing, 'I'd like to teach the world to sing in perfect harmony.' How could anyone hate a nation of peace-loving simpletons for whom the best part of waking up is Folger's in your cup?"[7]

Despite the media grumblings, Beers entered office with much fanfare and high expectations that she would accomplish the Brand America mission to change negative global attitudes toward the United States, particularly in the Arab Middle East, but also in Europe and Latin America. Charlotte Beers quickly identified George Bush and Colin Powell as the "poster people" of American public diplomacy around the world.[8] Her tenure was marked by the rather dubious outcome of the advertising campaign called "Shared Values," sponsored by the US State Department, which consisted of two-minute clips of Muslim Americans talking positively about their lives in the United States.[9] Beers resigned from her position in March 2003, just weeks before the US invasion of Iraq. Her successor, James Glassman, said that the American public diplomacy mission was a global war of ideas:

> Our mission today in the war of ideas is highly focused. It is to use the tools of ideological engagement – words, deeds, and images – to create an environment hostile to violent extremism. We want to break the linkages between groups like Al Qaeda and their target audiences. Indeed, in the war of ideas, our core task is not how to fix foreigners' perceptions of the United States but how to isolate and reduce the threat of violent extremism. Our task is not to build our brand but to help destroy theirs.[10]

Barack Obama's first under-secretary of state for public diplomacy and public affairs was Judith McHale. Appointed in May 2009, McHale did not receive the same media attention as Charlotte Beers or Karen Hughes. In her first major speech, McHale emphasized the people-to-people diplomacy (P2P) of her new boss, Secretary of State Hillary Clinton:

> This is not a propaganda contest – it is a relationship race. And we have got to get back in the game. So how do we rebuild our national credibility and renew our engagement with the people of the world? We need to develop a multidimensional, results-oriented approach that combines traditional outreach with cutting-edge technology to engage with people at all levels of society. Broadly speaking, public diplomacy operates on two levels. First, communication. This is the air game, the radio and TV broadcasts, the websites and media outreach that all seek to explain and provide context for US policies and action; and second, engagement, the ground game of direct people-to-people exchanges, speakers, and embassy-sponsored cultural events that build personal relationships.[11]

McHale's first address was entitled "Public Diplomacy: A National Security Imperative," and she referenced Secretary of Defense Robert Gates, the point man in both the Bush and the Obama administrations to elevate public diplomacy to the level of national security:

> We are not the only ones who see the significance of increased engagement. Friends, competitors, and adversaries are moving quickly. The Chinese are building infrastructure and cultural centers across the world, developing long-term relationships in Africa,

Latin America, and elsewhere. The Iranian public diplomacy network in the Middle East and beyond includes satellite television and radio networks in several languages, more than 100 newspapers and magazines, and thousands of websites and blogs. And of course Al-Qaeda and other extremists continue to engage aggressively using a range of new and old media.[12]

McHale's successor, Tara Sonenshine, who was appointed in April 2012, continued to emphasize "engagement" and public–private partnerships to raise the United States' profile and reputation until her departure in July 2013. US companies like Coca-Cola, the sports broadcasting network ESPN, the Aspen Institute think tank, and the consulting firm Booz Allen Hamilton are working with the State Department in support of public diplomacy goals, given the limitations of a $1 billion annual budget. Budget constraints in public diplomacy lead to more emphasis on charismatic leaders.

Secretary of State Hillary Clinton and President Barack Obama personalized American public diplomacy to a degree not seen before in previous administrations. Both used their global popularity and individual personalities – as well as social media engagement – to advance their policy agendas, even if those policies (e.g., the promise to close Guantanamo Bay prison in Cuba, and advancing a two-state solution in Israel) were not always fulfilled. By the time of Clinton's departure from the State Department in January 2013, she had visited 112 countries, was lauded for being the most well-traveled Secretary in US history, and had earned the moniker "Secretary of Schlep" from *Foreign Policy* magazine.

Public Diplomacy and Global Communication

It is clear that public diplomacy is a new subfield of global communication with old constituent ties to social influence, rhetoric, persuasive communication, and international exchange and engagement. As a modern concept, it is firmly ensconced in the ideological struggle of the twentieth century between the United States and the USSR; this was the era when public opinion management and winning the hearts and minds of global publics outside the two spheres, such as non-aligned nations, was supreme.

The continuum of persuasion between information and engagement has traditionally been the exclusive domain of governments in support of foreign policy interests. Traditional diplomacy is about relationships between state officials. It is top-down, elite, and driven by government officials who conduct business and negotiation privately, and have little contact or communication with the public. Public diplomacy refers to global communication efforts to inform, influence, and engage global publics in support of national interests. As opposed to traditional diplomacy efforts that take place behind closed doors and lead to sometimes awkward staged handshakes before the credentialed press, public diplomacy efforts are designed to be transparent in their mission and open-sourced in their function. It is the support of the overseas public, in particular non-official target groups, individuals and organizations, that a nation seeks, not just that of an individual head of state or foreign minister.

Public diplomacy is a global process oriented toward diplomacy to publics. Open communication, interaction, and reaching out to publics through news and opinion management are expected in public diplomacy. Unlike traditional diplomacy, which involves a small network of trained and educated individuals, public diplomacy's mission is open to everyone. It is a function and concern of all nations and citizens, including multinational organizations such as the European Union, UNESCO, and Medécins Sans

Frontières. In the short term, public diplomacy is about getting one's message out to foreign publics in a timely and understood fashion. At its core, the best public diplomacy is about building relationships and mutual understanding between the parties engaged in a communication exchange.

Public Diplomacy History

The Cold War (1948–91) between the United States and the Soviet Union played a primary role in maintaining public diplomacy's government mission. By the early 1990s, with the rise of global citizen activism and global media in service of such activism, public diplomacy took on a new dimension, with much more person-to-person and public-to-public activity. With an emboldened sense of purpose at having contributed to the demise of the Cold War, global citizens refused to remain sidelined in the post-Cold War era. Many took it upon themselves to shape the attitudes and opinions of their foreign compatriots outside the official channels of governments. By September 2001, with the declaration of a US-led global "war on terror" and the decline of traditional media's influence, global citizens created their own websites, email lists, and online meetings to educate, inform, influence, and engage on foreign policies that directly affected their livelihoods.

Public diplomacy's heritage is American, though its communicative attributes predate its twentieth-century origins wherever nations with ambition or at war cared about what others outside their national borders thought of them. Public diplomacy is like old wine in new bottles, those new bottles being the democratization of information and new information and communication technologies that have shrunk, if not collapsed, borders between global publics. Though public diplomacy has a dominant American patina, public diplomacy is an ancient phenomenon. As scholar Jan Melissen notes:

> Image cultivation, propaganda, and activities that we would now label as public diplomacy are nearly as old as diplomacy itself. Even in ancient times, prestige-conscious princes and their representatives never completely ignored the potential and pitfalls of public opinion in foreign lands. References to the nation and its image go as far back as the Bible, and international relations in ancient Greece and Rome, Byzantium and the Italian Renaissance were familiar with diplomatic activity aimed at foreign publics.[13]

Edmund Gullion, dean emeritus of the Fletcher School of Law and Diplomacy (1964–78) at Tufts University, is credited with coining the term in 1965 at the time of the dedication of the Edward R. Murrow Center of Public Diplomacy. It had been 12 years since the founding by Dwight D. Eisenhower of the independent federal agency responsible for public diplomacy activities, the United States Information Agency (USIA), in 1953. Gullion sought a term that would accomplish two functions:

1 disassociate public diplomacy from the loaded term propaganda with all its negative associations from World War II; and
2 elevate the role of the diplomat serving the public in the foreign service from that of a government public relations or advertising "sales" agent.[14]

Gullion was a highly decorated foreign diplomat who retired during the Lyndon Johnson administration as US ambassador to the Congo. The new Murrow Center emphasized direct communications and mutual understanding between the people of the United States and those in other countries. An early brochure described public diplomacy as follows:

> Public diplomacy ... deals with the influence of public attitudes on the formation and execution of foreign policies. It encompasses dimensions of international relations beyond traditional diplomacy; the cultivation by governments of public opinion in other countries; the interaction of private groups and interests in one country with those of another; the reporting of foreign affairs and its impact on policy; communication between those whose job is communication, as between diplomats and foreign correspondents; and the processes of intercultural communications.[15]

Traditional public diplomacy (TPD) has several features:

- government to publics (G2P);
- official in nature;
- necessary evil as technology and new media democratized international relations;
- linked to foreign policy and national security outcomes;
- one-way informational and two-way asymmetric (unequal partners in communication);
- passive public role; and
- crisis-driven and reactive.

The retired broadcast journalist Edward Murrow was named director of the USIA by President John F. Kennedy in 1961 and served in that position until January 1964. To this day, Murrow remains the iconic, if not ironic, face of public diplomacy. Though world famous as a foreign war correspondent who always reported the facts on the ground, Murrow had to transition from objective narrator of the fourth estate to the opinion management style required of a federal agency head tasked with "telling America's story to the world." While he viewed public diplomacy as a focus of non-governmental interactions that presented the unofficial and diverse views of private individuals and organizations, Murrow was also associated with a presidential administration that emphasized counterinsurgency and covert operations in developing countries.[16] The respected journalist said that harnessing the national interest overseas required credibility and integrity on the part of public officials:

> American traditions and the American ethic require us to be truthful, but the most important reason is that truth is the best propaganda and lies are the worst. To be persuasive, we must be believable; to be believable we must be credible; to be credible we must be truthful. It is as simple as that.[17]

After Murrow was kept out of the Kennedy Administration's secret Bay of Pigs invasion plans for Cuba in 1961, he said that the USIA must be brought in "on the take-offs and not just the crash landings."[18] Murrow sought to place the public diplomacy activities of the USIA firmly in the domain of policy decision-making inside the White House. Both Murrow and Walter Cronkite were known as the patron saints of broadcast journalism in the United States. To public diplomacy scholars and practitioners, Murrow is the lesser-known face of ethical and responsible public diplomacy. He was a visionary who understood that public diplomacy, like politics, is local and personal. The Murrowism "To be credible, we must be truthful" still holds today.

Defining Public Diplomacy

There is no one accepted definition of what public diplomacy is. Rather, every nation has its own definition in line with its stated goals and objectives. According to the Planning Group for Integration of USIA into the Department of State, "Public Diplomacy seeks to promote the national interest of the United States through understanding, informing and influencing foreign audiences."[19] A good elevator ride definition is that it is "an international actor's attempt to advance the ends of policy by engaging with foreign publics."[20]

The second definition incorporates a new dimension of public diplomacy – that it need not include just official public diplomacy representatives of governments. Today's global media and the global reach of celebrity can elevate a person without any formal elite education in foreign policy to a platform that can reach more global publics than any foreign minister or most heads of state. For example, the technological phenomenon known as Twitter has allowed Hollywood actors like Ashton Kutcher to compete for followers of his tweets with CNN broadcast journalists like Anderson Cooper. If Kutcher wants to make a statement about US foreign policy, he can tweet a short statement of 140 characters which instantly becomes part of the global conversation. On April 25, 2009 Kutcher did just that. He posted a tweet asking all his followers in turn to tweet the following: "Every 30 seconds a child dies from Malaria. Nets save lives. Support World Malaria Day."[21] Given the reach of social media and social networking sites like Twitter, Facebook, and MySpace, there are few, if any, government officials who have the virtual power of a television or movie star to influence the global public agenda.

From James Glassman to Brangelina

Who is more influential – a professional athlete, international film star, famous musician, or author; or the under-secretary of state for public diplomacy and public affairs? There is no question today that a person who is world famous for something apart from influencing public policy has the opportunity to be more influential as a public diplomat than a person walking the corridors of national governments. We live in a mediated environment dominated by infotainment and the comings and goings of celebrities around the clock. Should a celebrity – sometimes a person who is famous simply for being famous – decide to weigh in on some foreign policy issue, the mass media are likely to report it. This does not mean that foreign secretaries are going to give up making speeches or issuing press statements. But they will more likely follow the example of the new American president and make sure that everything that is said has a multimedia delivery system that favors the Internet and social media.

While traditionally public diplomacy has involved actors like public affairs and public information officers of governments, government broadcasters, and cultural mediators like sponsored exchange students and field workers, the new public diplomacy actors include anyone who challenges dominant assumptions in international relations and the foreign policies of governments. They may include international terrorists, sports stars and other celebrities, or any highly visible global public figures as well as non-governmental (NGO) and private voluntary organizations (PVO). James Glassman, Charlotte Beers, Karen Hughes, Judith McHale, and Tara Sonenshine may be the faces of public diplomacy in the American government, but they are hardly its chief agents of influence. Brad Pitt's work with Global Green USA in building eco-friendly houses in the ninth ward of New Orleans and Angelina Jolie's work with the United Nations on behalf of refugees are more influential on behalf of US public diplomacy, that is promoting the United States' image in the world. They are the new public diplomats of today.

New public diplomacy (NPD) is characterized by the following features:

- publics-to-publics (P2P) transmission;
- unofficial/non-governmental (NGOs, private citizens, practitioners);
- active and participatory public;
- dialogic and exchange orientation – two-way symmetric communication;
- generally more long-term in reference to behavioral change; and
- based on relationship, systems, and network theories.

No one knows if Angelina Jolie identifies herself as a public diplomat, but she has become the most recognized celebrity member of the foreign policy establishment. Since 2001, she has served as the face of global refugees. A goodwill ambassador for the United Nations High Commission for Refugees (UNHCR) who has traveled to over 20 countries to speak on behalf of refugees and internally displaced persons, Jolie was inducted into the Council on Foreign Relations in 2007. The council, which publishes *Foreign Affairs* magazine, is the most influential think tank of foreign relations in the world. Its select group of over 4,000 individual members includes ex-presidents, secretaries of state, CEOs, and elite media representatives, of which just 1,000 are women. Term members like Angelina Jolie must be under 40 years old and serve five years, after which they can be nominated for life membership. Corporate members (of which there are 250) include ABC News, AIG, Halliburton, PepsiCo, and Pfizer. Both Angelina Jolie and her partner, Brad Pitt, live their lives as actors on a world stage.

Compare the global attention paid to these two celebrities and a person in charge of public diplomacy at the State Department or Ministry of Foreign Affairs. Under-Secretary of State for Public Diplomacy and Public Affairs James K. Glassman is an international actor, but unlike "Brangelina," he could never attract the same attention for his causes. Glassman, who served as under-secretary from June 2008 to January 2009, linked public diplomacy to the war against violent extremism. James Glassman's public diplomacy focus is strategic:

Unlike traditional functions of public diplomacy like education and cultural exchanges, the aim of the war of ideas is not to persuade foreign populations to adopt more favorable views of America and its policies. Instead, the war of ideas tries to ensure that negative sentiments and day-to-day grievances toward America and its allies do not manifest themselves in the form of violent extremism."[22]

He likened successful public diplomacy to a competition between orange juice and lemonade:

Think of America's values and political system as orange juice; think of the Al-Qaeda system of violent extremism as lemonade. Our job for the short term is not to put all of our efforts into getting people to drink orange juice, but to get them not to drink lemonade. They can drink anything else they want: milk, ginger ale, tomato juice, Coke. We are confident that, ultimately, they will come around to orange juice or something close to it, but in the meantime, we want them to stay away from lemonade.[23]

Global Public Diplomacy

A country like Costa Rica, which has no standing army, will have a scaled-down public diplomacy compared to a major military power like the United States. North Korea and China have their own public diplomacy objectives, which are often indistinguishable from state propaganda goals. In many countries outside the United States, public diplomacy is used interchangeably with propaganda or strategic communication, because these activities involve mass communication efforts to effect behavioral changes that favor the sponsoring country. In order to fully understand public diplomacy, global communication practitioners and scholars have to consider other perspectives and to test their own cultural assumptions. A broad mind and intercultural orientation are helpful in transcending the dominance of the United States and the United Kingdom in public diplomacy schools of thought.

Layers of Public Diplomacy

The three main layers of engagement in public diplomacy are monologic (one-way) communication, dialogic (two-way or multidirectional), and collaborative (group ventures/ joint projects). An example of monologic communication in the service of public diplomacy involves public pronouncements with lasting global effects, like the words of American president John Kennedy who stood at Berlin's City Hall on June 26, 1963 and proudly declared himself a citizen of Berlin:

> Two thousand years ago, the proudest boast was *civis romanus sum* (I am a Roman citizen). Today, in the world of freedom, the proudest boast is "Ich bin ein Berliner." All free men, wherever they may live, are citizens of Berlin, and therefore, as a free man, I take pride in the words "Ich bin ein Berliner!"[24]

These words were meant to inspire all citizens living under the influence of the Soviet Union and behind the Iron Curtain, including the families divided between East and West Berlin by the Berlin Wall. A quarter of a century later, another American president, Ronald Reagan, once again stood in Berlin and said, "Mr Gorbachev, tear down this wall!" On July 24, 2008 Democratic presidential hopeful Barack Obama stood in Berlin and made his own promise of freedom to several hundred thousand people who knew only too well the significance of Berlin as an iconic monologic moment in history:

> Yes, there have been differences between America and Europe. No doubt, there will be differences in the future. But the burdens of global citizenship continue to bind us together. A change of leadership in Washington will not lift this burden. In this new century, Americans and Europeans alike will be required to do more – not less. Partnership and cooperation among nations is not a choice; it is the one way, the only way, to protect our common security and advance our common humanity. That is why the greatest danger of all is to allow new walls to divide us from one another. The walls between old allies on either side of the Atlantic cannot stand. The walls between the countries with the most and those with the least cannot stand. The walls between races and tribes; natives and immigrants; Christian and Muslim and Jew cannot stand. These now are the walls we must tear down.[25]

One-way communication strategies include international television and radio broad-casting networks like Voice of America (United States), Deutsche Welle (Germany), and the

British Broadcasting Corporation (United Kingdom). Following the attacks of September 11, 2001, the US government spent most of its State Department public diplomacy budget on international broadcasting efforts in the service of the "war on terror." Under the auspices of the Broadcasting Board of Governors, the US government launched Radio Sawa, a 24-hour radio broadcast to the Middle East. Its format was a blend of one-third news with two-thirds light music, mostly English, Arabic, and Spanish pop music that would appeal to young people (mainly males) under the age of 30. Critics referred to Radio Sawa using Britney Spears as one of the information warfare strategies of the United States. Al-Hurra Television (in Arabic, "The Free One") was launched on February 14, 2004. Like Radio Sawa, Al-Hurra has suffered credibility problems, most notably its symbolic brand. A network that calls itself a "freedom" network puts its target audience on the defensive. If the sponsor of the network is "free," does this imply that the viewing audience is unfree? In the case of Al-Hurra's target audience, whose governments are by and large autocratic and authoritarian, they generally perceive themselves to be free-thinking individuals independent from the controlling state bodies.

Two-way communication, or dialogue, is obviously important to international political engagement. Much of traditional diplomacy involves dialogue between principals. In public diplomacy, dialogue is expanded to the exchange of information and ideas across social and cultural boundaries.

The third layer of public diplomacy, collaboration, is often the least noted mode of communicative engagement in the literature, but it is no less important to our understanding of how public diplomacy operates in the global communication environment. As Cowan and Arsenault state, "Collaborative projects almost without exception include dialogue between participants and stakeholders, but they also include concrete and typically easily identifiable goals and outcomes that provide a useful basis and structure upon which to form more lasting relationships."[26] Collaboration is similar to the concept of superordinate goals in conflict resolution situations.

Many public diplomats in a dialogic or collaborative context view their roles as cultural mediators or peace negotiators engaged in Track Two citizen-based diplomacy. Track One diplomacy, the arena for formal, official, government-to-government interaction by designated representatives of sovereign states, is complemented by Track Two diplomacy, which refers to non-governmental, informal, and unofficial ties between private citizens and groups that relate to each other outside the constraints of formal power. Often these encounters are designed to bring groups of people together who are involved in conflict and require mediation. John McDonald, a diplomat for 40 years and co-founder of the Institute for Multi-Track Diplomacy, says:

> Track Two aims to reduce or resolve conflict by decreasing the anger, tension, and fear between peoples by improving the communication and understanding of the other side's point of view. In no way is Track Two a substitute for Track One; instead, it complements and parallels the goals of Track One.[27]

Elevation of Exchanges

One of the most important parameters of public diplomacy today is the valuing of person-to-person exchanges. Many universities host international visitors and tout the merits of overseas study in order to expand one's knowledge but also to promote a global understanding of political and social problems. On July 22, 2009 US Secretary of State Hillary Clinton was asked at a town hall meeting in Thailand which US foreign policy initiative had had the most positive impact on Thailand and Thai education. Her response was no surprise:

> We have been working together for 176 years, and there have been a number of important initiatives over that long period of time. But I think educational exchanges and student exchanges are among the most important, and I would like to see even more of them. I'd like more American students coming to Thailand. I'd like more American faculty coming to Thailand, and I'd like more students and faculty from Thailand coming to the United States.

She added:

> I think there's no substitute for person-to-person connection, because we are fighting against cultural media stereotypes. The media paints a picture of the United States which very often has not got anything to do with reality. And for a lot of people in Thailand, that's all they will know about the United States unless we create educational and cultural exchanges and opportunities. So that's what I'd like to see more of.[28]

Clinton's emphasis on educational and cultural exchanges over mass media to improve bilateral relations between Thailand and the United States illustrates a long-time tradition favoring what Edward Murrow referred to as "the last three feet" of communication. Mass media, for all their dominance, have a limited impact in changing attitudes and opinions in global populations. They serve more to reinforce pre-existing dispositions.[29]

Interpersonal communication is now viewed as being more influential in changing attitudes, beliefs, and behaviors because it provides a two-way (transactive) exchange of information. Media operate within a nexus of influences, including interpersonal forms like family, friends, and social networks. While mass media can be successful at bringing attention to important issues, greater and longer-lasting effects typically follow from interpersonal communication support for public communication campaigns.[30]

Public Diplomacy Goes Public

Public diplomacy is a function and a concern of all nations and their citizens, and of multinational security organizations such as NATO or non-governmental human rights organizations such as Amnesty International. Today, any international organization has to be mindful of its public diplomacy mission and include some understanding of its purpose in its external and internal communication statements. Gone are the days when nations could rely solely on trained diplomats from the most prestigious universities to represent the interests and concerns of their respective nations abroad. Likewise, non-governmental international organizations must be aware of their own brand image in an increasingly cluttered international information environment.

Public Diplomacy Actors

Traditional public diplomacy actors include public affairs and public information officers of the government, government broadcasters, and cultural mediators like sponsored exchange students and field workers in development who work closely with local citizens.

It is easy to see how a Fulbright or Rhodes scholar could be viewed as a public diplomat. A sponsored exchangee is funded by nation-states with a vested interest in the international education of that person. During the Kennedy administration, the Peace Corps was envisioned as an international development exchange program that would help to brand young Americans as international humanitarians in projects to meet the development needs of less-developed nations. New public diplomacy actors include those who challenge dominant assumptions in international relations and the foreign policies of governments (international terrorists, sports stars and other celebrities, NGOs). The new public diplomats do not toe the government line, but are often just as important agents of influence as those who run governments; they are also more often the targets of public diplomacy campaigns run by official sources.

Country Profiles

Germany

On November 9, 2009 Germany marked the 20-year anniversary since the fall of the Berlin Wall. The German magazine *Der Spiegel* captured the essence of the new Germany in its online photo essay with a 60-year timeline of the state (1949–2009): "Sixty years later, Germans are living in peace with their neighbors. Together they share a common currency – the euro – as well as the political institutions of the European Union. From a heap of bomb-destroyed ruins, Germany has evolved into the world's third-largest industrial nation and the world's leading exporter."[31] Like so many powerful nation-states with a mixed history, Germany is seeking to improve its image in the world through an orchestrated program of nation branding, presenting itself as a modern European nation of culture and a "Land of Ideas." The latter is a far cry from the World War II era symbols of swastikas, concentration camps, and National Socialism. As German scholar Oliver Zöllner writes, "The wording expresses a wealth of positive arguments and associations with Germany both within Germany and abroad: nation of science and culture – the land of poets and thinkers, innovative products that are 'Made in Germany.'"[32] Engaging foreign target groups in dialogue is the current fashionable leitmotif of German public diplomacy.

China

China's concern about its national image did not begin with the 2008 Olympics in Beijing, though in the years preceding it became a hot topic. While soft power is a well-known concept in academia, government, and the media, public diplomacy is not. More common are the concepts *wai xuan* (external propaganda), referring to China's image overseas, or *xuan chuan* (propaganda), which, unlike in the United States, has a positive connotation and is used interchangeably with words like "advertising" and "publicity."[33] In practice, Chinese public diplomacy is not unlike the French approach, with a strong emphasis on cultural exchange and diplomacy, seen in the development of culture years such as the Chinese–French Cultural Year in 2004 and the Chinese–Indian Friend Year in 2006, as well as the several hundred overseas Confucius Institutes.

The Chinese government established a division for public diplomacy in 2004 in the Information Department of the Ministry of Foreign Affairs. At its founding, Chinese officials placed a strong emphasis on courting the opinion of the Chinese people rather than that of an overseas public: "The basic goal of public diplomacy is to enhance the exchanges and interaction with the public in order to guide and win the understanding and support of the public for foreign policies."[34] In an interview with the *People's Daily*, Foreign Minister Zhaoxing Li said that "Inside China, we pay high attention to public diplomacy, often explain to the public China's diplomatic policies and practice, learn from the people how to improve our work, and have received more and more understanding and support from the people."[35] Zhao Qizheng of the Chinese People's Political Consultative Congress (CPPCC) wrote in an opinion editorial that good public diplomacy required to confront the Western media bias:

> We can't expect foreign media to portray China justly, or close the opinion gap they have created. China must present an accurate picture of itself to the world. The expansion of reform and opening up is necessary for the nation's peaceful development. In this regard, China should not only listen, but talk back.[36]

Just six months away from the Beijing Olympics in March 2008, Foreign Minister Yang Jiechi defined this image of China to the rest of the world:

> China is working to build a harmonious world of lasting peace and common prosperity. I believe this is also the goal mankind pursues. In ancient China, the idea of "peace and cooperation bring harmony" was already a popular one. We should strengthen our exchanges and cooperation to reduce elements of discord and increase elements of concord so as to promote cooperation among nations. This is a long-term goal for China, and we are working to achieve it. We will work with other countries for a more harmonious and better world.[37]

Despite these lofty words of peace and harmony, and the image of a "peaceful rise" over "global threat," China's national leaders continue to highlight economic growth and the preservation of the prestige of the Chinese national government over soft power. One of China's misconceptions about the cultivation of an international image, according to Yiwei Wang, is that "China has focused on expanding its economy internationally while neglecting culture, or – when culture has been considered – the Chinese government has just focused on expanding the traditional culture and ignored the cultivation of civil society abroad through cultural exchange."[38]

Israel

In 2008 the state of Israel celebrated its 60th anniversary, but without acknowledging the persistence of the Palestinian–Israeli conflict. In January 2009 the conflict in Gaza between Hamas and the Israeli Defense Forces increased global attention on Israel as a conflict-ridden state. Like Germany, the state of Israel is seen by the world as a country with a mixed reputation and history. Throughout much of its history – including the time of the First Gulf War in 1991 when Israeli citizens periodically donned gas masks to protect themselves from threatened attacks from President Saddam Hussein of Iraq[39] – global public opinion exhibited a great deal of support for the new state of Israel. Since the beginning of the twenty-first century, however, not only among Arabs in the Middle East but throughout most of the world, sympathy and solidarity have tended to rest with the Palestinian minority in Israel which seeks a Palestinian state, rather than with the Israeli government, its military, or Jewish settlers.

Many academics, media, and officials in Israel have been working to promote a "new" image of Israel, one that acknowledges the continuation of strife in the region but also highlights the technological, educational, and cultural merits of the state. Nevertheless, Israel, in spite of strong support from the United States, retains its image of a conflicted state that often comes in for criticism by non-governmental international organizations like Amnesty International and Human Rights Watch.

In an effort to overcome an information gap about itself, the country has begun to promote more international tourism, not just religious pilgrimages. It has sponsored media tours to show reporters and young bloggers how multicultural and secular Israel is, in an effort to confront the mediated image of Israel as a place full of religious extremists or warring parties. David Saranga, media consultant at the Israeli Consulate in New York City, explained the emphasis on youth and new media in the rebranding of Israel:

> The work is open-source, and transparent – as it has to be, to engage a younger generation. We are experimenting with what works, and encouraging interaction. With over 1,000 friends on Facebook, and 600 unique visitors a day to the isRealli blog, the numbers logging on are respectable, but not massive. However, what is happening on YouTube is noteworthy. Previously, if you searched for "Israel" on the video-sharing site, the vast majority of films found would be negative or anti-Zionist. Now you are just as likely to see positive depictions of the country. These are not "propaganda" films produced by the consulate, but are user-generated content.[40]

Tzipi Livni, the head of the moderate Kadima Party in Israel, has been involved in the rebranding, which includes encouraging more young Israelis to conduct civilian-based diplomacy through posting videos about life in Israel on YouTube. Despite these efforts, Israel's global image continues to be dominated by hard-power rather than soft-power images, and its military and economic alliances with the United States, particularly during the Bush administration, did nothing to help promote a new image of Israel independent of the world's sole superpower. Nevertheless, Israel has moved forward in recognizing the need to promote a more balanced and accurate image of its people, history, and culture. In this it has a huge advantage that the United States lacks – an enormous curiosity on the part of the global civil society to learn more about the modern state of Israel. The United States dominates global media coverage, while Israel dominates it only when there is news of conflict. The lack of good information about real life in Israel – including family life, school life, shopping, eating out – is a great opportunity for this modern state to take its rebranding in hand.

Conclusions

The future of public diplomacy will take on new dimensions; it will not be centered on the United States but defined by global civil society actors working both with and without government partners. It will be more personal, or *guanxi*, rather than being directed by the nation-state or government. The concept of *guanxi* refers to a core personal and social relationship network principle in Chinese society, which is often translated as "connections." It has been compared to social capital values advanced by Robert Putnam in his insightful book, *Bowling Alone*, and to the intermediary concept known as *wasta* in Middle Eastern culture. A person with good *guanxi* is someone who, through the influence of his or her personal contacts, can resolve a problem or fulfill a need quickly. The principle of reciprocity is a core value in good *guanxi*. One does not operate in a social vacuum but extends help and favors in order to receive such favors in the future, not necessarily from the person who has been helped. Public diplomacy's new dimensions will recognize and work within the parameters of a pay-it-forward global society where good social actors will be rewarded and bad social actors punished by the global civil society.

In the future, public diplomacy will become more ad hoc, spontaneous, and chaotic rather than state-room formal, as new social networks emerge to challenge the growing impotence of the nation-state system to resolve global conflicts or to fairly represent the aspirations of citizens. Iran's presidential election in June 2009 and the Arab Spring uprisings that began in 2010 illustrate the power of private citizens to reach out across national and virtual boundaries to challenge the power of the state. Though some would characterize the silencing of the Iranian street demonstrations as the reinforcement of state power, the documentation of these protests on YouTube and Twitter serves as a model of freedom and independence from both government and traditional media power.

We are in the age of a new mindset in public diplomacy. The focus has shifted from traditional one-way informational diplomatic objectives to two-way interactive public exchanges. Exchanges are being emphasized now more than ever, though support for exchanges still remains more rhetoric than resource-driven. Exchanges support reciprocity, establish rapport, show personal commitment, and build continuity and trust over the long term. Person-to-person exchanges allow more room to agree with a "target public" on the spot and shows liking better than mass media campaigns. They also defuse mistrust and the belief that a nation's public diplomacy is just propaganda or a marketing campaign in a new guise. These positive outcomes of exchanges in the long term are what make many countries jump on the mass media bandwagon in crisis situations. Nevertheless, public diplomacy today is more personal than ever and it is likely that collaborative approaches in public diplomacy will become more dominant in the twenty-first century as nations realize that do-it-alone management is neither practical, effective, nor affordable.[41]

Notes

1. President George W. Bush, Address to a joint session of Congress, September 20, 2001, at http://archives.cnn.com/2001/US/09/20/gen.bush.transcript/, accessed August 14, 2013.

2. Barbara Burrell, *Women and Political Participation: A Reference Handbook*, Santa Barbara, CA: ABC-CLIO, 2004, p. 160.

3. Margaret Tutwiler, Testimony before the Senate Foreign Relations Committee, Washington, DC, October 29, 2003.

4. Margaret Tutwiler, Testimony before the House Committee on Government Reform Subcommittee on National Security, Emerging Threats and International Relations, February 10, 2004.

5. Nancy Snow, "US Public Diplomacy: A Tale of Two who Jumped the Ship of State," Special Report, *Foreign Policy in Focus* (May 27, 2004), at http://fpif.org/us_public_diplomacy_a_tale_of_two_who_jumped_ship_at_state/, accessed August 20, 2013.

6. Margaret Carlson, "Can Charlotte Beers Sell Uncle Sam?" *Time* (November 14, 2001), at http://www.time.com/time/nation/article/0,8599,184536,00.html, accessed August 20, 2013.

7. Snow, "US Public Diplomacy."

8. Charlotte Beers, Under-Secretary of State for Public Diplomacy and Public Affairs; Richard Boucher, Assistant Secretary of State for Public Affairs, "Public Diplomacy in Support of the International Coalition," *Foreign Press Centers* (November 9, 2001), at http://2002-2009-fpc.state.gov/7533.htm, accessed August 20, 2013.

9. "Shared Values," at http://archive.org/details/SharedValues, accessed August 14, 2013.

10. James K. Glassman, "Winning the War of Ideas," speech before the Washington Institute for Near East Policy, July 8, 2008; see also James Glassman, "Winning the War of Ideas," *New York Sun* (July 23, 2008), at http://www.nysun.com/opinion/winning-the-war-of-ideas/82438/?print=0224157121, accessed August 20, 2013.

11. Judith McHale, "Public Diplomacy: A National Security Imperative," Address at Center for a New American Security, Washington, DC, June 11, 2009.
12. McHale, "Public Diplomacy."
13. Jan Melissen, "Wielding Soft Power: The New Public Diplomacy," *Clingendael Diplomacy Papers* 2 (May 2005), 1.
14. Geoffrey Cowan and Nicholas J. Cull (eds.), *Public Diplomacy in a Changing World*, Thousand Oaks, CA: Sage, 2008, p. 6.
15. "Origins of the Term Public Diplomacy," Public Diplomacy Alumni Association, at http://publicdiplomacy.org/pages/index.php?page=about-public-diplomacy, accessed August 14, 2013.
16. "The Life and Work of Edward R. Murrow: An Archives Exhibit," Edward R. Murrow Center, Fletcher School of Law and Diplomacy, Tufts University, MA, at http://dca.lib.tufts.edu/features/murrow/exhibit, accessed August 20, 2013.
17. Edward R. Murrow, Testimony to Congressional Appropriations Committee, quoted in Alexander Kendrick, *Prime Time: The Life of Edward R. Murrow*, Boston: Little, Brown, 1969, p. 466; also quoted in Nicholas J. Cull, *The Cold War and the United States Information Agency*, New York: Cambridge University Press, 2008, p. 189.
18. Nicholas Cull, "Public Diplomacy: Taxonomies and Histories," *Annals of the American Academy of Political and Social Science* 616(1) (2008), 31–54.
19. http://www.publicdiplomacy.org, accessed August 20, 2013.
20. Cowan and Cull (eds.), *Public Diplomacy in a Changing World*, p. 6.
21. "Ashton Kutcher Takes on Malaria with Twitter," Malaria Policy Center, April 8, 2009, at http://www.malariapolicycenter.org/news/ashton-kutcher-takes-malaria-twitter, accessed August 14, 2013.
22. James Glassman, "Winning the War of Ideas," *New York Sun* (July 23, 2008), at http://www.nysun.com/opinion/winning-the-war-of-ideas/82438/, accessed August 14, 2013.
23. Glassman, "Winning the War of Ideas," speech before the Washington Institute for Near East Policy, July 8, 2008.
24. Suzy Platt, *Respectfully Quoted: A Dictionary of Quotations*, Washington, DC: Barnes & Noble, 1993.
25. "Barack Obama's Speech in Berlin," at https://my.barackobama.com/page/content/berlinvideo/, accessed August 20, 2013.
26. Geoffrey Cowan and Amelia Arsenault, "Moving from Monologue to Dialogue to Collaboration: The Three Layers of Public Diplomacy," in Cowan and Cull (eds.), *Public Diplomacy in a Changing World*, p. 21.
27. John McDonald, "The Track Not Taken," *Harvard International Review* 22(3) (2000), 68.
28. "Townterview Hosted by Suttichai Yoon and Veenarat Laohapakakul of World Beat," at http://www.state.gov/secretary/rm/2009a/july/126335.htm, accessed August 14, 2013.
29. Joseph T. Klapper, *The Effects of Mass Communication: An Analysis of Research on the Effectiveness and Limitations of Mass Media in Influencing the Opinions, Values and Behavior of Their Audiences*. Glencoe, IL: Free Press, 1960.
30. R. E. Rice and C. Atkin, "Principles of Successful Public Communication Campaigns," in J. Bryant and D. Zillmann (eds.), *Media Effects: Advances in Theory and Research*, Hillsdale, NJ: Lawrence Erlbaum, pp. 365–87.
31. "1949–2009: The Federal Republic of Germany Turns 60," at http://www.spiegel.de/international/germany/0,1518,626308,00.html, accessed August 14, 2013.
32. Oliver Zöllner, "German Public Diplomacy: The Dialogue of Cultures," in N. Snow and P. M. Taylor (eds.), *Routledge Handbook of Public Diplomacy*, New York: Routledge, 2009, pp. 262–9.
33. Yiwei Wang, "Public Diplomacy and the Rise of Chinese Soft Power," in Cowan and Cull (eds.), *Public Diplomacy in a Changing World*, p. 259.
34. Ministry of Foreign Affairs of the People's Republic of China, academic seminar on China's public diplomacy, 2004.
35. Foreign Minister Li Zhaoxing, interview with *People's Daily*, December 16, 2004, at http://www.fmprc.gov.cn/eng/zxxx/t175545.htm, accessed February 16, 2005.
36. Zhao Qizheng, "Better Public Diplomacy to Present a Truer Picture of China," *People's Daily Online* (March 30, 2007), at http://english.peopledaily.com.cn/200703/30/eng2007 0330_362496.html, accessed May 30, 2007.
37. "Foreign Minister Yang Jiechi Meets the Press," March 14, 2008, at www.fmprc.gov.cn/eng/zxxx/t414877.htm, accessed May 14, 2008.
38. Wang, "Public Diplomacy and the Rise of Chinese Soft Power," 261.
39. Etyan Gilboa, "Public Diplomacy: The Missing Component in Israel's Foreign Policy," *Israel Affairs* 12(4) (October 2006), 715.
40. David Russell, "Meet David Saranga, the Man whose Campaigns are Rebranding Israel," *Jewish Chronicle* (May 23, 2008), at http://www.thejc.com/articles/meet-david-saranga-man-whose-campaigns-are-rebranding-israel, accessed August 14, 2013.
41. For more on the connection between public diplomacy and electronic colonialism theory (ECT), see Chapter 16.

5

The Medium

Global Technologies and Organizations

Introduction

Most of the concern about global broadcasting and communication focuses on ownership, content, impact, flows, and cultural issues, the global telecommunications infrastructure or the medium by which content is transmitted. Global information superhighways are not without their socioeconomic consequences. The access and penetration of satellite dishes, the laying of fiber-optic cables, broadband, the Internet, wireless telephony, and the deployment of mobile telephones are all part of Marshall McLuhan's "global village." Facebook, YouTube, Twitter, and other social media all rely on the telecommunication infrastructure. This chapter seeks to detail the major stakeholders in the evolution of telecommunication systems around the globe. As the information revolution progresses in core nations, the key to their success is their telecommunication systems. The global telecommunication system is the central nervous system of the global economy. Global broadcasting, for example by CNN or the BBC, could not exist without an internationally functioning technical transmission system or infrastructure. Global commerce relies on the same infrastructure.

The primary global telecommunication agency is the International Telecommunication Union (ITU), a specialized United Nations agency much like UNESCO. However, there are other major players, such as Intelsat, Vodaphone, AT&T, and Verizon, that bring to the telecommunications table a mix of philosophical, ownership, technical, and public policy perspectives. Core nations have long dominated ITU, but now semiperipheral and peripheral nations are calling for major structural changes to reflect their needs and concerns.

Global Communication: Theories, Stakeholders, and Trends, Fourth Edition. Thomas L. McPhail.
© 2014 John Wiley & Sons, Inc. Published 2014 by John Wiley & Sons, Inc.

International Telecommunication Union

- Govern by UN. (handwritten annotation)

The struggle between core and peripheral nations over the question of the future of telecommunications is currently at an uneasy compromise. The sense of victory felt by core nations over minimizing major tenets of the complaints has been short-lived. Observers note that another arena, the ITU, based in Switzerland, has become a battlefield between core and peripheral nations. The ITU sponsors major global conferences that look at global technical standards and other issues affecting global telecommunications. At these meetings, participants confer to assign worldwide frequencies from the usable electromagnetic spectrum available for broadcasting and a wide variety of communication services.[1] Historically, these meetings attracted little attention, as technicians and engineers from various nations around the world divided the spectrum led by a concern for technical harmony. Issues such as radio microwave interference between neighboring nations, technical standards, or equipment interconnection protocols dominated the meetings. When nations sent delegates to ITU meetings, industrial nations assumed that a highly technical and engineering delegation would suffice. Little attention was paid to social, cultural, or economic concerns. But times have changed. Peripheral nations now want a major voice at the ITU. They want their concerns on the agenda.

Global conferences are convened and organized by ITU, which is charged with coordinating the international use of telecommunication systems worldwide. The nations represented at these global conferences are members of the ITU. These conferences review and amend existing ITU international radio regulations. For instance, conference participants are empowered to amend regulatory procedures for settling differences between nations and for notifying, coordinating, and registering radio frequency assignments. They are also authorized to set new rules concerning technical and performance standards of telecommunication systems, including satellite issues. Probably the most significant set of regulations the general conferences review is the international table of frequency allocation.

By virtue of the range of their global authority, all ITU conferences are profoundly significant events. Major ITU conferences have been held twice in North America: in Atlantic City, New Jersey in 1947, and in Minneapolis, Minnesota in 1998. The 1998 conference lasted four weeks and set the ITU's general policies, adopted strategic and financial plans, and elected members of the ITU Council.

During the years between ITU conferences (which are held every four years), technological innovations such as satellite communications or mobile phones, and methods for using more and more of the high ranges of the spectrum, particularly microwave frequencies, have revolutionized telecommunications. New developments in communication have a profound influence on social, cultural, economic, and political organizations and have so radically transformed the way most people live and interact with each other and their environment that the present era has come to be known as the "information age." All core nations have the latest in communication technologies, whereas the peripheral nations have few computers, cable systems, or digital services.[2] A nation or region cannot be considered "modern" without a sophisticated, technically advanced, and globally interconnected telecommunication network.

History and Structure of the ITU

In 1865 the International Telegraph Union, the ITU's forerunner, was formed under the International Telegraph Convention signed by 20 European nations in Paris. This makes the ITU the oldest international organization surviving today. At that time, the organization dealt exclusively with technical problems. The establishment of international standards for the Morse code was among its first endeavors.

The invention and implementation of wireless systems such as the telegraph, radio, and cross-border telephony complicated the process of setting international regulations. In 1885 the union established the first international rules governing telephony. At the 1906 Berlin conference, the first international conference to deal with radio and to set standards for equipment and technical uniformity, certain sections of the radio frequency spectrum were allocated to specific radio services, most notably the wireless frequencies used by ships at sea. The sinking of the *Titanic* in 1912 led to the mandatory stationing of wireless operators around the clock on all large passenger ships. The 1927 International Radio Telegraph Conference decided the next major advance in radio spectrum management. At this conference, a table of frequency allocation was created.

John Howkins points out the rather simple procedures involved in early ITU activities:

> Users notified the union about the frequencies, which they were already using or wished to use, and the union registered these in its master list. Neither the union nor the user owned the frequency. What happened was that, through the union's processes of registration, the user had a squatter's right to a specific frequency. Furthermore, the union's recognition of a particular usage gave the user some protection in international law.[3]

This simple squatter's right on a first-come, first-served basis did not, however, take into account the limited nature of the resource. Also, the first comers were mainly from North America and Europe, all of whom were core nations. This procedure has been largely responsible for the congestion in some popular frequency bands, a problem that today makes efficient allocation difficult and regional meetings are required to sort out conflicting claims.

Initially, spectrum usage was confined to maritime activities such as radio navigation and ship-to-shore communication. During the 1920s, due to technological advances that provided new means of utilizing higher frequencies, the types of services that the radio spectrum enjoyed multiplied rapidly. As new commercial and public radio services began to compete for spectrum space, fears grew that unless each new type of service was given a separate and distinct band within the spectrum, overcrowding and interference between the services would occur.

The ITU responded to this concern at the 1929 World Administrative Radio Council (WARC), by resolving that the various uses of the spectrum be coordinated by allocating a certain stretch or band of frequencies to each particular service. By the 1947 Atlantic City conference, further advances in telecommunications capacity necessitated the revision of procedures for registering and securing recognition of spectrum uses. More detailed plans for services were adopted for each of the three newly created regions: Region 1 for Europe and Africa, Region 2 for the Americas, and Region 3 for Asia and the South Pacific.

As early as 1959, the ITU's approach to telecommunications management came under criticism. Critics noted that huge areas of the spectrum, such as the high-frequency bands, were unplanned, and pointed out that the ITU stepped in to coordinate national assignments of frequencies only after congestion and conflicting uses had occurred. Generally, the ITU gave priority to those nations that had had the economic and technological sophistication to occupy a frequency first. These were not necessarily the nations that most needed the frequency. The fortunate nations were primarily core nations that relied on the squatter's right tradition to claim prime spectrum positions.

Misgivings about the basic machinery of the ITU escalated in the 1980s and 1990s. The regulations the ITU had originally adopted to make international telecommunications manageable were becoming either overextended or obsolete with the rapid introduction of new demands such as frequency space for mobile telephones and other wireless devices.

To restate the original point, the history of the ITU has been punctuated by problems and doubts about the efficiency of its structural framework. The problems and doubts turn on questions that are essentially of a technical or administrative nature. One prime reason for this technical orientation was articulated in the *Economist*, which noted, "the ITU is full of engineers terrified of controversy and terrified of the press."[4] This fundamental fact is part of the ITU's culture today. The current ITU works through four major sectors:

1. *radiocommunication*, which focuses on satellite orbit issues and the international radio spectrum;
2. *standardization*, which focuses on internationally compatible rules and standards;
3. *development*, which was recently established to provide greater leadership and focus on information and communication technology (ICT) matters affecting the peripheral regions; and
4. *telecommunications*, where leaders from government and industry work together on major policy matters.

In recent years, critics of ITU have cautioned that although this narrow technical focus may have been acceptable when decisions about telecommunications were of concern only to a limited circle of specialists within the industry, it is no longer adequate. In an age in which telecommunications have become highly politicized because of their profound effects on the complexion of national and international roles, many nations are not only concerned about which medium or frequency they are carried on, but also about many non-technical matters. Semiperipheral and peripheral nations are aware of the pivotal role telecommunications play in the global economy. They are also demanding prime spectrum allocations well in advance of their actual use.

The ITU has received calls from many quarters to implement structural and administrative reforms designed to furnish mechanisms for recognizing and absorbing political and socioeconomic input. At the time of writing, the ITU has neither the ability to deal with political or ideological concerns nor the necessary administrative structure through which such conflicts could be channeled.

When peripheral nations threaten to turn ITU conferences into ideological and rhetorical contests, they trigger much apprehension. With no experience in dealing with such developments, ITU talks could collapse before technical issues could be resolved. This would jeopardize global spectrum management decisions and leave matters in an uncomfortable state of suspension. Of course, this is the last thing core nations want, who have vast sums of money invested in global telecommunications systems. These systems represent the central nervous system of the global economy. Therefore, core nations have a keen interest in maintaining a manageable and predictable telecommunications environment through the ITU.

Current Concerns

Two of the main reasons the international community devoted more attention to recent ITU conferences were the increase in the number of countries represented and the fact that peripheral nations, which accounted for almost all the increase, now constitute a majority in the ITU. In the 1950s fewer than 100 nations were members of the ITU. But by 2013 there were 193 nations in the ITU family. The level of preparation and negotiating skill required to manage a meeting of over 2,000 delegates, some 50 NGOs, and 700 sector and academic members discussing issues of unusual technical and social complexity was unprecedented in the ITU's history. They are also being confronted with the rapid pace of innovation in the telecom and information technology sectors.

The new majority status of the peripheral nations contributes to the high profile of these conferences, and these nations have been the source of a feature previously unheard of at ITU meetings: the use of political and ideological criteria in arriving at decisions concerning the "digital divide," spectrum management and allocations, as well as other issues which impact peripheral regions. Decisions at ITU are made on a one nation one vote basis. Core nations worry that if peripheral nations act in unison they will be able, by virtue of the majority they command, to push through measures relating to NWICO and thereby guarantee access for the developing world to highly desired spectrum space and geostationary orbits for satellites, as well as committing funds to reduce the digital divide. Many of the proposals concern the core nations, particularly the United States, which have a great deal to lose or which will have to bear the brunt of new expenditure. A new issue that the United States is pushing for, cybersecurity, has seen it become an ITU-D Sector associate with the International Information Systems Security Certification Consortium. Some of the issues it will be looking into are spam, viruses, malware, and the protection of data, as well as privacy.

Currently, a major initiative at ITU is the promotion of a global international mobile system called IMT-2000. This initiative will provide wireless access to the global telecommunication system through the application of both satellite and terrestrial systems. It will provide guidance for coordinating related technological developments in order to promote conversion in technical standards for wireless access technologies. This initiative also seeks to coordinate both public and private networks, which are emerging at various rates in different regions of the world.

The role of the ITU has expanded enormously as a result of technological innovation and the multiplicity of new stakeholders ranging from governments to broadcasters, to manufacturers, so that it has become the major global organization dealing with the substantial telecommunications sector. Many of the member states and related organizations now expect the ITU to take into account the cultural, social, and non-economic dimensions of issues in making frequency allocations and other major decisions.

Geostationary Orbits

Technically, the most effective positioning of a communication satellite is 22,300 miles above the equator in a geostationary or geosynchronous orbit (see Figure 5.1). At such an altitude, a satellite completes one orbit of the earth in the time it takes the earth to revolve around its axis once, that is, every 24 hours. Because the satellite is traveling at the same speed as the earth, it is always hovering over the same area and thus can provide continuous communication service to the same region. Satellites placed at lower or higher altitudes such as 15,000 or 30,000 miles above the earth do not travel at the same speed as the earth and thus, over time, disappear over the horizon. For there to be continuous communication, another satellite must appear to replace a satellite as it disappears over the horizon. This requires the use of expensive and elaborate antennae or receivers that can track the new satellite as it comes into range. Synchronous satellites, on the other hand, are always over the same spot on earth, and therefore their signals can be picked up by simple receivers or

Figure 5.1 A satellite orbiting Earth

ground stations. Moreover, because of their altitude, their transmissions cover much greater areas of territory, called a footprint, than their lower-altitude counterparts.

Unfortunately, there is limited space for satellites in the thin slice 22,300 miles above the equator in which synchronous satellites can operate or park for their lifetime. This is why the question of allotting orbital slots in advance, on a country-by-country basis, has become a pressing issue for peripheral nations, which trail far behind in satellite technology. If and when they catch up, there will not be sufficient usable prime parking spots remaining for their geostationary satellites.

The issue of geostationary parking spots took on additional symbolic meaning in the 1980s. Because the only position for these satellites was above the equator, and because the equator covers parts of peripheral nations in Latin America and Africa, some delegates from these regions seized on this important point. They argued at ITU meetings that the space above these nations should be reserved for them so that they would have appropriate parking spots for future satellite deployment. As already mentioned, these allocations have historically been awarded on a first-come first-served basis, which means that the core nations and the former Soviet Union came first to the table to make specific requests for operational satellite parking spots. By the time the peripheral nations, even those at the equator, are ready to operate satellites in the future, there will be no prime parking spots left, only suboptimal spots. And these suboptimal spots will be over some other nation, not the prime spots above their own nation-states. Naturally, the traditional operating system of first-come first-served did not please delegates from peripheral nations in relation not only to satellite orbital space, but also to spectrum allocation and management. The peripheral regions wanted to replace the first-come first-served process of ITU's spectrum management with a new system whereby they could reserve frequencies of all types for their future use.

They argued that this strategy would promote fair and equitable access to the international radio spectrum. Because the older industrialized nations had entered the field of radio telecommunications at a much earlier date than many newly emerging peripheral nations, they had obtained the rights to all prime frequencies by default. These core nations, led by the United States, naturally objected to any changes in criteria for allocation coming before ITU conferences. They claimed that the new policy would leave many allotted frequencies and orbital slots empty, awaiting some future point in time when the peripheral nations would be able to afford new technology.

The outcome of the push by peripheral nations for greater consideration in the allocation of the international communication spectrum, including orbital parking spots, was a substantial compromise. Even the United States agreed to allow Intelsat (see below) to promote the deployment of satellite communications in an equitable fashion across the world. This meant that peripheral nations would have appropriate ground stations for both unlinking and down-linking signals from the vast number of Intelsat satellites deployed around the world.

The Maitland Commission

A number of factors discouraged peripheral nations from pushing through their concerns at the ITU. First, they realized there would be other global meetings sponsored by the ITU at which they could state their case and make gains in their progress toward a fairer share of the radio spectrum and orbital parking spaces. Second, many nations, particularly the United States, applied pressure on them, and called in return favors to insure that an orderly spectrum remained intact, particularly for satellites. Third, almost all nations have some type of domestic system, regardless of how rudimentary, and want to see it continue operating without major adjustments. Fourth, divergent and often conflicting national interests among peripheral nations prevented the formation of a powerful, united, and well-orchestrated voting bloc that could have led to radical changes in ITU policies and procedures in the form of resolutions and amendments.

Although the industrialized nations sought to avoid the imminent controversy over the crucial role that telecommunications play in economic, cultural, and social developments, peripheral nations persisted in their criticism of the ITU. In response, during the 1980s the ITU established a commission chaired by Sir Donald Maitland from the United Kingdom. The formal title of the study group was the Independent Commission for World Wide Telecommunications Development. The two-year study submitted its report to the ITU in January 1985.[5] The report addressed the inequities in the distribution of telecommunications systems and services between core and other nations. It looked, for example, at telephone penetration levels and found some startling contrasts: three-quarters of the world's population live in countries with fewer than 10 telephones per 100 people, and more than half the world has access to less than one telephone per 100 people. In the Western industrialized world, however, individuals enjoy the use of more than one telephone per two people. The commission concluded that this imbalance could no longer be tolerated: "It cannot be right that in the latter part of the twentieth century a minority of the human race should enjoy the benefits of the new technology while a majority live in comparative isolation."[6] Moreover, the commission highlighted the benefits to the entire world if the disparities were removed:

> Given the vital role telecommunications play not only in such obvious fields as emergency, health, and other social services, administration, and commerce, but also in stimulating economic growth and enhancing the quality of life, creating effective networks worldwide will bring immense benefits. An increase in international traffic

will generate funds, which could be devoted to the further improvement and development of telecommunications services. The increased flow of trade and information will contribute to better international relationships. The process of creating effective networks worldwide will provide new markets for the high technology and other industries, some of which are already suffering the effects of surplus productive capacity. The interest industrialized and developing countries share in the worldwide development of telecommunications is as great as in the exploitation of new sources of energy. And yet it is far less appreciated.[7]

The Maitland Commission argued that although telecommunications systems were once considered a luxury, they are now viewed as essential components of development. Indeed, one may argue that a telecommunication infrastructure is a prerequisite for any type of social or economic development in peripheral nations. For example, the benefits of telecommunications include increased economic, commercial, and administrative efficiency; improved social and emergency services; and more equitable distribution of the social, cultural, and economic benefits of development. In addition, "The absence of a system which enables timely information to be sent and received engenders a sense of isolation and frustration, and so raises a barrier between different sections of the population. This cannot but undermine the process of development."[8] The Maitland Commission concluded that the best way to redress the imbalance and enhance the telecommunications ability of the developing world was through the expansion of telecommunications networks.

A final set of recommendations involved the role of the ITU and how it might be strengthened. The commission reasserted that telecommunications development should be given a higher priority. It charged the Secretary-General of the ITU with monitoring the implementation of the recommendations offered, reporting on the progress made, and stimulating further progress where necessary. The report concluded:

> There is no single remedy. A range of actions over a wide front and at different levels is required. Progress will be made only in stages. But, if the effort is sustained, the situation worldwide could be transformed in 20 years. All mankind could be brought within easy reach of a telephone by the early part of next century and our objective achieved.[9]

Follow-Up to the Maitland Report

The Maitland Commission altered the traditional role of the ITU forever. No longer was the ITU conference a simple technical and engineering meeting. In the future, it would have to take into account the peripheral nations' concerns about issues such as access to and equitable distribution of the radio spectrum. The Maitland Report focused on the inequities between nations, particularly the fact that core nations control telecommunications research, manufacturing, and fiscal resources. Although everyone knew that a telecommunication infrastructure was necessary for the promotion of telemedicine, education, banking, tourism, and eventually access to the Internet, the peripheral nations realized that they were not going to become part of the electronic global village if they did not receive support from the ITU. Therefore they did not want to undermine the ITU, but rather to reform it from within. Many of these reforms and genuine concerns came to the fore at the ITU in the 1990s and have continued up to the present. But new major issues emerged involving the role of the private telecommunications sector within ITU's decision-making apparatus, along with discussions about the privatization of major stakeholders such as Comsat and Intelsat. These crucial matters are dealt with in the following sections.

Intelsat

International Telecommunications Satellite Organization (Intelsat) was formed in 1965 to provide international satellite communication services. From the beginning, the United States was the major participant in Intelsat and the leading core nation in the ITU. Intelsat was controlled and owned by 144 member nations. It provided the satellite technology necessary to complete the global communication systems that were in place by 1969. Intelsat global satellite systems bring video, audio, voice, data, and Internet services to users in more than 200 nations around the globe. Basically, Intelsat operates as a wholesaler that provides satellite services to users through an Intelsat member in each country. The US member was Comsat Corporation. Intelsat operates a system consisting of high-powered spacecraft in orbit as well as thousands of earth stations around the world. Intelsat customers are primarily major telecommunications operators in nations throughout the world. In addition, it provides satellite communication services to major broadcasters, airlines, banks, multinational corporations, and international newspaper distributors, as well as disaster relief, health-care, and telemedicine organizations around the globe.

In the mid-1960s, Intelsat launched the world's first communication satellite, and by 1969 it was providing global television coverage of the moon landing to an audience estimated to exceed 500 million people. In 1978 Intelsat brought the World Cup football matches to over one billion TV viewers in 42 countries. By 1997 it had established three regional support centers to increase market awareness and to further develop its telecommunications business. These offices are in the Pacific Rim, southeast Asia, and Europe. Using a series of its satellites, Intelsat makes possible the broadcast of the Olympic Games and the World Cup to people around the world. In 2006 Intelsat purchased a major competitor, PanAmSat.

Intelsat Competition

In the global telecommunications environment in which Intelsat operates, it faces two new strong competing forces. First, there are a series of other satellite providers now operating in direct competition with Intelsat. For example, several companies now provide satellite-centric telecommunications services to a range of clients and compete directly with Intelsat for high-volume users and transoceanic telecommunications business. The second major competitor is transoceanic fiber-optic cable systems. These cables have exceptional broadband width, reliability, and speed, and fiber-optic systems now account for substantial amounts of telecommunications traffic over high-volume routes. These two competing groups service highly profitable routes. They do not serve peripheral nations, less populated areas, or low-profit routes where there is little demand for high-capacity, high-speed digital communications. Intelsat is the lifeline provider for universal access to satellite service thanks to its historic ownership and participatory structure. However, this field of telecommunications could radically change with deregulation and privatization.

Eutelsat Communications

Eutelsat was established in 1977 to operate satellite systems for Europe and elsewhere. It has since expanded to the Middle East, Africa, Asia, and the Americas where it offers a broad range of information and broadcasting services. It is the major telecommunications service provider for Eurovision, the trans-Europe television network. Future growth will come with HDTV and 3D and digital cinema. Six additional satellites are planned as the company continues to grow.

Inmarsat

The mobile satellite service company Inmarsat was founded in 1979. It began by providing ships at sea with a telephone service via satellite. Using new technologies, it now has a broad range of customers for its global satellite services – ships, airlines, media, oil platforms, governments, banking, utilities, construction, and NGOs. It is based in the United Kingdom and is a private company listed on the London Stock Exchange.

The Future of Intelsat

After 30 years, Intelsat is confronting a new reality. The competitive and regulatory international environment for satellites is substantially different from that of a global central monopoly when Intelsat was first formed in the 1960s. The environment today is rife with deregulation, competition, liberalization, and privatization. The original 144 partners in Intelsat find themselves with increasingly different goals, owners, and domestic policies. Many of the national partners have been or will be privatized. This is happening at a time when other global partners are vigorously advocating their own, different, business goals and policies. Of particular policy concern is the total privatization of Intelsat, which occurred in 2001. Intelsat had functioned as an intergovernmental operating organization based on a consensus that followed a series of negotiated global agreements. Because there is no global regulator of international telecommunications services or prices, Intelsat tended to promote agreements that would protect all members – core, semiperipheral, and peripheral nations alike. But the peripheral nations are now fearful that their interests will be totally neglected in a privatized environment in which the sheer weight of economics and profitability will dominate future decision-making. Some peripheral nations could even lose their lifeline access to Intelsat's satellites. Without access to Intelsat's infrastructures, they could lose connection to the outside world. In times of national disasters, such as a tsunami or earthquake, a lack of connectivity to the outside world could exacerbate the crisis.

ITU's Changing Role and Expectations

When ITU was founded in 1865, it was to coordinate agreements between 20 nations concerning interconnecting telegraph networks for international telegraph traffic. Over time other nations joined the union, and equipment manufacturers and telecommunication carriers from both the public and the private sectors participated in working groups to assist the ITU in establishing technical standards. The private sector firms never had any voting authority but provided the needed technical expertise so that the ITU could develop international agreements to permit the orderly deployment of telecommunication technologies.

During the first decades of the ITU's existence, most telecommunication carriers were monopoly providers already owned by the governments of various nations. For example, the government of France owned the Office of the Post Telegraph and Telecommunication, known as PTT. But with the rapid expansion of the global economy, along with rapid innovations in the telecommunications sector, a new environment now confronts the ITU. The demands of the information society and global economy find telecommunications systems and services being privatized in an era of deregulation. Liberalization, along with new stakeholders who have little or no connection to their own governments through ownership, oversight, or control, is now part of the telecommunications landscape. Thus, the balance of power has shifted with the liberalization of the telecommunications environment to the private sector. This movement is further complicated by the conversion of traditionally distinct analog technologies to digital communications. Telecommunications firms and broadcasting and computer corporations work with essentially the same basic digital technologies. Now Hewlett-Packard, Microsoft, Intel, IBM, and others are some of the ITU's private sector members, providing the much needed technical expertise as wireless telecommunications and satellite technologies continue to evolve. The current situation in the ITU is becoming awkward, as private sector members are providing an estimated over 90 percent of the intellectual and technical contributions that underpin the ITU's recommendations and technical standards. This new reality needs to be dealt with in order for the ITU to retain its global technical decision-making role. Speed and broad participation is not a hallmark of the ITU's style of bureaucratic management, yet the private sector wants greater influence at future conferences, and a say in the ITU's future direction. Faced with the growing private sector call for shared power arrangements, the ITU has been slow to respond even though liberalization and privatization have been part of the global information economy for over a decade. In 1998, at ITU's Minneapolis conference, the new environment confronting ITU was discussed. Documents supplied to delegates stated:

> With an increasing number of new fora created by the market itself, many users and experts now question the relevance of a slow-moving body such as the ITU, where all power is vested in government representatives rather than in those organizations who are investing in and developing new technologies.
>
> However, before writing off the ITU one should bear in mind that it is the only truly global impartial organization whose membership spans all aspects of the industry, from PTOs to manufacturers to satellite system operators to service providers and even user groups. Even in its current form ITU can largely take single-handed credit for the successful development of the world's current telecommunications networks over the last 100 years.[10]

ITU's slow and cumbersome procedures could cause regional groups to take over its role of setting technical standards. The same document goes on to state:

> Most ITU Members – State and Sector – at least agree that a declining role for the ITU is not desirable. Despite the burgeoning growth of industry- and technology-specific forums and lobby groups, the ITU still represents the only truly global, impartial telecommunications organization. It has no vested interests, represents the needs of the poor as well as the rich countries, and has succeeded where all other industry groups have failed – that is, in pulling together competing organizations and governments in a spirit of cooperation. And, in the ITU's case, this cooperative effort is much more than mere words; it has led to almost faultless interconnection of the global telecommunications network and a shared approach to radio frequency spectrum use for radio communications.[11]

Finally, peripheral nations enjoy their voting status at the ITU and do not want to see it diluted by adding private sector voting rights. They are also concerned that private sector voting rights will go to multinational corporations based in core regions such as the United States, Europe, or Japan. Over time the marginal voices of the peripheral nations could become even weaker if the ITU takes heed of the private sector's discontent with its current status. Yet the ITU realizes that if it fails to respond, many major telecommunications players could shift their interests, role, and advice to other regional groups – to the ultimate detriment of the ITU in the twenty-first century.

The ITU has not been blind to the calls for reform. In developing a strategic plan, it recognizes the crucial role that international telecommunications play within the broader context of the global economy.[12]

The ITU now has a concern for the growing gap between "the information rich" and "the information poor," or the digital divide, as the literature now refers to it. Yet at the same time, as it is attempting to reposition itself in the international telecommunications debate, it appears to be a potential big loser as large telecom organizations are privatized. If this occurs, these organizations will have to answer directly to their shareholders rather than seek solutions that take into account the needs of other nations.

World Summit on the Information Society

The United Nations endorsed the World Summit on the Information Society (WSIS) in 2001. The summit was held in two phases: the first in Geneva, Switzerland in 2003 and the second in Tunis, Tunisia in late 2005.[13] Both phases were coordinated by the ITU.

In general, the summit was to take a global approach to the impact of the information society (IS). It sought ways to make the IS equitable and inclusive by discussing issues such as access, capacity, and connectivity. Particular attention was paid to e-learning, e-education, e-governance, e-media, and e-trade. A final plan of action aimed at reducing the digital divide emerged from the second phase, but there are already two areas of contention.

The first relates to the NWICO. As discussed in earlier chapters, UNESCO, the ITU, and the United Nations all played a part in the contentious debate about NWICO. Yet, even in the tamer confines of the first phase in Geneva, issues such as reducing imbalances in IT systems and calls for greater diversity of media ownership appeared in the declaration of principles. These and other claims of chronic imbalances clearly reflect aspects of the earlier NWICO feud.

The second, and perhaps more explosive, issue relates to the governance of the Internet. As detailed in Chapter 6, the current assignment of Internet names is carried out by the Internet Corporation for Assigned Names and Numbers (ICANN). WSIS took up the issue and wanted ICANN, which is US-centric, to become a global agency where peripheral nations have some influence on future decisions. As WSIS expert Wolfgang Kleinwachter accurately notes, there is a growing concern about America's hegemonic control of the Internet:

> When the WSIS process started, a number of governments, mainly from the third world, began to question the legitimacy of ICANN. They pointed out that the digital divide was reflected in the distribution of domain names and IP addresses. They felt that they were unable to participate in ICANN's decision-making processes. And they criticized the role of the US government. Some governments suggested that the internet, like telecommunications and broadcasting, should be regulated top-down in order to protect national and political interests.[14]

World Trade Organization

In 1947 the General Agreement on Tariffs and Trade (GATT) was formed by most of the industrialized nations. Its basic aim was to establish international rules for promoting freer trade by reducing tariffs, government grants, or subsidies. The agreements were multilateral in focus, that is, several nations agreed to a certain timetable to mutually reduce tariffs in order to facilitate growth in trade and the global economy. On January 1, 1995 the World Trade Organization (WTO) succeeded GATT. Currently, the WTO has 158 member nations and is headquartered in Geneva, Switzerland. The entry of China to WTO represents a significant market for all core nations. It is also a clear signal to the world that China is on its way to becoming a core nation. The Russian Federation joined in 2012.

As global trade increases, alongside a substantial number of international mergers and acquisitions in the communications sector, the roles and influence of WTO have taken on additional importance. Yet these are not without controversy or consequence. The 1999 meeting in Seattle, Washington saw substantial protest from environmental activists, labor groups, and anarchists. Although the protest focused on environmental and labor issues, several of the peripheral nations' delegates complained that the imposition of US environmental regulations or salary and working conditions mandated by US labor unions was merely another form of imperialism, which they rejected. Peripheral nations, as well as some core and semiperipheral nations, were also concerned about the impact and relevance of US labor practices on their cultural industries. An important point of contention is that the United States views media properties such as film, books, and magazines as economic entities, whereas many other nations view these products as central to their history, national identity, language, and culture. As a result, several parties outside the United States vigorously defend their right to exclude cultural industries and products from WTO negotiations. These critics fear that the WTO is simply a pawn of American hegemonic intentions to grasp even greater global control for US-based communication conglomerates, such as Disney, Fox, or Viacom.

The major NGO contesting WTO's attempts to include audiovisual or cultural industries is the International Network for Cultural Diversity (INCD).[15] The INCD seeks to counter the homogenizing effects of the globalization and commercialization of culture. It seeks to preserve diversity and to promote choice in the cultural marketplace. This includes the production and distribution of indigenous goods.[16] The INCD is a citizens' movement with over 500 members from 70 nations. It is a prime mover in terms of supporting UNESCO's convention on the protection and the promotion of cultural diversity. This convention legitimates government's subsidies, grants, and so on, to their cultural industries and opposes the WTO's commercialization of this sector. Another active group opposing the WTO's potential adverse move on cultural matters is the Culturelink Network, based in Croatia.

A related controversial issue facing the WTO is intellectual property rights. Intellectual property refers to artistic and literary creations, most of which are protected by copyright. With the expansion of global communication corporations, the ability to reward and determine ownership of creative works is becoming more problematic. And with the expansion of international commerce, the WTO's role in establishing ground rules for all trade is receiving much greater attention.

Currently the WTO appears stuck on the Doha Round, which focuses on agriculture, because core nations will not drop tariffs that would permit access to key core markets for peripheral nations. China, India, and Brazil have provided the leadership at WTO meetings in terms of pushing forward the agrarian demands of the peripheral nations. Disputes between nations may be resolved through a complicated dispute settlement process. Such a process is clearly preferable to earlier times when colonial disputes about trade frequently led to skirmishes, and sometimes even open warfare.

Organisation for Economic Co-operation and Development

The Organisation for Economic Co-operation and Development (OECD) was established immediately following World War II. Canadian and US foreign aid under the Marshall Plan was initially administered by the Organization for European Economic Cooperation (OEEC). The goal of this organization was to rebuild Europe, which had been devastated by the war. Much of the motivation for funding what was a successful program was the effort to stop communism from spreading across Europe, which had been devastated by the war. As a follow-up, the Organisation for Economic Co-operation and Development was formed by 20 nations in Europe and North America in 1961. Since then, 14 nations have been added to the group. The OECD also has relations with 70 other nations and several NGOs. Under the leadership of the former Secretary-General Donald Johnson, a Canadian, the OECD has been attempting to add more development activities to its research agenda.

OECD members support research to develop international economic and social policy research. They investigate a broad spectrum of public policy issues that seek to identify the impact of national policies on the international economy. Currently, much of their work focuses on the impact of global trade, including everything from video to the Internet. For example, the OECD provides member nations with cutting-edge research and data on a variety of topics relating to the mass media. The following list gives examples of topics explored in terms of data and best practice from over 50 reports produced by the OECD which seek to assist member nations in planning for various aspects of media policy and emerging trends:

1 media mergers;
2 new social and economic approaches to a multimedia world;
3 the implications of convergence;
4 global information infrastructure;
5 competition and regulation in broadcasting;
6 competition law and policy;
7 telecommunications regulations: institutional structures and responsibilities;
8 better skills, better jobs, better lives.

Two other sectors within its research divisions which impact global communication are (1) information and communication technologies, and (2) digital economy and the information society.

The OECD attempts to forecast macroeconomic developments on behalf of the 30 member countries, which produce two-thirds of the world's goods and services. In a way, the OECD is a global think tank for core and some semiperipheral nations. It provides them with expert advice on how to further frame and expand international trade rules so as to increase the cooperation between member nations as well as others and to create a stable and expanding global economy. Most of their work is carried out from an economic perspective. New members are admitted to the OECD, which tends to be an exclusive club, who have a commitment to a democratic system of national government and function with a market economy. All potential new entrants realize that the OECD provides world-class advice on modernization and economic development. The nations that are excluded have no equivalent economic think tank with access to data and best practice policies to help them increase their role and influence in the global economy. The OECD publishes over 250 books a year to assist members.

Conclusions

The United States' withdrawal from UNESCO was a reflection and a consequence of the widespread negative view some UN member states have of the country. They do not like the arrogant and sometimes offensive actions of the United States, and hence do not fully cooperate in the multilateral agencies in which the United States often plays a vital role. In addition to problems with UNESCO, which hosted anti-Western projects, the ITU is no longer the private domain of technicians and engineers dealing with communications technology from a purely technical point of view. It is an international concern that sees economic, social, cultural, development, and political aspects as part of the global decision-making process. The ITU's character shift has, of course, drawn sharp criticism from those who used to either benefit from or control the "clubby" technical atmosphere which the core nations fostered. Some critics downplay the role of the ITU as well as its current changes, but a proper analysis indicates that the ITU is central not only to the future of international telecommunications, but also to the global economy. On any scale, the United States is the major net beneficiary of the global economy. Telecommunications is the central nervous system of the global economy, and the United States would be the biggest loser should the ITU fail in its various roles. Yet several peripheral nations within the ITU push for a parochial agenda that continues to frustrate the core nations.

A global village with a fractured ITU, or an Intelsat weakened as a result of privatization and competition, would set the scene for potential chaotic, conflicting, and competing assignments of the international frequencies related to the electromagnetic spectrum. Even though such a situation would adversely affect other nations, this would pale in comparison to the turmoil and commercial losses that core governments would suffer, as well as their vast private sector, which relies on instantaneous telecommunications every second of every hour without end. Core nations need to pay more attention to ITU issues because the consequences of neglect could cripple the global economy.

Basically, the ITU is seeking to retain global leadership as the pre-eminent inter-governmental organization where public (government) and private businesses work to develop global telecommunications and information services networks in an orderly and fair manner. This is no small challenge.

Finally, the impact and long-term outcome of the WSIS is still unknown. Some critics, particularly the group claiming to be a back-door attempt to resurrect aspects of the NWICO, are concerned. If there is a resurgence of NWICO then the ITU, its major patron, will be blind-sided, and this could hasten its demise. The other area of possible contention is the idea of UNESCO promoting an international convention on cultural diversity at the same time as the WTO is looking at cultural industries as a new frontier for its commercial trade rules. These rules could one day make subsidies, grants, radio, television, and film content regulations, and screen quotas, illegal. This has the potential to threaten government subsidies or license fees for publicly funded and other non-commercial media operations.

Notes

1. It is appropriate to introduce the concept of digital communication here. Digital communication represents the emerging technological standard for the transmission of voice, video, audio, graphics, and data. As a technology, it decodes incoming messages into electronic bytes that are then transmitted via a telecommunication medium, either a wired system such as a fiber-optics network, or a wireless technology such as a satellite or cellular network. The receiving technology reconstructs the digital information into the appropriate original format, such as a color telecast of an international media event such as the Olympics, or data transferred from one multinational corporation to

its various subsidiaries around the globe. Over time all current analog-based technologies will migrate to a digital format. This digitalization of telecommunications will eventually mean that traditional telephone companies will be able to broadcast television services or carry the Internet, and vice versa. This is a large part of the engine of change that is propelling many mergers between broadcasting and telecommunication entities that were historically separate. The convergence phenomenon began to overtake many regulatory bodies and their rule-making in the 1990s. In the twenty-first century, both national and international regulatory agencies will be found wanting as digital technologies and other technical innovations outpace the ability of regulators to devise guidelines to provide appropriate oversight or to structure to a plethora of competing global digital services.

2. Documentation of the interconnection of global communication networks, trade, and services can be found in George A. Barnett, Joseph G. T. Salisbury, Chul Woo Kim, and Anna Langhorne, "Globalisation and International Communication: An Examination of Monetary, Telecommunications and Trade Networks," *Journal of International Communication* 6(2) (1999), 7–19; Kyungmo Kim and George Barnett, "The Structure of the International Telecommunications Regime in Transition: A Network Analysis of International Organizations," *International Interactions* 26(1) (2000), 91–127; Anthony McGrew and David Held (eds.), *Governing Globalization: Power, Authority and Global Governance.* Cambridge: Polity, 2002.

3. John Howkins, "How the ITU Works," *Inter Media* 7(5) (1979), 22–3.

4. "Will You Keep My Space?" *Economist* (September 1978), 18.

5. *The Missing Link: Report of the Independent Commission for World Wide Telecommunications Development,* Geneva: ITU, 1985, http://www.itu.int/osg/spu/sfo/missinglink/The_Missing_Ling_A4-E.pdf, accessed August 15, 2013.

6. *The Missing Link,* p. 31.

7. *The Missing Link,* p. 65.

8. *The Missing Link,* pp. 7–8.

9. *The Missing Link,* p. 69.

10. "Reforming the ITU: New Roles, New Responsibilities for ITU Members," at http://www.itu.int/newsarchive/press/PP98/PressRel-Features/Feature1.html, accessed August 15, 2013.

11. "Reforming the ITU."

12. http://www.itu.int/osg/spu/stratpol/plan/, accessed August 19, 2013.

13. For more up-to-date information on the summit see its website at www.itu.int/wsis.

14. Wolfgang Kleinwachter," Internet Governance: ICANN vs. ITU?" Intermedia 32(1) (2004), 18. For additional information on ICANN-related matters, see, for example, James N. Duchesne, "Running Amuck: Using the Debacle of Recent Top Level Domain Expansions to Argue for Greater Governmental Participation in DNS Management," *CommLaw Conspectus* 21(1) (2012), 151–84. For an update on this evolving issue visit the websites of the Internet Governance Forum or WSIS.

15. For additional information on the INCD see its website at www.incd.net.

16. For a comprehensive discussion of the impact of globalization on popular culture, see Peter Grant and Chris Wood, *Blockbusters and Trade Wars*, Toronto: Douglas & McIntyre, 2004.

6

The Internet

The Evolving Frontier

Introduction

This chapter seeks to highlight salient aspects of the history and current role of the Internet. The Internet is to the information age what the automobile was to the industrial age. The Internet is now a mass medium in many nations and has created a new dimension for global communication. It had its origins in the 1950s as a response to a single crucial military question. Namely, how could the United States send strategic information across long distances electronically with a maximum guarantee of accuracy and likelihood of reaching its ultimate destination? This occurred during the early stages of the Cold War, when the fear of the spread of communism drove even scientific ventures. A team of eminent scientists was assembled from leading universities across North America. They set in motion research that established the foundation for the electronic transfer of information over vast distances. It was to become a marriage of computer technology and telecommunications which evolved into the Internet.

Before describing in detail the series of activities and decisions that collectively formed the foundation for the modern-day Internet, we need to note that only a few major innovations have affected international communications. These were the invention of the movable-type printing press in the fifteenth century, the telegraph and telephone in the nineteenth century, and the developments following World War II that led to the global communications infrastructure finally being put in place.

In the nineteenth century there were newspapers, which traveled by rail or private mail, and personal writing, which traveled as letters via international postal services. Electronic message systems consisted primarily of the telegraph, which tended to expand in tandem with railway systems. After the telegraph came the telephone, which saw a rapid expansion, along with a telecommunication infrastructure, in the early part of the twentieth century. Wireless signals started as ship-to-shore devices and morphed into radio. Radio broadcasting and networks emerged in the early part of the twentieth century. At the same time, the movie

Global Communication: Theories, Stakeholders, and Trends, Fourth Edition. Thomas L. McPhail.
© 2014 John Wiley & Sons, Inc. Published 2014 by John Wiley & Sons, Inc.

industry was taking shape in both Europe and the United States. The laying of submarine telephone cables under the Atlantic and then the Pacific oceans further expanded international communications capacity. Later, satellite services and cable broadcasting were introduced to further expand the telephone, radio, television, data, and other forms of telephony. The introduction of digital technologies and the Internet, which bring convergence, represent the next wave of global mass communication. The Internet relies extensively on the interconnection of widely dispersed but interconnected global personal and business computer systems.[1]

Background

The Internet system began in the Cold War era of the 1950s. The high level of anxiety over issues such as national security, the spread of communism, the Russians' successful launch on October 4, 1957 of Sputnik,[2] and the potential for nuclear destruction created a public will to undertake research on a massive scale. In retrospect, it is easy to see how these fears, combined with the military background of President Eisenhower, funding, and the intellectual critical mass came together during the 1950s to create the system that would eventually become the Internet. For example, it was widely feared during this era that the United States was vulnerable to a potential nuclear attack and that such an attack could disrupt nationwide communication systems, both commercial and military. The other concern was the high cost of computing, along with the physical size and awkwardness of mainframe systems, which used punch cards and bulky tapes. As a result, in 1958 the US government established the Advanced Research Projects Agency (ARPA) to promote advanced research in computing and to investigate related telecommunication matters. ARPA had the task of determining how computer technology could be successfully applied to military activities. About the same time, the Rand Corporation produced a national security report that documented the extreme vulnerability of the US national communication infrastructure in the event of a catastrophic event: it proved that national communication systems between the east coast and the west coast could be interrupted or severed by a nuclear attack. This, of course, had tremendous ramifications for the coordination of a military and civilian response. The United States' response to these concerns was to build what is described as a distributed network called ARPANET (ARPA Network), the precursor to the Internet.

ARPANET was constructed in 1969 as a distributed national network consisting of a number of stand-alone, remote systems. Each system controlled all the necessary data, like a number of backup systems. These systems collectively moved data from one system to another. This distributive network allowed for different possible routes, so that if one system was down the message or data would be relayed through an alternative telecommunication route that was also part of ARPANET. For example, if the network in Chicago was down, the system would reroute the data through St Louis or Houston until it reached its final destination, say Los Angeles. Eventually the entire message would be reconstructed as the data communication, arriving via several different networks, reached its final destination. The object was that, given a catastrophic nuclear attack in one part of the country, there would be enough ARPANET systems to bypass affected regions so that the Pentagon could communicate with military bases located strategically in the Midwest or on the west coast, for example. Today the ARPANET system might appear archaic, but it generated a large number of high-end host computers that had clear commercial applications for the technology and software being developed and supported by extensive federal research funds available through military and national security initiatives.

A second major outcome of the early computer research that eventually led to the Internet was the extensive utilization of academic resources. ARPANET was a project that interconnected the technical workings of four academic research groups based at the University of California, Los Angeles, the University of California, Santa Barbara, the University of Utah, and Stanford University. These groups had been selected because they were working on technical design issues and signal protocols for computers in different locations in an effort to communicate with each other and to share resources. These academics were the first generation of computer scientists. At the same time, the US Department of Defense was supporting networking and engineering projects at Harvard University and the Massachusetts Institute of Technology that would serve as the nucleus for east coast high technology research initiatives. Similarly, ARPANET provided the intellectual critical mass on the west coast that was necessary for the application of communication technologies to various military initiatives. Over time, universities and technical think tanks such as the Rand Corporation began to promote non-defense uses – some of which had commercial potential – of the networks. In the early days, newsgroups were based in academic disciplines. For example, physicists communicated with other physicists electronically, mathematicians with other mathematicians, economists with other economists, and so on. This produced an expanding universe of electronic mail users who were using personal or laboratory computers to communicate across a public switched network, which initially was under the control of the Department of Defense. ARPANET had become a packet (data) switching network that allowed researchers, via computers in different regions, to communicate using computer machines. By 1972 the four sites had grown to 23, which were all networked together and pushing the frontiers of new hardware and software design. By 1987 the Department of Defense had transferred responsibility to the National Science Foundation (NSF), partly in recognition of the substantial expansion of the Internet system that had replaced ARPANET by this time. The NSF was a logical choice because a large number of non-military applications and protocols were being pursued, and the NSF wanted to create a university-based network for a broad group of academics. Also, a number of commercial computer manufacturers were supporting research to create compatibility and open architectural features to assist an expanding market.

By 1990 the Internet was being used substantially by people who had significant computer programming experience. It was completely text-based, and users had to learn computer operating systems in order to send or receive e-mail or to participate in discussion groups. During the 1990s, the creation of the World Wide Web, the mouse, icons, browsers, and search engines that were user-friendly enabled the Internet to expand globally and rapidly. During the same period, the rapid decline in the cost of personal computers (PCs) also led to their widespread use in homes, schools, and businesses, which had not been foreseen by the developers of the original ARPANET system. In order to encourage the widest possible use of the Internet, in 1995 the NSF turned over control of the Internet to a number of commercial organizations and networks. Thus, today no one organization, government, or corporation owns the Internet. Rather, it is a global interconnection of telecommunications systems controlled by protocols and rule-making on a voluntary basis.

Although the Internet system was initially a technical medium for scientists and engineers, it has evolved into a mass medium. It has now become a network of networks. The Internet consists of four major elements or electronic services: e-mail, FTP (File Transfer Protocol), newsgroups, and two chat areas: IRC (Internet Relay Chat) and collaboration. Each of these elements has international communication potential.

The Department of Defense provided the initial funding, but since then the Internet has become a global network with major commercial applications. The Internet economy is now growing faster than other sectors of the economy. For example, according to a 2000 University of Texas study, e-commerce now employs more workers than insurance, public utilities, or the airlines. The same study forecasts an additional 62 percent annual growth rate for e-commerce companies.[3] The Internet did not become a global network overnight, but certain events highlighted its capacity for bringing together millions of geographically separated individuals. For example, following the deaths of international icons like Princess Diana or leading Hollywood stars, cyberspace became a popular meeting place for mourners. Other examples include the publication of NASA's Pathfinder pictures from Mars, or at times when the stock market is volatile. On these days, thousands of investors visit the financial web pages provided by Internet sites, broadcasting networks, cable systems, and investment houses.

Initially, the Web was viewed as an alternative news source, but it is now a mainstream news source. The Web is a mixture of special-interest information providers, ranging from governments to commercial systems, such as the Huffington Post, to global broadcasters such as CNN, the BBC, and Al Jazeera.

Over a billion people use the Internet each week and there are now over a trillion web pages. The world's fastest computer is Chinese. The second fastest is called Titan and is housed at the Oak Ridge National Laboratory in Tennessee. What is interesting about these new superfast and powerful computers is that more than 90 percent of their power "comes from technology originally developed for the video-game industry. Half of its 37,376 processors are ordinary CPUS. But the other half are graphics processing units, or GPUS. These are specialized devices designed to cope with modern video games, which are some of the most demanding applications any home machine is ever likely to run."[4]

The World Wide Web

The World Wide Web (WWW) is an Internet-based process that came about through the convergence of advancing technologies and increased sophistication in programming languages. The rapid development of the WWW is a result of distributed processing, which includes storing, displaying, searching, and formatting computer-based information; the global interconnection of PCs; the development of hypertext and a coding standard, HTML; and the development of browsers. Browsers are a key component and basically represent client application software that knows how to communicate through the Internet and capture appropriate documents. Browsers also include built-in tools for searches, e-mail, organizing information, and so on.

During the 1990s, there were two major browsers in competition with each other: Netscape Navigator, which was acquired by AOL, and Microsoft's Internet Explorer. Netscape dominated the browser market during the early years, but Microsoft took over the browser market in the late 1990s. This domination of the browser market came to the attention of the US Department of Justice, which in 1999 found that Microsoft was employing monopolistic tactics through marketing and by embedding its browser within its operating system, Windows, to the detriment of its competitors. Microsoft appealed the decision successfully in the United States, but the EU continues to challenge Microsoft, as well as Google, on a number of issues.

History of the World Wide Web

As a physicist at CERN Laboratories in Geneva, Switzerland, Tim Berners-Lee wrote a seminal paper in 1980 entitled "Enquire-Within-Upon-Everything." It contained a program that linked arbitrary computers but had the additional capacity to sort information according to certain categories. The computers could be located anywhere and search for select information, perhaps on particle physics. By 1990 Berners-Lee and others had progressed to the stage of writing papers and software using hypertext for the purpose of allowing European physicists to communicate with each other by computer. Berners-Lee proposed using a single simple interface to search various information sites spread about the Internet system without regard to location. He captured the concept of using HyperText Markup Language (HTML) to select certain words and then search a vast range of documents to discover similar words, listing them as a result of a computer search. The list also contained the remote computer's address (a uniform resource locator, or URL) to obtain the referenced document. This became the basis of the modern World Wide Web. Initially the WWW was limited to professional and academic organization users, but in 1993 the National Center for Supercomputing Applications (NCSA) at the University of Illinois developed a user-friendly client browser called Mosaic. Prior to this development there were about 50 web servers worldwide. By 1994, with the introduction of Mosaic, there were over 1,500. By 1995 the web had become the dominant mode for accessing information from remote personal computers over the Internet.

In 1994 Mosaic guru Marc Andreessen left NCSA to form the Mosaic Communication Corporation which in turn changed its name to Netscape Communications Corporation. Netscape produced the first version of Netscape Navigator, the early dominant browser for web users. In the 1990s Microsoft released Internet Explorer 3.0, which was to provide overwhelming competition for Netscape. The Microsoft browser was able to retrieve remote documents and provide greater speed and display capacity than its competitors. Each generation of browsers added several unique features, which further expanded the usefulness of the web for home, business, school, and a plethora of other uses.

With the advent of the each generation of browsers, the differences between Microsoft and other browsers became so pronounced that each system now interfaces with external pages that are dependent on the programming language of a specific browser. Thus, users who want the complete universe of pages or sites for any particular subject area have to load both browser programs in order to retrieve web pages that are systematically linked with one or other of the browser architectural protocols. It was this phenomenon, in part, that attracted the Department of Justice's attention, because the dominance of Microsoft's Internet Explorer browser was inclining new website developers to develop software that could interface with Microsoft's Windows but not necessarily with the Netscape or other browsers. As Microsoft has popular Windows products preloaded on almost every new PC, Internet Explorer is embedded in all Microsoft's product lines. PCs arrive with preinstalled Explorer browsers for users who do not have either the motivation or the sophistication to seek out competing browsers. Microsoft's browser claims to be faster and smaller, and to offer more features. However, owing in large part to the rapid growth of mobile devices and competing browsers such as Firefox, Chrome, Safari, and Opera, Explorer is no longer the clear-cut head of the class.

Video Games

Any history of the Internet would not be complete without acknowledging the place of video games. Video game systems – whether Atari, Nintendo, Sega, Electronic Arts, Ubisoft, Konami, PlayStation, or Xbox – have created a generation of computer users who appreciated high speed, enhanced graphics, and interactivity. Successful video games have served as a backdrop against which computer manufacturers must judge each new generation of PCs. As a result, video games continue to set new and higher standards for graphics, speed, and sophistication that each generation of PCs has to match, if not exceed. The other related phenomenon is that video games are a global enthusiasm. Early on, much of the software originated from Japan, but North American, European, and other affluent cultures quickly became willing markets for and manufacturers of increasingly sophisticated video games. Games became the common culture of pre-teens, teenagers, and adults in core nations partly due to the growth of online network platforms such as Microsoft's Xbox Live (XBL) and Sony's PlayStation Network (PSN). No doubt, over time semiperipheral nations will join in the video game sector.

Currently, video games are either pre-programmed within a cafeteria of software that is preloaded on PCs, or they are available externally to be downloaded for personal use through the Internet. A major point is that video games, although a separate technology using either a modem and a standard TV monitor or a hand-held device, had an impact not only on the technology of the Internet, but also on software development, particularly graphics capabilities. Games set the visual benchmark for PC graphics. It turns out that moving from a controller to a mouse is a small step for game users. The global interconnectedness has allowed for gamers in different regions of the world to participate simultaneously through the latest console technology like never before.

An example of the upward trend in graphics and costs is the BioShock game. Whereas the average cost of producing and advertising the game to date is $42 million, the new Bioshock Infinite, the third in the series, will cost $100 million to create plus another $100 million to market and advertise. It has taken four years and a team of 200 to create a game with 16 hours of play time.[5] It will be for PCs, Macs, and consoles. This will be the new bar for the industry and the maker, Irrational Games of Boston, knows it. Kyle Moody is a fan of their work: "Whether it's technology, interface, storytelling themes or all of these things, BioShock games mean a move to the future through the lens of the past."[6]

The World of Warcraft series has over 10 million customers and is an online multiple player game with a number of worldwide gamers. In 2013, a new record was set by GTA 5. On the first day, it took in a billion dollars.

The Internet Timeline

The following timeline shows the major historical events that cumulatively aided the global system called the Internet.

1955   US President Eisenhower approves funding for US satellite development.
1957   USSR launches the first satellite program, Sputnik, which consists of four satellites.
1958   US Department of Defense establishes ARPA.
1960s   A series of isolated academic papers in Europe and North America appear detailing packet switching, batch processing, spooling systems, time-sharing computers, and network alternatives.
1961   April: Soviets put first man in space.
        May: United States puts man in space.
        President Kennedy calls for massive funding for research and space exploration.
1965   Ted Nelson describes hypertext, a concept using word association to find similar words electronically.
1969   ARPANET created, with four university host sites.
        CompuServe established for home and business customers.
        United States succeeds with moon landing and walk on lunar surface.
1970s   Several new ARPANET host sites established, including European sites.
1971   USSR establishes first orbital space station.

1972   First e-mail program written.

Magnavox releases first home video game system, named Odyssey.

1973   United States establishes first US space station, Skylab.

1975   Microcomputers introduced.

Paul Allen and Bill Gates found Microsoft to develop programming languages.

1976   Apple Computers reach market.

1977   Owners of Apple, Radio Shack, Atari, Commodore 64, Texas Instruments, and others begin marketing personal computers designed for schools and home.

University of Wisconsin supports research to interconnect over 100 computer scientists via e-mail.

1980   Apple issues public stock to raise capital for extensive research and development infrastructure (leads to introduction of Apple Macintosh desktop computers in 1984).

Physicist Tim Berners-Lee of CERN Laboratories in Switzerland writes program to link colleagues' PCs.

1981   IBM enters personal computer market with two key partners, Intel and Microsoft. Because of size and market penetration, IBM sets new PC architecture standards. Smaller, lighter, and cheaper clones begin to appear as well, using Intel and Microsoft products and protocols

BITNET for e-mail and file transfers established between Yale and City University of New York; IBM adopts BITNET protocol to link IBM university computers.

Several of the Big 10 universities begin to establish protocols for networking services, e-mail, and list server activities between campuses.

1983   Desktop workstations established by scientists through grants from NSF.

1984   Newsgroups organized by researchers at universities, research institutes, and computer manufacturers.

1985   America Online (AOL) founded.

1986   Microsoft issues public stock and introduces Windows. Screen icons become the industry model.

1989   Steve Jobs creates new computer company, NeXT. This system introduces many innovations for desktop systems. Berners-Lee and others create web browser for NeXT workstations.

Commercial e-mail offered in limited markets by MCI and CompuServe.

Berners-Lee writes a paper detailing a system using hypertext (HTML) that would become the programming basis for the WWW.

1990   ARPANET disbanded.

1994   Netscape developed as Internet browser and establishes early lead.

Amazon.com launched.

1995   RealAudio developed for PC's audio use.

Microsoft introduces browser, Internet Explorer 4.0, to challenge Netscape.

Yahoo! and eBay founded – beginning of online auctions.

1998   More PCs sold than televisions.

CompuServe and Netscape acquired by AOL.

Google search engine launched.

1999   Microsoft charged by US Department of Justice with engaging in antitrust activities. Wins in United States but similar suits are still in play in the European Union.

Melissa virus swamps e-mail systems.

Napster, a music file-sharing program, released.

Internet advertising revenue exceeds $1 billion.

2000   AOL and Time Warner announce merger to create the largest global communications conglomerate; synergy fails to materialize.

Love Letter virus originating in Philippines attaches itself to e-mail addresses and infects hard drives around the globe.

Globally, old media companies begin to look for potential new media (Internet) companies for mergers, acquisitions, or partnerships.

2001   Microsoft enters the video game market with Xbox.

2002   Verizon introduces high-speed 3G cell networks.

Blackberry "smartphone" released in the United States.

2003   Digital cameras outsell film cameras.

Lawyers for Recording Industry Association of America (RIAA) representing recording artists and studios go after file-sharing and music-downloading.

MySpace launched, owned by Fox Interactive Media/News Corp.

2004   Google goes public with share offering.

Online advertising exceeds $10 billion, mostly from newspaper advertising.

Facebook premieres.

2005   Spyware and adware introduced to deal with problems of junk e-mail.

MPAA lawyers sue movie downloaders.

Apple's iPod sales set record.

YouTube founded (currently owned by Google).

2006   Twitter launched.

2007   Apple and AT&T release iPhone.

2009   Pirate Bay (Sweden) is a BitTorrent firm which allows file-sharing of audio and video productions. It was sued by the MPAA and others over Internet piracy. Pirate Bay lost the court case but later elected members to the European Parliament and continues to offer free access to movies, music, and television shows.

European Commission files a suit against Google over its scanning of millions of books to create an electronic database of primarily English-language books. Google's compensation of authors is an issue in both the United States and Europe.

The RIAA takes two students to the US federal court over music-downloading and file-sharing. It won both cases. One student was fined $675,000, and the other $222,000. But the latter opted for a second trial and the fine was raised to $1,920,000.

2010   Google releases PC operating system called Chrome, which competes with Microsoft's Windows operating system. Netbooks are primary marketing products for both companies.

Apple debuts the iPad.

European Union continues to investigate American communication conglomerates.

2011   The Internet gains on television as the public's main news source.

The Arab Spring contributed to this.

2012   Titan becomes the world's fastest supercomputer.

Online advertising revenue overtakes print advertising revenue.

Impact of the Internet

The Internet has had a major impact on many areas of life, from e-commerce to distance education. The following paragraphs highlight a single narrow yet important area – government reports – and illustrates some of the many unexpected influences of the Internet.

Table 6.1 Top four search engines in the United States, 2013, with year of founding

1	Google (1998)
2	Yahoo! (1994)
3	Microsoft (2009)
4	Ask (1996)

Source: Listofsearchengines.info.

The availability of government documents on the Internet has changed not only the access issue, but also the way information is now provided in an unfiltered fashion. Political pundits no longer have free rein to put their own personal spin, whether from the Left or the Right, on issues in order to direct viewers, listeners, or readers to an "appropriate" point of view. Because of the Internet, individuals can apply their own thoughts, ideas, and background to the interpretation of new information.

The Internet phenomenon began to expand rapidly in the 1990s. The system has grown enormously, much of the fuel for growth being generated by the creation of widely advertised commercial services. The original Internet system was designed as a narrow-casting system in which selected users would access unique data or share specialized information. Now it has become a 24-hour system, a mass medium in effect, ranging from full-service web information, to portals,[7] to news websites such as MSNBC or CNN, in addition to services aimed at the more limited high-tech users. Many utilize the Internet's search engines (see Table 6.1).

One of the largest uses of the Internet to date was on September 11, 2001. News websites were flooded with hits. A separate traffic phenomenon occurred with the 9/11 Commission in 2004. Televised hearings, numerous press appearances, and finally a bestselling government report – all followed by Internet users – led to significant pressure on the US federal government to act. Demand for copies of *The 9/11 Commission Report: Final Report of the National Commission on Terrorist Attacks upon the United States* swamped Amazon.com and other sales sites.

The important communication point to be made in all of this is that news editors, pundits, politicians, the US president, and others were no longer able to act as gatekeepers to restrict, alter, spin, or limit the information in the report. Millions of people around the world now had access to the full, unedited government reports at the same time as they were being presented to the national legislatures.

The Starr Report and summaries of the 9/11 report on the Internet fundamentally changed the potential for mass dissemination of information to a global audience. The reports represented unprecedented and unique examples of the pervasiveness of the Internet as a mass communication system. They represented the democratization of the mass media in that politicians or media elites were no longer able to control, filter, or interject their editorial viewpoints on a significant government document.[8] Individuals in the United States and elsewhere with access to the Internet were able to download the entire report, consume it, and draw their own conclusions. They did not have to rely on the next day's newspaper or on condensed sound bites on national newscasts to inform them about a major government document. Even the president of the United States, along with his substantial staff of spin doctors and press spokespersons, was left to consume these and other reports from their computers at the same time that millions of people around the globe were doing exactly the same thing.

As a result of the Internet, the global public is better informed. They can act as a more informed public jury on major political events, such as the invasion of Iraq. But the changes are not by any means limited to politics. The Internet is changing the nature and perception of the human environment. Users are creating a third culture, to which Featherstone referred in an earlier work to the origins and growth of a global culture.[9] There is a difference between users and non-users of the Internet, and this phenomenon is more pronounced among heavy users. To some extent Marshall McLuhan foresaw this as early as the 1960s when he was theorizing about the mass media being so pervasive as to totally consume all aspects of a person's being, leaving no aspect untouched.[10] Finally, along similar lines, electronic colonialism is about the mind being shaped more and more by external media, of which the Internet is simply the latest player. The Internet does alter, affect, and influence people in psychological ways yet to be seen or completely understood. The Internet is also primarily in English and has a bias toward the United States. These two realities have clear cultural consequences for Internet users around the globe. From rural villages in India with computer access, to Starbucks cafes in almost every major capital of the world, electronic colonialism is on a steady march 24/7.

The Internet has an obvious downside. It is capable of relaying to an international audience sordid details about what historically were personal matters. It can also spark erroneous claims that could end a politician's or CEO's career. When an Internet site runs a story, the story goes global. It is not restricted to a city, state, or nation. Rather, it becomes instantaneously available worldwide.

A final note is that the Internet's global and instantaneous communication ability, for good or ill, changed public life forever. In the age of the Internet there is no privacy. (Just ask the bloggers.) The release of government reports has made Internet history, but also opened the door for a two-way information superhighway. Various constituents e-mailed their elected representatives in record numbers with their thoughts and ideas about how to vote. Rather than sending a letter by mail, they could now quickly – and at no cost – e-mail a message to even obscure members of local and national governments. Many representatives are reporting that they have to reassign staff to deal with the flood of e-mails as the public uses the same computers to reply to the contents of government reports as well as to influence the position of their elected representatives. The messages tend to be short and full of typos, but in the final analysis the sheer volume of e-mails likely has a collective impact. Politicians or government agencies, such as the Federal Communications Commission (FCC) in the United States, do not have to wait for weeks for the regular mail to arrive to determine where their constituents stand on vital issues.

The British government began a series of investigations into News Corporation's phone-hacking activities (see Chapter 7).

Internet and Global Television Issues

The story of video on the Internet has yet to be written. The video materials available, whether they are music videos, television programming, or feature movies, have tremendous implications for current producers. With the ability of the Internet to broadcast video live, along with worldwide dissemination, current copyright holders could potentially see their materials appear anywhere in the world without their authorization or compensation. The following two examples illustrate the potential problems.

In June 2000 in California, a group of movie studios filed a suit in Los Angeles to close down a website that was allowing viewers to record television shows online. The site was attracting a large number of users and therefore caught the attention of television executives. Applying traditional copyright laws, the movie studios' legal team sought to close down the site immediately for unauthorized taping and redistribution of the video content, which originated from entertainment companies and was available via cable in the Los Angeles area for a cable subscription fee.[11]

A second situation reflecting the convergence of television and the Internet is represented by a company based in Toronto, Canada: iCraveTV began in December 1999 with nearly one million customers during its first month of operation and offering 17 online television stations. It provided free Internet access for its advertising-supported rebroadcast of Canadian and US television channels.[12] The 24-hour live streaming service included NBC, CBS, ABC (American Broadcasting Company), Fox, and PBS (Public Broadcasting Service). Within Canada, Internet broadcasting services are not regulated under the Canadian Broadcasting Act. What iCraveTV had done was create 10 Canadian Internet super stations for a potential global audience. This integration of television with the Internet has not been without its critics. Some claim that the Internet site violated copyright laws and constituted trademark infringement. For example, the US-based National Football League was part of a group that took legal action because US Internet users are able to access NFL games through stations that rebroadcast live on the iCraveTV Internet site. Other plaintiffs in the suit were ABC, CBS, Fox, Disney, and Time Warner. Using Internet video streaming or other Internet services can place firms in legal difficulties and liable to prosecution under US law. US law is aimed at protecting the copyright provisions of not only the major broadcasting networks but also major sporting events, which are contracted on an exclusive basis with US-based networks. The Internet's role in this had clearly not been anticipated even a few years ago in terms of providing a competing global alternative for the rights holders. Today, rather than confronting streaming video of copyrighted television shows, network and cable companies have developed free sites, such as Hulu, where visitors can watch their favorite shows with commercial breaks from sponsors.

These examples will likely be replicated when some entrepreneurial web provider makes European soccer globally available on the Internet. Also, North American professional sports organizations such as MLB (Major League Baseball) and the NHL (National Hockey League), which have fan bases worldwide, have developed online portals for people to watch their games for a fee, both domestically and internationally. Soccer and horse racing are also prime audiences for web services. The International Olympic Committee is another group that aggressively protects its trademarked products and symbols. To some, the convergence of television and the Internet is innovative and a new application, while others regard the users who watch these programs without paying for them as content pirates and rights thieves.

The Internet and Hollywood Films

Industries that have been surprisingly slow to change, such as Hollywood and the feature film studios, have been forced to re-examine their global distribution policies because of the Internet. Traditionally, Hollywood's major studios would release their films within North America first, and then later, sometimes many months later, distribute them around the world, primarily to other core nations and then semiperipheral nations. In a few instances, it could take a year for a major feature film to open in theaters in smaller nations. Now Hollywood is confronting the emergence of the global entertainment market. This market is increasingly sophisticated, with potential movie-goers using websites to obtain information about newly released Hollywood films or purchasing films through e-commerce businesses that specialize in film distribution, primarily DVD technology. The new Hollywood policy of rolling out global distribution of major movies within weeks is a direct response to the changing environment created by the Internet. All the major studios are re-examining their global marketing of new films, and the major reason is that Hollywood's hype machine has finally met a force it cannot control – the Internet.

Gone are the days when Hollywood could sell its movies in domestic isolation, with little fear that the US marketing message would spread quickly to countries where the films wouldn't be seen for months.[13] An example of this phenomenon was the global release of a co-production of Columbia and Universal Pictures, *Erin Brockovich*, starring Julia Roberts. During the opening week, the film became the number one attraction in seven major markets, including the United States, Canada, and five European nations. The global market for films is being approached more as a single market than as a series of isolated markets. Sony is also marketing new releases on an international rather than a national basis.

Hollywood's Expansion

Canada has long been known as "Hollywood North." For decades studios from Hollywood and New York have been filming a wide range of television and feature movies across Canada, but particularly in Vancouver, Toronto, and Montreal. Television shows such as *The X-Files*, and other series and movies are being made across Canada. Toronto is the third largest video production center in the world after Los Angeles and New York. It has become an almost $2 billion industry employing about 70,000 people thanks to nearly all the major American studios filming there.

Canada recognized the employment and economic benefits of courting the film industries of New York and Hollywood early on. They also discovered the bonus accompanying the final productions in terms of a strong boost to the tourism industry. Now New Zealand, Australia, and Ireland are attempting to replicate Canada's success.

For example, New Zealand is now competing aggressively for Hollywood blockbusters. The government has been generously courting Hollywood studios with incentives for both the production costs as well as other expenses, such as marketing and advertising. In 2011 US$200 million was spent to attract New York and Hollywood productions. Films like *Avatar*, *The Lord of the Rings* trilogy, and *The Hobbit* all benefited from the millions invested by the New Zealand federal government. The long-term gains in international tourism are a major justification, as well as short-term employment boosts, ranging from the use of extras, to animation, and post-production work. Yet some critics complain that New Zealand is becoming the fifty-first US state and that the local independent film industry is suffering.

There are three other interesting facets of this new policy shift, which recognizes the globalization of the Hollywood feature film industry. The first is that the new releases come out only in English; dubbed or translated versions are not available on the initial release date. The second by-product of the change is that the marketing strategy and advertising copy, including photos, for these releases are now all standardized. Identical promotional materials are used across the globe in other core nations. Hollywood's latest blockbuster promos seen in the United States are the same promos seen in Europe and other nations. Hollywood's approach to the global market had to change or face a growth in the pirating of films or alternative purchasing, which would have adversely affected the profitability of the studios' investments in what are in most cases expensive feature films. This is what has led to the third policy shift. In 2005, following the lead of the music industry going after illegal online file-sharing through the courts, the Motion Picture Association of America (MPAA) began a series of law suits to stop the illegal online copying of movies. The MPAA is seeking to reduce file-swapping or peer-to-peer (P2P) activities involving Hollywood productions. Although the copyright violation and movie sharing constitutes only about 2 percent of online illegal activity (music represents more than 60 percent), the movie industry is worried about the future. Today things such as torrent files have made downloading large video files easier than ever. Many foreign websites create large P2P communities where videos can be found and downloaded within the United States using programs that break down and recreate the files more quickly than ever. With each new generation of computers both speed and space will be less of a problem or deterrent. Complicating matters for the MPAA is that each new version of file-sharing software is becoming more user-friendly and more difficult to track. Facing these technical realities, Hollywood studios are seeking to make some online pirates pay and to use these cases to stop others. Even if they are successful in the US courts, the studios still have little hope of pursuing compensation for the infringement of their property rights outside the United States.

Internet Users

Yet another example of how the Internet has let to a re-examination of traditional ways of doing business concerns Internet users. The distribution of Internet users in 2012 by regions according to Internetworldstats.com is shown in Table 6.2.

The core nations were the early inventors and adopters of the Internet, but today new nations are showing how quickly they are developing technologically. Due to the exponential increase in users in Asia North America only accounts for 11.4 percent of Internet users today. The core nations have all three requirements for Internet access: technical expertise, the financial resources to buy the required computers and hook-ups, and communication infrastructures to deliver interactive Internet services. In many cases, peripheral nations lack at least one of these requirements, and in some cases they lack all three. There is clearly a digital divide. Africa lags further and further behind Asia, Europe, and North America.

In cyberspace, peripheral and semiperipheral nations rarely communicate directly with each other; almost all Internet traffic flows through the United States. The nature of the Internet today can be partly explained using world system theory. Its language, technological, and cultural advantages help the US remain the most powerful and influential nation in the information age. The US is also home to key stakeholders such as Google, Microsoft, Apple, Amazon, and social network companies.

Table 6.2 Distribution of Internet users by region, 2012

1	Asia	44.8 percent
2	Europe	21.5 percent
3	North America	11.4 percent
4	South America	10.4 percent
5	Africa	7 percent
6	Middle East	3.7 percent

Source: http://www.internetworldstats.com/stats.htm, accessed August 19, 2013.

Another factor that seems to encourage greater Internet use is geography. Six nations have geographically isolated populations yet have substantial per capita users. These are the Scandinavian countries of Finland, Sweden, and Norway, as well as Australia, Canada, and New Zealand. Semiperipheral nations in central and eastern Europe, and now the Middle East, will likely see the largest per capita gains in new Internet users. E-commerce on the Internet is now generating significant revenue in all core nations. Internet sales are rapidly increasing at the expense of brick and mortar stores. This will fuel additional demand for Internet access as well as growing commercial competition as the market share for the electronic purchase of goods and services around the globe expands at a rapid pace.

Computer Viruses

With the advent of the Internet came the birth of computer viruses. Some are merely nuisances, while others, such as the Melissa, Love Letter, MyDoom, and Resume viruses, have affected electronic mail and other files with extremely damaging results. Major corporations have had to shut down their systems because of some of the more pernicious viruses. These have the potential to erase data, release secure data, change data, or totally freeze or take over computer systems. It is estimated that there are now over 100 new viruses per week, and by the end of 2012 nearly one-third of all computers were found to be infected with viruses. With e-commerce expanding on a daily basis, the impact of viruses can be catastrophic and, within a matter of minutes, can run into millions of dollars in lost time and business. Although computer viruses first appeared in the early 1980s, macro viruses that spread worldwide with the extensive use of the Internet system are a more recent phenomenon. There are also many reports of hoaxes, which are more than major annoyances. Given the recent impact of viruses that embedded themselves in complex and massive ways, even hoaxes have to be taken seriously.

Cyber crime is another new by-product of, as well as a legal challenge to, the Internet. For example, the "I Love You" virus, which originated in the Philippines in May 2000, moved via e-mail across Asia to Europe and from there to North and South America. Thousands of individual PCs were infected, as well as computer systems of major organizations such as the British House of Commons, Yahoo!, the US Central Intelligence Agency, CNN, and the Ford Motor Company. While the overall cost of damage from this e-mail worm is difficult to assess, it was well into the millions of dollars. By 2012 the greatest virus to wreak havoc was the Stuxnet. The authorities are attempting to determine who is behind this virus.

Basically, computer viruses are uninvited guests that run on your PC. They can attach themselves to other files – mainly e-mail addresses. As computer programming languages become more user-friendly, and because they are transferable, viruses can now switch from one platform to another without any difficulty. The virus problem is huge. Viruses can be initiated by novice programmers, but their consequences can be catastrophic as the viruses spread globally and in seconds worm their way from system to system. Malicious hackers or simply nerdy computer groupies can unleash viruses at any time. Today there is anti-virus software that has helped to reduce the problem. Yet new categories like adware, pop-ups, spyware, and malware continue to infect computers. Removal software is available from several vendors.

Here is another example of how the Internet has altered the ability to control information, according to the European Journalism Centre Media News for February 11, 2013:

Two of the biggest names in the Internet freedom debate, The Pirate Bay and WikiLeaks, are connected in the release of the infamous "Collateral Murder" video, it is now reported.

One of the first and biggest stories WikiLeaks broke was the "Collateral Murder" video, which contained classified footage of a 2007 U.S. airstrike in Baghdad. The military opened fire on what it said were armed insurgents but turned to be civilians, two of whom, Saeed Chmagh and Namir Noor-Eldeen, were war reporters for Reuters. The footage, shot from the helicopter's cockpit, was released in 2010 and made WikiLeaks, and Julian Assange, household names.

The release of the "Collateral Murder" video was aided by one of the founders of The Pirate Bay, Gottfrid Svartholm. Svartholm, who is currently is in jail for creating the file-sharing site Pirate Bay. The hacker Julian Assange has his own legal problems in Europe. He founded WikiLeaks in 2006. It became world famous for publishing US military and diplomatic cables in 2010.[14]

Finally, in 2013 both the *New York Times* and the *Wall Street Journal* reported that their Asian bureaus had been hacked. The *New York Times* hired the computer security firm Mandiant to investigate. They discovered that a branch of the Chinese army had been responsible and that they had hacked into several other corporations and government agencies as well.[15]

Blogging

A new Internet-driven phenomenon, called weblogs or blogs, arrived in the mainstream media around 2004. Some of the early bloggers, such as engineers or technicians, were adding personal or political comments to their discussion websites as early as the mid-1990s. They used coding languages such as HTML. In the late 1990s web publishing software was created which greatly expanded blogging. In addition, a few seminal events occurred in the early 2000s, which moved blogging to a new level.

The first substantial blogger-driven event was a focused Internet attack in 2002 on the then powerful Republican senator Trent Lott. Lott had made some inappropriate and racist comments at a party and the mainstream media, as usual, covered the story, but only for a few days. However, some tenacious bloggers kept the heat on Lott for weeks and called for his resignation. This web-based chorus forced the national media to take another look at the entire episode. Lott did eventually resign because bloggers were able to build enough pressure via the Internet to put his story back on the evening newscasts and talk shows in a negative light. A decade earlier he could have avoided such scrutiny and shame.

In 2003 other creative blog users were able to mount a substantial fund-raising drive via the Internet for Howard Dean, a candidate for the Democratic presidential nomination. His star rose rapidly as he was the Internet favorite but he and others lost out to Senator John Kerry. Dean also set the gold standard of fund-raising by using the Internet in creative ways. Barack Obama was to take the matter several steps further by implementing a host of political Internet activities which helped him win the presidency in 2008.

In 2004 bloggers became mini-celebrities by being accredited as media representatives at both the Democratic and Republican national conventions.[16] In a record space of time "blogging" became a household word much as "Google" had done. Finally, in late 2004 Dan Rather and CBS carried a piece on documents alleging that President Bush was not as solid a National Guard soldier as he had claimed. The documents turned out to be false. Again it was the bloggers who kept the profile and bias of the CBS network alive and forced the mainstream media to pursue the issue. Eventually both Rather and CBS issued apologies for their major lapse. CBS was forced to set up an investigation, and as a result senior CBS personnel were fired. Some websites were calling for Rather to be fired as well. Rather announced his retirement but later sued CBS for wrongful dismissal. CBS was forced to acknowledge that the White House had pressured the network to let Rather go.

A recent development has been "multi-author blogs" (MABs). These are blogs that have a number of writers. MABs from magazines, newspapers, television, think tanks, interest groups, and others are expanding the blogosphere. They are also becoming news sources from citizen journalists as well as professionals.

Another manifestation of this phenomenon is video blogging. This combines the text-based blog accompanied by video. Amateur video footage by holiday-makers in the regions affected by the Indian Ocean tsunami in December 2004 presented vbloggers on several continents with a huge opportunity. Vbloggers observe no protocols, obtain no permission, and have no copyright concerns. Dramatic footage, be it of a televised confrontation or of a natural disaster, will find its way around the world in future thanks to the growing cadre of vbloggers.

So the debate about the role and eventual fate of bloggers continues. Some claim that they are pretend journalists in T-shirts with a laptop, while others see the new phenomenon as the next significant trend in journalism. Bloggers can be rude or crass, and seem to spent a great deal of their time discussing sex, yet they have made the political process more open; clearly they have a voice and opinion on high-profile issues, whether or not people or political parties like it. Large news corporations cannot ignore their impact, and several now give people the opportunity to weigh in on their own websites or cable television shows.

Social Networking

Another new and booming phenomenon is social networking. Sites such as MySpace, Facebook, Twitter, and LinkedIn have created a new global interface. Although MySpace and Facebook began as social sites, they have developed, both positively and negatively, as ways for professionals to network or for businesses to profile. Twitter, a more recent addition to this group, is a way for people to keep fans or friends up to date on their daily activities. It has become so large that news corporations can now quote people of interest from the site, rather than contacting them personally. LinkedIn, founded in 2002, is a website for professionals to create a web of connections through their peers in their industry. It is business-oriented and it gives people the opportunity to provide a miniature résumé to people looking at prospective employees. These websites have become incredibly popular, and businesses are trying to find out how to optimize their image to attract those using these sites.

ICANN

The Internet Corporation for Assigned Names and Numbers (ICANN) has become both powerful and controversial. It is the outcome of years of recognizing the growth and significance of the Internet for the global economy. Domain names and various Internet protocols, which carry a unique numerical address, are at the center of the Internet's orderly expansion. All computers need an address in order to participate in the Internet's growing role in all aspects of modern life. The global Internet community "created a need for a new kind of social contract."[17] Milton Müller refers to the various functions that ultimately provide for unique Internet names and addresses as "the root."[18] It is clear that ICANN has become powerful because it controls the rights to add top-level domain names, such as .com, .edu, .net, or. org. ICANN is a private company which controls the technical standards of cyberspace. To some extent it controls global information-sharing in the online environment. It raises the bar on the construct of power.

Internet names and related protocols emerged out of and along with the growth of ARPA. Since the funding for ARPANET came from the US military at the early stage, some controversy over who was getting the preferred names was bound to emerge. ARPANET was disbanded in 1990, when the US-funded NSF took over part of the naming function for a period, and then in 1993 the US federal government gave governance control to Network Solutions, Inc. A rash of "cyber squatting" took place whereby people would register domain names with the hope of selling them on later.[19] By 1998 this and other problems led the US Department of Commerce to create a private entity, ICANN, based in California. ICANN was given substantial gatekeeper control over new access to the Internet's registries. Challenges to what appeared as a powerful monopoly role emerged.[20] In the United States much of the challenge to the function of ICANN came under the umbrella of antitrust laws, specifically the tough Sherman Antitrust Act.[21] Even though ICANN is governed by an international board of directors, who attempt to insure that technical elements of the Internet's infrastructure serve global needs, this oversight has not kept the global community of users included or content. Currently there are calls for a shift from coordinating role of ICANN from a US-centered base to a multilateral one.[22] This controversial matter has unexpectedly been taken up with some zeal by peripheral nations within the World Summit of the Information Society (WSIS). This will set a politicized tone for what ICANN and others see as being technical rule-making.[23] It also means that the future of Internet governance may benefit the International Telecommunication Union (ITU) or the Organisation for Economic Co-operation and Development (OECD) – as possible new ICANN oversight and structures. Online access in non-Latin languages, such as Arabic or Chinese, for domain names is one step toward accommodating the genuine criticism from peripheral nations.

In closing, this is not a trivial matter. The future of the Internet and how and who governs it internationally are central to the emerging electronic information environment. If fair and equitable access is not spelled out, the peripheral regions will fall further behind in the digital divide. The core nations to date have controlled the "global village" with its Internet connectivity through ICANN and its predecessors. Many civil society groups have been critical of ICANN's closed and tone-deaf corporate culture. Some opening up of rulemaking and greater access is now being challenged in several forums. A good example is the Internet Governance Project, which is an alliance of academics seeking to influence Internet policy by sponsoring events and publishing position papers about ICANN's policies and procedures. They have a significant following.

At the ITU's 2012 World Conference on International Telecommunications a new multi-stakeholder model featuring intergovernmental oversight was put forward to essentially replace ICANN, but there was strong opposition from the United States and others.

Conclusions

Any description of the Internet, as well as projection of the future of global communications, deals with history on the run. Given the major technological and software advances being promoted by major corporations and research institutions, there are going to be several additional generations of Internet hardware and software. Likewise, the merger phenomenon of old media stakeholders and new Internet players, such as Time Warner, is in its infancy. In the future, there are likely to be more mergers of transnational corporations, whether they are based in Europe, North America, or Japan. The Internet personifies a dynamic, rather than a static, state of affairs. The Internet economy is growing at a "much faster pace than the industrial revolution that began in the eighteenth century. Perhaps more importantly, the potential scope, size, and overall economic impact of this system is much larger than what we can comprehend today. The key characteristics that distinguish the new economy are information, knowledge, and speed."[24]

Before drawing some general conclusions, we should note a significant point relating to indigenous Internet sites. Various linguistic or ethnic groups have created sites that focus on and promote smaller cultural sectors. Many of these are aimed at keeping expatriates informed or to inform children of their ancestral roots. Yet for every page on the Internet that is non-English, there are at least 100 pages of English text. The Internet is both US-centric and English-dominated. That is a major reason why the Internet is a leading purveyor of electronic colonialism around the globe.

Even so, we can draw six general conclusions. First, while the origins of the Internet may be traced back to the 1950s with the sponsorship of the US Defense Department, we can still say that the origin, description, and role of the Internet as it has evolved to date occurred within the core nations. Innovations and expertise in North America, Europe, and to some extent Japan permitted the development of the hardware and software necessary to establish a global Internet system. Semiperipheral nations played only a catch-up role as they attempted to mimic innovations first established and demonstrated within core nation markets. Semiperipheral nations also tend to face the dual problem of the lack of investment capital to underwrite new Internet ventures, and of the high-tech entrepreneurs and the critical mass of necessary talent needed to develop and promote more indigenous Internet sites and services. For peripheral regions, the situation is simply exacerbated.

The Internet revolution is in progress. Some nations with progressive public policies that encourage foreign capital and reward entrepreneurs will benefit, but other nations may stall or regress over time, and this will weaken their global economic and social positions. Semiperipheral and peripheral nations are distant users of the Internet. In those areas where the Internet exists, it is primarily available only to elites, whether they are government officials, military, academics, businesses, or religious leaders. In far too many cases, the average person in peripheral regions is waiting for a first telephone and is not concerned about browser technologies, e-commerce, Kindles, iPods, or social media.

Second, the Internet represents change. Its impact among information gatherers and providers, whether they are in the media, business, or universities, has been profound. The situation will continue to escalate as e-commerce, e-education, and social media begin to displace traditional mechanisms and modes of behavior across the Internet. Just as Amazon.com revolutionized the bookselling industry and eBay changed shopping, so virtually every industry will experience similar Internet intrusion and some global opportunities or competition in the near future.

Third, e-commerce and e-multimedia will take on more global trappings. The ability to advertise and market on the Internet is a global electronic phenomenon. It has transformed commerce beyond the traditional bounds of the nation-state. The BBC, MTV, CNN, Google, and other media enterprises have long recognized this; there is a clear demarcation between the old media firms and the new. A firm without an Internet presence is destined to a strategic reality of declining market share and influence. The Internet represents the globalization of the marketplace in a fashion unprecedented in human history. It brings with it values and economic rituals, such as credit cards and advertising, that reflect the electronic colonizing of both the mind and the marketplace. Internet global advertising exceeds $15 billion and is increasing annually. Much of the online ad revenues appear to be coming primarily from newspapers and to a lesser extent from network television. Strategically, over time – since the amount of online advertising is going to increase – a growing number of newspapers and magazines will close.

Fourth, capturing consumer behavior and consumer-purchasing power for products and services offered over the Internet will become a greater economic force and reality over time. The global success of the Big Five – Amazon, eBay, Google, Microsoft, and Yahoo! – as both viable commercial and electronic leaders, bodes well not only for them but for many others as well.

It is not so much an issue of cultural imperialism, as some critics have maintained, as the economic common sense of following the success of various individuals, corporations, and systems that have migrated successfully and quickly to the world of the Internet. This phenomenon might more reasonably be called electronic imperialism. The Internet is to our future what automobiles and transportation were in the past. Now we are looking at digital nations, virtual spaces, e-commerce, and global systems that link individuals and the Internet without regard for time, space, or borders. Whereas time and space were the defining characteristics of the industrial era, so now the Internet, where time and space no longer pertain, is the defining medium of the information age.

Fifth, China is set to be the largest Internet user nation. Also, the greatest growth will be across all semiperipheral nations since many core nations represent mature markets in terms of computer sales. Nations such as India and Brazil represent huge untapped markets. Even the International Monetary Fund (IMF) and others are recognizing the emergence of China as the leading global economy in the near future, replacing the United States.[25]

Sixth, Internet technologies are not neutral. They impact a broad range of behaviors from information processing, to research strategies, to e-commerce, and e-living. Just as the invention of the printing press had widespread consequences for the industrial revolution, so too the Internet will impact on this and future centuries in profound ways. Marshall McLuhan detailed the printing press's impact on society and individuals in his seminal work *The Gutenberg Galaxy* (1962). A similar classic has yet to be written about the impact of the Internet, but there are early indications that this impact will be substantial. For example, with reference to the Internet and information technologies, Alan Hedley states: "what is at stake are the very thought processes of those dominated. Only powerful nations currently have the ability to choose the type of information society most compatible with their cultural institutions."[26] This viewpoint is fully consistent with the theory of electronic colonialism. Basically, the Internet, whether in China, the United States, or some remote part of India, will have parallel consequences for social systems (e.g., education, commerce, discussion groups, and friends) and the mindsets of individual users. Internet users, regardless of time and space, will mentally converge over time with other widely dispersed users. They will come to have more in common with individuals scattered around the planet than with non-users in their neighborhoods, family, schools, or work.

Notes

1. There is a vast literature on the subject, including J. Levine, C. Barondi, and M. Young, *The Internet for Dummies*, Foster City, CA: IDG Hooks Worldwide, 1999; K. Hafner and M. Lyon, *Where Wizards Stay Up Late: The Origins of the Internet*, New York: Touchstone, 1998; and Paul Ceruzzi, *A History of Modern Computing*, Boston: MIT Press, 1998.

2. The symbolic role of the series of four Russian Sputnik satellites cannot be underestimated. These relatively unsophisticated satellites successfully launched by the Soviet Union demonstrated to US military, political, and industrial leaders that Soviet technology was much more advanced than many had believed. The science that could propel a Russian satellite into orbit could also be

easily modified to launch a nuclear payload at North America. In response, US President John Kennedy in 1961 committed the nation to putting a man on the moon by the end of the decade. Thus began the space race, along with the necessary rocketry to propel not only satellites into space but also manned orbital missions. In July 1969 the Apollo 11 module landed on the moon with Neil Armstrong and Buzz Aldrin. Sputnik's signal had lasted only 18 days, but it was sufficient to galvanize the United States to engage in a space race that provided substantial funding for the development of satellites for broadcasting as well as military uses, and for the development of manned space vehicles, which led to the miniaturization and increased sophistication of computer systems. Although it is highly possible that US academics and scientists would eventually have developed much of the communication technology of today even without Sputnik, Sputnik provided the impetus, focus, and substantial federal funding required to propel the United States into the global leadership role it currently holds in computers, satellites, digital devices, mobile telephony, e-commerce, and telecommunications.

3. *United States Today* (June 6, 2000), 1A.

4. *Economist* (November 17, 2012), 74.

5. Harold Goldenberg, *New York Times* (March 24, 2013), A&L 1, 20.

6. Kyle Moody, quoted in Harold Goldberg, "The Nerd as Auteur in BioShock Infinite," *New York Times* (March 24, 2013), at http://www.nytimes.com/2013/03/24/arts/video-games/the-nerd-as-auteur-in-bioshock-infinite.html?hpw&_r=3&, accessed August 19, 2013.

7. Portals are essential navigating tools for searching the Internet. They fall into two categories. The first type of portal, available through AOL, Yahoo, MSN Worldwide, Excite, Lycos, and others, helps users search for general interest and broad categories of content. The audience for these major portals has given rise to a second category called niche portals, which specialize in more narrow areas and condensed searches. Good examples are portal sites for graphic artists, gardening, golf, sports, gambling, or health, or sites in Spanish such as www.quepasa.com for the global Latino market. These specialty portals have unique features that appeal to specific segments or niches of the broader Internet audience. Over time, as new niche segments are identified, these types of portals will expand significantly and ultimately draw more users.

8. The Internet has changed the nature and role of the mass media. Just how much is a story yet to be told. At this point, some may argue, with good reason, that the traditional media still set the agenda of public discourse and that Internet traffic is a function of the old media, which retain elite power. But we are rapidly reaching the point in core nations where the Internet will set the agenda and traditional media will be forced to follow. Blogging and tweeting are contributing to this shift in agenda-setting.

9. Michael Featherstone (ed.), *Global Culture: Nationalism, Globalization and Modernity*, London: Sage, 1990.

10. Marshall McLuhan and Quentin Fiore, *The Medium Is the Message*, New York: Bantam, 1967.

11. *Wall Street Journal* (June 16, 2000), B8.

12. In the early 1990s Mark Cuban, now an owner of the Dallas Mavericks and chair of HDNet, married a PC to a high-speed telephone line to get a distant college basketball game. He subsequently created an Internet site using similar connections for distant events that became so popular that he sold it to Yahoo! in 1999 and became a billionaire. Yahoo! now offers its users hundreds of radio and television stations. Yahoo! pays all the necessary fees up front for audio and video programming that appears on the Internet by way of its portal.

13. *Wall Street Journal* (June 12, 2000), A1.

14. Elizabeth Dickinson, "The First WikiLeaks Revolution?" *Foreign Policy* (January 13, 2011), at http://wikileaks.foreignpolicy.com/posts/2011/01/13/wikileaks_and_the_tunisia_protests, accessed August 16, 2013.

15. "China's Army Seen as Tied to Hacking against U.S.," *New York Times* (February 19, 2013), 1.

16. Matthew Klam, "Fear and Laptops on the Campaign Trail," *New York Times Magazine* (September 26, 2004), 24.

17. Milton Müller, *Ruling the Root: Internet Governance and the Taming of Cyberspace*, Cambridge, MA: MIT Press, 2002, p. 5 (Müller is an expert on Internet matters and a key force in the Internet Governance Project).

18. Müller, *Ruling the Root*, p. 6.

19. Lily Blue, "Internet and Domain Name Governance: Antitrust Litigation and ICANN," *Berkeley Technology Law Journal* 19 (2004), 387–403.

20. Susan Schiavetta and Konstantinos Komaitis, "ICANN's Role in Controlling Information on the Internet," *International Review of Law, Computers and Technology* 17(3), 267–84.

21. Blue, "Internet and Domain Name Governance," 393.

22. Wolfgang Kleinwachter, "Beyond ICANN vs ITU?" *Gazette* 66 (2004), 233–51.

23. Milton Mueller and Lee McKnight, "The Post-.com Internet: Toward Regular and Objective Procedures for Internet Governance," *Telecommunications Policy* 28 (2004), 487–502.

24. Anitesh Barua and Andrew Whinston, *The Internet Economy Indicators*, Austin: University of Texas, June 8, 2000, p. 2.

25. Mahbubani, Kishore, "Is the US Ready To Be Number Two?" *YaleGlobal* (February 11, 2011), 1. In 1980 the US economy was more than 10 times larger than China's, yet by 2017, China with its rapid growth could have the largest share of the global GDP, more than 18 percent, according to International Monetary Fund projections. US leaders have not prepared their citizens for this "great convergence," suggests Kishore Mahbubani, author and dean of the Lee Kuan Yew School of Public Policy, Singapore. Still, much of the world has moved toward US values and standards. Education, science, and technology have united the world around some best practices. Cooperation is still needed on global challenges like climate change, Mahbubani argues, and a system of global governance would be useful. He argues that principles of democracy, recognition of power balances, and the rule of law should guide any systems of global governance. This era of convergence is well suited to adjusting old systems and building new ones.

26. Alan Hedley, "Technological Diffusion or Cultural Imperialism? Measuring the Information Revolution," *International Journal of Comparative Sociology* 39(2) (1998), 210.

7

American Multimedia Conglomerates

Introduction

Not long ago, US productions, particularly feature films and television shows, dominated theater screens and television sets around the globe.[1] Foreign productions provided relatively little competition. Today, other major global firms own US production houses, share co-productions, or produce world-class competitive products for a global media market elsewhere. Sony of Japan, the BBC of the United Kingdom, and Bertelsmann of Germany are good examples of foreign multimedia firms that compete daily with US media companies. Yet US firms still control a majority of foreign sales in the global communication market. They are also expanding through regional partnerships, international joint ventures, or outright take-overs. Time Warner, Disney, Viacom, News Corp, and Comcast (the owners of NBCUniversal) represent the major US media owners that dominate many global media, global communication, and global media-related markets.

This chapter details the origins, assets, and global interests of these major US multimedia firms, along with a few others. Table 7.1 shows the top six media companies in the world. Disney, the largest of them, controls ABC, ESPN, Miramax and Touchstone Pictures, and more. News Corp, the second largest, owns the Fox properties, MySpace, and the *Wall Street Journal*. Time Warner controls CNN, HBO, Warner Music Group, AOL, and several other media properties. Viacom owns MTV, CBS, BET, and Showtime, while Comcast owns NBC (National Broadcasting Company) and is the largest cable television operator, with over 22 million subscribers. All are headquartered in the United States, the dominant core nation, and all have extensive semiperipheral and some peripheral market activities.

It is important to note the profiles of such multimedia firms. First, in terms of revenue, the three largest global media empires are all American. Second, in terms of electronic colonialism theory, all of the US multimedia empires along with their extensive advertising networks project, encourage, and promote US values, mores, history, culture, language, and tastes around the world. To a considerable extent, it is this influence – the impact of US

Global Communication: Theories, Stakeholders, and Trends, Fourth Edition. Thomas L. McPhail.
© 2014 John Wiley & Sons, Inc. Published 2014 by John Wiley & Sons, Inc.

Table 7.1 Top six media companies in the world, 2013

1	Disney (United States)
2	News Corporation (United States)
3	Time Warner (United States)
4	Viacom (United States)
5	Comcast (United States)
6	Sony (Japan)

multimedia fare on other countries' domestic media, in terms of production standards, box office receipts, and worldview – that concerns other core,[2] semiperipheral, and peripheral countries. In terms of the latter, think Disney, SpongeBob, Barbie, Bart Simpson, or Justin Bieber and Beyoncé. Foreign nations' concerns cover a vast range of cultural products such as music, movies, television series, magazines, books, and now the Internet. In terms of world system theory, the United States' activities in semiperipheral nations, which have large, accessible markets with growing disposable incomes, as well its activities in some peripheral nations, illustrate the broad range of off-shore economic activities undertaken by major US communication corporations. Major US global multimedia empires define relations with other nations along several product lines, as well as advertising, on an expanding number of foreign commercial television networks, radio networks, outlet stores, movie screens, and print publications.

Hollywood and New York-based communication corporations do well on a global scale because they have four substantial advantages. First, they operate in English, the language of the largest global segment of media outlets with purchasing power. Second, they have access to substantial fiscal resources and capital markets, which allow them to finance multimillion-dollar productions or take-overs. A single Hollywood feature film costs more than what most other nations spend annually on all their feature films. Third, US television networks overwhelmingly prefer US-made prime-time shows. ABC, CBS, Fox, and NBC seldom purchase foreign-made programs. Fourth, Hollywood and New York have access to the broadest range of acting talent, producers, writers, and directors. Some of the talent is from other core nations such as Australia, Canada, the United Kingdom, France, or Japan. The best global actors and actresses work primarily or exclusively on US productions. Most foreign actors, actresses, and musicians dream of the day they have a contract from an American company. That is their gold standard for defining success across the media and cultural sectors.

The critics of US cultural imperialism are at a loss about what to do. Some call for media protectionist policies, which emerge from time to time around the globe. Quotas limiting US media imports are a good example. Others simply lament the fact that the business is all about economics and job opportunities and there are scant opportunities for actors, writers, or producers from semiperipheral and peripheral nations to obtain employment and needed exposure in core nations. Most foreign commercial markets buy US television and movies for their television and theater outlets. For example, across Europe, 60 to 80 percent of their purchases of foreign television programming are from the United States. At least 50 percent of the movie screens in Europe show Hollywood productions as well as local ones. Across Latin America, 60 percent of the movie screens show Hollywood productions. In the future, as the number of channels increases in other core and semiperipheral nations thanks to cable, satellite, and digital technologies, the need for content will only increase the demand for American productions of all genres.

Disney

Disney is the world's largest communication empire, with an annual revenue of around $38 billion. The company was started in the early twentieth century under the leadership of Walter Disney, who had a vision for using animated cartoons and feature films as major commercial ventures.[3] His brother, Roy Disney, provided the financial acumen to help build what has now grown into a media giant.[4] The venture produced global icons and widely recognized characters including Mickey Mouse, Donald Duck, Cinderella, and Snow White. During the 1950s, the major film subsidiary Buena Vista was established, and a number of Disney shows were made for television. Disneyland opened in 1955 in California. In the 1960s Disney had several successful feature films including *101 Dalmatians*, *Mary Poppins*, *The Jungle Book*, and *The Love Bug*. In the 1970s further theatrical successes included *The Aristocats*, *Robin Hood*, and *The Rescuers*. Today Disney still has a strong line-up, with movies such as *Toy Story* and *Star Wars*. Walt Disney World, another major theme park, opened in Orlando, Florida, in 1971. In 1983 Tokyo Disneyland opened, and the same year the Disney Channel began as a cable TV service. In the early 1990s Disneyland Paris opened and quickly became controversial because of its US cultural orientation. Also, the Disney Corporation purchased Capital Cities/ABC in 1995 and became a major television broadcasting network owner (see Table 7.2).

In the late 1990s several Disney subsidiaries started websites that allowed products to be purchased anywhere in the world directly from Disney. Most recently a new park was opened in Shanghai, China, and Disney plans to open more parks internationally. In 2006 it bought Pixar and in 2009 Marvel of comic book fame. In 2012, building on its acquisition of Pixar and its tradition of animation, Disney purchased Lucasfilm for $4 billion from George Lucas, its sole owner. Disney immediately announced plans for a new *Star Wars* movie to be followed by two more over a decade. Lucas's first big movie success was *American Graffiti* in 1973, and his studio went on to make the hugely successful *Indiana Jones* and *Star Wars* movies. Lucasfilm also developed new digital technologies for special effects and computer animation. Disney's new *Star Wars* movies will be tied in to their theme parks and vast merchandising lines as well.

In 2005 Hong Kong Disneyland opened and attracted over five million customers during its first year of operation. The park consists of four themed areas: Main Street USA, Fantasyland, Adventureland, and Tomorrowland. This Disneyland is jointly owned by the Chinese government (57%) and Walt Disney Company (43%). Plans are already underway to expand the park's size and perhaps add Frontierland to its themes. All themes have a direct connection to electronic colonialism theory since they represent American themes and history. This is difficult to miss when one of the major attractions is called Main Street USA.

In 2007 Disney joined with General Electric (GE) and News Corporation to start the website Hulu. Hulu offers streaming video of movies and television shows. It is funded by commercials and Disney owns 27 percent of it, as do the other two media companies.

Disney currently operates as a global entertainment company with four major business divisions: Media Networks, Parks and Resorts, Studio Entertainment, and Consumer Products.

A major global asset is Disney-ABC-ESPN Television (DAET). DAET is now available in 240 territories around the globe to over 1,300 broadcasters. The media fare includes a cartoon channel for children, named Toon Channel. It carries Disney animation shows, movies, and cartoons. Internationally it is offered as part of cable or satellite packages aimed at a children's audience. Given Disney's vast library of video productions, much of it decades old, non-American networks have considerable difficulty competing with DAET and the appeal of Toon Channel.

Table 7.2 Major Disney holdings, 2013

A&E Television Networks (38%)
ABC Television Network
Biography Channel
Buena Vista International
Citadel Broadcasting
Disney Channel Worldwide
Disney Consumer Products
Disney Games
Disney Interactive Media Group (PCs, mobile phones, video games)
Disney Junior
Disney Live Family Entertainment (ice shows)
Disney Music Group
Disney Publishing Worldwide
Disney Stores Retail Chain
Disney Stores Worldwide
Disney Theatrical Productions (Broadway musicals)
E! Entertainment (35%)
ESPN (80%)
Euro Disney (39%)
Hollywood Pictures
Lifetime Entertainment Services (50%)
Lucasfilms
Marvel Entertainment (Avenger films)
Miramax
Pixar
Radio Disney Network
SOAPnet
The History Channel (38%)
Toon Channel
Touchstone
Walt Disney Internet Group
Walt Disney Parks and Resorts
Walt Disney Studios and Pictures
Walt Disney Studios Home Entertainment
Walt Disney Studios Motion Pictures International
Walt Disney Television International

The Disney Interactive Media Group has two main interests: entertainment websites and news websites. These sites include Disney Online, ESPN, ABC, and ABC News. The Internet group also offers searches, chat rooms, message boards, and e-mail. As a full Internet service provider, Disney competes directly with other major portals such as AOL, Microsoft, and Yahoo!

Today Disney is a highly diversified communication conglomerate, ranging from broadcasting, to feature films, to the Internet, to theme parks and resorts, to Disney stores, which operate in hundreds of locations worldwide.

History

The roots of Disney date back to December 30, 1890, when Walter Disney was born in Chicago, Illinois. Through his early years, Disney held several jobs including volunteering for the American Ambulance Corps, sorting and delivering Christmas mail for the Kansas City Post Office, and eventually forming a company with Ubbe Iwerks called Iwerks-Disney Commercial Artists. By 1920, Disney and Iwerks had joined the Kansas City Slide Company, which was renamed the Kansas City Film Ad Service. The same year, Disney produced what he called "Laugh-O-Grams." Essentially, the production of Laugh-O-Grams was Disney's introduction to the world of animated film and the beginning of the Disney empire. In 1937 *Snow White and the Seven Dwarfs* arrived in cinemas. A full-length animated feature, it represented a new breed of film. After *Snow White*, Disney went on to produce 35 animated feature films. Some of the company's most famous works include *Cinderella*, *Sleeping Beauty*, *Pinocchio*, *Dumbo*, *Peter Pan*, *Mary Poppins*, *The Jungle Book*, *The Little Mermaid*, *Beauty and the Beast*, *Aladdin*, *The Lion King*, and *Hercules*.

To increase exposure and sales, Disney opened several theme parks, which are the most successful theme parks in the world in terms of number of visitors. Disneyland Paris is 39 percent owned by Disney and is the largest tourist destination in all of Europe, with over 15 million visitors per year. In 2001 Disney opened Disney California Adventure Park and Tokyo DisneySea.

When the Walt Disney Company bought Capital Cities/ABC for $19 billion in the mid-1990s, it entered network broadcasting in a big way. Disney bought Capital Cities/ABC because it was having problems getting its programs on television at desirable times. The purchase of Capital Cities/ABC allowed Disney to reach larger prime-time audiences. After all, ABC was the network credited with the highly rated prime-time shows – and audience favorites – *Home Improvement*, *The Drew Carey Show*, and *Monday Night Football*. ABC's Wednesday night line-up was just as popular with one of the network's newest and most watched programs, *Dharma and Greg*. ABC was also popular with Sunday night prime-time audiences, who enjoyed the return of *The Wonderful World of Disney*. Some other solid shows are *Grey's Anatomy*, *Scrubs*, *Lost*, and *Ugly Betty*. Finally, the network picked a winner in *Who Wants to Be a Millionaire?* Winners are defined in the industry as programs which command a premium advertising rate.

News is another important element of ABC Broadcasting. ABC News continues to attract large audiences with *World News Tonight*. The news division was enhanced with a second launch of *20/20*, the successful late-evening show *Nightline*, and *Primetime Live*. Furthermore, *ABC World News* has always been the leader in foreign news coverage.

In 2002 senior Disney and ABC executives tried to cancel the award-winning *Nightline*. The news magazine, which began in the 1980s with coverage of the Iran hostage crisis, has a loyal following and is a credit to moderator Ted Koppel and ABC's News Division.

But the senior staffs of Disney and ABC attempted to hire NBC late show star Jay Leno without informing Koppel or his producer. The industry and viewers alike were upset by the crass, secretive move. ABC was perceived to be abandoning its public service mandate in pursuit of a few more dollars. Leno quickly declined the offer, sensing that being part of a plot to end a high-quality news show in a post-9/11 environment would be a career mistake. But in the end, the "bean counters" at Disney are likely to prevail and quality broadcasting will take a hit for the sake of profits. Other than NBC's *Today Show* and CBS's *60 Minutes*, news and public affairs programming is not a big commercial success for Disney.

ABC Broadcasting also has a vested interest in the following cable networks: A&E (37.5%), the History Channel (37.5%), Lifetime (50%), E! Entertainment (34.4%), and Walt Disney Television International. A&E has been the winner of 20 Emmy Awards, and the network has reached more than 70 million subscribers in North America. The History Channel serves more than 42 million subscribers; the History Channel International was launched in 1998 and is available in 51 countries. E! Entertainment has become a leading worldwide provider of entertainment and news information on both television and the Internet. In fact, E! Online Entertainment is one of the leaders of the World Wide Web and has a large teenage audience.

ESPN Inc.

Disney-controlled ESPN is the worldwide leader in sports, reaching over 80 million homes. All ESPN networks and services are 80 percent owned by ABC. It was founded in 1979. Its main telecast is *SportsCenter*, and in 1987 it negotiated with the National Football League to broadcast Sunday night NFL football. ESPN's audience jumped dramatically and now they are a fixture in the global sports culture. ESPN2 was launched in 1992, has 65 million subscribers, and is one of the fastest growing cable networks in the United States. ESPN also operates internationally. This 28-year-old network now reaches 150 million households in more than 150 countries and territories and in 20 languages. In 2004 it launched a Spanish network, ESPNU. ESPN.com is one of the most visited websites in the world. In 2003 the US Office of Foreign Assets Control, as part of its anti-Castro stance, fined ESPN for broadcasting sports in Cuba. Finally, Sega is licensing ESPN shows for its video games worldwide. ESPN is a 24-hour sports cable franchise that is a media wonder and is now worth over $40 billion. By 2013 ESPN's three-decade run and profits had convinced Rupert Murdoch to start a competing sports network, Fox Sports 1.

Theme Parks: Marketing Media Heroes

To further reach audiences internationally through television, radio, cable, and the Internet, Disney expanded its theme park business in Europe and Asia. Based on the success of Tokyo Disneyland, which opened in 1983, Disney opened Euro Disney Resort in 1992 to further expand international markets. It currently owns 40 percent of the French-based theme park and resort, which has been renamed Disneyland Paris. Euro Disney operates two parks outside of Paris, Disneyland Paris and Walt Disney Studios. The latter was constructed in 2002 at a cost of over $500 million. Since inception the parks have welcomed over 150 million visitors. Disneyland Paris is still losing money and its largest personal shareholder with 16 percent is the Saudi Arabian Prince Alwaleed. Disneyland Paris also contains a McDonald's restaurant.

Disneyland theme parks have been successful and profitable in the United States, Hong Kong, and Tokyo because the American style of doing business worked. However, this was not the case during the early years in Europe. Europeans did not accept or understand the American way of doing business, nor did they like it. Cultural differences created some hostility in France, and the Walt Disney Company did not enjoy the success in Europe it had expected. Disney executives had also failed to do the preliminary research, approaching France as though it were a foreign market similar to Japan.

Understanding a country's unique culture is vital to the success of a US company. The Disney training manual provides a good example of the problems Disney encountered in France. Before Disneyland Paris opened, the company built offices and a training center to recruit cast members. After passing Disney's pre-hiring procedures, candidates were then trained. Every employee hired needed to meet and pass Disney's strict personality requirements. Recruits had to practice the "Disney smile" and saying "Have a nice day." They also had to follow the 13-page manual outlining Disney's dress code, otherwise known as the "Disney look." The manual outlines the ideal look – well scrubbed, happy, all-American – and spells out everything from the appropriate size of earrings, to the appropriate length of fingernails, to its absolute intolerance of facial or dyed hair. The young European employees did not understand or appreciate the "Disney look." It was difficult for them to subscribe to the American look since they were not Americans, and they believed the requirement stripped them of their individuality. As a result of this major culture clash, the French, who contested the strict dress policy, took Disney to court. Ultimately, the Walt Disney Company modified and instituted a new, more relaxed European dress policy.

The Walt Disney Company also failed to research the pros and cons of selling alcohol at Disneyland Paris. Alcoholic beverages are not served in the California, Florida, and Tokyo theme parks, and the same policy was instituted at Euro Disney, which failed to respect the European custom of drinking wine with lunch. Needless to say, the French rebelled against the no-alcohol policy and stayed away in droves. As a result, in 1993 the Walt Disney Company changed its policy to allow the sale of wine and beer at Disneyland Paris. Despite several other examples of Disney's failure to understand local tastes and traditions, it has made adjustments by adopting other European practices. It also expanded its hotel offerings, and the parks now feature seven hotels, with a total of 8,000 rooms, plus two major convention centers.

Also the Disney expansion into Asia represents a straightforward example of a core-based multinational organization entering a semiperipheral area, in this case China, which has an enormous population of 1.3 billion; thus, China has the potential to become part of Disney's major global network in the twenty-first century. The Hong Kong and Shanghai investments are likely the tip of the iceberg in terms of Disney's future expansion plans across China – and all with the blessing of the communist Chinese government.[5]

Pixar

In 2006 Disney bought out Pixar Animation Studios. Pixar is a world-class computer animation firm which began in 1979 as the Graphics Group, part of the computer division of Lucasfilm. In 1986 Steve Jobs, of Apple fame, purchased it and renamed it Pixar. In 1991 Disney signed with Pixar for a series of computer-animated feature films, and thus began the important relationship from both creative and monetary angles. The first film was *Toy*

Story in 1995. It was the first fully computer-animated feature film. Before this, animated films were hand-drawn frames which took enormous amounts of time. *Toy Story* was a huge global success and the highest-grossing movie that year. *Toy Story 2* followed in 1999, and grossed almost half a billion dollars worldwide. In 2012, focusing on its tradition of animation, Disney purchased Lucasfilm for $4 billion from George Lucas, its sole owner. Disney immediately announced plans for a new Star Wars movie. Lucas's first big movie was American Graffiti in 1973. Lucasfilm is also renowned for new digital technologies and computer animation. Future Star War movies will be tied into their theme parks and merchandising lines.

Summary

The Walt Disney Company began as a small, creative firm established by two brothers: Walter Disney, who was responsible for the animation activities, and his brother Roy Disney, who handled the company's finances and strategic planning. The initial years of the company were extremely successful with the creation of several popular culture icons such as Mickey Mouse and Donald Duck. After World War II, the company began to add theme parks, one in California and later one in Florida. They then expanded internationally with Disneylands in Japan, France, and now China. During the 1980s, the company expanded through Disney stores and greater diversification into related fields. Several highly successful children's and family films were produced during this period, and they ventured into new territory such as the NHL hockey team, the Mighty Ducks, the addition of Disney cable channels, and the addition of Disney Music. In the 1990s, the take-over of the national television network ABC was a major move for the corporation. Currently, Disney's largest unit is its film labels, which include Disney, Touchstone, Buena Vista, Dimension Films, Hollywood Pictures, Pixar, and Miramax Films. These units produce films for the global market, and they market select ABC shows. Finally, the move into Asia with a second theme park in Hong Kong represents a major global move for the Disney Company. Asia represents a vast new market, and Disney appears to be ahead of Time Warner in strategically identifying new opportunities in Asia. But all is not well at the Magic Kingdom. In 2004 major shareholders, including Roy Disney, Walt Disney's nephew, were calling for the resignation of the CEO, Michael Eisner. He simply announced his desire to retire in 2006.[6] The take-over of Pixar was also a successful venture which has increased Disney's global footprint. Pixar has studios in California and now China.

Finally, in the context of electric colonialism theory (ECT), Disney is a classic example. It operates on a global scale with American cultural products across a broad range of media and platforms. It utilizes the latest technology and marketing information to increase market share annually, whether through music, movies, merchandise, or theme parks. More children around the world know Mickey Mouse than any other cultural icon. For other non-American cultures, Mickey and Minnie represent a distinct challenge to indigenous characters, practices, and sales of indigenous goods. For example, in Mexico, children's parties have traditionally featured a piñata, a papier mâché donkey, filled with candy. Now, most piñatas are made in the likeness of either Mickey Mouse or SpongeBob. Another example is Europe. Disney has 45 television channels across Europe which carry their vast library of cartoons and movies. Their sports channel ESPN is offered in seven countries.[7]

News Corporation

History

In 2004 News Corporation, the second largest global media company, announced that it was moving its corporate headquarters to the United States, confirming the status of the United States as the most important multimedia market in the world. It represented a significant loss to the image and future of Australia as a major player in the information age. As one of the largest vertically integrated media conglomerates on the planet, News Corp gave three major reasons for the move. First, it was seeking to expand the shareholder base, scope, and demand by becoming an American company. This allows News Corp to be listed on major US indices which list only US stocks, and to open up the company to the many pension funds that are limited to purchasing US stocks. Second, more than 75 percent of News Corp's revenue and profits come from US multimedia operations. Only a very small portion of their revenues comes from Australian operations. Third, such a move provides News Corp with access to much larger capital markets. These markets may become crucial as News Corp attempts to create a global satellite sports and entertainment network similar to CNN's all-news network. Access to capital is also important in terms of underwriting blockbuster movies for Fox Studios. New Corps is divided into the following communication segments: cable, television, film, direct broadcast satellites, publishing, and a few smaller areas.

The largest shareholder of News Corp is Australian-born Rupert Murdoch, a naturalized US citizen who resides in Europe. He is a media mogul unlike any other.[8] Murdoch has created in News Corp an international empire of media, technology, and sports franchises. Murdoch himself is conservative and hires senior management of the same persuasion. For example, his US Fox network is headed by Roger Alles, a well-known conservative Republican who has worked for and advised Republican presidents. Alles's news divisions have learned how to slant both foreign and domestic news to guarantee that it will be aired and that they will not be fired for failing to follow the company's line. In general, Fox lacks a culture of professionalism and objectivity in the handling of news. Rather it prefers to go with a right-wing agenda rather than a balanced format, as personified by Bill O'Reilly and others. They run with the latest rumor or anti-Democratic story with glee.

Murdoch has used sports teams as a vehicle to obtain large audiences for his networks, not only for sports programming but for other broadcasting initiatives as well. The interconnection of sports and television is simply a growing international phenomenon. Murdoch is also part owner of a new sports channel in Canada, CTV Sportsnet. The growing convergence of sports and television continues, with almost monthly announcements of major corporate agreements. Part of the strategy is to control the sports franchise, but these companies also want an advantage in the form of the media rights of the sports league. Murdoch is no stranger to either controversy or sports. His Fox network came out of nowhere to purchase the broadcasting rights of the National Football League. Although the Fox network was initially perceived as a distant fourth national network in the United States, it has since become a serious challenge to the "big three" – ABC, CBS, and NBC – with hit shows. Through a separate company Murdoch has a substantial sports cable following that competes directly with Disney's ESPN. In 2013 Murdoch raised the stakes by creating a larger all-sports network, Fox Sports 1. In the United Kingdom, Murdoch is a major player with his BSkyB television satellite network, which experienced start-up difficulties until it purchased the rights to broadcast Premier League soccer matches. Now BSkyB is a major player, with more than seven million subscribers in the United Kingdom. News Corp intended to purchase 100 percent of the company but a major scandal in 2011 forced it to back off. Its corporate strategy is to use soccer as the engine to sell satellite dishes across Europe. Other European media-related sports and television marriages are easy to find. Italian media giant Silvio Berlusconi owns the AC Milan soccer team, while the international car-maker Fiat controls Juventus. In the Netherlands, Philips Electronics owns AFC Ajax, Amsterdam's soccer team.

News Corp is a global media firm with significant interests in television, film, books, newspapers, magazines, satellites, cable systems, and sports.[9] It is a diversified global communications corporation with operations and holdings in every core and semiperipheral country as well as most peripheral regions, excluding Africa, due to the vast range of its satellite networks. For example, it has 29 television channels across Europe. Table 7.3 shows News Corp's vast and widespread holdings. In 2007 Murdoch purchased the Dow Jones Company for $5 billion. Dow Jones is the publisher of the *Wall Street Journal*, and Murdoch intends to use its staff to aid his Fox business channel with commentaries and business news and stories.

Table 7.3 Major News Corporation holdings, 2013

20th Century Fox (and subsidiaries)
20th Century Fox Home Entertainment
American Idol
The Australian (newspaper)
Beliefnet
Blue Sky Studios
BSkyB (39%)
Channel [V] Asia Stations America
The Courier-Mail
DIRECTV (38%)
Dow Jones
Fox Broadcasting
Fox Family Channel
Fox Interactive Media
Fox Music
Fox News
Fox Searchlight Pictures
Fox Sports Latin
Fox Sports Net
Fox Television
Foxtel
FX
HarperCollins (and subsidiaries)
Herald Sun
Hulu (27%)

Table 7.3 (cont'd)

IGN Entertainment Games
MyNetworkTV
MySpace
National Rugby League
NDS
New York Post
Rotten Tomatoes
Sky Italia and Sky Deutschland
SmartSource
STAR TV
The Sun
The Sunday Mail
The Sunday Telegraph
TATA SKY (20%)
The Times (and subsidiaries)
The Times Higher Education Supplement
The Times Literary Supplement
TV Guide
The Wall Street Journal
Zondervan

The Murdoch family, including Rupert's sons and daughter, own about 30 percent of News Corp. The firm currently makes about 25 percent of its sales from global businesses and 75 percent from US media businesses. This mix may change, perhaps dramatically, with global initiatives, particularly in the Far East, growing substantially. Murdoch's family situation could easily be confused with the script of one of his soap operas. Rupert Murdoch, now nearly 80, appointed his eldest son, Lachlan, as deputy chief operating officer and heir apparent to become president of News Corp. But in 2005 Lachlan abruptly resigned and moved his family back to Australia. His other son, James, stepped down as chief executive of BSkyB in 2007.

British Sky Broadcasting Group

British Sky Broadcasting Group (BSkyB) is the United Kingdom's leading pay-television provider. News Corp owns 40 percent of it. Since 1989 it has distributed television programming to customers in both the United Kingdom and Ireland. It offers 650 radio and television channels via satellite.

BSkyB has over 10 million customers. It provides news, sports, and entertainment programs through channels covering nine sectors. They are entertainment, news, children's, movies, sports, music, radio, adult, and specialty offerings. For example, Sky Sports offers over 36,000 hours of sports programming per year over five satellite channels, and is seeing a consistent growth in number of viewers. In August 2003 an episode of the US Fox network program *The*

Simpsons featuring then British prime minister Tony Blair attracted over one million viewers on Sky One. Sky News continues to receive industry awards and now has foreign bureaus in Washington, Mumbai, Brussels, Moscow, Beijing, Jerusalem, and Johannesburg.

BSkyB has pioneered the introduction of digital television to Europe. This service, known as Sky Digital, provides the clearest available picture quality technically, along with CD-quality sound. Sky Digital offers 10 documentary channels, five sports channels, and up to five different movies every hour, along with all the BBC television channels.

Finally, a look at BSkyB's multichannel entertainment offerings is informative. Sky One now outdraws the five terrestrial networks with programs such as *Las Vegas*, *24*, *Cold Case*, *Scrubs*, *Malcolm in the Middle*, and the globally popular *Simpsons*. Sky Movies offers 450 movies per week on 11 different pay channels. Some of the movies that attract more than 10 million viewers a week are *Men in Black*, *Pirates of the Caribbean*, *My Big Fat Greek Wedding*, and *Bruce Almighty*. Some of the satellite channel offerings are Bravo, Paramount, E!, Hallmark, Hollywood TV, Bloomberg, CNN, Disney, Nickelodeon, MTV (with 5 channels), and VH1 (with 3 channels). As the above lists demonstrate, American media fare is embedded in foreign satellite services to a very large extent. Since many of these channels are pay channels, there must be an audience for them. ECT deals with the collective impact of these audiovisual products over time. Their effect is becoming evident, from British boys who prefer to play basketball rather than soccer to teenagers dancing and dressing like American pop icons. In the case of BSkyB, this Americanization phenomenon is further reinforced by Murdoch's ability to direct the placement of his vast US-oriented Fox television and movie studio productions on British and Irish satellite systems.

STAR TV

In the mid-1990s Rupert Murdoch's News Corp acquired control of STAR (Satellite Television Asian Region) TV, and in 1998 STAR TV acquired Hutchvision Hong Kong Ltd. Hutchvision Hong Kong was the first Hong Kong-based satellite television licensee; it started broadcasting satellite television services, known as the STAR network, in 1991. The STAR TV network offers both subscription and free-to-air television services, reaching more than 300 million people across Asia (including India) and the Middle East in a multitude of markets, making STAR distinct among broadcasters. STAR TV is the dominant satellite broadcaster in Asia and has viewers in 53 other countries as well. In addition, it is the only broadcaster to offer such a broad range of programs to all of Asia and the Middle East, with coverage from east Africa to Japan. STAR TV transmits more than 45 programming services in eight languages. It controls more than 10 channels in Hong Kong alone, all of them broadcasting 24 hours a day. Programs feature a mix of movies, news, music, sports, and general entertainment. STAR TV is a commercial network relying on advertising from more than 20 global brands.

STAR TV runs four divisions: China, India, Middle East, and Fox International Channels Asia. Services carried on the network include ESPN, Fox News, and National Geographic. Several other satellite television broadcasters uplink their signals from Hong Kong, including CNN and CNBC. Clearly STAR TV is a strong foot soldier for electronic colonialism theory.

Increasing government deregulation and liberalization, as well as technological advances in satellites and receiving dishes insure a solid future for the broadcasting industry everywhere. Although audiences welcome the local-language programming, the net result is that larger STAR TV audiences are being built at the expense of local, and frequently government-owned, television networks. Most local stations are still non-commercial and lack the flair and broad scope of STAR TV's multiple channel system. Therefore, the impact of STAR TV, and to a lesser extent other networks such as the BBC and CNN, offer Asia and other nations a new commercial model that is a direct application of electronic colonialism. These advertising-supported networks need audiences to sell to their global brand sponsors in order for both the new networks and the global products to succeed in these vast new markets.

Dow Jones

The Dow Jones Company was acquired by News Corp in 2006. It is widely known for two assets yet it also has significant global activities. Its flagship publication is the *Wall Street Journal*, which was first published in 1889. In 1896, it started the Dow Jones Industrial Average (DJIA) which today consists of 30 blue chip US corporations, one-third of which are in the information or media sectors. Examples of these companies are IBM, AT&T, Verizon, Microsoft, General Electric, and the Walt Disney Company. In terms of international assets, Dow Jones started the prestigious *Far East Economic Review* in 1946, and launched the *Asian Wall Street Journal* in 1976, and the *Wall Street Journal Europe* in 1983. In 1994 it established the *Wall Street Journal Americas*, published in Spanish and Portuguese, and in 2004 the *Wall Street Journal India*. Dow Jones is also partnered with the *Financial Times* of London and the *Independent Media* to put out a Russian business daily called *Vedomosti* (Record).

The various *WSJ* editions, both in the United States and abroad, have a conservative tone or bias. One could make the case that the *WSJ* is a development journalism enterprise on behalf of free enterprise. It promotes an editorial mantra of hostility toward social issues, activists, and critics of business practices. For example, the *WSJ* has historically campaigned against universal health care, environment legislation, the United Nations, and affirmative action programs. In terms of the Iraq War, it provided coverage that supported the Pentagon's line. Rather than seeking balance and objectivity in its stories, it stooped to ridicule, much like Bill O'Reilly of Fox News, or Rush Limbaugh's radio rants. The *WSJ* had earlier complained about US and foreign media focusing on the photos of the Abu Ghraib prisoners' abuse. For the *WSJ*, its uncritical support for the United States' military policy translated into easier access to senior Washington officials for a broad array of upcoming stories during the Bush administration. Since the election of President Obama, there has been substantial negative coverage of his attempt to pass universal health-care legislation. The basic point is that the conservative tone of the *WSJ* properties panders to a global niche, which is an audience defined by wealth.

On the electronic side, in addition to its Internet sites for various print properties, Dow Jones has had a major global alliance with CNBC since 1997. Across both Europe and Asia, Dow Jones provides CNBC with business and news programming. With the change in ownership, the talent at Dow Jones and the *Wall Street Journal* now have a window on Fox News as well. As the global economy evolves and corporations become more global in scope and talent, the Dow Jones Company is well positioned to expand its business-oriented multimedia properties around the globe.

UK Scandal

A phone-hacking scandal in the United Kingdom in 2011 involved a number of News Corp journalists and editors. The activities under scrutiny actually dated back to 2002 when a 13-year-old schoolgirl was kidnapped and killed. Her mobile phone was hacked by a private investigator hired by the *News of the World*. In 2005 the same paper intercepted the Queen's family voicemail messages. There was a police investigation, and two people associated with the *News of the World* were jailed. In 2009 News Corp reportedly paid out over $1 million to settle cases where employees had hacked into the private phones of celebrities, union leaders, and politicians. In 2011 the British police started a broad investigation into illegal phone hacking by News Corp papers. Many new claims emerged and the *News of the World* management admitted its journalists had engaged in widespread illegal phone hacking. Several new pay-offs were approved by News Corp, but the scandal did not go away.

Public anger and the media storm hit a peak in July 2011, when a lawyer for the schoolgirl killed in 2002 revealed that her voicemail had been hacked into and that phone messages had been erased by the hacker, which likely misled the police in their hunt for her. That same month the *News of the World* paper closed down, and it was revealed that senior management had also been paying off police and others for tips and leads on news stories. The bribery probe alone resulted in over 50 arrests.

As public and parliamentary anger grew, Rupert Murdoch took over from his son and heir apparent James to limit the damage. He even had a series of secret meetings with the prime minister during the preceding months. Rupert and James Murdoch and a senior executive of News International (another News Corp property) were questioned extensively and the hearings were covered live on the Internet. An international audience was now riveted to the fall-out from the scandal. There was even an attack on the octogenarian Murdoch by an audience member at an open hearing, who was intercepted by Rupert's wife. The video segment went viral and appeared on nightly newscasts around the globe.

The final report, titled "News International and Phone-Hacking" by the House of Commons Committee, concluded:

Corporately, the *News of the World* and News International misled the Committee about the true nature and extent of the internal investigations they professed to have carried out in relation to phone hacking; by making statements they would have known were not fully truthful; and by failing to disclose documents which would have helped expose the truth. Their instinct throughout, until it was too late, was to cover up rather than seek out wrongdoing and discipline the perpetrators, as they also professed they would do after the criminal convictions. In failing to investigate properly, and by ignoring evidence of widespread wrongdoing, News International and its parent News Corporation exhibited willful blindness, for which the companies' directors – including Rupert Murdoch and James Murdoch – should ultimately be prepared to take responsibility.[10]

The extent of the problem was illustrated by a revelation at the hearing that previous members of the committee had also had their phones hacked. Further criminal charges and trials are likely to emerge from this decade-long debacle. The hacking scandal, investigations, and pay-outs to settle some of the lawsuits have cost News Corp over $350 million so far and this sum is likely to more than double over time.

Finally, in 2012 a report by Lord Justice Leveson concerning British media ethics, or the lack thereof, called for the creation of stiffer oversight of media systems and a stronger code of ethics. The British Parliament will have the final say, but these recommendations have raised other concerns in relation to press freedom.

As Alan Cowell wrote in "Britain: Newspapers Protest New Press Rules":

An array of newspapers protested a new press code on Tuesday that empowers a press watchdog to investigate abuses, order corrections and levy steep fines for misbehavior.

The Newspaper Society, which represents 1,100 newspapers, said those provisions would impose a "crippling burden" on publications struggling against the inroads of the Internet. "A free press cannot be free if it is dependent on and accountable to a regulatory body recognized by the state," said Adrian Jeakings, the president of the society. The conservative Daily Mail commented in an editorial, "The bitter irony is this long-drawn out debate comes when the Internet – which, being global, has no regulatory restraints – is driving newspapers out of business." Newspaper owners and editors have so far not signed on to the agreement, which lawmakers agreed to early Monday in the wake of the phone-hacking scandal.[11]

Summary

Rupert Murdoch controls all News Corp properties on a daily basis and makes sure that they follow his political and corporate leanings. His vast multimedia holdings have always been global in nature. His Fox holdings in the United States are increasing their audience share, and the decision to move the corporate headquarters from Australia to New York in 2004 further solidified the focus on the Fox sector of the company. With satellite systems in Europe (BSkyB) and Asia (STAR TV), Murdoch may be well on his way to creating a global media infrastructure. His purchase of Dow Jones as well as MySpace illustrates the power of News Corp to make big deals. The big unknown for the company is who will succeed him.

A final point: Hollywood has long been the gold standard for foreign actors and actresses but it has now also become the stage for foreign directors as well. For example, the 2013 release by Fox Searchlight films of *Stoker* starred the Australians Nicole Kidman and Mia Wasikowska and British Matthew Goode and was directed by prominent South Korean director Park Chan-wok, even though he spoke little English and needed a translator. Another example is Taiwanese director Ang Lee who won a Best Director Oscar in 2013 for his work on *Life of Pi*. Leading directors from Canada, Australia, Latin America, and Europe all seek exposure and Hollywood fame.

It is anticipated that News Corp will be split into two new entities by 2113, one focusing on video, television, and film, and the other on print publications, such as the *Wall Street Journal* and *The Times* (of London).

Time Warner

In 2000 the merger of America Online and Time Warner created the largest communication organization in the world at the time. The merger and anticipated synergies have not gone nearly as well as expected. In 2009 AOL was spun off as a separate company.

Even as a separate company AOL has had branding and fiscal problems but in a surprising bold move in 2011 it acquired *Huffington Post* for $315 million. Led by outspoken Internet-savvy Arianna Huffington, the *Huffington Post* is news, liberal opinion site, and several niche blogs. It has international sites in the United Kingdom and Canada and aggressive global expansion plans.

The major properties of Time Warner include CNN, HLN, TNT, Warner Bros., HBO, Cinemax, Time Warner Cable, Time Warner Books, Warner Music Group, Time Inc., its publishing arm, Cartoon Network, and TBS (Table 7.4). Time Inc. accounts for 15 percent of Time Warner's sales. Warner Bros.' movies and the WB Television Network generate almost 50 percent of Time Warner's sales. They also publish over 30 feature magazines

Table 7.4 Major Time Warner holdings, 2013

ADTECH/Advertising.com
Adult Swim
AIM/ICQ
Atlantic Records
Cartoon Network (and subsidiaries)
Central European Media Enterprises (31%)
Cinemax (and subsidiaries)
CNN (and subsidiaries)
Comedy Central (50%)
CompuServe
Court TV (50%)
The CW Television Network (50%)
DC Comics and DC Nation
Elektra Entertainment Group
Entertainment Weekly
Essence
Fortune
HBO (and subsidiaries)
HLN (and subsidiaries and offshoots)
In Style
IPC Group Limited (Europe)
Kids' WB!
Lightningcast
MAD magazine
MapQuest
Money
Moviefone
Mushroom Records
NASCAR.com
Netscape
New Line Cinema
People
Pogo.com
TheSmokingGun.com
Spinner.com
Sports Illustrated
TACODA

Table 7.4 (cont'd)

Telepictures Productions
Third Screen Media
Time (and subsidiaries)
Time Warner Books UK
Time Warner Cable
truTV
Truveo
Turner Broadcasting Station
Turner Classic Movies (and subsidiaries)
Turner Entertainment
Turner Network Television (and subsidiaries and offshoots)
Warner Books
Warner Bros. Entertainment (and subsidiaries and offshoots)
Warner Bros. Pictures
Warner Music Group
WB Network
Winamp

such as *Time*, *People*, and *Sports Illustrated*. The Time Warner video group controls close to 6,000 feature films, including all eight Harry Potter films, *The Dark Knight*, *Gran Torino*, and *Slumdog Millionaire*; 32,000 television shows; and 14,000 animated titles. It operates major book clubs and book publishing through Warner Books and Little, Brown, and promotes print and videos through the Time–Life series. Finally, Time Warner controls 50 percent of both Comedy Central and Court TV. Time Warner has 34,000 employees worldwide.

Reflecting the growing role of off-shore income for all American media conglomerates, WarnerFilms is now making almost twice as much on foreign box office receipts as on domestic ticket sales. More and more movies will be produced for the global audience rather than the declining domestic market. Scripts with international potential will trump those with a domestic theme.

History

In 1922 24-year-old Henry Robinson Luce founded Time Inc.[12] Beginning with *Time* magazine and later *Life*, *Fortune*, and *Sports Illustrated*, Luce became the leading global magazine publisher. Time Inc. lost its print persona almost overnight when it merged with Warner Communications in 1989. Warner brought a major video culture to the print culture of Time. The new combined entity, Time Warner Entertainment (TWE), experienced some merger woes. The two different corporate cultures took time to blend, and senior management experienced turmoil, but eventually Gerald Levin of Time Inc. became chairman and CEO of Time Warner in 1992.

The new focus for TWE was further expanded with the addition of Ted Turner's empire in 1996. Today, journalism and entertainment history coexist at TWE. Gerald Levin recalls Luce's legacy at TWE:

> Luce was adamant that economic progress was inextricably linked to political systems that actively encouraged individual initiative and free enterprise. For me, the advent of a digitally based economy gives Luce's view fresh urgency.
>
> Luce also insisted it wasn't enough for business leaders to pursue efficiency and productivity. Those who entered the executive suites of American business had to have a heightened sense of their responsibility to the common good.
>
> I share this conviction. [13]

Levin also comments on his grasp on the new role for video and cable at Time:

> At the heart of what I envisioned was a world-class news operation in print and electronic media, with the size and resources to immunize it from those who had no regard for its heritage …
>
> I believe that if Luce had entered the media business when Ted Turner did his instincts as an entrepreneur and journalist would have led him to grasp cable's potential for creating a new kind of global journalism. In the same way I believe that the 24-year-old Luce who conceived *Time* or the media revolutionary who proclaimed that *Life* was more than a new magazine – that it was a new way of seeing – would have jumped on the internet and been a formative influence on its evolution as a news medium.[14]

Luce was a print man, whereas Levin brought with him expertise in video, and through the merger with AOL, he also brought Internet expertise. Levin was sacked in 2002 and AOL's Steve Case a short time later.[15] Also, Time Warner's major competitors – Disney, Viacom, News Corp, Sony, Bertelsmann, NBCUniversal, and others – compete in the same global communication market with many competing brands.

CNN Connection

Although CNN, a Time Warner enterprise, is discussed more thoroughly in Chapter 11, an important issue involving CNN is relevant here. Ted Turner's video empire competed with Time's print focus and culture. Turner's various media properties greatly supplemented Time Warner's strategic moves in the video business.

The AOL side of the merger brings global leadership covering web brands, interactive services, Internet connectivity, branded portals, and an expanding range of e-commerce services. The AOL network's handling of over two billion instant messages per day is an indication of its size. AOL was founded in 1985 and has four major product lines.

1   The Interactive Services Group includes AOL's major Internet provider activities including CompuServe and Netscape, which are Internet portals. This business group also contains AOL Wireless Services, which is designed to deliver AOL properties to an expanding global group of wireless customers. Whereas most AOL customers today hook up to the Internet through a PC, in the future, particularly in Europe and Asia, more and more clients will opt for wireless Internet connectivity.

2   The Interactive Properties Group contains branded properties such as Digital City; ICQ, a portal; AOL Instant Messenger, a popular electronic text message service; as well as Moviefone, Inc., and MapQuest. In 2008 AOL acquired a global social media network, Bebo.

3   AOL International Group is responsible for all AOL, CompuServe, and Netscape opera-
    tions outside the United States. This is a rapidly expanding segment of AOL's overall
    business. Outside the United States AOL has more than 10 million subscribers. In many
    nations, AOL properties are the second leading Internet provider. In foreign countries,
    the main Internet provider is generally the domestic telecommunications company,
    such as France Telecom or Bell Canada. Some of the 38 nations covered by AOL world-
    wide are: Argentina, Australia, Brazil, Canada, France, Germany, India, Japan, Puerto
    Rico, and the United Kingdom.

4   Netscape Enterprise Group included software products, technical support, and consult-
    ing and training services. As of May 2008, AOL no longer supports or develops Netscape
    products.

The number of AOL subscribers around the world was once close to 30 million,
approximately 24 million of whom were in the United States. However, subscription
numbers have plummeted in recent years and according to the latest numbers, around six
million subscribers remain.

AOL competes directly for Internet subscription revenues with Microsoft, AT&T, Prodigy,
and others. Their web-based search services and portals also face considerable competition
from Google, Yahoo!, MSN, Disney, and Excite At Home. Even though it functions in a highly
competitive environment, AOL has structurally maintained a distinct global lead as the
major Internet provider. By merging with Time Warner, AOL had hoped to move to a new
level in its ability not only to provide connectivity and e-commerce services, but also to
deliver a vast array of content through a mix of free and subscriber services around the globe.
This major corporate merger is not being universally applauded. A number of key executives
have been replaced. The firm still does not have a national television network.

Summary

Time Warner became one of the world's largest media companies through a long-term
strategic plan involving major mergers. In 1989 Time Inc. merged with Warner
Communications and in 1996 with Turner Broadcasting. Time Warner now operates in six
major communication sectors: cable, publishing, films, music, broadcasting, and the
Internet. Its cable systems provide some of the most technologically sophisticated digital
fiber-optic systems available anywhere. The company has also focused on global markets.
This is especially true of its broadcasting, particularly CNN International, which produces
exclusive programming for Asia and Europe and reaches over 150 million TV-viewing
households in over 212 countries and territories. It is undertaking this without the advantage
of a national television network based in the United States such as ABC, CBS, Fox, or NBC.

Finally, it is important to keep in mind that within the United States domestic market
CNN is number two, behind Fox and sometimes behind MSNBC as well, but globally it is
number one, pushing BBC World Television Service into second place.

Viacom

History

In 1971 Viacom was spun off from CBS. But in 2000, the Federal Communications
Commission (FCC) approved the merger of Viacom with CBS. Viacom, as part of the
consolidation in the broadcasting industry, was able to purchase CBS Corp for $30 billion.

This immediately gave Viacom control of more than 35 percent of the US broadcasting market. The deal covered all CBS properties, which at that time included 38 television stations, 163 radio stations, and interests in 13 Internet companies. Viacom is now the fourth largest communication giant in the world. The purchase constitutes an interesting role reversal. Originally CBS, like other networks, produced a great deal of in-house programming. But in 1971 the FCC forced CBS to sell all internal production and cable programming units, which it did by creating Viacom.[16] Now, 27 years later, Viacom has been so successful that it is in a position to buy its parent, CBS. The FCC dropped the prohibition against networks owning production houses in 1995. As a result, major television networks are now producing more in-house shows in order to contain costs, control the process, and reap the syndication income from successful drama series or sitcoms. Viacom is a massive video syndication company with a global reach, which includes properties such as MTV, Paramount Pictures, King World International (*Jeopardy* and *Wheel of Fortune*), United Paramount, Infinity Broadcasting, the publisher Simon & Schuster, and hundreds of movie theaters in Canada, Europe, and South America.

Federal regulators' decision to allow the merger reflects a current policy of permitting competition among corporate giants in order to facilitate the efficient and effective use of the market, rather than ruling them with a heavy hand. Now several Viacom brands will have to fight it out with the brands of other major conglomerates such as Disney, which owns ABC; News Corp, which owns Fox; Comcast, which owns NBC; and Time Warner. All of these corporations have major international holdings. They are able to use their North American consumer and studio base to produce videos and movies for domestic and foreign television and theaters, as well as software for their Internet sites. Their Internet activities are expanding globally as these firms put greater resources and strategic emphasis on Internet initiatives, many of which are joint ventures. These North American communication conglomerates almost always cover the costs of production through US revenues, and thus foreign markets, through syndication, represent substantial profits based on two large income streams – the US and global markets.

Viacom is an international stakeholder in major media markets ranging from motion pictures, to television, to publishing, to recreation, to video distribution (Table 7.5). Viacom owns Paramount Pictures, which began producing feature films as long ago as 1912, and controls Paramount's 2,500-strong (and growing) library of titles, which contains a number of classic feature films, along with the *Star Trek* and *Indiana Jones* movies, *Braveheart*, and *South Park*. In 2006 Paramount Pictures purchased DreamWorks and in 2013, not to be outdone by Disney, agreed to open three new theme parks in Russia. Animated characters from the *Shrek*, *Kung Fu Panda*, and *Madagascar* films will likely find a substantial role at the new theme parks.

In terms of television, the major products are produced through Paramount Television as well as CBS, MTV, Nickelodeon, VH1, Nick at Nite, Black Entertainment Television (BET), and Showtime. Through its holdings, Viacom controls the libraries of major series such as *I Love Lucy*, *The Honeymooners*, *Star Trek*, *Beverly Hills 90210*, and *Cheers*. It also controls Spelling Entertainment, which in turn controls the syndication rights of 16,000 television episodes, including international markets.

Viacom also offers the Paramount channel in Europe, distributed as part of a multichannel package on Rupert Murdoch's satellite system BSkyB. In television broadcasting, Viacom owns 19 TV stations in the United States through its subsidiary Paramount Stations Group. These stations are located primarily in major cities and reach 25 percent of US TV-viewing households.

In Latin America, Paramount, MCA, MGM, and Fox have a joint interest in Cinecanal for Spanish-speaking Latin America and in Telecine for Brazil. These two networks combined reach approximately two million subscribers.

Table 7.5 Major Viacom holdings, 2013

Addictinggames
BET Networks
CMT
Comedy Central
Gametrailers
Logo
MTV (and subsidiaries)
MTV 2
mtvU
Neopets
Nick at Night
Nick Junior
Nickelodeon (and subsidiaries)
Paramount Pictures
Paramount Television
Paramount Vantage
Parentsconnect
Shockwave (online and mobile games)
Spike TV
Teen Nick
TV Land
VH1 (and subsidiaries)
Viacom International Media Network

Viacom is a diversified entertainment and publishing company with operations in four areas: networks and broadcasting, entertainment, video and music/theme parks, and publishing. Viacom's future plans are clear. The major changes will be dealing with the growth and expansion of MTV, which went international in 1986, Nickelodeon, and BET. Nickelodeon and the Media Group have introduced plans to launch Nickelodeon in Turkey as well as other countries. Viacom hopes to have Nickelodeon spread worldwide so that it can meet the demand for expanding markets with network shows and movies that have proved successful in the United States. That is why Viacom created a new international media network in 2011.

CBS Corporation

In 2005, under the direction of the controlling shareholder and chairman Sumner Redstone, the assets of Viacom were split into two separate companies – CBS and Viacom. CBS consists of 22 units (see Table 7.6).

Table 7.6 Major CBS Corporation holdings, 2013

CBS Connections
CBS Consumer Products
CBS Entertainment
CBS Films
CBS Home Entertainment
CBS Interactive
CBS News
CBS Sports
CBS Outdoor
CBS Radio
CBS Scene
CBS Sports Network
CBS Studios International
CBS Television Distribution
CBS Television network
CBS Television Stations
CBS Television Studios
The CW
ECOMedia
Showtime
Simon & Schuster
The Watch Magazine

Why is ECT reflecting the global scene, particularly as it pertains to the spread of a Western model of culture and media influence? The following is one example of how the industry in general is spreading its influence around the globe.

> CBS Studios International is the leading supplier of programming to the international television marketplace, licensing to more than 200 markets in more than 30 languages across multiple media platforms. The Studio participates in international channel ventures, currently comprised of 22 channels in 20 languages across 87 territories, reaching more than 100 million international households. CBS Studios International also exports a diverse lineup of formats for local production around the world. The division distributes content from CBS Television Studios, CBS Television Distribution, Showtime, CBS News, CBS Films and a library of more than 70,000 hours of programming. CBS Studios International is a division of CBS Corporation.[17]

This unit of CBS, along with similar ones across the industry, represents the foot-soldiers advancing the application of ECT.

In 2006 CBS hired Katie Couric as the first female solo anchor of a network newscast. She came from NBC's *Today Show* and signed a contract that made her the highest-paid anchor in the world. But to CBS's chagrin the ratings did not follow their bold move. Couric consistently lagged behind her two competitors on ABC and NBC. Couric had replaced Dan Rather who had been the anchor for 24 years but was pushed out by CBS senior management over the veracity of a piece Rather had done which was critical of President Bush's military service. Rather has filed a lawsuit for wrongful dismissal which is working its way through the US court system; he claims that CBS management caved in to White House pressure to remove him.

Summary

Viacom has major global interests ranging from Paramount Pictures, BET, and MTV, which are particularly attractive to advertisers because of their global niche market; to strong publishing interests in CBS's Simon & Schuster; and syndicated television programming on various global satellite systems. Viacom and CBS International have been active in promoting regional global markets, including Australia, Latin America, and particularly Asia. Viacom is also a major player in international theatrical exhibition operations, with a number of cinemas around the globe. CBC Radio, formerly Infinity Broadcasting Corporation, operates nearly 200 radio stations. Finally, Viacom's profits come from a mix of revenue sources. The primary source is advertising revenue from its media brands, particularly MTV and BET; another source of revenue is sales of books and movie ticket purchases for its Paramount Productions.

Comcast

In 2011 the largest US cable operator, Comcast, purchased NBCUniversal from General Electric for $30 billion. Comcast itself owned the Golf Channel, E! Entertainment, and Versus, plus an NHL hockey team and its arena in Philadelphia. As a cable operator, it offers multichannel video programming, Internet, and phone service. The merger with NBCUniversal brought with it several properties, such as the NBC Television Network, Brave, CNBC, MSNBC, Oxygen, Syfy, Telemundo, part interest in Hulu, Universal Pictures, Focus Features, Weather Channel, and a 50 percent interest in Europe's Canal+ and StudioCanal (see Table 7.7). NBC Sports is a major player across several professional leagues, and has the rights to the Olympic Games. Comcast's cable systems offer international fare in the following languages: Arabic, Chinese, Filipino, French, German, Greek, Israeli, Italian, Japanese, Korean, Polish, Portuguese, Russian, and Vietnamese. It is too early to determine the success and synergy of cable and video being merged, but as discussed earlier the 2000 merger of Time Warner and AOL did not turn out well.

NBC operates the 24-hour cable channels CNBC and MSNBC. While it is home to such hits as *The Tonight Show with Jay Leno*, *Saturday Night Live*, *Late Night with Carson Daly*, and *The Apprentice*, the network is losing market share to cable channels and the Internet.

NBC is a global media company with broadly diverse holdings that consist of the following elements: NBC Television Network, NBC-owned and operated stations, NBC Entertainment, NBC News, NBC Sports, CNBC, MSNBC, NBC Cable, NBC International, NBC Interactive, and MSNBC Desktop Video. NBC has been setting industry standards in technology and programming for more than 70 years. It was the first network to broadcast in color, the first to broadcast in stereo, the first to present a made-for-TV movie, and the first to offer an early morning news program. It was also the first television network to broadcast both online and digitally.

Table 7.7 Major NBCUniversal holdings, 2013

Bravo
CNBC
CNBC Europe
CNBC Asia
Focus Features
MSNBC (82%)
Mun2
NBC Television Network
NBCUniversal Television
Oxygen
SyFy
Telemundo
USA Network
Universal Pictures
Universal Production Studios
Universal Studios Theme Parks

NBC's first major organizational change came in 1986 when GE acquired RCA and thereby became NBC's parent company. Then in 1993 NBC launched Canal de Noticias NBC, a 24-hour Spanish-language news service, across Latin America. In 1994 Canal de Noticias NBC debuted on cable stations in the United States. In 1996 NBC became the number one prime-time network in every category, ahead of ABC and CBS. In 1999 NBC agreed to acquire a 32 percent stake in Paxson Communications Corp, based in West Palm Beach, Florida, for $415 million. The agreement combined NBC's powerful brand name and broadcast group with Paxson, owner of the largest number of television stations in the United States. NBC said the move provided a second national distribution outlet for NBC programming while giving Paxson additional resources to strengthen its broadcast group and PAX TV network. In 2004 GE made a dramatic and significant media move in acquiring an 80 percent stake in Universal Television and Movies. The renamed NBCUniversal is now a much larger global stakeholder in the evolving global multimedia sector.

NBCUniversal operates in four divisions: network, production, film, and theme parks. The networks are now extensive and most are carried on cable and satellite channels around the world. NBCUniversal television has 14 owned and operated stations along with 200 affiliates. It also controls Telemundo, a large Spanish-language network, with 15 owned and operated stations and 32 affiliates. Telemundo is carried by nearly 450 cable systems. Telemundo Internacional is available in over 20 of the largest markets across Latin America.

The other NBCUniversal networks are mun2, a Latino network aimed at MTV's teenage audience; the SyFy channel; and the USA Network. Off-shore, there are NBC Europe; CNBC Europe, which reaches 85 million households; and CNBC Asia Pacific, which reaches 30 million. In film, it is a major stakeholder in Universal Pictures. Under its new ownership the corporate strategy is aimed at global expansion. It also controls Focus Feature, which is a worldwide film distribution company. Finally, in addition to Universal

Studios theme parks in the United States, it also has parks and resorts in Japan, Singapore, and Spain, among other places.

NBC also became the main broadcaster for the international Olympic Games. NBC broadcast the Summer Olympics from Atlanta, Georgia in 1996; from Sydney, Australia in 2000; and from Athens, Greece in 2004, marking the fifth straight Summer Olympics broadcast by NBC. NBCUniversal Sports also broadcast the 2008 games from Beijing, China. NBC also had the rights to the 2006 and 2008 Winter Games.

Bravo

Acquired by NBC in 2002, Bravo is an arts and culture network with over 80 million households across North America having access to it. A number of foreign satellite and cable systems also carry the upscale shows, such as the Montreal-based Cirque du Soleil.

CNBC

Two of the world's leading media companies, Dow Jones and NBC, came together in December 1997 to create the Consumer News and Business Channel (CNBC). This global alliance was a powerful combination: Dow Jones produces vital world business and financial news and information, while the NBC is the leading television network in the United States. This move united the world's most recognized business news brands including the *Wall Street Journal*, CNBC, and Dow Jones. CNBC is available to 175 million households worldwide, and is watched by millions of people around the globe every day. As baby boomers start worrying about retirement, they focus on investing their money, and CNBC has the pertinent information to answer their questions.

Discovery Communications

Discovery Communications is the world's leading non-fiction media company. It reaches more than 1.8 billion viewers in over 218 countries. It has 155 networks and works in 35 languages. Some of its more popular channels are Animal Planet, Discovery Kids, Discovery Channel, Science Channel, TLC, and Planet Green.

It was founded in 1985. In 1987 it began televising live Russian shows to its US subscribers and launched its Discovery Channel in England in 1989 and across Latin America in 1994. The company also owns patents for e-books and has four digital media sites, HowStuffWorks, TreeHugger, Revision3, and Petfinder. The firm also has a joint venture in the United States with the Oprah Winfrey Network (OWN).

Gannett Company, Inc.

The Gannett Company is an international, diversified news and information company. It is the United States' largest newspaper company in terms of circulation, owning 84 dailies, including *United States Today*. *United States Today* has a circulation of over 2.3 million and is available in over 60 nations worldwide. In the United States Gannett also owns 23 television stations, reaching millions of viewers. Gannett also produces *USA Today*, one of the major Internet newspaper sites in the world. It is also expanding its digital presence on the Internet and developing mobile apps in both the United States and the United Kingdom.

Recently it increased its online presence with CareerBuilder, JobsCentral, 10Best, and MobestreamMedia.

Gannett has operations in the United Kingdom, Belgium, Germany, Italy, and China. In the United Kingdom it owns 17 dailies and NewsQuest, which controls over 200 regional papers, magazines, and trade publications. NewsQuest also has over 80 Internet sites.

Walmart International

This retail juggernaut now has stores in 27 foreign regions. Walmart International employs over 800,000 workers in Argentina, Brazil, Canada, Chile, China, Costa Rica, El Salvador, the European Union, Honduras, India, Japan, Korea, Mexico, Nicaragua, and other countries. Annual sales in these foreign nations are over $100 billion and growing rapidly. It plans to open over 200 new stores in outside the United States annually.

Walmart controls over 2,300 stores in Mexico alone. The international division is the fastest growing part of the entire company. In time there will be more stores outside the United States than within it, and eventually the top management will come from the international division.

In terms of multimedia, Walmart has two sectors: retail store sales and Internet sales. It is the fastest growing media seller in both categories. For example, its stores sell computers, iPads, iPods, tablets, DVDs, CDs, video game systems, and books. They sell more DVDs than any other retailer and are the largest retailer of new blockbuster films. They are Hollywood's largest customer, with over 50 percent of all DVD and Blu-ray sales.

On Walmart.com four media products are offered: (1) DVD rentals via mail in direct competition with Netflix and Blockbuster; (2) music downloads at less than $1 per song from any genre; (3) sales of DVDs, Blu-rays, and other products with an audiovisual connection; and (4) a streaming video service, Vudu, which is number three behind Netflix and Microsoft's Xbox music/video.

Another example of Walmart's power lies in consumer electronics. Sales of these units are second only to BestBuy, and more than all other outlets combined. When Walmart sells the hardware, like a DVD player; gaming devices like Nintendo, Xbox PlayStation; or a CD player, it also sells the software as well. This connection gives it a major advantage over competitors who tend to sell or rent one or the other.

Some musicians are now signing exclusive contracts with Walmart. For example, Garth Brooks released an exclusive box set through Walmart and on the first day alone sold more than a half million copies. It also set records for pre-orders on Walmart.com. Other artists, such as Journey and the Eagles are lining up to be the next commercial success via a Walmart exclusive. The Eagles' first double CD set for Walmart has sold over three million.

Walmart is a new global stakeholder not only in terms of international communication but also because of its enormous purchasing power and number of global outlets. It represents a major future player in the telecommunications sector. It also brings with it market clout, controversy, and a strong orientation to free enterprise. It is a serious and effective promoter of electronic colonialism wherever it goes. Walmart personifies US values and commercial culture. But it is also known for being anti-union and seems to actively promote an adversarial labor management environment. For example, senior management made a grave error of judgment when they openly campaigned against the election of Barack Obama, who supports fair wages and non-discrimination, particularly against women. Walmart has faced a large number of class-action lawsuits filed by women over wages and other discrimination issues. Finally, the company and the founder's family foundation have provided millions of dollars in funding to right-wing extremist groups such as the Heritage Foundation to attack pro-union legislation everywhere.

Virgin Media Inc.

Virgin Media came from the merger of Telewest and NTL in 2006 and the subsequent merger in 2007 with Virgin Mobile. It is an American-owned company which operates primarily in the United Kingdom and Ireland, offering digital cable, digital terrestrial television, Internet, mobile, and telephone services. Its main competitors are BSkyB and Freeview. Virgin Media Television also operates several cable channels and websites in the United Kingdom.

Advance Publications Inc.

Advance Publications is a private American company controlled by the Newhouse family. It owns 25 newspapers, business journals, cable interests, Fairchild and Parade publications, *Golf Digest*, Condé Nast publications, and Internet and website businesses. Condé Nast publishes some of the world's most prestigious magazines, including *Vogue*, *Glamour*, *Allure*, *GQ*, *Brides*, *Vanity Fair*, *Wired*, and the *New Yorker*, and also oversees 28 websites.

The Nielsen Company

The American Nielsen Company was formed in 2007 as a result of the buy-out of the Netherlands-based VNU. VNU, founded in 1964, was a global information and multimedia company with interests in over 100 countries. In 1999 VNU bought Nielsen Media Research and formed the subsidiary ACNielsen, which lasted until 2007. Nielsen Media Research dates back to 1923, when Arthur C. Nielsen founded a research company which evolved into the ratings giant which provides clients with data on what consumers watch and buy.

Nielsen provides data on television, radio, Internet, mobile, and print in over 100 countries. Through Nielsen Monitor Plus, a media-buying and advertising information service, Nielsen measures over 85 percent of the globe's advertising expenditures. Nielsen/NetRating is the leading service for monitoring and analyzing Internet use, including tracking online advertisements. This firm tracks more than 70 percent of the globe's Internet traffic.

Finally, Nielsen Media Research provides detailed information of television viewership in the United States for over one million households. This unit accounts for one-quarter of the company's revenue. In recent years some of its data collection methods and analysis have come under criticism.

In terms of ECT the Nielsen subsidiaries are prime examples of how core-based firms control much of the data about electronic and print media. The wealth of data, knowledge, and analysis provided by Nielsen to subscribers is enormous, across a vast range of commercial multimedia lines. The advertising giants, for example, are all based in core nations. They have clients in almost all the semiperipheral nations and some peripheral ones as well. Yet the data and research provided to them by Nielsen serves a twofold purpose: (1) to strengthen and fine-tune what they are already doing for their existing client base, and (2) to recruit new clients by impressing them with their arsenal of data and services. For any totally new ad firm to emerge or for any firm based in a semiperipheral nation to become a major ad agency is almost impossible. This phenomenon and the reality of the global role and scope of the existing ad agencies, in partnership with Nielsen, make the quest for more customers for core media products easier because the basic research and strategy works relatively well.

The goal of expanding its base to understand in greater detail how the mind works prompted Nielsen to two specific acquisitions. The first was a move to acquire IAG Research in 2008. IAG Research deals with research into advertisement performance and effectiveness. It measures all ads and product placements on television every night. IAG Research also tracks ad effectiveness on the Internet and in movie theaters. The second was the acquisition, also in 2008, of NeuroFocus, a company using cutting-edge neuroscience brainwave monitoring of customers with offices across the United States, Europe, Israel, and Asia. They study how the human brain works, particularly as it responds to ads and messages using the medical procedure called electroencephalography (EEG). EEG monitors the electrical activity of the brain. NeuroFocus offers clients, including some of the biggest brands in the world, six product lines or services: advertising effectiveness, brand and image analysis, competitive advertising intelligence, product pricing analysis, and neuroinformatics database.

These two companies add to the global arsenal of Nielsen as it moves to the next level of its measurement activities, whereby it does not ask viewers what they think, but rather looks directly into the brain and records on a monitor what they are thinking. This is central to the theory of electronic colonialism. And Nielsen is not alone in this type of cutting-edge research. Google, Microsoft, Yahoo!, Netflix also have confidential algorithms which predict human behavior.

In 2010 a new consortium emerged to attempt to compete with Nielsen Ratings. This group, made up of major media companies as well as advertisers and advertising firms, has lodged a series of complaints concerning the accuracy of Nielsen's ratings. In particular, it plans to focus on measuring new media such as websites and mobile devices. It also plans to focus on streaming video or peer-to-peer (P2P) file-sharing and Skype in order to determine what will happen to traditional communication networks and Hollywood productions.

Conclusions

Globally there is an expansion of movie theaters, cable systems, satellite distribution systems, personal computers, music, DVDs, CDs, video outlets, and mobile digital devices. This infrastructure is fueling substantial expansion by global communication firms. In particular, US multinational communication corporations such as Disney, News Corp, GE, Time Warner, Dow Jones, Gannett, Viacom, Walmart, and others are strategically repositioning themselves as global corporations rather than as US communication firms. Their future success and earnings are more and more dependent on emerging markets and international sales. As their Internet and other off-shore assets grow, they are being propelled into a highly competitive global marketplace. In their corporate annual reports, as well as in other company documents reflecting strategic planning, the dominant theme is globalization and their increasing role in that milieu. In the future, continuing global off-shore growth for these US-based communication companies will exceed domestic corporate growth.

The growth and impact of US multimedia firms have changed considerably. The move of News Corp from Australia to America represented an enormous net gain for the US media sector. At the same time it represented a net loss to another core nation, Australia. For Australia, the advantage of having the English language could further propel it to become even more of an electronic communication colony of US popular culture. Some Australian critics of the News Corp move to New York City cited cultural and employment issues in their futile opposition to the relocation. Australia and several other nations are likely to continue to lose their bright young talent to Hollywood and New York. The likes of Nicole Kidman, Mel Gibson, Russell Crowe, Paul Hogan, Helen Reddy, and Olivia Newton-John represent a talent drain that is only going to increase as Australia becomes an even greater media outpost and electronic colony of US cultural goods. For most foreign actors, directors, and musicians, working in the United States represents the epitome of success, both professionally and financially.

Because the United States is the leading core nation, these corporations have become aggressive in other core nations in both Europe[18] and Asia.[19] At the same time, they have expanded into the semiperipheral nations because these nations represent substantial new markets where there is strong demand for US products of all types, ranging from CDs and DVDs, to iPods, to the Internet. These semiperipheral nations also have the greatest number of potential new customers with discretionary disposable income. They represent a new customer base for all the major US communication empires. The emerging markets, particularly Brazil, China, and India, will grow faster than the more mature markets across core nations.

A good example of global expansion is Disney's theme park in Hong Kong, developed in conjunction with Chinese authorities. Clearly, Disney is positioning itself to use the Hong Kong site as a gateway to the immense Chinese market during the twenty-first century. There are already moves to expand the park. A related expansion into China took place in the 1990s as Rupert Murdoch recognized that his Asian satellite system, STAR TV, could potentially attract a multitude of new customers across China and the entire Pacific Rim. (See Chapter 14 for more on media activities in China and Asia.)

US media giants, with their advertising, products, and services, have inundated only a few peripheral nations. Most peripheral nations lack the necessary technical infrastructure, ability to provide security, or sufficient disposable income to make it economically worthwhile for these companies to establish major activities in these regions. At the same time, some of them are actively seeking to avoid contact with US popular and media culture. They are motivated by a desire to protect and promote their indigenous culture and traditional way of life, which is characterized by low technology, or by religious beliefs. Or it may be that authoritarian governments or anti-democratic leaders are limiting the contact they have with the developed nations.

Finally, these global media firms need to continue to grow if they want to remain competitive. Because the potential growth is greater off-shore, they will continue to direct greater efforts toward, and to place their best corporate executives in, global regions in order to produce the rate of return demanded by senior management and shareholders. This expansion occurs in unison with the activities of their advertising agencies. As such, the nations where they operate need to have a market-based economy for these firms to thrive, profit, and expand. Obviously, some of this expansion comes at the expense of indigenous production houses, or local advertising agencies. Because these US media conglomerates have enormous libraries of television and feature films, which have already been paid for as first-run productions in the large domestic market, they can compete aggressively internationally with an arsenal of video and audio products that can collectively swamp any foreign network or production house through sheer volume.

Notes

1. The emergence of global television has always had its critics. They focus primarily on the social, cultural, and political aspects of the global dissemination of popular shows. Most of the shows were American, with a few British shows doing well on a global scale. In the 1980s, the global success of Dallas became the rallying symbol for cultural nationalists in several nations. For a broad critique of this phenomena, see Cynthia Schneider and Brian Wallis (eds.), *Global Television*, Cambridge, MA: MIT Press, 1988, and Richard Gershon, *The Transnational Media Corporation*, Mahwah, NJ: Lawrence Erlbaum, 1997.

2. Europe and most of Europe's former colonies refer to multimedia as audiovisual products. A prime example of this, including a broad, detailed description of the concerns and challenges, is contained in the European Commission's *Study on Economic Implications of New Communication Technologies on the Audio-Visual Markets*, Brussels: European Communities, 1998.

3. Steven Watts, *The Magic Kingdom: Walt Disney and the American Way of Life*, Boston: Houghton Mifflin, 1998.

4. Bob Thomas, *Building a Company: Roy O. Disney and the Creation of an Entertainment Empire*, Boston: Hyperion, 1999.

5. The Chinese government's approval of a major Hollywood-based theme park occurred in the same year that China entered the World Trade Organization (WTO). The two events were not unrelated. China is attempting to reposition itself as a modern global player in the communication industry. By joining the WTO, it has agreed to open its telecommunications market, to allow foreign firms to provide Internet services, and to increase the number of US feature films it imports. Beijing was the host city for the Summer Olympics in 2008. Clearly, these activities, along with Disney's activities in Hong Kong, reflect the acceptance of US business practices, information technologies, and popular culture. In return, China will no doubt attempt to export more of its goods and services to core nations, particularly the United States. At the same time, however, China has become market-sensitive – it wants to participate and to follow the rules and regulations, including the dispute resolution mechanisms available through the Geneva-based WTO. Although China still cracks down on cyber cafes and is repressive with dissidents, it still aims to move from semiperipheral status to core status by 2020. The European-based Reporters Sans Frontières (Reporters Without Borders) lists China as one of the worst countries for press freedom on the planet. Finally, the Disney Corporation, along with other major US corporations, would not be making major long-term investments in China if it thought these investments would either fail or be confiscated by the Chinese authorities. Although there is no written agreement that the Chinese will not do this, they are clearly indicating through a broad range of activities that they want to participate in the global information society of the twenty-first century, and eventually on an equal basis. However, their repressive practices against progressive media systems surface far too frequently.

6. James Stewart, *Disneywar: The Battle for the Magic Kingdom*, New York: Simon & Schuster, 2004. Two additional books which trace Disney's influence are Janet Wasko, *Understanding Disney: The Manufacture of Fantasy*, Oxford: Blackwell, 2001; and Janet Wasko, M. Phillips, and E. Meehan (eds.), *Dazzled by Disney?*, London: Leicester University Press, 2002.

7. In 2007 the European Commission asked the European Audiovisual Observatory (www.obs.coe.int) to collect information on all pan-European television broadcasting channels. The data base on more than 6,000 channels is available through MAVISE (www.mavise.obs.coe.int). It is the most up-to-date and comprehensive data about the television sector across Europe. It also contains foreign, mostly American, channels as well. The impact of these American channels and other cultural matters in Europe is detailed in Chapter 9.

8. Rupert Murdoch's various dealings have come under criticism around the globe. One of the better summaries is contained in Russ Baker's piece in the *Columbia Journalism Review* of May/June 1998.

9. News Corp's global media ventures have a major strategic asset that other global competitors frequently do not. Its control of STAR TV in Asia, BSkyB in Europe, as well as several other satellite and cable ventures, allows these networks to draw from the extensive library of software produced by the various Fox production facilities. Through their control of 20th Century Fox Studios, Fox Broadcasting, Fox News, Fox Family Channel, Fox Sports Net, and 22 US-based Fox television stations, News Corp media and systems managers around the globe have a ready and lucrative arsenal. Fox shows and channels provide the Murdoch Group with an enormous competitive advantage compared to the competition, which must attempt to outbid each other in order to purchase syndication game and drama shows, movies, or other programming materials.

10. "News International and Phone-Hacking," British House of Commons Culture, Media and Sport Committee, 11th Report of Session 2010–12, May 2012, p. 84.

11. Alan Cowell, "Britain: Newspapers Protest New Press Rules," *New York Times* (March 20, 2013), A6.

12. W. A. Swanberg, *Luce and His Empire*, New York: Scribner's, 1972.

13. Gerald Levin, "The Legacy of Henry Luce: Values for the Digital Age," speech to the Aspen Institute, August 7, 1999, Aspen, CO, p. 2.

14. Levin, "The Legacy of Henry Luce," pp. 2, 4.

15. Nina Munk, *Fools Rush In: Steve Case, Jerry Levin, and the Unmasking of AOL Time Warner*, New York: Harper Business, 2004.

16. Tony Chiu, *CBS: The First 50 Years*, New York: General Publishing, 1999.

17. http://www.cbscorporation.com/portfolio.php?division=99, accessed August 19, 2013.

18. Reinhold Wagnleitner, "The Empire of the Fun, or Talkin' Soviet Union Blues: The Sound of Freedom and US Cultural Hegemony in Europe," *Diplomatic History* 23(3) (1999), 499–524.

19. Srinivas Melkote, Peter Shields, and Binod Agrawel (eds.), *International Satellite Broadcasting in South Asia*, Lanham, MD: University Press of America, 1998.

8

Stakeholders of Multimedia Conglomerates Outside the United States

Introduction

Although some global media systems such as CNN, MTV, BBC, Disney, News Corporation, and the Internet come to mind as high-profile stakeholders in the global media world, there are clearly other major players. This chapter details the major global media stakeholders outside the United States and describes their various communication interests. Although the United States frequently attracts substantial criticism for exporting a culture of Hollywood sex and violence and for dominating music videos, television, and theater screens around the world, some of the major global enterprises, such as Sony, Vivendi, Bertelsmann, and others, are foreign-owned multimedia corporations.

For example, Japan's Sony Corporation controls Columbia Pictures; properties and brands of Germany's Bertelsmann include Random House, GEO, ArvatoAG, and the RTL Group; France's Lagardère publishes *Elle*, *Car and Driver*, and several other magazines; Vivendi controls Universal Music Group and video-game maker Activision Blizzard. This chapter details these global media conglomerates and others. The British Broadcasting Corporation, frequently regarded as the gold standard of public broadcasting, is covered in Chapter 11, as a global competitor to CNN.

Cultural Imperialism

In the 1960s and 1970s, critical scholars produced a body of literature on the subject of cultural imperialism.[1] These scholars condemn the United States' role in global media expansion. Some of this criticism found its way into the rhetoric of UNESCO in the 1980s

Global Communication: Theories, Stakeholders, and Trends, Fourth Edition. Thomas L. McPhail.
© 2014 John Wiley & Sons, Inc. Published 2014 by John Wiley & Sons, Inc.

and continues to be repeated by people promoting an anti-American agenda. The agenda seeks to re-ignite the support for NWICO and to promote a more equitable and balanced flow of media in the international arena. Without going into detail about the origins of cultural imperialism, it is worth noting that there is simply no monolithic US global media empire. Although there is a global media empire, the media corporations are from various nation-states, which are all located in core nations. They work in different languages with different interests and strategies, rather than promoting a simplistic New York–Los Angeles plot to capture the minds of unsuspecting foreigners. From records and CDs, to movies, magazines, television, and the Internet, there is a great global mix of ownership among the current major multimedia stakeholders. This globalization and consolidation of the communications industry is going to increase and expand over time. About the only common denominator of the several far-flung global stakeholders is the desire to make a profit by expanding their audience size or share. They seek more customers to generate greater profits in order to keep their respective senior management, owners, and shareholders happy. All are looking at emerging markets for future growth.

Concerns about the possible effects of the mass media on individuals and cultures have been a preoccupation of academics since World War II. Much of the research focused on the impact of the media on developed core nations, particularly the United States, Canada, and Europe.[2] But a small number of critical scholars began to examine the impact of the media on the less developed peripheral nations and look at issues such as power, domination, economic determinism, and other variables.[3] The "Made in America" label began to take on different meanings to different researchers. But it was Herbert I. Schiller[4] who focused in a theoretical way on issues such as global ownership, one-way flow of information, power, cultural aspects, and the impact of advertising. Schiller studied the ways in which core-based media industries were having a deleterious effect on indigenous industries in peripheral and semiperipheral countries, as well as how these industries were drawing economic resources, such as box office revenues, from both industrialized and non-industrialized nations around the world for the financial benefit of Hollywood or New York. In the 1970s the literature on cultural imperialism began to look at other media systems as well, from records, tapes, video games, and television, to advertising and children's paraphernalia, particularly Disney products and parks. There was growing criticism and documentation of US media giants by a small cadre of critical scholars. But in 1988 many of these scholars were taken aback when Japan's Sony Corporation paid $5 billion to acquire Columbia Pictures. The Hollywood film landscape began to change dramatically as this merger was rapidly followed by other US industries being bought by foreign corporations as part of the expanding global economy. Many of these transactions and the foreign stakeholders involved are detailed later in this chapter.

The significant point here is that, although the theory of cultural imperialism was gaining credence as a negative model of global relationships, Sony's deal forced scholars to rethink the question of who owns what and for whom. The problem became a transnational issue rather than a purely Hollywood or "Made in America" one, as critics had contended for decades. The literature and momentum of critical scholars became stale and lost their spark during the 1990s as major foreign media corporations changed the global media landscape. At one point in the 1970s, the United States dominated the global media system to an extent it had not done before or since. Beginning in the 1980s, with the take-over of some Hollywood studios by foreign corporations; the move of British, German, French, and Canadian companies into global cultural industries; and the entrance of the then Australian-based News Corporation into television and satellite businesses in North America, Europe, and Asia, a highly competitive global media marketplace began to develop. It functions to maximize profits from various global profit centers with little regard for national concerns, culture, language, or academic critics, except when they interfere with the economic goals of these far-flung media empires.

The following sections document the extensive penetration of Europe, Japan, and other countries into US and global markets by virtue of their investments in a broad range of cultural products that are made and primarily consumed in the United States. A model example of this is News Corporation, formerly based and incorporated in Australia but which received 75 percent of its revenues and profits from operations in the United States. Reincorporating in the United States was a logical move for News Corp. All giant foreign media corporations are in direct and daily competition with US giants such as Time Warner, Viacom, ComcastNBC, and Disney.

The United States of Europe

Europe's television, movie, music, cable, and satellite industries are experiencing an unprecedented frenzy of consolidation. The 28 EU nations are working more and more as a collective rather than as individual nations when it comes to international media. In addition, the European Union is constructing trans-European communication policies. Thus, the concept of a United States of Europe (USE) is a valid construct.

Historically, the origins of the United States of Europe can be traced to the period immediately after World War II. In 1951 the European Coal and Steel Community was established under French leadership. The six members were Belgium, West Germany, Luxembourg, France, Italy, and the Netherlands. The agreement reduced barriers hindering cooperation and encouraged joint ventures in the two strategic industries, coal and steel. The idea was such a great success that the six countries decided to expand the concept to other sectors. They did so and created a "common market" free of trade barriers and tariffs with the 1957 Treaty of Rome. Institutions, laws, regulations, policies, strategic planning, and in 2002 a new currency, the euro, were designed to create a single seamless market leading to the United States of Europe. This standardization and consolidation also impacted their cultural industries, or as Europeans refer to them, audiovisual industries. Today the USE stands at 28 member nations with eight more nations seeking admission. In 2004 alone 10 new members, mostly former Soviet-dominated countries, joined the union, followed by Bulgaria and Romania in 2007. One of the possible new entrants is Turkey, which has a large Muslim population – this will alter the cultural environment across the USE. The current population of the USE is larger than that of the United States.

Considering that prior to 1980 almost all European television and cable systems were either strictly government-controlled or government-owned, the recent merger mania is new to the European communications industry. With liberalization and deregulation in the 1980s, there was a substantial wave of privatization of radio, television, and cable systems across Europe, as well as the addition of several new commercial channels. A third wave of activity is now taking place in which transnational communication corporations are becoming larger and larger as they purchase smaller systems across Europe, start entirely new channels or networks, or buy foreign multimedia outlets, prompting some critics to call these countries collectively the "United States of Europe" (Table 8.1).

The motivation for this activity is straightforward. John Tagliabue puts it this way: "What is causing this frenzy of reorganization? Mainly, the global economy, which is forcing Europe's relatively small players to join forces to cover the costs of switching to digital and pay per view TV and of marketing integrated bundles of television, telephone and Internet services."[5] These combined and larger media companies are in a better competitive position because they can offer a larger audience to advertisers, or a larger number of cable subscribers, to generate the revenues necessary to upgrade cable systems to make them Internet-ready. A

Table 8.1 Top 10 European major communication stakeholders by revenue, 2013

1	Bertelsmann (Germany)
2	Vivendi (France)
3	Lagardère (France)
4	BSkyB (United Kingdom)
5	Pearson (United Kingdom)
6	Reed Elsevier (The Netherlands/United Kingdom)
7	ARD/Deutsche Welle (Germany)
8	BBC (United Kingdom)
9	Mediaset (Italy)
10	Virgin Media (United Kingdom)

Source: Nordicom.

related phenomenon in the United States of Europe is that more commercial corporations are designing advertising and programs for a pan-European audience. Advertisers want to deal with major trans-European broadcasters for a single package rather than with small individual media outlets on a city-by-city or country-by country basis.

The future media environment of the United States of Europe will ultimately resemble the US model of large national entities such as ABC, CBS, Fox, and NBC, in which each has a number of major regional affiliates. In Europe there will be major new conglomerates, created through the consolidation of smaller national-based systems that are reaching out to a pan-European audience. Many European communication corporations realize that they need to engage in pan-European merger activities or they will be purchased by some other major stakeholder, or be left behind altogether. If they do not expand, they will be left with smaller audiences and reduced revenues in an era when production costs and competition for both European and US television series and movies continue to escalate.

Seen through the lens of world system theory, the following communication corporations are all based in core nations much like the United States. These nations exhibit similar traits that make them highly competitive: a high gross national product (GNP), heavy deployment of information technologies, and a sophisticated and well-educated labor force. These European core nations are also expanding as rapidly as possible into other core as well as semiperipheral nations. Geographically, they have an advantage because many of the semiperipheral nations are adjacent to the European community. Peripheral nations around the globe are in many cases former colonies of European nations. On the one hand, this may give the USE an advantage in marketing their communication products and systems to peripheral nations. On the other hand, deep-seated antagonism and a legacy of hostility between the colonies and their former European masters might prevent some peripheral nations from doing business with their former colonizers.

A final point is that in the United States cultural industries and their products are viewed as economic entities, but across Europe and elsewhere these same industries are viewed through a very different prism. Cultural industries or audiovisual industries are regarded as part of European culture, history, and artistic heritage. Europeans are much more concerned with their language, culture, and employment opportunities in media industries, and with preserving their history, and do not regard media productions as being economic products like cornflakes, apples, lumber, or cars. This is reflected in the many public policies on and significant financial subsidies for cultural activities that are promoted and encouraged in

European nations. The USE is concerned about the cultural homogenization of media industries if they follow a US formula and model. The leadership for the cultural sectors across Europe is assigned to various ministers of culture, which is a high-ranking cabinet post in almost all nations. An example to illustrate this important point follows.

The European Union provides specific grants to stimulate the development and distribution of European media productions. The goal is to increase quality and make available trans-European films and television programs across five genres or formats: fiction for television and cinema, movies, documentaries, animation, and new media. The European Union also underwrites writing workshops for various media and seminars about new media technologies. Since 2000 this program, entitled Media Plus, has a budget of over $2.5 billion. Most of the funding goes toward increasing the circulation of European films across Europe and the world. Media Plus funded the post-production and marketing of the films *March of the Penguins* (2005), *The Lives of Others* (2006), and *The Counterfeiters* (2007), all three of which won Oscars. About 300 new films are funded by this program annually. The goal is to push a trans-European perspective onto global screens of all sizes. The hope is to compete with Hollywood for eyeballs as well as revenue.

One of the key acts was to create the European Audiovisual Observatory in December 1992:

> the only centre of its kind to gather and circulate information on the audiovisual industry in Europe. The Observatory is a European public service body with 39 member States and the European Union, represented by the European Commission. It owes its origins to Audiovisual Eureka and operates within the legal framework of the Council of Europe. It works alongside a number of partner organisations, professional organisations from within the industry and a wide network of correspondents.[6]

The goals of the observatory are twofold: (1) to create transparency in the audiovisual sector, and (2) to provide data for experts in the business and academic sectors. The observatory's stated mission is "a challenge for Europe."

Basically the EU is trying to create a pan-European effort to stem the growing threat of becoming an electronic colony of US media empires. The EU wants the audiovisual talent and media profits to remain in European hands.

> The audiovisual sector is one of the fastest growing areas of the European economy and a leading global market. The internationalisation and integration of what were previously mostly national media landscapes, boosted by rapid technical progress, mean that the audiovisual sector now stands out above other branches of the economy.[7]

In general, European leaders are well aware of the significance of developing supportive public policies as well as of financial incentives in order to have major stakeholders in a audiovisual sector that can compete on the world stage – primarily against American players.

Bertelsmann

The German-based Bertelsmann group of companies has a strong media presence in over 50 countries worldwide. It is the seventh largest media company globally. Carl Bertelsmann established the company in 1835 as a religious publishing house. While remaining a private company, it now has five major operating units worldwide and a revenue in the billions. Its interests lie in newspapers, magazines, printing, print distribution, broadcasting, music rights management, and various media investments.

Bertelsmann's interests in magazine and newspaper publishing are carried out through its Gruner + Jahr subsidiary, which publishes 285 magazines and newspapers in over 20 countries. Bertelsmann holds a 75 percent stake in Gruner + Jahr. It is also the sole owner of Random House, the world's largest book publishing company. Through its Direct Group division, Bertelsmann markets books to more than 15 million people throughout Europe, North America, Australia, and New Zealand through book clubs and book stores.

Bertelsmann also has major interests in television, owning 90.5 percent of the RTL Group (formerly CLT-UFA), the largest TV and radio group in Europe. The RTL Group was formed through the 2001 merger of CLT-UFA, Pearson TV, and Audiofina. The company has television stations in Germany, France, Spain, the Benelux countries, United Kingdom, Croatia, Greece, Hungary, and Russia. The German RTL Channel alone is the most successful advertising-financed commercial TV station in Europe. In addition to its TV station, RTL Radio targets listeners within a similar geographical market. Finally, the VOX station began airing in 1993, offering nationally informative programs and broadcasting live events. However, this proved unsuccessful and in the late 1990s, after a series of buy-outs, VOX switched its programming toward airing more US-produced series and movies, such as *CSI: New York*, *Gilmore Girls*, and *Six Feet Under*. RTL holds a 99.7 percent stake in the VOX channel. M6 is one of Bertelsmann's television stations in France. Within 10 years, M6 developed into the most profitable advertising-financed private TV station in France. The RTL Group holds a 48.8 percent stake in M6. In addition to the television stations, Bertelsmann owns UFA Film and TV Production. This division is located in Potsdam, Germany and produces 2,000 hours of television each year, making it one of Germany's largest production companies. Finally, one of Bertelsmann's television interests, UFA Sports in Hamburg, is Europe's leading TV sports marketing company.

In 2008 Sony music acquired what was until then known as the Bertelsmann Music Group (BMG), leaving behind only the BMG Rights Management division as a part of the Bertelsmann portfolio. In July of 2009 the American investment firm, Kohlberg Kravis Roberts & Co. (KKR), purchased 51 percent of BMG Rights and since then it has expanded its music catalog.

Internet investments and web-based activities have been uneven and troublesome for the company. In 2000 Bertelsmann ended its five-year partnership with AOL. It also helped prolong the life of Napster through a series of investments totaling more than $85 million and thus became a target for copyright infringement lawsuits which cost the company upward of $60 million in settlements. Bertelsmann's investment in Lycos ended when the company shareholders decided to liquidate it in 2008. Bertelsmann's online book site was a partnership with Barnes & Noble, and many of its multimedia activities were carried out in conjunction with the Axel Springer publishing house of Germany. In 2004 it sold its interest in Barnes & Noble Online back to Barnes & Noble, Inc. at a substantial loss. In 2008 the company published a hard-copy, condensed edition of the German Wikipedia site to a mixed reception. In 2009 Bertelsmann, under the RTL Group, purchased a German social networking site called Wer-Kennt-Wen (Who Knows Whom) which claims over 6.5 million users and has expanded into Austria and Switzerland. Additionally, Bertelsmann has also invested in Qeep, a social network for mobile phones. Both efforts have been touted as an attempt by Bertelsmann to break into the MySpace market to become a direct competitor with the American-based social networking giant.

Vivendi

France's Vivendi SA is a major player in France, across Europe's audiovisual sector, and globally, with Activision Blizzard and other properties. The company was established in the nineteenth century with major interests in public utilities and construction, which continue today. In 1997 it added communications to its corporate interests by purchasing a 30 percent stake in France's Havas. In 1998 the company changed its name from Generele des Oeaux to Vivendi to reflect its new communications interests. It has four divisions: television and cinema, music, games, and telecommunications.

In 2000 Vivendi acquired the Seagram Company of Canada in a $55 billion merger. Vivendi was after Seagram's three major communication units: Universal Studios and Pictures, as well as the Universal Music Group (UMG). Today it has retained only the UMG unit. It had hoped to create the synergy to become a major global player in the rapidly evolving communications sector, but overall it failed.

Vivendi also merged with Canal+ in 2000. Created in 1984, France's Canal+ is the European leader of pay-TV, offering premium programming on several channels. After an initial launch in France, Canal+ is now available across Europe. StudioCanal, the company's film division, also produces over 50 films annually and its film library is the third largest in the world. StudioCanal seeks to bring together European film providers for both television and theater distribution in order to encourage the development of a unified, pan-European film industry. As a corporation, it sees itself as the European alternative to Hollywood. The current cost of producing blockbusters for a global audience is beyond the fiscal reach of most European film studios.

Recent years have seen Vivendi gain new interests in the video game industry. In 2007 Vivendi merged with Activision to form Activision Blizzard, with Vivendi owning 62 percent of the company. The company's headquarters is in California and it has operations in 14 countries, including China. Activision Blizzard's game portfolio contains such well-known titles as *Call of Duty*, *Spider-Man*, *Guitar Hero*, *X-Men*, *James Bond*, and *World of Warcraft*. One version of *World of Warcraft* sold 3.3 million copies on the first day and in 2011 its *Call of Duty* exceeded one billion in sales in just 16 days. Finally, Activision Blizzard runs successful subscription-based multiplayer online role-playing games around the globe.

Universal Music Group began as a part of the Universal Pictures film studio and has been owned by various other corporations over the years. In 2006 it became part of Vivendi SA. In 2013 it completed the purchase of EMI Music of United Kingdom, some of whose artists include Lady Gaga, Rihanna, and Justin Bieber. The company focuses on emerging markets in Brazil, China, India, the Middle East, and Russia. In the telecommunications sector it has operations in France, Morocco, and Brazil where it offers telephone, Internet, and mobile services. (For more on UMG and other music companies, see Chapter 10.)

Lagardère Media

Lagardère Media is an extremely diversified French conglomerate with major publishing and media interests as well as military-industrial activities. It produces the Dr Seuss books, CD-ROM encyclopedias, and several consumer oriented magazines published internationally, including *Elle*, *Car and Driver*, *Woman's Day*, *Metropolitan Home*, and *Harlequin*. It is now the tenth largest US magazine publisher overall and the largest foreign magazine publisher in the United States. Globally, Lagardère is the number one magazine publisher. The focus of its various magazines is primarily on advertising and then on circulation. *Elle* has 39 editions around the world. Lagardère also publishes several newspapers in France. Lagardère properties claim close to 40 million readers on a monthly basis. It became one of the first global marketers by promoting the Elle Channel with Parisian cosmetic firm Estée Lauder's cosmetic brand Clinique. The corporation views itself as a global, highly diversified industrial and multimedia group. Lagardère also owns Interdeco Global Advertising, the top advertising agency in France. In 2008 Lagardère acquired Doctissmo, a company that publishes content directed at women on the Internet, as a part of their move to expand their magazine enterprise onto the Internet.

Pearson PLC

Pearson, based in the United Kingdom, is a global media company with three main branches: the Penguin Group, the Financial Times Group, and Pearson Education. The Penguin Group is the second largest publisher of books globally. It has branches in North America, Australia, New Zealand, South Africa, India, and China. Authors published by the Penguin Group include Tom Clancy, Nora Roberts, Alan Greenspan, Al Gore, Nick Hornby, and the Dalai Lama. Pearson also publishes the *Financial Times* (*FT*), which competes directly with the *Wall Street Journal*. The *Financial Times* is aimed at the global business community and has been a successful newspaper since its introduction in 1888. The Financial Times Group owns 50 percent in shares of the weekly global magazine the *Economist*. Additionally, Pearson has sought a niche in educational and reference publishing. Pearson Education owns Prentice Hall, Addison-Wesley, Pearson Longman, Pearson Higher Education, and Pearson Scott Foresman. As part of its educational niche, Pearson also controls the largest number of websites directly related to major leading textbooks.

Pearson's 2008 sales figures based on geography clearly demonstrate the strategic importance of the US marketplace to all non-American communication firms. The company realized 27.9 percent of total global sales from its domestic market in Europe, but by comparison the North American market accounted for 69.7 percent. All European-based communication companies must be successful in the US market in order to be a global stakeholder.

Reed Elsevier

In 1993 Reed International, a British publisher, merged with Elsevier Scientific Publishers to form Reed Elsevier. Reed Elsevier is based in London and Amsterdam. It is primarily made up of three divisions: Elsevier, LexisNexis, and Reed Business Information. Elsevier publishes textbooks, journals, and other reference material within the medical and scientific fields. It is the largest such publisher in the world and has a strong presence online. In the last decade, Elsevier has come under fire for its rather expensive subscription fees, with entire editorial boards resigning and launching new competing publications. Another controversy arose over the conflict of interest between publications on medical advancement and scientific enlightenment and Reed Elsevier's investment in the arms trade, which resulted in the parent company selling its weapons division in 2008. LexisNexis provides online archives of legal documents through www.lexis.com and news stories through www.nexis.com. The company also publishes textbooks, magazines, and newspapers in the legal and business fields, as well as offering training courses in the area of taxation law. Reed Business Information publishes over 30 titles, including *Publishers Weekly* and *Variety*. In 2008 Reed Elsevier bought ChoicePoint, an American information aggregator which collects personal and business information and sells it to the US government and private corporations.

Mediaset

Mediaset is the largest private television or commercial broadcaster in Italy. It controls seven channels in Italy and four in Spain, plus two additional satellite channels. The majority owner is the former Italian prime minister Silvio Berlusconi, who is also president of the AC Milan soccer club. Mediaset is seeking international expansion for its vast library of soap operas and sitcoms. Started in 1997, Mediaset acquired Italian broadcasting rights for all NBC movies and miniseries. In 2004 it began a 24-hour commercial children's channel, named Boing, in partnership with Time Warner. It also jointly produces major productions for the international market. Mediaset networks are delivered through cable and satellite, which facilitate further global expansion, particularly for the Italian-speaking market. Mediaset also controls the top Italian advertising agency Publitalia.

Mediaset owns three-quarters of the Dutch television production company Endemol. It produces over 40,000 hours of programming yearly and has some major global hits. Endemol operates across 26 countries globally, including the United States, India, Australia, and the Philippines, where it is frequently the largest TV producer. Some of the company's TV success stories are *Big Brother* (on CBS), *Fear Factor* (on NBC), and *Extreme Makeover* (on ABC), which it licenses to major television networks around the globe. From time to time, US multimedia firms seeking a solid television production foothold in the European Union have attempted to buy Endemol.

European Broadcasting Union

The European Broadcasting Union (EBU) is a significant transnational entity for public broadcasters across Europe, the Middle East, and North Africa. Given that almost all nations outside the United States have had large and successful non-commercial (i.e., public service) broadcasters since 1950, the EBU has been a crucial professional association of national, non-commercial broadcasters. Working in 56 countries, it operates Eurovision and Euroradio networks. It also facilitates the exchange of programming and negotiates broadcasting rights for major sports events, such as soccer matches and the Olympics, and finally works to facilitate original co-productions between member broadcasters. In 2005 it issued the Madrid Declaration. The five main issues covered by the Declaration are:

1   the major role played by public service broadcasters to further European integration;
2   a proactive approach on the part of the EBU and its members to support public services;
3   the need for public service broadcasting to be at the forefront of new initiatives regarding digital terrestrial broadcasting;
4   a comprehensive delivery of public service content on the full spectrum of new digital platforms; and
5   the crucial importance of guaranteed stable and long-term funding to allow the full implementation of public service duties.[8]

Finally, the EBU will be busy monitoring the proposed actions of the World Trade Organization (WTO) as they impact the public broadcasting sectors. The EBU does not view broadcasting as a commercial commodity to be included in WTO's free trade undertakings. (The WTO and its move into the media and cultural sectors are discussed in Chapter 5.)

Multimedia Corporations Outside the United States and Europe

European-based multimedia corporations are by no means the only non-US stakeholders in the global communication industry (see Table 8.2). The following sections detail the primary global communication stakeholders located in nations outside of Europe and the United States.

Aboriginal People's Television Network (Canada)

Aboriginal People's Television Network (APTN) was launched in 1999 as a means of promoting positive images and messages about Aboriginal peoples and their lifestyles. The new specialty channel is attempting to reverse the long-standing trend of negative mainstream media coverage of Aboriginal peoples. AFTN presents Aboriginal programming from Canada, the United States, Australia, and New Zealand. The schedule includes children's, educational, and cultural programming as well as news, current affairs, and political programming. Most programming is produced, written, and staffed by media professionals of Aboriginal ancestry.

Approximately 56 percent of the shows are in English, 16 percent in French, and 28 percent in a variety of Aboriginal languages, primarily Inuit. APTN is a clear example of development communication. The goal of the network is to present pro-social and proactive messages on behalf of Aboriginal communities as an alternative to the traditional mainstream TV networks, which are staffed almost entirely by non-Aboriginal personnel. Also, mainstream TV and movies tend to portray Aboriginal characters in a less than favorable light.

NITV (Australia)

A government-supported network, NITV began in 2007. Its goal is to portray the voices and image of Australia's first people in a positive manner. According to their website:

> National Indigenous Television (NITV) is part of the SBS family of free-to-air channels broadcasting across Australia providing a nationwide Indigenous television service via cable, satellite and terrestrial transmission means and selected online audio visual content. The content for these services is primarily commissioned or acquired from the Indigenous production sector.[9]

Much of NITV's programming comes from the Canadian Aboriginal network APTN.

Table 8.2 Major communications stakeholders outside the United States and Europe, 2013

WETV (Canada)
Aboriginal People's Television Network (Canada)
NITV (Australia)
Televisa (Mexico)
Globo Communications (Brazil)
Cisneros Group (Venezuela)
Sony Corporation (Japan)
Bollywood (India)
Zodiac Entertainment (Italy)

Televisa (Mexico)

The roots of the Azcarraga family empire date back to the radio era. Emilio Azcarraga Milmo began his media career with the radio station XEW-AM in Mexico City during the 1940s. The Azcarraga family subsequently owned the station. In 1972 they formed the giant television network Televisa by combining two other television companies. Emilio Azcarraga Milmo died in April 1998, leaving Latin America's largest multimedia corporation, Televisa, to his son, Emilio Azcarraga Jean. The Azcarragas now control a sprawling operation that includes four network channels with 260 affiliate stations; a publishing company called Editorial Televisa; two record labels (EMI Televisa Music and EMI Latin); 17 radio stations; several cable channels; a satellite system; a movie company; Estadio Azteca (a massive 120,000-seat stadium); three soccer teams; and an airline. In addition, they have investments in the US Spanish network Univision; the stateside cable channel Galavision; and a Venezuelan television network. With the rapid growth of Spanish media in both the United States and Europe, the Azcarraga empire is growing, with hopes of competing with the Disney and Sony corporations.

Univision Communications

Univision is the largest Spanish-language network in the United States. It was launched in 1961 and is currently experiencing substantial growth. The Hispanic population in the United States is growing rapidly and has now become the largest minority in the United States. Univision features telenovelas, soap operas that last for several months. The Univision network reaches the vast majority of US Hispanic households through a number of stations it owns and operates, as well as through several broadcast affiliates. Univision also operates a number of radio stations. Univision works in partnership with Televisa to broadcast a large number of Spanish-language programs that appeal to the growing US Hispanic audience. Univision is a major, sometimes the dominant, channel in US cities such as Miami and Los Angeles, and in several Texan and Arizonan cities. Univision is also beginning to attract substantial advertising revenue from major US corporations as reaching the Hispanic audience is becoming more critical to the increasing market share for media and consumer products alike.

In 2013 Univision announced another joint venture with ABC network, to be known as Fusion:

> Fusion capitalizes on Univision's news leadership and expertise in reaching U.S. Hispanics and ABC's global news leadership to serve over 50 million Hispanics, the youngest and fastest-growing demographic in the US. Currently, Hispanics represent 16 percent of the total population in the United States, a number that is projected to double to 30 percent by 2050. Hispanics wield considerable spending power of over $1 trillion, and have an increasing impact on social, economic and political trends.[10]

Globo Communications (Brazil)

Globo is a multimedia giant with a television network, newspapers, magazines, books, radio, cable systems, movies, Internet, and records. In addition to owning Rio de Janeiro's largest circulation newspaper, *O Globo*, the company's television interest attracts over 60 percent of the Brazilian audience and is the largest television network in Latin America. The company is privately owned by the Marinho family who started it in 1965. Historically the Marinho elders have had a close relationship with the political masters of Brazil. They started Globo International Network in 1999. Recently they started TV Globo Japan/Asia, and the company plans further global expansion.

Cisneros Group (Venezuela)

Established in 1929 in Caracas, Venezuela, Cisneros is now one of the world's largest multimedia firms in private hands. The chairman and CEO is family member Gustavo Cisneros who directs its vast holding across the Americas. The company seeks to serve the 500 million Spanish across Europe and the Americas with high-quality audio and video entertainment. The flagship television station is Venevision, the largest in Venezuela. In addition, it has interests in AOL Latin America and DirectTV Latin America, and in the global market, Venevision International. Based in Miami, Venevision International provides Cisneros products in 20 languages in over 100 countries across five continents. Venevision International has won a number of awards and produces the number one telenovela in the Americas from its Miami studios.

Sony Corporation (Japan)

Originally established in 1946 under the name Tokyo Telecommunications Engineering Corporation, Sony Corporation got its new name in 1958. Company founders were determined to create new markets with communication technology. The company produced the first Japanese tape recorder in 1950. In 1955, after receiving a transistor technology license from Western Electric, it launched the first transistor radio. It then produced the first Sony trademark product, a pocket-sized radio.

In 1960 Akio Morita, one of Sony's founders, moved to New York to oversee the company's major US expansion. At this time, Sony launched the first home video, a solid-state condenser microphone, and an integrated circuit-based radio. Another decade of explosive growth was launched by Sony's 1968 introduction of the Trinitron color television tube. The VCR and the Walkman were other early Sony successes. Competition, especially from other Asian countries, was affecting the Sony Corporation by the 1980s. For this reason, Sony, under Morita's leadership as chairman since 1976, used its technology to diversify beyond consumer electronics. In 1980 it introduced Japan's first 32-bit workstation and became a major producer of computer chips and floppy-disk drives. Sony expanded its US media empire by acquiring CBS Records from CBS for $2 billion and Columbia Pictures from Coca-Cola for $4.9 billion, both in 1988. Sony was now in the US entertainment industry in a big way. In 1992 it allied with Sega to develop CD video games, and with Microsoft to produce electronic audio, video, and text books.

Sony Corporation is headquartered in Tokyo, Japan; the sister company in the United States is called Sony Corporation of America. The company employs 180,500 people worldwide. Sony's major products include audio and video equipment, televisions, and information, communications, and electronic components. Some of the products produced for the audio division include CD players, MP3 players, headphone stereos, hi-fi components, radio cassette tape recorders, radios, car stereos, and digital audiotape. The video division produces DV-format VCRs, DVD video players, video CD players, digital cameras, and videotapes. The television division produces color TVs, projection TVs, flat display panels, and large color video display systems. Sony products also include computer monitors, personal computers, Internet terminals, telephones, the PlayStation, and car navigation systems.

Sony's music division offers recordings from acts ranging from Alicia Keys, Carrie Underwood, Paul Simon, and Rage Against the Machine. Sony Music includes among its divisions Columbia Records, Epic Records, and RCA Music Group. Globally Sony works through four divisions: electronics, games, movies, and music.

Bollywood: India's Film Industry

The cinema of the semiperipheral nation of India deserves specific mention. The first Indian-made silent feature film was produced in 1913. From these humble origins the film industry in India is now producing over 800 films per year. The vast film industry has been nicknamed "Bollywood" (a combination of Hollywood and Bombay). The films are primarily Hindi productions, with a number of regional centers producing other films in their own languages.

Bollywood is a major focus of India's popular culture both at home and abroad. The commercial films are shown both in the Indian subcontinent, and to the large number of Indian expatriates across the Middle East, Africa, Asia, Europe, and North America. The genres of musicals, romance, comedy, and melodramatic themes dominate. A typical budget for a feature-length movie with export expectations is still only $2 million compared to Hollywood actors commanding more than $10 million each for a single movie. Also, Indian censors are very strict and restrict the sexual content in movies. Across India more than six million workers are employed in the cinema sector and leading stars are national heroes. The growth of cable channels and DVDs is providing additional outlets for Bollywood productions and increased revenue growth. Though a niche cinematic industry in terms of global reach, the Bollywood industry has survived surprisingly well in the face of major core nation competition.

However, it took a British-made Bollywood-themed movie, *Slumdog Millionaire*, to deliver the first global critical and popular success for the genre. Produced in Hindi and English for $15 million in 2008, the movie won eight Oscars, including Best Picture and Best Director, and has grossed over $360 million so far. Like most non-US films, *Slumdog Millionaire* had global distribution problems and turned to Warner Bros. and Fox for assistance. As a result, the two American studios made millions from the production. More recently an Indian-made Bollywood comedy, *3 Idiots*, has been another large global success but such successes are rare, given the large number of Bollywood films made annually.

Global Trends

This review of global broadcasters illustrates two important points, which will be developed in some detail here. The first is the connection between sports and the mass media. This partnering is particularly common in Europe, where many major broadcasting conglomerates also own, in part or in whole, major European soccer teams. US media firms also own several sports teams. The second point is the substantial and ever increasing role that non-US media stakeholders are playing in global communication.

The Sports Connection

The connection between sports and the mass media has had a long and checkered career. During the 1950s and 1960s attempts to link the International Olympic Movement (IOC) and the Summer and Winter Olympic Games with the world television audience were tenuous. It was not until the 1970s that the value of media rights for the Olympic Games escalated dramatically because of bidding wars between ABC, NBC, and CBS. In the 1990s the gray area between amateur and professional sports became even shadier when, for the first time, professional basketball and hockey players participated in the Olympic Games. Today the Olympics enjoy substantial revenue from a combination of media and marketing funds that were created as part of the selling package for host cities. Host cities incur enormous local expenses but recoup those expenses, plus revenue from tourism, thanks to the huge sums paid almost exclusively by US television networks. The sums paid by US firms for marketing rights supplement this revenue. It should come as no surprise that sponsorship of the Olympics makes sense, and that this sports connection should work for corporations with other sports as well. Even now, the National Football League holds exhibition games in Europe and the National Hockey League holds exhibition games in Asia and Europe, as part of their attempts to go global. European football, known in the United States as soccer, has limited exposure in the United States except during the World Cup. The 1999 US women's World Cup victory, shown live on television, had a dramatic influence on soccer and media exposure in North America. In the future, global sports leagues will emerge, and global broadcasting will parallel that movement. Current media outlets such as News Corporation, Disney, Time Warner, and others may aggressively purchase international sports teams in order to influence the allocation of, or to obtain, international sports broadcasting rights, primarily for teams that draw enormous global audiences that would be drawn to global products such as Coca-Cola, American Express, McDonald's, Kodak, IBM, Google, and UPS.

It appears that Rupert Murdoch's News Corporation strategy concerning sports may be changing in Europe. Previously, he had announced large-scale attempts to purchase major media systems which frequently ran into regulatory trouble as the culturally sensitive Europeans looked with disfavor on the Australian-born media giant. Also, he has been acquiring part ownership in non-major media outlets across Europe. For example, in 1999 he acquired 35 percent of an Italian digital pay-TV service known as Stream. Murdoch, along with other partners, is now acquiring the rights to broadcast Italian soccer games, In Germany, News Corporation bought 66 percent of the niche channel called TM3. This relatively obscure channel outbid Germany's number one commercial TV channel for all domestic broadcasting rights to Europe's major soccer league for four years.

Global Stakeholders

These descriptions of transnational media conglomerates reflect the basic fact that global communication systems are only partly American in shape, content, and ownership. Many powerful non-US global corporations are extremely active in the global communication marketplace. Even though these non-US firms compete with Hollywood and New York, they do so while sharing the same commercial values. The goal of these global media corporations is to maximize profits for owners and shareholders, much like their US counterparts; they entered the global arena to increase market share. The global communication stakeholders are all based in core nations. All global media firms rely heavily on foreign customers, whether they are in other core nations, or in semiperipheral or peripheral zones. These non-US firms need to have a significant presence in the US market to be profitable and to be considered major global players. They have taken advantage of the significant structural changes in the 1990s that encouraged privatization and deregulation at the same time as satellite technology, cable systems, DVDs, and the Internet were expanding rapidly.

In Europe, where government-controlled and government-owned media lost market share, and in some cases became a phenomenon of a previous era, aggressive corporations quickly sought either to extend their traditional interests in the mass media, beginning with print products, or to move into new areas and make strategic decisions to diversify previously non-media corporations. The outcomes are similar. All major global multimedia corporations are seeking to maximize profits in order to increase or improve the rate of return for their shareholders. They do this through a combination of expanding current markets and adding new market share through acquisitions or joint ventures. Ultimately, they seek the expansion of electronic colonialism. Just as US global media firms seek foreign customers in Asia and Europe, so Asian and European firms are aggressively pursuing customers in North America. They do so by producing shows and other media products that will attract a substantial customer base along with healthy advertising revenues. Bertelsmann and Sony are prime examples; Sony Pictures Classics spent over $10 million to market a single film, *Crouching Tiger, Hidden Dragon*. But the reality for most foreign firms in the feature film business is that the costs have moved the bar far beyond their reach. The example of female movie stars speaks volumes. Julia Roberts and Cameron Diaz command between $20 to $30 million per movie, while producers have their pick of Halle Berry, Drew Barrymore, Nicole Kidman, Reese Witherspoon, Sandra Bullock, Renée Zellweger, or Angelina Jolie for between $10 and $20 million. The vast majority of foreign-produced feature films do not have total budgets in this league, let alone for a single star.

Clearly, customers with disposable income are free to make choices between a plethora of books and magazines, movies and television channels, records, tapes, Internet sites, and other communication products around the globe. Most are unaware of who owns the content, who controls the delivery system, or how important advertising is in terms of revenue for these global empires. Few people could identify, or would care, which firm actually owns the product they are viewing, listening to, or reading.

Early in the twenty-first century, the biggest global communication firms are conducting most of their business abroad, or capturing more customers in foreign markets, and have less to do with the nation-state their corporation was established in. A global mindset or outlook, global advertising, and global strategic planning reflect the successful communication management of tomorrow. Business without borders will be the norm rather than the exception for global multimedia corporations. Like the Internet, global communication systems and products will transcend national boundaries.

A new policy issue is looming on the horizon, which could impact the non-American multimedia stakeholders. The World Trade Organization, as part of its new round of negotiations, is looking to include the audiovisual sector in new multilateral talks.[11] As part of its broad tariff reduction goal, the WTO may include government subsidies as well. For many nations, particularly in Europe, this could result in the ending of government grants or programs that seek to bolster their film and television industries. (For more on this cultural policy issue see Chapter 16.)

A final point about the United States of Europe. Beginning with radio and now television, there are government-funded networks with no commercial/advertising on them across Europe. The BBC is a prime example. Also the European Union is actively funding audiovisual projects that are appealing to a global audience. To a large extent, policymakers and production houses are trying to reduce the likelihood of becoming an electronic colony of the United States' multimedia conglomerates.

Notes

1. See, for example, Juan E. Conradi, "Cultural Dependence and the Sociology of Knowledge: The Latin American Case," *International Journal of Contemporary Sociology* 8(1) (1971), 35–55; Kaarle Nordenstreng and Tapio Varis, *Television Traffic: A One-Way Street?* Reports and Papers of Mass Communication no. 70, Paris: UNESCO, 1974; and Thomas Guback, *The International Film Industry*, Bloomington: Indiana University Press, 1969.

2. See, for example, Ben Bagdikian, *The Media Monopoly*, Boston: Beacon, 2000; Jeremy Tunstall, *The Media Are American*, New York: Columbia University Press, 1977; Thomas McPhail and Brenda McPhail, *Communication: The Canadian Experience*, Toronto: Copp Clark Pitman, 1990; and Anthony Smith, *The Geopolitics of Information: How Western Culture Dominates World*, New York: Oxford University Press, 1980.

3. See, for example, Andrew A. Moemeka (ed.), *Communicating for Development*, Albany: State University of New York Press, 1994; Oliver Boyd-Barnett, *The International News Agencies*, London: Constable, 1980; Tsan Kuo Chang, "All Countries Not Created Equal to Be News," *Communication Research* 25(5) (October 1998), 528–63; Rob Kroes, "American Empire and Cultural Imperialism: A View from the Receiving End," *Diplomatic*

History 23 (1999), 463–78; and Thomas L. Mcphail, *Development Communication: Reframing the Role of the Media.* (United Kingdom: Wiley Blackwell, 2009)

4. Herbert I. Schiller, *Communication and Cultural Domination*, White Plains, NY: International Arts and Sciences Press, 1976); see also J. Tomlinson, *Cultural Imperialism: A Critical Introduction*, London: Pinter, 1991.

5. John Tagliabue, "A Media World to Conquer," *New York Times* (July 7, 1999), 5.

6. Caroline Pauwels and Jan Loisen, "The WTO and the Audiovisual Sector," *European Journal of Communication* 18 (2003), 291–314.

7. http://www.obs.coe.int/about/oea/org/mission.html, accessed August 22, 2013.

8. For the full text of the Declaration see http://www.ebu.ch/en/union/news/2005/tcm_6-34614.php, accessed August 25, 2013.

9. http://www.nitv.org.au/about-nitv/dsp-default.cfm?loadref=67, accessed August 22, 2013.

10. http://corporate.univision.com/2013/press/abc-and-univision-introduce-fusion/#ixz, accessed August 22, 2013.

11. Caroline Pauwels and Jan Loisen, "The WTO and the Audiovisual Sector," *European Journal of Communication* 18 (2003), 291–314.

9

Euromedia
Integration and Cultural Diversity in a Changing Media Landscape

Alexa Robertson

Introduction

Once upon a time, a long time ago (that is to say, before Harry Potter and Gandalf found their way onto the big screen), parents and children across Europe lined up at the cinema and at McDonald's to experience Disney's version of the story of Hercules. This social and cultural ritual occasioned an outburst in what was then Europe's own weekly newspaper, *The European* (Figure 9.1). The front page cried "Plunder! Disney tears up our heritage" and depicted Hercules tearing apart a book, Mickey Mouse gleefully counting the dollars, and Pinocchio, Winnie the Pooh, and Quasimodo looking on in dismay. On the editorial page and in a number of articles inside the paper, *The European* lamented that "the guardians of European culture" were worried about what the paper referred to as "the Disney effect." The creative, intellectual, European treasure trove was juxtaposed with a US business empire called "Mauschwitz" because the Disney empire was thought to be something quite other than free. Disney has often said that its strategy is to "think global, act local" – a virtual paraphrase of Roland Robertson's notion of glocalization. But in the view of *The European*, it was precisely the other way around.

In fact, *The European* was a commercial interest, like Disney, a media company that targeted an international audience. But the stance it adopted on its editorial pages bears a striking resemblance to that reflected in European Commission directives such as "Television without Frontiers," which stipulated that a majority of broadcast time in the ether media of EU member states should be earmarked for European products. The same argument resulted in the founding of Euronews, the channel that was meant to be Europe's

Global Communication: Theories, Stakeholders, and Trends, Fourth Edition. Thomas L. McPhail.
© 2014 John Wiley & Sons, Inc. Published 2014 by John Wiley & Sons, Inc.

Figure 9.1 "Disney tears up our heritage," *The European* (August 28–September 3, 1997)

answer to CNN and that underpins such ventures as the European Film Promotion network and the MEDIA Mundus audiovisual cooperation program. This argument is that Europeans should be the ones to decide how Europe is seen and understood – not Disney, or CNN, or Hollywood. It resonates with the UNESCO Declaration on Cultural Diversity, which states:

> In the face of current imbalances in flows and exchanges of cultural goods and services at the global level, it is necessary to reinforce international cooperation and solidarity aimed at enabling all countries, especially developing countries and countries in transition, to establish cultural industries that are viable and competitive at national and international level.[1]

In Europe, a continent with 24 official languages, a historically unprecedented project to develop and reinforce international cooperation had been taking place for several decades, and was about to enter a new phase. *Hercules* premiered a few months after the Maastricht Treaty was signed in 1992, transforming the European Community into the European Union. As the hero of Mount Olympus was cleaning out stables to the chorus of the Muses, the European single market was coming into being, stipulating the free movement of goods and services between EU member states. The number of states swelled, two years after the *Hercules* premiere, to 15, after Austria, Finland, and Sweden joined. A decade later it had grown to a union of 27 members, including eight former Warsaw Pact states – some of them developing countries and all of them certainly countries in transition. It was a sprawling and ethnically and linguistically diverse family of nations that observed the fiftieth anniversary of the foundational Élysée Treaty in January 2013. The fact that British Prime

Minister David Cameron announced, the following day, that he would give Britons the chance to vote to leave the European Union were his Conservative Party to be re-elected, highlighted how fragmented the Union had become. Age-old divisions had grown deeper and wider in the course of the "eurocrisis".

The media landscape had grown as fragmented as the political one. Barely a generation ago, most Europeans had access to one or two state-funded (and, in the case of the former Warsaw Pact countries, state-controlled) radio and television channels. Deregulation started in the early 1980s in the United Kingdom under Margaret Thatcher, and spread quickly eastward, notably to France (where advertising crept into all broadcasting), Italy (where Berlusconi leveled the distinction between media and political empires), and beyond. In Sweden, legislation had to be changed when a renegade channel began broadcasting to the country by satellite from London, and thus circumvented the law against advertising in ether media. By 2012, over 8,900 television channels were available in the European Union and candidate countries, up 375 from the previous year.[2] Most European countries had completed the transition to digital television, and television was holding its own against – and in some respects benefitting from – social media, and remained the most important source of information and entertainment for Europeans.

The European Commission nevertheless saw the media landscape as the site of radical changes, "characterised by its blurred borders in both geographical and technological terms" and marked by globalization and digitalization.[3] The radically altered media landscape in Europe can at times seem a battlefield on which business interests, developers of technology, journalists (often with a strong sense of mission and professional integrity), and policymakers struggle to gain the higher ground. To this have been added networks of bloggers and citizen journalists who often have the resources to publicize their own social and political agendas. While often in conflict, these different sorts of actors increasingly work in tandem with increasingly active audiences, to transform the European media scene.

This chapter takes a look at the intersection of politics and media globalization in the European context. Most European countries have strong public service traditions, and the ethos remains despite the inroads of commercialization and digitalization. National governments thus continue to be important players in the European media game. But the focus will be on the European Union, as it has come to play an increasingly central role in communications policy, and because its reactions to technological and economic developments can teach us a lot about globalization in general. It is for good reason that Europe has been called "an exemplary landscape for comprehending globalization."[4] A key question throughout is what has been done to create a communicative space or public sphere that is uniquely European, to counter the impact of US media influence and to forge a common European identity.

The Power of Culture

Shortly before the turn of the millennium, UNESCO launched a fundamental review of cultural policies in light of transformations in the media world. Delegates met in Stockholm to discuss a document entitled "The Power of Culture," which noted that while technology was yielding a broader range of choices, the increasing concentration of media ownership under globalization was actually limiting access. "How can we ensure," the delegates were asked, "that in every country, the media provide diversified programmes which not only promote a shared national identity but also give pluralistic expression to the variety of social, political and cultural values?"[5] The adaptation of public service broadcasting to the "enormous" changes in the sphere of communication was thus identified as a key issue. In a variety of documents adopted over the years, UNESCO has sought to protect the "fruitful diversity of cultures." In 2009 it called for a renewed discussion, thought necessary not just because of ongoing and deepening globalization, but because of the global financial crisis, the impacts of which "are challenging our very understanding of cultures and identities."[6]

One UNESCO text in particular is often invoked by European institutions and actors, and must thus be considered a starting point for any account of communication and cultural regulation in Europe. It is the UNESCO Convention on the Protection and Promotion of the Diversity of Cultural Expressions, adopted in Paris in October 2005, and usually referred to as "the UNESCO Convention." Its objectives include the creation of conditions in which cultures can "flourish and freely interact," more balanced cultural exchange in the world, and working to make policymakers in the corridors of power and media consumers in the home aware of the value of diverse cultural expressions. Translated into everyday language, this means that UNESCO thinks it important to resist what some call Americanization, and others refer to as "cultural homogenization" when talking about the results of media globalization.

The UNESCO Convention urges international cooperation and solidarity to enable countries "to create and strengthen their means of cultural expression, including their cultural industries, whether nascent or established, at the local, national and international levels."[7] The aim of the convention and other UNESCO agreements is to insure that all societies remain open to the cultural expressions of others. "When States adopt measures to support the diversity of cultural expressions," it is argued, "they should seek to promote openness to other cultures of the world."[8] The idea, in other words, is for states to work together, for the benefit of an internationalized community, rather than go it alone for the economic gain of individual corporations. This take on the sort of action required of regulators in a globalized world resonates with the aims and language of EU communications policy.

EU Communication Policy

As the Berlin Wall was toppling in 1989, and barbed wire throughout eastern Europe was being penetrated, not by NATO soldiers but by Western media, the European Union agreed on a directive symbolically entitled "Television without Frontiers." Its main objective was to create the conditions necessary for the free movement of television broadcasts within the European Union, to promote the development of programs with a European dimension, and to stem the deluge of American imports in an era of deregulation.

Sans Frontières

In the view of the European Commission, the single European market that came into being in the early days of globalization applied to television broadcasts as much as anything else. "Just as any of us is free to buy chocolate, wine or a new car in any EU country," it explained to Europeans, "we can also watch TV channels from all over Europe."[9] For the single European television market to function, it was thought that a minimum set of common rules was needed to govern advertising, program production, and the protection of minors. Beginning in 1989, these rules were enshrined in the "Television without Frontiers" Directive, which was a response to the communications revolution of the early 1980s and the growing deficit in audiovisual trade with the United States.

The directive was updated over the years, and eventually replaced in 2007 by the Audiovisual Media Services Directive (AVMSD). The national governments of EU member states had until December 2009 to apply the new directive: 10 failed to make it in time. Unlike its precursor, the AVMSD was specifically formulated to address a digital mediascape. In 1989 the challenge was to regulate media production and distribution in an age when satellite broadcasting showed how porous national borders were. A decade later the issue was less one of top-down developments and "linear" services (with satellite and other broadcasters providing a schedule) as bottom-up and "non-linear" services. The question now was how to respond to consumer behavior: what rules should apply to films supplied at the request of the user, who has control over what he or she wants to watch and when?

According to the European Commission, the new rules were yet another response to more technological advancement – which regulators refuse to be outstripped by. They "create a level playing field for Europe" in a new media context and "seek to preserve cultural diversity" and "safeguard media pluralism."[10] When the High Level Group on Media Freedom and Pluralism, set up in 2011, published its long-awaited report in 2013, it stressed the urgent need for policy to protect media freedom in the face of commercial interference and media concentration. It requires no in-depth textual analysis to conclude that the language of EU media regulations is redolent of UNESCO discourse.

The European Union, GATS, and a Digital Agenda

European Union policy echoes UNESCO stances in other respects as well. Given the European view that the media play a significant social, cultural, and political role, the European Union has consistently resisted liberalization of the audiovisual market, an issue that has been hotly debated in the context of the General Agreement on Trade in Services (GATS), a World Trade Organization (WTO) treaty that came into force in 1995. In a number of arguments, the UNESCO Convention has been invoked in support of the view that cultural products are not like other commodities, and must therefore be exempt from free trade deals. There has been concern at the growth in the audiovisual trade deficit between the European Union and the United States. In 1995 the deficit was $4.8 billion. By 2013 it had almost doubled.[11] Another example of a trade imbalance that the European Union has identified as a threat is the domination of the Internet by US companies. Against this background, a Digital Agenda for Europe (DAE) was launched in May 2010. The Commission argued that decisions about the Internet had to be taken in an accountable and transparent manner (despite the European Union not being well known for its strengths in these respects) and promoted aid for the provision of high-speed Internet in countries that lacked it. All in all, the view from Europe has been that producers, broadcasters, and distributors from some countries are at a disadvantage, in economic terms, when it comes to competing in audiovisual markets worldwide.

A problem related to the GATS, which has been pointed out by various European actors, is the lack of multinationally agreed standards on cultural and audiovisual policies. This makes it difficult for individual states to limit their commitments to liberalization (liberalization being the thrust of GATS) to preserve and promote specific cultural identities. In theory, GATS allows flexibility in this respect. In practice, trade panels rather than cultural actors end up deciding where the limits to liberalization should be set. This tends to be done with economic rather than cultural considerations in mind, and the concern is that they promote uniformity rather than safeguard diversity. EU actors have complained that under GATS it is impossible to distinguish between policy measures that legitimately protect and promote cultural diversity (which the European Union favors), and measures that are protectionist (which is its *raison d'être* to discourage).

Another problem with GATS is that it is seen as conservative, at a time when technological change was requiring regulators to be imaginative and willing to adapt to innovations. In various policy documents, EU actors have emphasized the huge uncertainty about future developments in digital and interactive audiovisual services. According to one:

> the acceptance, under the GATS, of the mere right to maintain existing measures, or to adopt safeguards with regard to traditional services only (such as cinema, radio and television) would completely fail to conserve the necessary scope for future policy measures.[12]

But the view from Europe, above all, is that GATS and the pressure for liberalization are a threat to the foundations on which the European audiovisual model rests: co-production agreements with other countries, financial support for production and distribution, and the requirement that a certain amount of broadcast time be earmarked for European content.

The European Union and Culture

The Maastricht Treaty of 1993 enabled the European Union "to take action in the field of culture to safeguard, disseminate and develop culture in Europe."[13] This action covers, of course, the fields of media and communication.

Since the beginning of the twenty-first century, the European Union has had a development plan known as the Lisbon Agenda. Its aim is to make the European Union "the world's most dynamic knowledge-based economy."[14] The Lisbon Agenda includes a strategy for culture, said to be a response to globalization. Taking its cue from the UNESCO Convention, the new European strategy is based on the conviction that culture is a vital dimension of international relations.

As should be clear by now, the European Union considers the audiovisual industry, including film, to be an important part of the cultural sector. But museums and historical documents and artifacts belong here too; and the European Commission has been promoting the digitization of "cultural heritage and material" in order to make it accessible online.

The Media Program of the European Union

Financial and other support is offered by the European Union to the European audiovisual industry under a program called MEDIA. It contributes to the financing of films, television drama, documentaries, and animation projects. For the 2007–13 period, its budget was €755 million (approximately $1,400 million).

US feature films have an over 50 percent share in most markets throughout the world, and over 90 percent in the domestic market. Against this backdrop, European Film Promotion (EFP) was launched in 1997. A network of film organizations and institutions, the EFP receives generous support from the European Union's MEDIA Programme. By 2009 it had 30 member organizations representing 31 different European countries.[15] The

EFP mandate is to increase opportunities for European film to compete in the international marketplace.

In 2009 the European Commission adopted a new program within this framework, called MEDIA Mundus, for cooperation between Europeans and third countries in the audiovisual sector. The commission said it hoped to create business opportunities and to increase consumer choice by bringing "more culturally diverse products" to European and other markets. "It's time to go global," said the EU Media Commissioner:

> The international audiovisual landscape has changed significantly over the last two decades, notably through the impact of technological developments like video on demand, internet TV or multichannel digital television. This has created growing demand for more audiovisual content, and we need to "fill" these new technologies with new and exciting content.[16]

The background to the program was the structural weakness in the international audiovisual landscape, which has prevented European producers from taking full advantage of emerging new platforms. The program is also meant to address the paradoxical situation that has arisen under globalization, whereby consumers have increasingly limited choice and access to products of more limited cultural diversity at a time when the number of media outlets is exploding. The soundtrack to this venture could well be the song in which Bruce Springsteen complains, "57 Channels (and Nothin' On)."

The problem identified here is related, but not identical, to that of liberalization and flexibility in the GATS negotiations. Individually, the EU member states – big countries like the United Kingdom, Germany, France, and Spain; small countries like Sweden, Denmark, and the Netherlands; and countries with relatively new capitalist economies like Poland, the Czech Republic, and the Baltics – have relatively small markets compared to the United States. They lack the critical mass to compete successfully. And viewers are not helping, given their propensity to consume US programs and box office blockbusters. While the ideology behind the MEDIA Programme and MEDIA Mundus is naturally the same, the objectives and mechanisms set out in the latter are said to be radically different.[17]

Protecting Diversity while Encouraging Integration

To sum up, it can be said that, while the European Union lacked a communication policy for much of its history, the spread of globalization in general, and cultural globalization in particular, and the enduring and even increasing distrust of its citizens, resulted in the European Union paying closer attention to communication from the mid-1990s onward. It now has an audiovisual and media policy that is implemented in four ways. The first is via the regulatory framework: the Audiovisual Media Services Directive aims to bring about a single European market for broadcast media and film. The second consists of funding programs such as MEDIA. The third measure is to enhance the free flow of online content and to promote media pluralism. The fourth way in which the European Union acts is to defend European cultural interests outside Europe – significantly in the context of the WTO. EU policy is thus somewhat reminiscent of Dr Dolittle's Pushmi-pullyu character, striving as it does to defend cultural specificity, while at the same time investing heavily in bringing Europeans together in a single market and culture.

Apart from the need to protect European cultural products and industries from the onslaught of Hollywood, Bollywood, and Australian imports, the European Union has been faced with the challenge of consolidating an internal European community as well as the single market. The problem that has plagued the architects of the European project over the years can be summed up in one key phrase – the "democratic deficit" – and it is on this that many of the steps taken by the European Union in the area of communications have been predicated. The most important task currently confronting the European Commission – in its own view and in the view of numerous commentators, after the poor turn-out in the 2009 elections to the European Parliament – is to restore public confidence in the European Union. The media, both traditional and new, are seen as essential to its accomplishment.[18]

Europeanization and the European Public Sphere

At this point, it might be useful to pause and consider the scholarly debate raging around European integration and communication. Hallin and Mancini have demonstrated how dangerous it is to generalize about "the media" or even "European media," as countries in different European regions have profoundly distinct traditions governing the interaction between political systems and media cultures.[19] Arguing that European media systems fit uneasily in the largely Anglo-Saxon accounts of how media and politics interact, they introduce three media systems models. The "liberal" model is most reminiscent of the US system, characterized by the dominance of market mechanisms. According to Hallin and Mancini, this conforms to the situation in the United Kingdom and Ireland. Northern European countries such as Germany, Sweden, and Denmark, however, have a different system, in which public and commercial media coexist, but where the state is also more active and civil society more involved. This they refer to as the "democratic corporatist" model. The "polarized pluralist" model is the third, and describes the systems of the countries of southern Europe, grouped around the Mediterranean. The media in these countries tend to be integrated more closely into party politics, and there is a different tradition of journalistic professionalism compared to the countries that conform to the two other models.

Given these different traditions, it is perhaps not surprising that many scholars and commentators are more skeptical than the European Union about the prospects for Europeanization, the possibility of creating a common European media culture, and – what is often thought to be the cure for the democratic deficit – a European public sphere (EPS).

The notion of the public sphere is very influential in European media studies. The concept comes from a book written by Jürgen Habermas in the early 1960s, which only became widely known when it was translated from German into English in 1989.[20] What Habermas had in mind was a hypothetical space between the private realm of the family and the realm of the state, inhabited by citizens who shared ideas and information that mattered to their political choices. The concept is now often applied in such a way that the media become the public sphere, rather than simply supplying its inhabitants with input. The media are thought to promote the pluralism that is necessary for healthy democracies by offering a place for different actors to be heard.[21] The European Union in general, and the European Commission in particular, has indicated that it hopes there will be a European public sphere one day from where feelings of affinity and democratic dependency can be nurtured. It lamented in 2006 that there had been an "inadequate development of a

'European Public Sphere' where European debate can unfold," that the public sphere and media in Europe continued to be largely national, and that there are "few meeting places where Europeans from different Member States can get to know each other and address issues of common interest."[22]

A number of scholars have argued that if the same European or EU news is reported by different media in Europe at the same time, it would be possible to say that an EPS existed.[23] According to this view, the EPS is a "pluralistic ensemble" of issue-oriented publics and the EPS, like the village of Brigadoon in the old musical, comes into being when all of those publics think and talk about the same thing at the same time. Schlesinger – who views the formation of an EPS as an impossible project – claims it would be necessary for the European Union to have the same news agenda in all European languages, and for people to think of themselves first and foremost as EU citizens, and only secondarily as members of nations.[24] He is an example of a skeptic who thinks an EPS must fulfill the same conditions as those of a national public sphere. (This view has been criticized by those who point out that if a common language, a common nation-wide media system, and citizens with a common identity were preconditions for a national public sphere, few states would qualify for one.) Another way of conceptualizing the EPS is to see it as built from the infrastructures of national public spheres, and filled with reporting and discussion of European issues seen in a European perspective.[25]

Europeanization, in turn, is thought by some to be a bottom-up process through which national public spheres move closer until they finally merge in an EPS.[26] Others see it as a top-down process in which the agenda is set by the European Union, with the sort of policy measures outlined above. The red thread running through all of these discussions is the lack of European (rather than national) media, and the unsatisfactory nature of the European media that do exist.[27] This is not necessarily the fault of journalists. Statham interviewed 110 correspondents working the Europe beat for national and regional newspapers, and found that national source strategists were more engaged, more professional, and more successful in their dealings with journalists reporting European issues than EU strategists and spin doctors. He observes that "the EU makes little effort to compete with national political actors to influence normal beat journalists."[28]

Media coverage throughout the continent thus tends to remain national in focus. While Europeans show little enthusiasm for European Parliament elections, however, they tend to be more enthusiastic about following the Eurovision Song Contest when it is broadcast live on television, and the number of votes cast for the best melody continues its steady climb to unprecedented levels. When the contestants took to the stage in Malmö in 2013, an estimated 170 million people watched the same event at the same time in the same communicative space. Voting in the Eurovision Song Contest went further than voting in the European Parliament elections in another way that matters to Europeanization. EU citizens could only vote for politicians from their own states to represent them in the European Parliament: a British Conservative could only vote for a British party, not for a Finnish or a Greek Conservative candidate; nor could a Swedish Green vote for a Green candidate from Germany. In their cultural as opposed to their civic capacities, however, Europeans could vote for songs and singers from other European countries. Under Eurovision, European enlargement had also gone further than political enlargement: as well as viewers from the EU member states, "Europeans" from Russia, Turkey, Israel, Iceland, and other parts of the continent are also eligible to vote.

The Eurovision Song Contest is one piece of evidence that Gripsrud draws on when challenging the EPS skeptics.[29] Citing Eurobarometer opinion surveys as further evidence, he points out that a majority of Europeans are interested in knowing the opinion of citizens in other EU member states on important political and social issues – the sort of behavior one would expect in a public sphere. Together with Chalaby,[30] Gripsrud points to the increasing importance of transnational, pan-Eurovision television. They argue that significant things are afoot when it comes to European broadcasting, and that the traditional connection between national territory and media culture is breaking down:

> The great social, cultural and political differences within the European Union make expectations of a uniform, completely integrated European public sphere totally unrealistic. But, importantly, that is not to say that such a public sphere does not exist … Television already contributes to a Europeanization of national public spheres and the minds of citizens.[31]

For Gripsrud, the European Broadcasting Union (EBU) clearly fulfills one criterion for the existence of a European public sphere, however defined.

The European Broadcasting Union and Euronews

Thirty years before CNN moved into the global village, the European Broadcasting Union (EBU) was linking broadcasters throughout the continent in a non-commercial, non-governmental collaborative network. Its nascence coincided with the demise of Pope Pius XII, which prompted the chief editor of Dutch television to famously declare: "I want the dead Pope live!"

The very act of cooperation can be thought to contribute to the emergence of a shared professional culture with common news values. The largest association of national broadcasters in the world, the EBU is larger than the European Union, with 75 members from 56 countries in and around Europe. It is for this reason that the Eurovision Song Contest – which is one EBU product – involves participation from non-European Union states.[32] Its member broadcasters reach an audience of 650 million each week.

As well as promoting cooperation and exchange between European public service broadcasters, the EBU serves as a lobby organization for them, working to insure that the role of public service broadcasting is recognized and taken into consideration by decision-makers. It represents its member organizations when the European Union deliberates audiovisual policy, and works closely with the UN and UNESCO to insure that the voice of European broadcasters is heard in the global debate on media policy. In the view of the EBU, "Europe's public service broadcasters are different to other market players; they are committed to public service values."[33] This means that the debate must be about content, and not just delivery mechanisms "or what kind of screen is being viewed," and above all that what is transmitted should be attuned to what is best for society, and not what is best for the market.[34]

The EBU calls itself the "hidden link" in the distribution chain of programs to European households. Its Geneva-based office coordinates daily and sometimes hourly transfers of programs, news, sports events, and music between members. This means that relatively poor countries are not at the mercy of expensive commercial operators like Reuters to buy news footage: these broadcasters trade material with each other and together decide which events are most relevant for each "feed." By 2012, more than 45,000 news items a year were being exchanged in this way.

Euronews

The EBU was one of the actors behind the launching of Euronews, the channel widely known as Europe's answer to CNN . It calls itself "the leading international news channel." Launched in 1993, it is now a multilingual, multi-platform service with a mandate to cover world news from a European perspective.

Euronews is based in Lyons, where journalists working the same news beat and at the same news desk put together bulletins from the same raw material, and broadcast them in English, French, German, Spanish, Italian, Portuguese, Russian, and Arabic. It also differs from most other channels in that there are no anchors, and reporters are rarely seen on camera. In this respect, it is "news from nowhere." On the other hand, many programs are retransmissions of national broadcasts. Through the Euronews portal, viewers in Germany and Greece get to see Portuguese programs about Poland, and so on. Apart from news reports every half-hour, flagship programs such as *Europe*, *Agora*, and *Parlamento* focus on European news.[35] According to its website, "Euronews' ability to understand and decipher the various political debates and implications of political decisions made within Europe and their effects not only on a global scale but on day to day living make it the only channel best positioned to deliver true 'European' news."[36]

The channel takes in commercial revenues, receives €50 million from the EBU each year, and lists 22 public broadcasters as its shareholders. According to a contract signed by the European Commission in 2005, Euronews was to receive €25 million between 2005 and 2010.[37]

Euronews broadcasts to more than 251 million households in 139 countries. It cites statistics which indicate that 171 million households in Europe receive Euronews, compared to 135 million receiving CNN International and 89 million receiving BBC World. The figures are interesting, because, while it is common to encounter Europeans who regularly watch CNN and BBC World, it is rare to come across Euronews or someone who is even aware of its existence.[38] Interviewed in 2008, managing director Michael Peters said (somewhat confusingly) that while Euronews was the most watched international news channel in Europe, no one knew that.[39] This was one factor behind the "extreme makeover" the channel underwent in 2008. It got rid of the blue and gold EU color scheme, toned down the European perspective and toned up the global take on the news, went in for more aggressive marketing, and tapped into new delivery modes. Apart from cable, satellite, and terrestrial broadcasts, it distributes news via mobile phones and live video streaming on GPRS, 3G, WAP, and i-mode services, and links its unedited, raw news footage "No Comment" segment straight to YouTube.

Despite its engagement with emerging technology, the channel has a very traditional view of the role of the news provider. This is to keep the well-informed citizen nourished with a regular dose of the sort of input thought essential to the health of the public sphere. "At Euronews," says the website www.euronews.net, "we believe that the growing use of sensationalism in news influences and distorts the viewers' perception of current global events … The work of the journalist is not to take sides, but rather to transcribe reality objectively and with complete integrity."[40] The Euronews philosophy, then, is that the role of a news channel is to supply individuals with "sufficient information to allow the viewer to form his own opinion of the world."[41] And it does tend to be "his" view. No fewer than 73 percent of Euronews viewers are men with high salaries and liquid stock investments, opinion leaders, and frequent fliers. As such individuals also tend to be staunch supporters of the European Union and a single euro currency, it is not immediately clear what Euronews can contribute to solving the problem of the European Union's democratic deficit.

As the EBU pointed out, the global media debate must not just be about delivery systems and screens (or, it could be added, economics). It must also concern content, if the power of communication is to be understood and if the media's democratic role is to be scrutinized. More than that, attention must be paid to form. Euronews might be popular among busy elites, but it is worth reflecting on whether its short, telegram-like bulletins contribute to engaging Europeans as well as informing them. In this respect, Euronews – like most other global broadcasters – is under-researched. Among the few studies that have been done, one compared coverage of Europe in Euronews and a national broadcaster.[42] Frydén Bonnier used a combination of quantitative and qualitative methods to find out which of the two channels could be thought to be most "Europeanizing." Studying a month of daily reporting, she compared the amount of attention devoted to Europe (a traditional indicator) but also paid attention to communicative style. Was the news reported in a way that made it likely viewers would feel it had something to do with them, so they could identify with Europe, the European Union, or other Europeans? Frydén Bonnier found that Euronews had (perhaps unsurprisingly) a larger proportion of European reports in the sample period and that they made up a larger part of the total broadcast time than in the domestic channel. But after having analyzed more than 150 reports, she also concluded that the telegraphic reporting style was much less personalized and engaging than the reports of domestic broadcasters: "So while Euronews has many more news reports on the European Union and European issues, only four percent of them convey to the viewers a feeling of identification with the European Union, with Europe, or with other Europeans,"[43] in contrast to a quarter of the reports from the domestic broadcaster. The importance of content and form – and not least narrative tradition – is the focus of the remainder of this chapter.

Shared Histories, Different Understandings

In 1989 former French Prime Minister François Mitterand said: "Europe does not have a common language yet … Television can be that common language."[44] That has yet to happen. As Bourdon points out, rather a lot of research suggests that global satellite television has contributed to the persistence of old national communities (albeit deterritorialized ones) rather than the creation of new ones.[45] After two decades of technological revolution, people have abundant opportunities to become informed about what is happening in their world: the explosion of commercial broadcasting and Internet resources means that Europeans are no longer reliant on public service channels to become well-informed citizens. But as skeptics about the EPS gleefully point out, they continue to be faithful to their national broadcasters. In a setting with proliferating outlets, television can play a more profound role, and help viewers engage with the world, as well as observe it. Parallel to a "thinning" out of political reporting, there is evidence to suggest a "thickening" of reportage culture. This brings us to an important question: what does cultural diversity mean in practice? Despite all that has been said about "the global newsroom," there is strong evidence that journalists rooted in different media cultures, or speaking to different audiences, are using the semiotic materials circulating in the global mediascape in different ways. This means that members of those different audiences are liable to arrive at different understandings of the way the world works.

In a study that compared how six Europe-based broadcasters reported the world in a six-week period, it was found that there was rather less "breaking news" than expected, and that a lot of news was actually "olds," that is, about historical events.[46] A striking example was reporting of the sixtieth anniversary of the Normandy invasion, known as D-Day. A total of 60 news items about the D-Day commemoration, amounting to 190 minutes of news, was found in the daily reports of six European channels, three of them broadcasting to national audiences, and three of them to international audiences. Looked at more closely, these stories seemed to be making sense of current affairs, and giving viewers messages about how to solve problems that transcend national borders. The findings, which illustrate the diversity that UNESCO and others mentioned here have held to be so important, can be briefly summarized as follows.

The "master" story told by the BBC – the recurring theme in all its reports – was about the liberation of the oppressed by stalwart heroes. In speeches given significant airtime by the British channel, US President Bush tried to equate the liberation of Europe with the liberation of Iraq. The BBC resisted this frame to some extent. In the days surrounding the commemoration, Iraq came across as an American mission, flawed and fraught with problems. The D-Day invasion, on the other hand, was a British story (albeit with an international supporting cast). In contrast to Iraq, it was depicted as combat in an irrefutably good cause and a glorious success. The heroes in question are unusual figures in BBC discourse, which other studies have shown tends to privilege elites. Here the focus was on the ordinary men, often with working-class and regional dialects, who were repeatedly celebrated as the most noble and self-effacing of their generation. The story told to BBC viewers was about the experiences of these men. It was about something that happened six decades ago, and had little to say about the current state of international relations.

The story told by the public service broadcaster Heute to viewers at home in Germany, on the other hand, was about the present. D-Day had to do with the birth of modern Germany, the importance of having friends and keeping them. The people in this story were Europeans who had overcome their differences and learned to respect each other. While war veterans featured in this narrative, the main actors were German Chancellor Schröder and French President Chirac, or the Germany and France they symbolized.

In contrast to the profoundly gendered BBC discourse, the Swedish public service broadcaster offered viewers the perspectives of women and non-combatants. Instead of reveling in the enthusiasm of the military replay as the BBC had done, nurses gave voice to all those who lived through the carnage, and felt saddened by the thought of so many young lives lost. Also in contrast to its British counterpart, the Swedish newsroom understood the D-Day anniversary to be only ostensibly about the past. What made it interesting was that it provided an occasion for world leaders to have a summit, and to sort out their differences over the ongoing US occupation of Iraq.

Rather than painting a different picture from the newsrooms servicing domestic audiences, the European global channels tended to reinforce national tendencies. The stories told by BBC World News were strongly reminiscent of those told in the domestic British newsroom, with their *Boy's Own* tone of coverage and the situating of the D-Day story – and by corollary those listening to it – firmly in the past. The BBC World narrative of the Normandy invasion was all about liberation and heroism. By contrast, the global German newsroom, Deutsche Welle, told the story of D-Day in a respectful but not reverential tone of voice. Its master narrative was not one of American and British liberators who long ago fought shoulder to shoulder for a just cause, but one of Europeans who were living in the present, as the best of friends. The metaphor employed was actually stronger: the D-Day anniversary provided the opportunity to reaffirm the marriage vows between a partner who had once been raped and her violator, who had repented his evil ways and become trustworthy and steadfast.

But of all the channels, it was Euronews that made most of the theme of reconciliation. It made it clear that wars tend to bring out the worst in people – both now, in Iraq, and then, in Auschwitz and Paris, where women who had fallen in love with men from the wrong country were treated as pariahs. But Euronews acknowledged, like the others, that many had behaved in a human and altruistic fashion as well. The BBC and American and British soldiers were among the heroes. But in the Euronews account of the liberation of Europe from barbarity, the heroes also came from the new EU member states. Euronews did more than echo the Deutsche Welle metaphor of mixed marriage. It amplified it. On Euronews, the sixtieth anniversary of D-Day was celebrated by a Europe that was, as it put it, reconciled with itself. What it said about contemporary international relations was that the world had moved on and was no longer a place in which differences could be resolved by military conflict. Where both BBC programs had symbolized D-Day with logos featuring a gun, Euronews epitomized it by the passionate embrace of the French and German leaders.

In reports of the D-Day commemoration – as in reports of breaking news and most other events – the six European newsrooms used similar, and sometimes identical, footage. Much of it emanated from the EBU exchange. They talked about the same event at the same time to Europeans across the continent, many of whom shared the same history. For a moment, it was almost as if the revisited Normandy beaches served as a temporary European public sphere. Certainly, many of the requirements for an EPS outlined above were fulfilled by these reports. But to look at the evidence in this superficial way is to miss an important point, as attention to the master narratives reveals. The facts do not always speak for themselves.

Conclusion

The emphasis in this chapter has been on that which is "European," and support has implicitly been given to those who argue that a European public sphere is taking shape, that media production and use is contributing to a European identity, and that European publics do have things in common and are apparently aware of it. But the power of national traditions and *Weltanschauung* remains strong – just as UNESCO says it should. Within Europe there are not just different models of media and politics; there are also different historical experiences and narrative traditions which mean that the same event often takes on different meanings in different media.

Different accounts of the world, and messages about the relationship of the intended audience with that world, vary from one media culture to another. In some European countries, established themes and understandings are reinforced in foreign news coverage rather than reworked. At the same time, other outlets are moving away from the very notion of "foreign news," some (like Euronews, BBC World, and Deutsche Welle) by their remit, others by the narrative techniques they employ, which invite their audience members to think of themselves as cosmopolitans and members of a transnational community rather than as citizens of nation-states. They can even make different sense of shared histories.

Even if it predated the actions stipulated in the European Commission's "Europe for Citizens" program for 2007–13, the Euronews take on D-Day was a good fit with the objectives of this part of the EU cultural plan. Part of the budget allocated to the Europe for Citizens program was earmarked for projects to preserve "active European remembrance."[47] Although these are mainly projects designed to preserve the places and archives associated with mass deportations and former concentration camps, it could be argued that the media are one of the sites in which collective memories are kept alive.

From the heroes of World War II to those of Mount Olympus: whatever happened to Hercules? In *The European*, Hercules had lost his Greek identity. Pinocchio was no longer

Italian, Quasimodo was no longer French, and Winnie the Pooh was no longer English. These cultural icons had all become Europeans in the newspaper article which opened this chapter. Some would say that such media discourse is as much a form of cultural imperialism as any commercial strategy devised by a US conglomerate. This is certainly a question to which any student of the media and cultural regulation should give thought.

Not long after Disney cashed in on Hercules, *The European* went belly-up. In the midst of an economic crisis that was accentuating the divisions between Europeans rather than hastening integration, five well-established national newspapers decided to do something about it. Rather than reinforcing stereotypes, they challenged them and invited their readers to get to know their neighbors. The "Europa" series was published simultaneously by Germany's *Der Spiegel*, France's *Le Monde*, Spain's *El País*, Poland's *Gazeta Wyborcza*, and the United Kingdom's *Guardian*. In the digital media age, the articles can easily be found on the Internet. Readers of this chapter are invited to look them up.

Notes

1. http://unesdoc.unesco.org/images/0012/001271/1271 60m.pdf, accessed August 22, 2013.
2. These figures change all the time. To access to the most up-to-date figures at any given time, and other background information, visit the European Audiovisual Observatory at www.obs.coe.int.
3. http://www.eu4journalists.eu/index.php/dossiers/english/C98, accessed August 29, 2013.
4. Stylianos Papathanassopoulos, "Europe: An Exemplary Landscape for Comprehending Globalization," *Global Media and Communication* 1 (2005), 46.
5. UNESCO, "The Power of Culture," at http://portal.unesco.org/culture/en/ev.php-URL_ID=18717&URL_DO=DO_TOPIC&URL_SECTION=201.html, accessed August 29, 2013.
6. "The UNESCO World Report on Cultural Diversity," at http://www.unesco.org/new/en/culture/resources/report/the-unesco-world-report-on-cultural-diversity/, accessed August 29, 2013.
7. http://unesdoc.unesco.org/images/0012/001271/1271 60m.pdf, accessed August 22, 2013.
8. http://unesdoc.unesco.org/images/0012/001271/1271 60m.pdf, accessed August 22, 2013.
9. http://ec.europa.eu/avpolicy/reg/tvwf/index_en.htm, accessed August 22, 2013.
10. European Parliament and Council, Directive 2007/65/EC, December 11, 2007, *Official Journal of the European Union* L332/27.
11. http://ec.europa.eu/digital-agenda/, accessed August 22, 2013.
12. European Broadcasting Union, "Audiovisual Services and GATS Negotiations," January 17, 2003.
13. http://europa.eu/legislation_summaries/culture/index_en.htm, accessed August 22, 2013.
14. http://www.europarl.europa.eu/summits/lis1_en.htm, accessed August 22, 2013.
15. The EFP was officially founded in 1997 during the Berlin International Film Festival. Its founding members were organizations and institutions from Belgium, Germany, France, Greece, the United Kingdom, the Netherlands, Austria, Switzerland, and the five Scandinavian states as a country grouping. They were joined by Iceland, Portugal, and Spain shortly afterward, by Luxembourg and Italy in 1999, by the Czech Republic and Hungary in 2002, and by Estonia, Latvia, and Lithuania in 2003. By 2009 the EFP ranks had swollen to include Slovenia, Bulgaria, Poland, Romania, and Serbia.
16. EU Media Commissioner Viviane Reding, press release, January 9, 2009, at http://europa.eu/rapid/press-release_IP-09-26_en.htm, accessed August 29, 2013.
17. Decision No 1041/2009/EC of the European Parliament and of the Council of 21 October 2009 establishing an audiovisual cooperation programme with professionals from third countries, MEDIA Mundus.
18. "Commission Recommendation of 20 August 2009 on media literacy in the digital environment for a more competitive audiovisual and content industry and an inclusive knowledge society," at http://eur-lex.europa.eu/LexUriServ/LexUriServ.do?uri=CELEX:32009H06 25:EN:NOT, accessed August 29, 2013.
19. Daniel C. Hallin and Paolo Mancini, *Comparing Media Systems: Three Models of Media and Politics,* Cambridge: Cambridge University Press, 2004; Daniel C. Hallin and Paolo Mancini, *Comparing Media Systems Beyond the Western World*, Cambridge: Cambridge University Press, 2011.

20. Jürgen Habermas, *The Structural Transformation of the Public Sphere*, Cambridge: Polity, 1962/1989.

21. Darren G. Lilleker, *Key Concepts in Political Communication*, London: Sage, 2006; Monroe E. Price, *Television, the Public Sphere and National Identity*, Oxford: Oxford University Press, 1995; Peter Dahlgren, *Television and the Public Sphere: Citizenship, Democracy and the Media*, London: Sage, 1995.

22. European Commission, "White Paper on a European Communication Policy," COM 35 final, 2006, 4–5, at http://europa.eu/documents/comm/white_papers/pdf/com2006_35_en.pdf, accessed August 7, 2013.

23. See, for example, Hans-Jörg Trenz, "Media Coverage on European Governance," *European Journal of Communication* 19(3) (2004), 291–319.

24. Philip Schlesinger, "The Babel of Europe? An Essay on Network and Communicative Spaces." In Dario Castiglione and Chris Longman (eds.), *The Language Question in Europe and Diverse Societies: Political, Legal and Social Perspectives*, Oxford: Hart, 2007; Philip Schlesinger, "A Cosmopolitan Temptation?" *European Journal of Communication* 22(4) (2007), 413–26.

25. S. Lingenberg, S. "The Audience's Role in Constituting the European Public Sphere: A Theoretical Approach Based on the Pragmatic Concept of John Dewey," in N. Carpentier et al. (eds.), *Researching Media, Democracy and Participation*. Tartu, Estonia: Tartu University Press, 2006, p. 123.

26. See Michael Brüggemann, "How the EU Constructs the European Public Sphere," *Javnost: The Public* 12(2) (2005), 57–74; Risto Kunelius and Colin Sparks, "Problems with a European Public Sphere: An Introduction," *Javnost: The Public* 8(1) (2001), 5–20; Minna Frydén Bonnier, "Europeanization in European News Broadcasts? A Comparative Study of Euronews and Rapport," Master's thesis, Department of Political Science, Stockholm University, 2007.

27. Barrie Axford and Richard Higgins, "The European Information Society: A New Public Sphere?," in Chris Rumford (ed.), *Cosmopolitanism and Europe*, Liverpool: Liverpool University Press, 2007; Michael Brüggemann, "How the EU Constructs the European Public Sphere," *Javnost: The Public* 12(2) (2005), 57–74; Frydén Bonnier, "Europeanization in European News Broadcasts? A Comparative Study of Euronews and Rapport"; Hans J. Kleinsteuber, "Habermas and the Public Sphere: From a German to a European Perspective," *Javnost: The Public* 8(1) (2001), 95–108; Marcel Machill, Markus Beiler, and Corinna Fischer, "Europe-Topics in Europe's Media," *European Journal of Communication* 2(1) (2006), 57–88; Schlesinger, "The Babel of Europe?"; Schlesinger, "A Cosmopolitan Temptation?"; Holli Semetko, Claes H. de Vreese, and Jochen Peter, "Europeanised Politics – Europeanised Media? European Integration and Political Communication," *West European Politics* 23(4) (2000), 121–41; Slavko Splichal, "In Search of a Strong European Public Sphere: Some Critical Observations on Conceptualizations of Publicness and the (European) Public Sphere," *Media, Culture & Society* 28(5) (2006), 695–714.

28. P. Statham, "Making European News: How Journalists View Their Role and Media Performance." *Journalism* 9(4) (2008), 408.

29. Jostein Gripsrud, "Television and the European Public Sphere," *European Journal of Communication* 22(4) (2007), 479–92.

30. Jean K. Chalaby, *Transnational Television Worldwide: Towards a New Media Order*, London: I. B. Tauris, 2005; *Transnational Television in Europe: Reconfiguring Global Communications Networks*, London: I. B. Taurus, 2009.

31. Gripsrud, "Television and the European Public Sphere," 489.

32. In 2009 the competition took place in Moscow, as Russia's Dima Bilan had won in 2008; the 2009 winner, Alexander Rybak, represented Norway, which is not a member of the European Union.

33. http://www.eurovision.tv/upload/media/EBUcorporate.pdf, accessed August 29, 2013.

34. European Broadcasting Union, "Who We Are and What We Do," at http://www.eurovision.tv/upload/media/EBUcorporate.pdf, accessed 31 August 2013

35. For an analysis of the content and structure of Euronews programming, and a comparison with other global broadcasters, see Andreas Widholm. "From Television Flows to Generic Structures: Reflections on Form and Content of Euronews and BBC World News," Unpublished conference paper, Department of Journalism, Media and Communication, Stockholm University, 2009.

36. http://www.euronews.com/the-station/, accessed August 22, 2013.

37. "Communication from the Commission to the Council, the European Parliament, the European Economic and Social Committee and the Committee of the Regions on implementing the information and communication, Brussels, 20.4.2004," COM(2004) 196 final, at http://eur-lex.europa.eu/LexUriServ/site/en/com/2004/com2004_0196en01.pdf, accessed August 29, 2013.

38. This, at least, is the experience of someone who lectures at a European university, at two departments who send and receive a significant number of students on exchange to other European countries each year.

39. "Euronews Rebrands to Take on Rivals," *Guardian* (2008), cited in Richard Rooke, *European Media in the Digital Age: Analysis and Approaches*, Harlow, UK: Longman, 2009, p. 94.

40. https://www.facebook.com/euronews.fans/info, accessed August 29, 2013.
41. https://www.facebook.com/euronews.fans/info, accessed August 29, 2013.
42. The national program was *Rapport*, the main evening newscast of Swedish Television, a public service broadcaster.
43. Frydén Bonnier, "Europeanization in European News Broadcasts?"
44. Quoted in J. Bourdon, "Unhappy Engineers of the European Soul: The EBU and the Woes of Pan-European Television," *International Communication Gazette* 69(3), 276.
45. Bourdon, "Unhappy Engineers of the European Soul," 277.
46. A. Robertson, *Mediated Cosmopolitanism: The World of Television News*. Cambridge: Polity, 2010.
47. http://eacea.ec.europa.eu/citizenship/programme/action4_en.php, accessed August 22, 2013.

10

Global Issues, Music, and MTV

Introduction

In the twenty-first century, communication, media, and information exports are becoming the primary engine of the global economy for the United States and other core nations. Since the end of World War II, US aerospace industries have provided the primary US export product, with sales of both commercial and military aircraft to various nations around the world. These sales greatly assisted the US balance of payments as well as domestic employment. But with the end of the Cold War, the aftermath of 9/11, and the economic recession the global demand for aircraft has subsided. In addition, the passenger airline manufacturing business has become a global duopoly between Boeing and its European competitor, Airbus. As a result, makers of US cultural products ranging from movies and TV programs to music and computers are overtaking aerospace as the primary US employers and exporters. A good example of this export phenomenon is Viacom's Music Television (MTV) which is available on every continent and has a potential audience of 500 million households. It has numerous websites, as well. In the United Kingdom alone it offers 25 video channels for all ages. The primary demographic is the age group 10–24. This is also the prime group sought by advertisers.

According to the US Department of Commerce, the sale of feature films and TV shows and home video rentals to foreign markets increased significantly during the 1990s. It is projected that global revenues will exceed $35 billion by 2016. The same reports estimate that the US music industry will account for 50 percent of global sales.[1] American films and music are now global commodities and future sales increases have to come from foreign, primarily emerging, markets. These video commodities are the foot-soldiers of electronic colonialism.

When imported products consisted of military aircraft or jumbo jets, there was little widespread concern among foreign populations. But when they began to consist of mass media products with cultural, linguistic, as well as economic implications, animosity began

Global Communication: Theories, Stakeholders, and Trends, Fourth Edition. Thomas L. McPhail.
© 2014 John Wiley & Sons, Inc. Published 2014 by John Wiley & Sons, Inc.

to grow toward the prevalence of core nations' cultural artifacts, video talent, as well as moral and economic values. Clearly, not everyone or every nation welcomes the globalization of the mass media. Many peripheral nations and some industrialized nations, particularly Canada, Ireland, Australia, and France, are concerned about the dominance of US global media exports.[2] David Rothkopf explains the issues:

> Globalization has economic roots and political consequences, but it also has brought into focus the power of culture in this global environment – the power to bind and to divide in a time when the tensions between integration and separation tug at every issue that is relevant to international relations.
>
> The impact of globalization on culture and the impact of culture on globalization merit discussion. The homogenizing influences of globalization that are most often condemned by the new nationalists and by cultural romanticists are actually positive; globalization promotes integration and the removal not only of cultural barriers but of many of the negative dimensions of culture. Globalization is a vital step toward both a more stable world and better lives for the people in it. Furthermore, these issues have serious implications for American foreign policy. For the United States, a central objective of an Information Age foreign policy must be to win the battle of the world's information flows, dominating the airwaves as Great Britain once ruled the seas.[3]

The world's information and media flows have been enhanced by the widespread surge in sales of televisions, computers, DVD players, CD players, iPods, satellite dishes, cable, Kindles, Nooks, and personal mobile devices. In addition, there have been infrastructure advancements such as the growth of streaming video from various vendors. On the print side, the amount of US content exported around the world is significant. Even the Hearst-owned *Cosmopolitan*, a niche magazine for women, has global sales of close to five million copies, with 40 foreign editions in 25 languages. Time Inc. has several globally successful magazines as well.

US media companies frequently enjoy an economic advantage denied to almost all of their off-shore competitors. The domestic US audience is not only large and wealthy, but it also has a substantial and varied taste for entertainment and media products of all types. This continent-wide market provides the economic resources necessary to support a global culture. In addition, the latest mass media technologies are frequently introduced in the US marketplace, thus allowing US producers to experiment with and to refine technical and marketing strategies before moving off-shore to an ever expanding group of global customers. These customers are in other core nations as well as in all the semiperipheral and some of the peripheral nations. As domestic markets become mature and the room for growth decreases, the strategic focus is now on emerging markets elsewhere.

This chapter reviews communication exports and the globalization of the media marketplace. The export market for US-produced television programming and the international music industry is examined in detail. Particular attention is given to MTV, a network that personifies the marriage of global television with leading musicians, and a global youth culture.

As noted earlier, foreign television networks consume large quantities of US movies and television shows via syndication. Particularly attractive are US-made situation comedies and dramas with high production values.[4] Major series such as *Dallas, Columbo, Star Trek, Baywatch, Seinfeld, ER, The Simpsons, The Cosby Show, Friends, SpongeBob*, and *Sex and the*

City dominate many foreign television schedules. For example, it is estimated an audience in excess of one and a half billion in 148 nations had viewed *Baywatch*. *Baywatch* began in 1989 and lasted 10 years, with 210 episodes available for syndication. *The Simpsons*, an animated prime-time show about a dysfunctional family, is available all over the world and is the longest-running animated comedy. In 2009 it passed *Gunsmoke* as the longest-running prime-time show and in February 2012 it showed its five-hundredth episode. It also has served as a catalyst for other animated series, such as *South Park*, *Family Guy*, and *King of the Hill*.

However, in the 1990s an interesting shift occurred. The major networks replaced expensive dramas and sitcoms with reality shows, talk shows, or shows based on the news magazine format (similar to CBS's *60 Minutes*). Today, the news genre on national television networks is in trouble from the three competing all-news networks, CNN, Fox News, and MSNBC. But reality shows and others continue to fill the void. One of the consequences of this trend is a steep increase in the price of the fewer remaining successful sitcoms, such as *The Simpsons*, *Seinfeld*, *Friends*, *Everyone Loves Raymond*, *Scrubs*, and *Frasier*, and a stable of children's shows available for syndication.

Cost Escalations

Among the reasons why networks are cutting back their production of prime-time drama is the high cost of such programming. The cost of prime-time episodes now averages about $1.75 million an hour, about double the cost of an equivalent episode a decade ago. Some series are substantially more expensive: each instalment of *ER* cost $13 million; Tim Allen of *Home Improvement* received a fee of $1.25 million per episode; and even the *The X-Files*, which was for a time filmed in Vancouver, Canada to keep costs down, cost $2.5 million per episode. Each of the six leading actors on *Friends* received $1 million per half-hour episode – and they walked away from money despite the success of the show. With high-profile stars demanding higher salaries and with competition for experienced writers and cast, production costs are increasing dramatically. In comparison, news programming costs about $500,000 an hour. Even "reality" shows such as *America's Most Wanted*, *Survivor*, *Hell's Kitchen*, *You're Fired*, *American Idol*, *X Factor*, *Undercover Boss*, or *Biggest Loser* are relatively inexpensive to produce compared to the cost of producing leading dramas or sitcoms, or of broadcasting rights for major sports events.

Audience Fragmentation

As costs escalate, US networks also need to face the reality of a fragmenting audience. CBS, NBC, and ABC dominated the television market from the inception of the medium until the 1980s, when the Fox network joined them. In June 1998, however, these four networks were for the first time out-watched in prime time by audiences viewing cable options. During the 1990s viewers deserted the major networks to tune into what are often called "narrowcasting" or niche channels. Now the growth of mobile devices is also impacting their audience size. The rapid growth of alternative cable options, including both specialty channels (ESPN, MTV, A&E, CNN, and MSNBC) and super channels (such as WGN and TBS), had a significant cumulative impact on the audiences for the major television networks. The major networks have had their audiences reduced to less than 50 percent of the total prime-time audience. They have been forced to scramble to maintain an audience share sufficient to sustain high advertising rates.[5] The addition of time spent on the Internet and mobile apps has also taken a toll on broadcasters.

Clearly, one of the factors making the new media offerings so attractive is their ability to target specific or niche audiences. Another is their programming flexibility, which permits them to address unique high-interest events. Take, for example, the infamous white Ford Bronco low-speed chase and the subsequent trial of former football star O. J. Simpson. This case, involving a well-known personality and a lengthy and sordid trial about sex and murder, captivated enormous audiences in North America and abroad. As the dominant news story of its time, it provided audiences with niche news and public affairs networks, with thousands of hours of programming over several months that not only filled their schedules but also attracted a new and larger audience. While the new players focused on the trial, the "big four" networks found themselves in a no-win situation. Leery about abandoning their traditional audiences by pre-empting afternoon soap operas or prime-time sitcoms, they limited their coverage to the traditional newscasts. Although these networks retained a portion of their audience, many viewers were motivated to tune into Court TV or other all-news alternatives they had never watched before. All-news networks cover every detail of these major stories, whereas the Big Four networks are forced to select when and how to pre-empt their schedules. The media's handling of the hearings before the 9/11 Commission or the British investigation of the News Corp phone hacking are cases in point.

Clearly, technology is responsible for this proliferation of media options and the continued fragmentation of the viewing audience. The number of cable channels is expanding more rapidly than anticipated. With the advent of digital television, viewers will have access to over 100 channels. Even if only a small number of individuals watch these channels, such as the History Channel, the Spanish Channel, or the Golf Channel, the total impact on the networks in the long run will be staggering. In the final analysis, the Big Four networks are not only losing audiences, but they are also losing revenue. Thus their ability to experiment with the number of sitcoms as in the early days of television, when they collectively controlled the entire audience base, is limited. This reduction in the number of successful sitcoms means that fewer are available for foreign syndication, and thus the price tag for what is available has increased substantially.

At the same time it may be that a corresponding increase in the audience of CNN – particularly when global news stories break, such as the Gulf War, the death of Princess Diana, or an act of terrorism – is likely to insure that foreign media continue to carry extensive US programming options. (CNN is covered in detail in Chapter 11.)

As costs escalate, audience size shrinks, and advertising revenues decrease, the major US television networks are re-evaluating their positions and strategies, not only with respect to each other, but also with respect to the myriad cable channels now available. As more broadcast, cable, DVD, smart phone, mobile, and Internet options become available to viewers, Comcast NBC, CBS, Fox, and Walt Disney's ABC network are cutting staff. These decisions reflect the reality of escalating programming costs and decreasing numbers of viewers. Of the original Big Three networks, NBC is well situated, primarily because it responded to the cable challenge by introducing its own specialty channels – MSNBC and CNBC – as a means of competing for the advertising revenue available to these niche markets. NBC also established channels in Europe and Asia. Yet many analysts suggest that these efforts may be insufficient and predict that major industry restructuring, including mergers or joint ventures, will continue in the future.

New International Realities

Despite the problems, foreign markets are still lucrative for US producers. The proliferation of media options is increasingly an international phenomenon, and this creates new opportunities for US program sales abroad. As technology has led to increased media choices, so also governmental media and regulatory policies have had to adapt. Historically, much of broadcasting, originally radio and then television, in the industrialized countries outside the United States was dominated by public government-supported systems. The British Broadcasting Corporation (BBC) served as the model for many national media networks, particularly in the British colonies. For many years, most European viewers had access to only one or two public television channels, which were publicly financed and carried no advertising. Private networks and cable and satellite services were not available nor could they be licensed. This situation changed substantially in the 1980s when privatization, deregulation, liberalization, and commercialization took hold around the globe. Prime Minister Margaret Thatcher of the United Kingdom and President Ronald Reagan of the United States spread their conservative views and promoted pro-business policies.

In an era when broadcasting options were limited to one or two public media outlets, regulation was significant. In fact, the rationale for public, as opposed to private, broadcasting relied on the notion that the electronic mass media were social institutions with certain public accountability goals. These media were entrusted with the responsibility for providing educational broadcasting and children's programs, promoting democracy and human rights, and providing balanced programming. With the introduction of private broadcasting outlets, government regulation was reduced in favor of market forces. Today, this duopoly between public and private broadcasting systems coexists in most industrialized nations. As a result, the viewing and listening public now has substantially more media choices, and US producers have larger markets for their products. Not surprisingly, a growing number of the foreign options have a distinct made-in-America flavor. It is still cheaper to buy US content compared to original programming.

Modeling: Creating Indigenous Programs with US Cultural Values

Most foreign nations, with significantly smaller audience bases, are unable to compete with the expensive, high-quality production values of US dramatic television programming. In order to fill the available broadcast schedule and maximize their revenues, they purchase US syndicated programming. Consequently, many nations, industrialized and less developed alike, experience significant erosion of their own cultures. But the issue does not end with the direct importation of US programming.

A more insidious practice has emerged which further threatens national cultures. As mentioned earlier, US networks have introduced lower-cost "reality"-based programs or game shows. Although these programs are attractive to US audiences, they do not export well. Because their themes tend to be parochial and time-sensitive, their chances for foreign syndication and release are marginal. Instead, foreign producers tend to copy the news magazine or reality show format, inserting local content, announcers, or venues. In Australia, for example, which imports a significant number of US feature films and television productions for domestic consumption, home-grown productions increasingly look very much like US programming. A few examples illustrate the point. Australia has its own version of NBC's *Today Show*, an equivalent of *The Newlywed Game* called *A Current Affair*, a clone of MTV's *Real World* entitled *A House from Hell*, and its own *Wheel of Fortune*, *Funniest Home Videos*, and *60 Minutes*. Thus, even when there is indigenous production capacity, the US influence is visible on foreign television throughout the industrial world, particularly in English-speaking countries. The United Kingdom, Canada, Ireland, and New Zealand, also major consumers of US television and feature films, model many local productions on US originals. From time to time, US media outlets also remake television shows and films from other core nations.

The tendency to produce adaptations of US models has both cultural and programmatic implications.[6] Of significant concern is the different manner in which the United States and other nations view cultural industries. The US rationale for promoting television, feature films, DVDs, records, CDs, and other cultural products is based on the notion that the marketplace will determine winners and losers. Sometimes the winners, such as the movies *Titanic*, *Slumdog Millionaire*, and *My Big Fat Greek Wedding*, reap enormous rewards for their producers. Other films are duds and force their parent studios into bankruptcy. This is the price investors are willing to pay to insure that the marketplace rules. This attitude contrasts dramatically with the perception of almost all other nations, which view cultural industries from a non-economic perspective. For them, films, DVDs, radio, music, CDs, and other media products are an expression of their historical roots, current culture, identity, and future destiny. In order to insure an indigenous media presence, many of these countries subsidize their national radio and television networks, feature film industry, and other cultural sectors.

France provides an outstanding example of the extent to which a country is willing to use tax revenues to subsidize media productions and products to compete directly with US cultural industries. Primarily, although not solely, because of language constraints, domestic French productions tend to fare poorly in the open global market. The French government helped finance the film *Asterix* – at a cost of $50 million, the most expensive French film ever made – in an attempt to recapture part of the French domestic market. Currently, French films attract less than 50 percent of the French market.

The French and other European markets are facing an additional threat – the growth of the US-style multiplex cinema. Although the cineplex has increased the number of screens and cinema attendance, it has failed to create an increase in audiences for European films. Rather, it has promoted the further penetration of US movies into foreign markets, and US box office receipts continue to escalate. Today Hollywood reaps more than half of its profits from off-shore audiences, compared to only 25 percent in the early 1980s. Given this shift in profit figures, Hollywood producers are now spending significant sums to market major blockbusters internationally. These multimillion-dollar marketing budgets dwarf the amounts available to produce entire films by independent competitors around the globe.[7] Finally, these same Hollywood production houses have added merchandise and DVDs to their revenue stream, with non-US sales of DVDs exceeding domestic DVD sales.

Global Media Marketplace

The global media marketplace is perceived as being under the control of the United States, which exports its culture through television shows, movies, music, McDonald's, smartphones, tablets, sportswear, and shopping malls. However, Rod Carveth, who agrees that the economy is becoming globally integrated, suggests that the United States may be losing its competitive advantage.[8] According to Carveth and others, the United States needs to change its strategy if it wants to regain its dominant position in the global media industry. These analysts contend that a number of developments, such as global media mergers and acquisitions; legal and cultural import barriers in the European Union, Canada, and Japan; as well as strategic miscalculations by US media firms, has eroded the country's competitive advantage.[9] In order to reassert itself, strategists suggest that the United States must adopt a cooperative rather than a competitive strategy in international media. Co-productions come to mind.

For years the United States maintained an international advantage because of its superior technical and marketing talent, its audience size, and its capital resources. The domestic industry also benefited from the export of its products to foreign markets. In addition, foreign talent wanted to work in New York or Hollywood. Throughout this period, US superiority in electronic media was evident, but the United States failed to anticipate any competition from foreign markets.

As an early leader in the electronics industry, the United States was unprepared when it began to lose its competitive advantage to Japanese and European manufacturers. During the 1980s, major US consumer electronics manufacturers such as RCA abandoned the industry. While research and development fell off in the United States, it blossomed internationally, particularly in Germany, Japan, and France, where substantial advances were made. The US international media presence was further weakened when many countries, including Canada,[10] began to impose restrictions on US media exports at the same time as they began to subsidize their own media productions, thus creating more programming to compete with US video products. In addition, when 12 European nations joined together to form the European Union in the 1950s, they began to open up the former Soviet Union and eastern European countries to freer trade with Europe and Japan. European media companies such as Bertelsmann, Hachette, Canal+, and Pathé began to compete in the global marketplace. Moreover, they were prepared to meet the increasing demand for European-produced programming that reflected the unique identities of Europeans.

Another factor that weakened US domination was a series of mergers or acquisitions through which foreign corporations gained control of US media undertakings. The trend of merger and acquisition activity began when Australian-born media baron Rupert Murdoch and his company News Corporation acquired newspapers such as the *New York Post*, the *Chicago Sun-Times*, and the *Boston Herald*. Another player was the Holtzbrinck Publishing Group who purchased Macmillan Publishers and Publicis Omnicom Group who purchased Saatchi & Saatchi, the successful international advertising conglomerate. Perhaps the most high-profile acquisition of a media company was that of Columbia Pictures by Japan's Sony Corporation, but others included Hachette's (France) purchase of the Diamond's magazine chain, the sale of A&M Records to Philips (The Netherlands), Bertelsmann's (Germany) acquisition of RCA/Ariolas Records, Vivendi's (France) controlling of a significant segment of the games sector with Activision/Blizzard, and VNU's (The Netherlands) take-over of the Nielsen rating company. Non-US companies have consolidated as well, in order to strengthen their combined market share.

In all of these cases, the players were motivated by an appreciation of the manner in which the mergers would permit the companies to combine their strengths to achieve savings in production, distribution, and exhibition of media products on a global scale. They anticipated some positive synergy. Moreover, these foreign companies wanted to gain access to the vital US market.

Given the changing global media marketplace and barriers preventing the United States from becoming an international broadcaster, Carveth and others contend that it is important for US firms to merge with and/or to acquire international companies if the country wants to regain its competitive edge internationally. The US needs to jump on the merger and acquisition bandwagon. Virtually every other nation in the world, including those in the European Union, lack sufficient domestic programming to meet their future media goals.[11] The best strategy for insuring US access to these markets is for domestic companies to form alliances with international players. The resulting co-productions will open new markets. In 1990, for example, NBC and London-based Yorkshire Television formed a joint venture called Tango Productions, which enabled NBC to avoid or at least minimize the import regulations of the European Union when selling its media products. Other joint ventures have developed between US and non-US firms. Clear Channel Communications of San Antonio, Texas now holds interests in several global firms.

The International Music Industry

By 2012 global music sales were over $16.5 billion. The five leading nations in terms of sales are the United States, Japan, Germany, United Kingdom, and France. English is by far the dominant language for the artists, with one notable exception. The exception is the growing niche market for Spanish music and this is primarily due to artists Ricky Martin, Gloria Estefan, Salina Gomez, and Enrique Iglesias. The global industry is in a state of flux for two reasons: (1) there is a series of potential acquisitions as the industry consolidates on a global basis; and (2) it has to find a way of dealing with both legal and illegal downloading of music from the Internet.[12]

In examining the music industry, it is important to recognize that most of the relevant information is collected and maintained by Billboard using SoundScan data. SoundScan data collects point-of-sale information on all music formats and configurations sold at about 80 percent of US retail outlets, and then projects sales for the entire US marketplace. These data provide a wealth of knowledge about the industry.

Historically the international music industry was dominated by five major global players, all from core nations: Universal Music Group (France); Sony Music Entertainment (Japan); EMI Group (UK), purchased by Vivendi (France) in 2012; Warner Music (US); and Bertelsmann (Germany). In 2003, however, Sony Music merged with Bertelsmann's BMG, cutting the number of major players to four. But a new firm, Live Nation Entertainment, has now taken the fourth spot (see Table 10.1). Of the top four, only two are American-owned. Most recording artists need to rely on the US market to recoup their companies' investments in the first album, which now requires the additional expense of video production as part of the initial promotion package. It is estimated that first video album costs now exceed $1 million.

Table 10.1 Major music companies, 2013

1	Universal Music Group (France)
2	Sony Music Entertainment (Japan)
3	Warner Music Group (United States)
4	Live Nation Entertainment (United States)

The major players usually control every aspect of the supply chain from copyright on the music through the distribution cycle to the consumer. They have extensive sales outlets in all core nations, all semiperipheral nations, and now some peripheral nations. The dominant artistic language is English, giving a substantial advantage to British and North American artists and bands. Finally, as discussed elsewhere, MTV's global television niche for the teenage market has also served to promote the global expansion of the video music industry.

Although there are several independent labels, and some occasionally do well with individual records – for example, Disney soundtracks for movies such as *Pocahontas* or *The Lion King* – the bulk of the global sales, approaching 80 percent, are controlled by the Big Four. The largest digital music seller is Apple's iTune stores. Further details concerning the Big Four's activities and artists are discussed below, along with the role of MTV in the global music scene.

Universal Music Group (France)

The largest global music company is Universal Music Group (UMG). It has two core business units, recorded music and music publishing, and is owned by Vivendi of France. UMG has ventures in 80 countries, over 10,000 employees, and more than 25 percent of the world's market for music of all types. UMG took over the British EMI Records in 2012, adding to its music assets. It also controls the third largest music publishing group. UMG also owns the world's leading Latin music company, UM Latin Entertainment. Leading Latin musicians sign up with this New York-based, French-owned company. It is a clear example of electronic colonialism since all Latin countries are in the semiperipheral or peripheral zones.

UMG has 18 record labels, including Decca and UMG Nashville. Some of UMG's artists include ABBA, Brian Adams, Elton John, Rihanna, Justin Bieber, Enrique Iglesias, Sheryl Crow, Rolling Stones, Sting, Bon Jovi, Black Eyed Peas, and Shania Twain. It also has almost half of the global sales in the classical music genre.

Until 2000 UMG was a division of Seagram's of Canada. It is also aggressive in online music sales. A major factor in UMG's size and success was the acquisition of PolyGram Records in 1998 by the Seagram group. PolyGram was a major European-based music giant that traced its origin to Siemens, established in 1898. Mergers and acquisitions have been the hallmark of the music recording industry as illustrated by the size and activities of the major record conglomerates.

Sony Music Entertainment (Japan)

The second largest music conglomerate is the Sony Music Entertainment Group, the product of a 2004 merger between the music divisions of Sony Corporation of Japan and Bertelsmann of Germany. After buying out the 50 percent Bertelsmann stake in 2008, Sony Music now controls approximately 25 percent of the global music market.

Sony entered the record business when it acquired CBS Records Group in 1988. Sony's music labels include Columbia, Arista, Epic, RCA Victor, Sony Classical, and Legacy. It has major recording artists under contract like Alicia Keys, Carrie Underwood, Celine Dion, Mariah Carey, Will Smith, Ice Cube, Barbra Streisand, Charlotte Church, and Bob Dylan. Sony jointly owned the Columbia House record club (which folded in 2011) with Warner

Music. Sony has always geared its musical interests to a global, as well as English-language, platform. This global reach reflects its corporate desire to be a Japanese-based corporation, with the bulk of its corporate activities carried out in other core nations, as well as semiperipheral and some peripheral nations.

The Sony music group also provides the music for PlayStation 3 and has a content deal with YouTube.

Warner Music Group (United States)

When Time Inc. took over Warner Bros. in the late 1980s, it also acquired the Warner Music Group, which is the third largest record company, after UMG and Sony. The record labels controlled by Warner Bros. are Warner Music International, Elektra, Atlantic, Maverick, Reprise, and Rhino. Some of its 1,000 artists are the Red Hot Chili Peppers, Eric Clapton, Faith Hill, and Sammy Davis Jr. In addition to being available at record stores around the globe, Warner Bros. artists' music is also available through Warner's online site or through over 150 Warner Bros. stores located in core nations as well as in Mexico, the Middle East, and the Pacific Rim. Warner is also a major music publisher. More than half its revenue comes from outside the United States, but it is still seeking a larger share of the EU market.

Live Nation Entertainment (United States)

This is a distant fourth music and events company formed in 2005. Live Nation's music interests are run by Live Nation Artists. Under contract are Madonna, U2, Jay-Z, Shakira, and Nickelback, a Canadian band. Madonna left Warner Music to join Live Nation. Live Nation owns Ticketmaster, the House of Blues, and promotes over 2,000 concerts with leading artists globally. In the future it hopes to sign more artists who are dissatisfied with the onerous terms in their current record contracts with other companies.

Summary

The four global music groups outlined above have extensive corporate activities in many nations. The bulk of the artists, whether contemporary, alternative, rap, classical, country, or rock, are English-speaking artists. The music producers also control as much of the production process as possible, from finding new talent to web-based purchases. The four giant music producers have corporate roots in the United States, Japan, and Europe. They have become industry leaders through a series of mergers and acquisitions, which are likely to continue in the future despite the anti-US bias of the European Union's merger commission.

A second significant aspect is that all the major record companies have established significant web-based marketing, retail, and promotion sites for their artists. Yet, as digital distribution systems become available through the Internet, some speculate about the long-term consequences for the global recording industry. In response, some recording companies and groups have initiated legal action against the rapidly expanding Internet sites that provide non-royalty copies in digital format to Internet clients. Future Internet online music business is estimated to be worth billions of dollars. The issue is whether consumers will purchase or simply download the necessary software to create audio files, which are technically equivalent to CDs. Several firms are offering MP3 solutions, which permit high-quality digital audio to be recorded and downloaded by home servers. MP3 is the industry term for a new data compression system that allows the pirating of music over the Internet, an activity that could clearly undermine and change, perhaps forever, the economics of the global recording industry. The move toward a free virtual jukebox has been altered, as both UMG and Sony have become shareholders in MP3 format firms and have now established a fee structure. Although the Internet is discussed elsewhere in this book, it is worth noting here that every single electronic medium is susceptible to change in the Internet environment.

Finally, it is worth noting that a number of high-profile individual artists have been trying to get out of their lifetime recording contracts. They sign these agreements when they are virtually unknown and the contracts are heavily weighted in favor of the recording studios. Many refer to the terms as servitude.

MTV: The Dominant Global Music Connection

Music recordings are a powerful entertainment medium in their own right. When they are offered in conjunction with the excitement of video, their appeal is even stronger. Not surprisingly, young people are tuning in to Viacom's Music Television (MTV) channels around the world. MTV reaches over 350 million viewers in 145 countries, particularly in Europe and Asia. It is currently the world's largest television network, broadcast in one-third of the world's TV-viewing households. Viewed primarily by pre-teens, teens, and young adults, MTV is an impressive global youth television phenomenon. Composed of 100 affiliated international networks including MTV Latino, MTV Brazil, MTV Europe, MTV Mandarin, MTV Asia, MTV India, MTV Australia, MTV New Zealand, and MTV Africa, the MTV network already has the ability to reach a large proportion of the world's youth each day. Moreover, new MTV networks are under consideration. MTV has signed a licensing deal with Russia, anticipating that the country's youth are now ready to tune in to a 24-hour music television network. MTV Russia will likely reach more than 10 million households and feature musicians such as Madonna, U2, Prince, Nirvana, and the Spice Girls, as well as local Russian groups. Over 80 percent of MTV's total audience is now outside the United States.

MTV was the first 24-hour, 7-day-a-week music video network. It is supported by advertising and constitutes a basic service on most cable networks. Targeted at the 10- to 24-year-old age group, MTV's international satellite-delivered music programming reaches millions around the globe daily. Owned by Viacom, MTV operates several cable television programming services – Music Television, MTV2, VH1, Nickelodeon/Nick at Nite, Country Music Television (CMT), TNN, and TV Land (see Table 10.2). MTV is also experimenting with the Internet and its own websites in order to examine the possibilities of providing music in online ventures.

Although there are an estimated 80,000 websites devoted to music, many of which have become digital shrines to major recording artists, MTV.com is the most popular music website in the world. MTV has an Internet subsidiary called MTV Group, which controls all MTV websites; the number of websites is enormous. The Internet properties are MTV.com, VH1.com, SonicNet.com, various international websites, chat rooms, news, streaming audio, and MTV merchandise.

Because music tastes are highly localized, MTV's global airtime is filled with locally produced programming and American shows. Despite that fact, teens around the world are basically listening to and viewing the same music videos. For example, in 1996 Madonna, Queen, and the Rolling Stones topped the charts of MTV Latino. Although MTV Europe reserves 30 percent of its broadcast hours for indigenous European groups, American artists dominate MTV Europe's top 10 artists. In 2001 MTV Japan went on the air as a 24-hour

Table 10.2 MTV holdings worldwide, 2013

MTV Adria
MTV Africa
MTV Arabia
MTV Asia
MTV Australia
MTV Base UK and Ireland
MTV Brand New Italy
MTV Brazil
MTV Canada
MTV China
MTV Estonia
MTV Europe
MTV France
MTV Germany
MTV Hits Italy
MTV Hits UK and Ireland
MTV Hungary
MTV Idol France
MTV India
MTV Israel
MTV Italy
MTV Japan
MTV Korea
MTV Latin America
MTV Latin America Revolution
MTV Latvia
MTV Lithuania
MTV Netherlands
MTV Networks Europe
MTV New Zealand
MTV Nordic: Norway, Sweden, Finland, Denmark
MTV Pakistan
MTV Philippines
MTV Poland
MTV Portugal
MTV Romania
MTV Russia
MTV Spain

Table 10.2 *(cont'd)*

MTV Tawain/Hong Kong
MTV Thailand
MTV Turkey
MTV UK and Ireland
MTV Ukraine
MTV2 UK

Japanese-language service. Of course, it goes without saying that musical groups who fail to produce a video to accompany their recording releases are simply excluded from MTV's playtime. Just as CNN has altered the global news business forever, so MTV has altered the global music trade.

Given MTV's popularity, advertising is another issue that deserves attention. According to Jay Pettegrew and Roy Shukar, MTV worldwide is one large continuous commercial advertising network.[13] Not only are the music videos "commercials" designed to enhance the sale of albums, but they are also surrounded by advertising for other products, and many artists openly promote commercial products within the music videos themselves. Many critics assert that MTV is a commercial propaganda outlet specifically aimed at impressionable teenagers.

Clearly, MTV promotes Western popular culture worldwide. Any reciprocal play is limited by the nature of MTV's North American broadcasting schedule. The Westernization of global culture is further enhanced by the basic fact that much of MTV programming and most music videos are produced in English. Even MTV Asia's interactive chatline, which requires Internet access, functions in English. Concerns about the pervasive commercialism and cultural imperialism of MTV programming worldwide are growing. Jack Banks puts the global influence this way:

> Music video is at its core a type of advertisement for cultural products: films, soundtracks, recorded music, live concerts, fashion apparel depicted in the clip and even the music clip itself as home video retail product. Omnipresent play of music videos on MTV (and elsewhere) helps shape global demand for this array of products.[14]

Similarly after examining MTV's impact across Asia, Stacey Sowards concludes:

> While MTV Asia has made appropriate, culturally aware marketing decisions that has allowed it to establish a firm base in Asia, the programming is still largely a manifestation of American culture. The differences in comparison to MTV in the United States are surface structural changes at best. There are several programs that are Asia specific; however, many of them are not, but are simply exported from the United States in the same way that *Dallas* and *Baywatch* are. More than 50 percent of MTV Asia's programs are imported directly from MTV in the United States. Additionally, American popular culture is ubiquitous throughout programs; even those that attempt to include Asian cultures. The programs that incorporate Asian cultures reflect American culture, through the way the VJs speak, the music that is aired, and the image that is portrayed. Even the use of Asian VJs fails to avoid the hegemonic nature of MTV Asia, since they also speak English, and attempt to represent American cultures and ideology through fashion and music selection. In fact, the American essence of MTV Asia is probably what attracts such a large Asian

viewership. Additionally, MTV Asia also has the effect of Americanizing Asian music, as seen by Asian musicians whose key influences are American bands. Furthermore, to be able to watch MTV Asia, one must have access to a satellite dish, excluding most of Southeast Asia, except those that have enough money, usually the elites.[15]

In 2008 the MTV network incorporated political coverage of elections into a segment called *Choose or Lose*, which called on young people to "vote loud." Viewers aged between 18 and 24 accounted for nearly 20 percent of the voters in the United States. Presidential contenders and companies such as AT&T and the Ford Motor Company now recognize the potential of MTV's campaign coverage to bring their messages into the homes of twenty-somethings. By focusing on the "three Es" – education, economy, and environment – *Choose or Lose* became the primary broker for 30 million young voters who were MTV viewers, while simultaneously providing a venue for candidates and major companies that wanted to target younger audiences for their commercials.

Another example of MTV's social commitment is its AIDS awareness campaign, "Staying Alive," which started in 1998. Its aim is to educate young people about the risks of AIDS and about safe sex practices, with the support of performers Beyoncé, Justin Timberlake, Sean Combs, and others.

MTV and Electronic Colonialism

One clear example of the application of the theory of electronic colonialism is found in music television, globally known as MTV. MTV has attempted to colonize not a broad range of viewers and listeners, but rather a select niche, namely the youth culture (see Table 10.3). MTV wants the minds of this global youth culture to follow them and buy the products which surround the music videos as commercials. They also want to influence how these viewers look and think. They indirectly promote the homogenization of culture.

Demographically this is an important group, particularly for advertisers of youth-oriented products, which range from clothes to cultural products such as films, records, PCs, DVDs, and iPods. MTV seeks to influence the attitudes, preferences, and purchasing behaviors of teenagers and people in their twenties around the globe. It promotes a mainstream diet of primarily British and American artists, plus non-Anglo musicians who usually mimic the format of individual artists or bands that are mainstream in either the

Table 10.3 MTV's global youth culture, 2013

Comedy Central
Country Music Television
Logo
MTV2
mtvU
Music Television
Nickelodeon/Nick at Nite
Spike
VH1

United States or Europe. It also offers "reality" shows. MTV does this in order to continue expanding its reach and influence on the attitudes of younger people in as many nations as possible. MTV is not solely concerned with music or the issues and themes surrounding the music industry; its goal is to influence the global teenage audience into accepting commercial habits and products that are predominantly from core nations. In this market-oriented process MTV is reaping a handsome profit for its parent, Viacom.

In order to further colonize and capitalize on the global youth culture, MTV has turned to the Internet. Its own Internet service, MTVi Group, seeks young customers with credit cards who can download music materials from the Internet for a fee. MTV is banking on the notion that around the globe there are a number of teenagers with sufficient disposable income to purchase music and merchandise over the Internet. MTV hopes that years of promoting relentless consumerism will ultimately pay off in the form of Internet-based purchases.

Through electronic colonialism, MTV has managed to marginalize many indigenous artists and indigenous genres of music, including Aboriginal music in Australia, African music, and non-traditional Indian music.[16] MTV gives little time or exposure to these alternative genres. As Jack Banks in his article, "MTV and the Globalization of Popular Culture," notes, MTV has become so influential that both Hollywood film studios and the global record conglomerates not only use MTV as a major advertising vehicle to reach the teenage audience, but also coordinate the release of new films or new videos on a preferential basis through MTV's global network.[17]

MTV was one of the first cultural industry giants to recognize the expanding global economy and to become a key part of it. Individual artists around the globe will lament their marginalization due to MTV, but, as Banks further notes, "Clearly MTV and music video are influencing the emerging global economy as well as the contours of a global popular culture – what remains uncertain is the role played by MTV in molding a global consensus about the shape of this economy and culture."[18] Given the expanding global strategic plan of Viacom, MTV's parent company, MTV has come to represent the music video juggernaut. That is, if you are a musician who is part of it, you will reach a global audience and become rich and world famous virtually overnight, but if you are not part of MTV, your chances of succeeding as a music video artist in any significant way are substantially reduced.

Conclusions

The global media market is in a state of constant change. Much of the change is fueled by the new communication companies, technologies, and business practices of core nations. The expansion of cable satellite delivery systems and mobile devices has provided huge growth internationally for video audiences. Audiences around the world are familiar with US movies and television shows and, as the number of television channels expands through global privatization, the liberalization of regulations, and in some cases total deregulation, there will be a host of new customers and viewers for Hollywood sitcoms, TV movies, music videos, and network syndicated shows. Concomitantly, this expanding foreign market has facilitated the growth of cultural industries in the United States and increased their role and influence within the US economy substantially. Their future also looks bright, as there is an almost insatiable demand for made-in-America television, music, and movie productions – particularly coupled with their very sophisticated advertising and marketing campaigns (as outlined in Chapter 15).

One particular company that has done exceptionally well both domestically and globally is MTV. The marriage of music and video, with most musicians from core nations, has permitted the rapid expansion of this major music television network. The only cloud on the horizon is the emergence of the Internet and the strong possibility of digital quality music and shows being illegally downloaded from Internet sites. This phenomenon could allow listeners to bypass local music outlets, thereby affecting how the music of international stars is packaged, distributed, and priced in the near future. However, the industry, along with its trade associations, has been fairly successful in recent attempts to protect copyrights (and therefore profits) against the threat posed by Internet file-sharing or the Swedish Pirate Bay.

The Pirate Bay is the world's largest bittorrent tracker. Bittorrent is a filesharing protocol that in a reliable way enables big and fast file transfers. This is an open tracker, where anyone can download torrent files. To be able to upload torrent files, write comments and personal messages one must register at the site. This is of course free.[19]

Finally, there are still a number of vocal critics of the cultural imperialism of the core nations. Much of the criticism is aimed at US-based industries, particularly Hollywood, but also to a lesser extent television shows with large global export markets, such as *Baywatch* or *The Simpsons*, or the MTV network. What is interesting is that communication giants based outside the United States such as the BBC, Bertelsmann, and Sony have managed to avoid the storm of criticism directed at Hollywood in general and at Disney, Viacom, and Time Warner, in particular. Yet, at the same time, they have enjoyed the financial gains from the growing market for cultural products around the globe. These firms have recognized the increased importance of US cultural industries, particularly the profitability associated with successful global sales, but they have somehow managed to dodge the hostile criticism that continues to emanate from critical school theorists in Asia, Europe, Latin America, and North America. The ubiquity of music and other mass cultural products is spread globally but produced by a few core nations, yet the shrill rhetoric of concern and protest about cultural imperialism is aimed mainly at one core nation: the United States.[20]

Notes

1. *Entertainment and the Electronic Media*, New York and Washington, DC: McGraw-Hill and US Department of Commerce, 1999, pp. 321–9. For a detailed decade-by-decade analysis of US television sales abroad, see Kerry Segrave, *American Television Abroad: Hollywood's Attempt to Dominate World Television*, Jefferson, NC: McFarland, 1998.
2. Some nations have gone to great lengths to counter the intrusion of Western popular culture. The overthrow of the shah of Iran was motivated in large part by distaste for the Western values, media, and culture he was promoting in Iran. When the Taliban controlled Afghanistan, it took drastic measures, ordering the removal of all televisions, VCRs, and satellite receivers from the country. Canada has taken a less draconian approach. For decades it attempted to reduce the influence of US mass media through the promulgation of Canadian content rules that require the media to produce and distribute Canadian material. The French-speaking province of Quebec has gone even further to protect its cultural heritage by instituting a provincial language policy that requires the use of French as the predominant language of business and culture in the province. Language "police" oversee the use of French in all commercial enterprises, going so far as to demand that the French lettering on signs be twice as large as their English counterparts.
3. David Rothkopf, "In Praise of Cultural Imperialism," *Foreign Policy* 107 (1997), 39.
4. As a general rule, TV sitcoms or dramas need to have at least a three-year run to be successfully syndicated. This provides approximately 66 episodes that can then be sold as a package for either the domestic rerun market or international syndication. Clearly, shows with successful runs of five or more years in syndication enjoy substantial secondary revenue streams in addition to their lucrative initial showings. Now, with DVDs, the ownership rights for some shows or movies are like a license to print money.
5. Because of high costs, the number of foreign network news bureaus has also been reduced. For example, CBS foreign news bureaus, which once numbered 12, now operate in only four cities – London, Moscow, Tokyo, and

Tel Aviv. They continue to hire brilliant foreign journalists, such as Sheila McVicker in Europe.

6. The use of US media models and strategies is not limited to the mimicking of cultural industries but extends even into the field of politics. The United Kingdom's former prime minister Tony Blair hired media consultants to model his political campaign, emulating the successful style of former US President Bill Clinton. Former German chancellor Gerhard Schröder also employed made-in-America campaign techniques, including the extensive use of sophisticated polling in order to conduct his successful election campaign. US political consultants now have branch offices located in Europe, Latin America, and elsewhere. They offer assistance to political candidates who wish to utilize the successful media strategies and tactics developed over the last three decades in the United States. This breadth of experience gives these US political media consultants a global market advantage.

   This trend is not without its critics. During the 1999 Israeli election campaign, a Washington-based pollster's role became a controversial part of the Labor Party's campaign. In Sweden the Social Democratic Party's hiring of a high-profile US consultant became an issue in the campaign. Clearly, just as there are critics of the Americanization of television and popular culture, so too are there vocal opponents of the Americanization of the political process, particularly during national election campaigns. Much of the US consultants' advice is about how to use and to appear on television, as well as how to run negative commercials about their opponents. But in the final analysis this phenomena is just another niche example of the pervasiveness of electronic colonialism theory.

7. Additional details about the plight of the European movie industry can be found in the *Economist* (February 6, 1999), 68. For a more in-depth analysis, see *European Audiovisual Conference: Challenges and Opportunities of the Digital Age*, Brussels: European Commission, 1997.

8. Rod Carveth, "The Reconstruction of the Global Media Marketplace," *Communication Research* 19(6) (1992), 705.

9. Alison Alexander, James Ovens, and Rod Carveth (eds.), *Media Economics: Theory and Practice*, Mahwah, NJ: Lawrence Erlbaum, 1998.

10. Thomas McPhail and Brenda McPhail, *Communication: The Canadian Experience*, Toronto: Copp Clark Pitman, 1990.

11. R. Carveth, J. Ovens, A. Alexander, and J. Fletcher, "The Economics of International Media," in A. Alexander, J. Ovens, and R. Carveth (eds.), *Media Economics: Theory and Practice*, Mahwah, NJ: Lawrence Erlbaum, 1998, pp. 223–45.

12. A look at the turmoil caused by the Internet is also detailed in the *Economist* (June 16, 2001), 617.

13. Jay Pettegrew, "A Post-M Moment: Commercial Culture and the Founding of MTV," in G. Dines and J. Hunez (eds.), *Gender, Race, and Class in Media*, Thousand Oaks, CA: Sage, 1995, pp. 488–98; Roy Shukar, *Understanding Popular Music*, London: Routledge, 1994.

14. Jack Banks, "MTV and the Globalization of Popular Culture," *Gazette* 51(1) (1997), 58.

15. Stacey Sowards, "MTV Asia: Cultural Imperialism in Southeast Asia," Paper presented at the National Communication Association Annual Conference, New York, 1998.

16. Tony Mitchell, "Treaty Now! Indigenous Music and Music Television in Australia," *Media, Culture and Society* 15(2) (1993), 299–308.

17. Banks, "MTV and the Globalization of Popular Culture," 51. For a detailed analysis of music videos, see Jack Banks, *Monopoly Television: MTV's Quest to Control the Music*, Boulder, CO: Westview Press, 1996.

18. Banks, "MTV and the Globalization of Popular Culture," 59.

19. http://thepiratebay.se/about, accessed August 31, 2013.

20. To counter this phenomenon, the United States needs to focus more attention and funds on the area of public diplomacy. That is why this edition has a chapter on the subject for the first time.

11

CNN
International Role, Impact, and Global Competitors

Introduction

Memories from major global breaking news stories – such as the Tiananmen Square protest, both Gulf Wars, the death of Princess Diana, the Asian tsunami, the fall-out following the 2008 Iranian elections, the *News of the World* hacking scandal, and, in the United States news stories involving celebrities like O. J. Simpson, Kobe Bryant, Martha Stewart, Scott Peterson, Robert Blake, Bernard Madoff – are reminders that the press is on site to bring the viewing public up-to-the-minute news stories. Newsgathering in the United States is plentiful and apparent on ABC, CBS, Fox, NBC, and other news outlets. In addition, there are now three US all-news channels: CNN, MSNBC, and Fox News. There are two global all-news networks: CNN and the BBC World Television service.

Major US, European, and Asian radio and television broadcasters have been covering international events since the 1920s. Outside the United States, broadcasters such as the British Broadcasting Corporation (BBC) and Germany's Deutsche Welle, along with international bureaus of major television networks, have been covering global events on their evening newscasts for decades. Any election of the Catholic pope is widely covered. What is different now is that the Cable News Network (CNN) has changed the global media format in a dramatic way. Viewing went from a format based on 30- or 60-minute prime-time newscasts to a 24-hour format focusing on news and public affairs programming from both national and global perspectives. CNN and other all-news networks thrive on controversy, breaking news stories, coups and earthquakes, and stories that go on for days, or even weeks, such as the response to the Indian Ocean tsunami in December 2004. Another example is the 2000 Florida election recount saga which saw CNN's audience rating increase sixfold, while four-year-old MSNBC experienced its highest ratings ever. CNN has attracted competition

Global Communication: Theories, Stakeholders, and Trends, Fourth Edition. Thomas L. McPhail.
© 2014 John Wiley & Sons, Inc. Published 2014 by John Wiley & Sons, Inc.

because it proved there was a niche market for all-news television. CNN is a media property of Time Warner and has been losing market share, particularly to Fox News and more and more to MSNBC as well. (I will discuss this phenomenon further below.)

News crosses domestic and international boundaries without regard for time or space. International communication and new technologies have had a profound effect on news institutions, news sources, newsgathering techniques, and audiences almost everywhere. The global media trend grew throughout the twentieth century, along with the global economy. This was made possible by radio, wire services, magazines, newspapers, satellites, videophones, and the advent of global all-news networks in the 1980s. As more countries opened their borders to imported signals, both news and entertainment took on greater importance as media firms of all varieties sought larger audiences. These larger audiences were often from other core nations, as well as from semiperipheral nations, and occasionally peripheral nations. Media firms sought out these larger audiences in order to increase advertising revenue for the commercially based global television networks. From the electronic colonialism perspective, the potential impact of advertising on consumer behavior was frequently a greater cultural concern than the programs themselves. The implications of global advertising and its relation to world system and electronic colonialism theories are detailed in Chapter 15.

Along with international news coverage comes growing competition. By the 1980s, the world had developed a huge appetite for television programming of all kinds, including news and information. Interestingly, in the early 1980s it was Ted Turner who took the bold initiative to establish the first 24-hour all-news network. It was based in Atlanta, Georgia. He saw a need and stepped in with his Turner Broadcasting Company. On June 1, 1980 Turner introduced the Cable News Network, otherwise known as CNN. In addition to CNN, Turner launched CNN Headline News in 1981 and the Cable News Network International (CNNI) in 1985, in response to increasing competition. CNNI's goals were to expand internationally oriented programming, upgrade satellite carriage, expand its newsgathering capabilities, and become the primary global television network for news. Ted Turner deserves credit for his tenacity, vision, and deep pockets in terms of realizing that there was a market out there for 24-hour news. He sought to create a better informed public.

Without a doubt, CNN is the godfather of global television news reporting to audiences around the world. Millions in over 200 nations now watch the 24-hour all-news format. Historically, the markets for the United Kingdom's *Economist* or the American *International Herald Tribune* were early indications that there was a niche market in print for the international news sector. What CNN managed to do was to make the development of the niche television news market a global phenomenon. As the global economy evolves and expands, people are defining themselves in terms of television viewing more as regional (e.g., European or Latin) or as world citizens. They are concerned about world events as well as local, regional, and national events. Turner understood this desire for global information. He had the crucial financial resources to keep CNN on air during its early years. It was not until the mid-1980s that CNN broke even, let alone made a profit.

Before CNN, the prestigious French newspaper *Le Monde* (The World) had the definition and concept right. The trouble was that it never had the distribution system to become a world newspaper, and possibly the fact that it wasn't in English disadvantaged it. Originally, radio faced similar barriers, with one major exception – the BBC World Service. Although there were other world radio services, none had the network clout, the vast number of colonies as a captive audience, or the international respectability of the BBC World Service. In terms of television, originally only nation-states, for the most part, developed and licensed television networks. Many of these television networks were frequently just an extension of national radio networks. They were delivered by way of limited terrestrial microwave networks or via telephone lines within a nation's borders. No transnational television systems were created until the reality of CNN's success forced other nations, particularly within the European Union, to consider competing services, such as Euronews. Satellites were the major technical development behind CNN's success, as well as the creation of other networks, such as France 24 and Al Jazeera.

CNN was so successful that it attracted competition. Currently, two of CNN's main competitors in Europe and Asia are Rupert Murdoch's satellite channels, including BSkyB and the BBC. In 1994 the BBC launched a 24-hour television news service, starting in Asia. Although the BBC had previously run a limited European service, the Asian initiative made it a full-fledged competitor of CNN. Another CNN competitor is the EU's Euronews, an effort to present foreign news and analysis from a pan-European perspective.

The French government announced plans for a satellite-based French equivalent of CNN in order to bring a French public policy perspective to international issues. Launched in 2006, this has been branded as France 24. The new channel received millions of euros in start-up funds from the French government and represents the French challenge to the CNN editorial stance on world events, much as Al Jazeera and Al-Arabiya represent the Arabic viewpoint and challenge to CNN as well as the BBC. France 24 wants the world to understand the French perspective as well as French cultural values. It broadcasts in French, Arabic, and English 24/7. France 24 is using the Internet as its major distribution system as well as being a video broadcaster via cable/satellite. It sees CNN as its major competitor and has put together a staff of 700 full-time employees, who are complemented by over 1,000 foreign correspondents or "stringers" around the globe. Their goal is to make France 24 the leading video site for international news.

Because of its national and international successes, CNN has managed to attract US-based as well as global competition. Two new 24-hour all-news networks – MSNBC and Fox News – now provide strong domestic competition for CNN and its headline news networks, rebranded as HLN (see Figure 11.1).[1] This chapter details CNN's major international media role from its

Figure 11.1 CNN's foreign and domestic competitors, 2013

inception to its current activities. It also deals with other major global media organizations such as the BBC, Voice of America, Radio Martí, and Deutsche Welle.

International news and information gathering changed because of Ted Turner's CNN. A new era of global reporting was born in 1980 as domestic boundaries became obsolete in an era of satellite and cable. Although several countries and companies were entering the global information marketplace, no one news source was to be as successful as Turner Broadcasting and its crown jewel, CNN.

CNN, originally a division of Turner Broadcasting System, is the world's international news leader. In October 1996 Time Warner acquired Turner Broadcasting for $6.54 billion, and Ted Turner became vice president of Time Warner and its largest shareholder. He has since resigned and lost a fortune, as the later merger of Time Warner with AOL has been a financial disaster. The CNN merger created an unparalleled media giant with the ability to bring the most thorough, immediate, and live coverage of the world's news to a worldwide audience. In the pursuit of timely, unbiased, and in-depth news reporting, CNN pioneered innovative techniques and broke new ground for the television news industry. The high-energy environment at CNN and its sister networks is home to over 4,000 employees worldwide. Currently, CNN has 36 bureaus worldwide. It has also reached several milestones. Besides launching CNN Headline News and CNNI, CNN has also branched out into CNN Radio. This division provides all-news programming to nearly 500 radio stations nationwide. In 1988 the division introduced Noticiero CNNI, which produces six hours of Spanish news for distribution on CNNI in the United States and throughout Latin America. And in 1995 CNN was launched into cyberspace. CNN Interactive is the world's leading interactive news service. Its staff of world-class journalists and technologists are dedicated to providing 24-hour-a-day access to accurate and reliable news and information from any location.

As a unit of Time Warner, CNN has not fared well. A series of senior management changes and missteps at Time Warner have adversely impacted CNN. With budget cuts looming, CNN is stuck in second place, after Fox, and sometimes even slips to third, after MSNBC, in the weekly ratings war. Its problems have not gone unnoticed. The internal pressure is from Time Warner, which is demanding more profit and a return to top ranking. Consider this devastating commentary by Michael Wolff in the widely read *USA Today*:

> CNN the news network that nobody likes, or watches or can fix, is looking for a new CEO. Even if you actually believe you can fix it, it's far from clear that anybody would want you to. Although the network is an embarrassment to everybody who works there, as well as to the industry as a whole … So the main job for new CNN CEO may be just to bear the humiliation of it all.[2]

The new CEO of CNN was appointed in 2013 and he will have to keep a constant eye on expenses and ad revenues which will likely translate into keeping expensive foreign bureaus and reporting to a minimum.

First Live Broadcast

CNN's first live broadcast involved the high-profile black civil rights leader and well-known Democrat Vernon Jordan. On May 29, 1980 Jordan was shot in Fort Wayne, Indiana. President Jimmy Carter visited him in hospital. CNN distributed the story live during the day before the other major networks had a chance because traditional networks held back such breaking stories for their major evening newscasts. The networks were scooped during the day and this was to be repeated frequently as CNN broke stories at whatever time the events took place.

Tiananmen Square

Another major news opportunity in the late 1980s had drastic and unexpected consequences for CNN. In May 1989 the USSR president Mikhail Gorbachev made an official visit to China. Because this was the first summit meeting since 1958 between the leaders of the two largest communist nations, all major US networks were granted permission to broadcast from China. CNN, with anchor Bernard Shaw, received permission to establish a temporary outdoor studio in Beijing, close to the Sheraton Hotel. CNN set up a portable satellite earth station in order to transmit its signal to its headquarters in Atlanta, Georgia. After six days, President Gorbachev left China, but CNN had permission from the Chinese authorities to transmit for another day. Fortuitously for CNN, the Tiananmen Square confrontation occurred within the next 24 hours. The Chinese authorities were devastated by the global coverage provided by CNN. President Bush, who was at his vacation home in Kennebunkport, Maine, stated that he was watching the events unfold live on CNN and that all he knew was what CNN was showing – just like the rest of the world. The drama escalated as the Tiananmen Square demonstrators continued to defy Chinese troops and tanks. A separate drama began to emerge as Chinese authorities attempted to cut off the live CNN coverage. The CNN crew refused to disconnect their equipment and the entire incident and confrontation was broadcast live. The Chinese authorities were outraged, but CNN would not cease live coverage until it received an official letter from the Chinese Ministry of Telecommunications revoking the original seven-day transmission agreement. A kind of double coverage ensued when ABC began covering CNN's situation along with its own coverage of the confrontation. During CNN's coverage, Bernard Shaw explained how the network managed to break its live news:

> If you're wondering how CNN has been able to bring you this extraordinary story … we brought in our own flyaway gear, about eighteen oversized suitcases with our satellite gear … We unpacked our transmission equipment and our dish. So whatever you've seen in the way of pictures and, indeed, in the way of words, came from our microwave units at Tiananmen Square bounced right here to the hotel, through our control room on one of the upper floors – I won't mention the floor for protective reasons – back down through cables up on the CNN satellite dish, up on the satellite, and to you across the world … And I have to say this, for those cable stations that want to cut away, and I can't believe that any of you would want to cut away, you're gonna risk the anger and angst of all your viewers if you do … We have about two and a half minutes left on the satellite.[3]

The letter from the Chinese Ministry of Telecommunications finally arrived; it was delivered live and within minutes CNN coverage stopped. The drama and the replays out of Atlanta placed CNN in a new light. It was now truly the global news network it had always claimed to be. But it needed another major global story in order to demonstrate that it had the flexibility, equipment, and personnel to deliver live news coverage that was either comparable or superior to that of the major US and European networks. The Gulf War provided that opportunity.

The First Gulf War

CNN was well prepared to be the media outlet for live coverage of the 1991 Gulf crisis. It carried not only the bombings but also Saddam Hussein's meeting with British hostages. And when Jordan's King Hussein wanted to broadcast a message about the Gulf crisis, he delivered it live on CNN. World leaders began to communicate about the Gulf crisis through CNN; world leaders in North America, Europe, and the Middle East updated themselves on the status of the war by following CNN's live coverage. It also made CNN reporter Peter Arnett a media superstar. Previously, both Ted Turner and CNN executives had courted Middle Eastern governments and television officials and now that groundwork was paying off. CNN was granted permission to broadcast live from Baghdad. The other US networks watched in envy as CNN produced the only global live coverage from the war zone, frequently from behind enemy lines. Bernard Shaw joined the CNN crew in order to provide 24-hour coverage. Despite warnings from the White House to vacate the region, CNN reporters and production crew decided to stay. When the bombing began on January 16, 1991 all major US and European networks had crews in the Middle East. But four days after the war began, only 17 remained of the hundreds of journalists and crew members in the Middle East. Nine of these were from CNN. Following Operation Desert Storm, CNN, and particularly Peter Arnett, were criticized for granting Iraqi officials too much airtime during the war. American officials wanted a cheerleading tone. The US military sought propaganda to persuade the American public that the war was necessary. Given the foibles of live coverage, some mistakes were inevitable, but internationally CNN became the new global medium for breaking world news. It was considered the new gold standard because it had now beaten all television networks with its war coverage.

The 1991 Gulf War presented challenges as well as opportunities for CNN. The challenges were twofold. First, was the US public willing to support military action against a foreign country, particularly after the debacle of the Vietnam War? Second, would CNN crews, including production staff, be permitted, as well as technically equipped, to send live signals from Baghdad, the capital of Iraq? The opportunity was straightforward: CNN would be able to broadcast a major international conflict live not only to its vast US audience, but also to a substantial number of viewers around the globe. What made the First Gulf War all the more pivotal for CNN's success was the fact that it was not just the first but also one of the few broadcasters permitted by both Iraqi and US military authorities to continue shooting video. Their European, Canadian, and Asian broadcasting counterparts were denied access to frontline footage.

The First Gulf War turned out to be another defining moment in CNN's history. Even the leaders of the two nations engaged in the conflict – the United States and Iraq – openly conceded that they were following the progress of the war on CNN. CNN was interpreting the war for the world. This war was CNN's war. This fact bothered many foreign broadcasters, public policy experts, and politicians in other nations since they were reduced to viewing events and interpreting history in English and at least a step behind CNN. As a result, after the war several governments, particularly those in Europe, established competitor or alternative television services so that, when major international events occurred, they would have their own broadcasters, analysts, and film footage to be able to present their perspectives, rather than having to rely on a foreign broadcaster such as CNN. These competitor networks include France 24, Euronews, as well as an expanded the BBC World Television service, which is covered in greater detail later in this chapter. The First Gulf War heightened the context in which the news media covered and defined international news and information stories. Philip Taylor summarizes the significance of CNN's new role as a result of the First Gulf War:

> Throughout the autumn and winter of 1990, thanks to the role which Cable News Network (CNN) had defined for itself as an instant electronic interlocutor between Baghdad and Washington, it became clear that television would play a particularly prominent role in any conflict, with Saddam and Bush frequently exchanging verbal blows via the ten-year-old television network once lampooned by rivals as the "Chicken Noodle News." But it was already apparent that, by providing a public forum to the traditionally secretive world of diplomacy, CNN was quite simply changing the rules of international politics and that, as a consequence, it was also likely to alter the way in which modern warfare would be projected onto the world's television screens.[4]

The reporter known for this unprecedented coverage, which made him one of the world's most visible reporters, was Peter Arnett. Arnett's success in Baghdad is cited as his most significant accomplishment simply because his coverage of the war was broadcast live on television around the globe. CNN positioned Arnett as the archetypal journalist, the reporter who met newly defined professional challenges at great personal risk and hardship. By staying behind enemy lines to report the story, he exemplified the reporter's responsibilities in an age of live satellite-fed communications.

While some loved Arnett, others were critical of him, for his supposed lack of loyalty to the United States because he insisted on staying behind enemy lines. When Arnett reported that the allies had bombed a plant producing infant formula rather than biological weapons, as the US military insisted, public fears intensified that his dispatches were being used for propaganda purposes. At one point, US lawmakers pressed for control over his broadcasts: the Pentagon wanted him fired, and the CIA and the FBI also sought to discredit him.

CNN's news coverage of the First Gulf War again highlighted the network's unprecedented coverage in the international marketplace. But CNN wants to remain the "first choice" provider or gold standard of international news and information coverage. On an average day, CNN has a domestic audience of more than a million households. When major news events break, however, whether in China, Asia, or the Middle East, the ratings go through the roof. CNN captures the majority of the global television news audience. Interestingly, CNN did not send Arnett to Kosovo, after which his status at the network plummeted. He was dismissed by CNN in 1999.

CNN's presence is felt in every part of the world. It has become synonymous with news from every corner of the world. Its founder, Ted Turner, transformed his Atlanta-based company into a creditable international news service with the help of first-class journalists. The network has launched a new era of global news and information coverage using aggressive strategies that include covering news whenever and wherever it happens, breaking the news first, and providing live coverage from the scene. All of these strategies have made Turner's company the leader in shaping international events.[5]

A brief history of CNN is in order here. Turner dedicated the network to around-the-clock news operations in the early 1980s. Satellites were used to deliver CNN to cable operators, but only about 20 percent of TV-viewing households in the United States received cable television. Turner needed more viewers if his new venture was to succeed. To increase cable access, he introduced ESPN, HBO, Nickelodeon, Arts & Entertainment (A&E), USA, Disney, Showtime, and C-SPAN to attract a larger cable-viewing audience (see Figure 11.2). By 1985 Turner's original news channel was reaching more than 33 million households, or

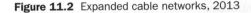

Figure 11.2 Expanded cable networks, 2013

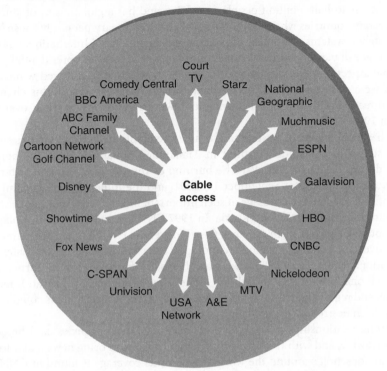

four out of five US homes with cable TV, and nearly 40 percent of all US homes with televisions. Headline News alone had 18 million subscribers. These numbers were vital to CNN's economic success because larger audiences meant greater advertising revenues, and by this time CNN was attracting national advertising accounts. By the mid-1980s Turner wanted to attract an even larger audience, so he turned to the global market for growth. As international trade and shifts in the world markets became more relevant to the US economy, these activities created a demand for more up-to-date information about the international scene. CNN also became a model niche cable channel that others began to mimic.

CNN's family of networks has grown to nearly a dozen news channels and a wholesale news service (CNN Newsource) that sells video news to approximately 700 broadcast affiliates worldwide. With Turner's array of 24-hour networks and services, today CNN is a major player in domestic and international programming. CNN's networks include CNN, HLN, CNN Radio, CNNI, CNN *World Report* news exchange, CNN Newsource, CNN Airport Network, CNN Interactive, CNN Money, and CNN en Español. CNN now has web pages in English, Arabic, Spanish, Turkish, Portuguese, and Korean. In 1999 it launched a Spanish-language channel in Spain. This service was the first CNN local-language news channel that was completely controlled and operated by staff outside its US corporate headquarters in Atlanta.

In a move that enhanced Turner's presence in global markets, state media monopolies around the world began to allow modest competition from the 1980s. Countries such as India, Japan, Hong Kong, Russia, and South Africa wanted news services in addition to the local coverage that was brought to them by their state (public) broadcasters. Turner moved quickly to reach these new audiences by distributing CNN internationally. CNN now employs a satellite system that covers six continents; it reaches over 200 countries with potential access to half a billion people every day, and has a global team of almost 4,000 people. Even in countries where CNN is unavailable to ordinary people, because of limited cable or satellite systems or because of political censorship, CNN International has become the first choice of viewers in major hotels, government offices, and presidential palaces. A remarkable aspect of CNN's expansion in the 1990s was that it occurred while other US networks were slashing the budgets of their foreign bureaus. Clearly this changed in a negative direction with the global economic downturn, after it was taken over by Time Warner in 1996.

CNN has built much of its reputation as a creditable news source from such news coverage stories as the student protest in Tiananmen Square in 1989, the bombing of Baghdad during the First Gulf War, the burning of the Moscow Parliament building in 1993, the terrorist attacks of September 11, 2001, and the Indian Ocean tsunami in 2004. Because of CNN's extensive coverage of such important international news stories, it is now doing business in China, Iraq, and Russia. In 1997 CNN opened a bureau in Cuba, though it had to obtain US government approval first. One reason CNN has had such a rapid rise is its innovative use of communication technologies to reach larger audiences. Satellites gave CNN a national audience in 1980, and since then satellites have enabled Turner to be the first international broadcaster to link the globe using a mixture of Intelsat, Intersputnik, PanAmSat, and regional satellite signals when existing land-based systems could not do the job or had been destroyed by the calamity.

The strong relationships it has built with networks, news agencies, and broadcasting unions worldwide, and with freelancers have enabled CNN to bring news and information coverage to households around the world. Much of its coverage is found in CNN's *World Report* program.

World Report

What has CNN *World Report* brought to the newsgathering table? Since 1987, *World Report* has been an internationally distributed news program consisting of news items contributed by foreign broadcasters. It has been an outlet for news organizations of any political persuasion to report news about their countries from their own perspective. As of 2013, over 350 stations representing 150 countries participate in the *World Report*. This suggests that it continues to serve the needs of world broadcasters. Various news items have been aired from public and private stations such as CCTV in China, Cubavision in Cuba, CyBC Bayrak TV in Cyprus, MASTV in Mexico, TV Asahi in Japan, RNTV-Radio which is a division of Radio Netherlands Worldwide, SABC in South Africa, and ZBC in Zimbabwe.

World Report has had a considerable effect on CNN and its coverage of high-profile, controversial news and information stories. According to Ted Turner:

We never would have been allowed to stay in Iraq during the Iraqi war if it hadn't been for the *World Report*. We've gotten a lot of access as a result of our making a real effort to having people from other countries and other news organizations feel comfortable about us. We've got a lot of access to world leaders and so forth, and then, allowed to be behind the lines and allowed to stay in circumstances where other news organizations weren't allowed to. Partly that was the case that we'd been allowed because so many world leaders were watching us when there's a conflict anywhere in the world, or anything controversial, where people, where leaders need to get their point across. Like Saddam Hussein did. At least we gave him some access that they otherwise wouldn't have gotten if CNN wasn't there, because basically we believe that everyone has a right to be heard.[6]

Turner Broadcasting Company's international success is also its curse. CNN's managers know they are no longer playing in a field of one. Imitators will strive to equal or surpass the US news company's global reach. But CNN's ability to watch its competitors and stay one step ahead will leave little room for a takeover. Competition is healthy for CNN because it keeps forcing the network to re-examine fundamental strategies of global versus niche programming.

Today, executives at CNN state that their goal is to get people around the world to watch CNN. This means being more international in scope and more local from the standpoint of viewers in other parts of the world. To meet the information needs of the global market, CNN generates news programs that are compelling and relevant to a global audience. It also means that CNN reports on important events whenever and wherever they happen. By doing so, the network is trying to expand its role as a global communicator, the channel for diplomats and generals, and even angry crowds in streets and town squares – with the potential to shape public life in every corner of the planet.[7] As mentioned, however, CNN's success has attracted competition. Some of its chief competitors are discussed in the following sections.

Merger Matters

With AOL and Time Warner's merger, CNN faced a new reality and a different set of new bosses. CNN's founder, Ted Turner, left the company in 2003. In 2001 CNN laid off almost 10 percent of its employees when it let 400 of them go. During the same era it failed to replace its president Rich Kaplan, who was dismissed in 2000. The current president is not well liked by some staff members. CNN has also been losing market share to MSNBC, Fox, Internet news sites, and competing international services, such as BBC World TV. John Cook, in his piece "CNN's Free Fall," writes about the lack of strategic planning, downsizing, and new ownership as "the changes have fostered discontent and disillusionment among the rank and file, many of whom were perfectly content with the old CNN."[8] Cook also makes the point about a new, major shift away from the former model of news being the central focus to a personality-centered schedule focused on stars such as Christiane Amanpour, Wolf Blitzer, Brian Nelson, and Jeff Greenfield.[9] With this repositioning of CNN, along with new owner's focus on the bottom line, the honesty, creativity, risk-taking, and media acumen pioneered by Ted Turner have come to an ignominious end.

The CNN Effect

The CNN effect or factor refers to the process by which the coverage of a foreign event by CNN causes that event to be a primary concern for its audience, which in turn forces the federal government to act.[10] What CNN chooses to focus on becomes a major public policy issue, or headache, for the US State Department. CNN has such an impact that it cannot be ignored in Washington. It has the effect of being an outside agenda-setting voice for US foreign policy. This factor is extended when other networks begin to match CNN's focus on a foreign news event. When other networks begin to match CNN's coverage, the matter then becomes an issue for the governments of core nations. Others also argue that what

CNN fails to cover and its growing budget cuts mean that there is no public outcry for action and thus little assistance or policy attention is forthcoming.[11]

For example, the US and British administrations were forced to respond to the Somalia crisis because CNN would not drop its coverage of it, whereas a civil war has raged for years in Sudan with no core nation response because for a time CNN chose not to focus on that plight. Even former US secretaries of state have admitted that they have to keep abreast of what CNN is covering abroad.[12] In 2005 Florida governor Jeb Bush, reviewing the tsunami damage in Asia, lamented the fact that as soon as CNN left, so would the aid workers and public pressure to assist in the lengthy repairs and costs.

If foreign affairs events are not reported on CNN, the story disappears – whether for the US secretary of state, the British minister of foreign affairs, the head of the United Nations, or a Japanese ambassador. The ability of CNN to set the global agenda is new to the role of the global media. When CNN ignores an issue, the issue languishes and fails to make the radar of editors around the world, with few exceptions. A report on the Congo civil war in 2012 is an example:

> The Congo conflict was characterized by passive effects stemming from media inattention: coverage was not voluminous, and there was little framing of stories that could be seen as advocating international involvement. Indeed, the conflict was framed as "intractable," and UN peacekeeping efforts were generally criticized, thus providing little encouragement that additional international intervention would likely be effective.[13]

But the phenomenon of the CNN effect, its agenda-setting, may be short-lived as it loses market share. Yet at the same time the media's public policy role will likely increase as other networks, as well as the Internet with its bloggers, pick up the role of focusing greater attention on foreign policy, global issues, and aid. At other times, when CNN focuses on an issue, such as Abu Ghraib and other scandal and torture violations, the governments of the United States and the United Kingdom are forced into a damage control mode. Their spin masters are mere amateurs when it comes to taking on the major media outlets, particularly CNN. An indication of CNN's influence is the amount of research it has attracted. For example:

> The Alerting function clearly is of some importance. And, while this by no means constitutes a wholesale endorsement of the CNN effect, it does appear to indicate that in the overall mix of factors leading to an international intervention, *the international community is more likely to respond to a serious crisis in a country of marginal strategic or economic importance if the mainstream media are effective in alerting the population to the crisis.*[14]

How CNN Was Out-Foxed but Not Out-Classed

CNN was the global media king in 1991, with its strong coverage of the First Gulf War. Yet less than a decade later Fox News overtook CNN in the US market, by using brash personalities like Bill O'Reilly, being in the right place at the right time,[15] and supporting the wars and all things Republican. Now the leading critics of the Obama administration and even the president have acknowledged the fact.

In the early 2000s CNN was overtaken in the US domestic all-news market by News Corp's Fox News. CNN continued to attract the largest global news audience (BBC World TV is second), but in the crucial and enormous home market it was beaten to second and sometimes third place. This quickly translated into lower advertising rates, and at its parent Time Warner, which was bleeding due to AOL's failure to turn a profit, CNN lost its top status. Several management changes at CNN mandated by Time Warner also failed to stop the ratings slide. With Fox News proudly catering successfully to a right of center audience, CNN has been left with an identity crisis as to what and how to attract back its own departed audience.

To put CNN's problem in perspective, consider the results of the 2004 US presidential election. Basically, CNN has tried to be an objective and middle-of-the-road network, and under Ted Turner's leadership this formula worked very well. (It is worth noting that since the merger of AOL and Time Warner in 2001, Turner has lost billions in Time Warner stock and he is no longer with the company.) But overall the US audience shifted, as reflected in the federal election breakdown. The right wing of the political spectrum, as represented by the Republicans, won 51 percent of the popular vote, and the liberal wing 49 percent, most of which were votes going to the Democrats. The problem is that CNN had claimed the center of the electorate – where fewer Americans are positioned. The media audience either perceived themselves to be conservative and viewed Fox News, or as liberal, or they viewed a range of media outlets, including CNN and the Internet. The end result was that CNN was positioned in a declining part of the political spectrum as the center ground collapsed and audiences moved mainly to the right or to the left for Obama. In essence, the CNN network is now going through an identity crisis in terms of what it wants to be and where it wants to place itself in relation to its competitors.[16] The polarizing effect of the elections hit CNN's strategic position hard. Meanwhile Fox News delighted in its newfound audience niche and increasing ad rates. This has left CNN in a quagmire with few repositioning options – unless it makes a direct attack on Fox News by shifting its editorial slant to the right and thus risks losing the audience it has now.

The Second Gulf War: Embedded Journalists

War coverage took a different track during the Second Gulf War in Iraq. The US military, which had a legacy of hostility toward the media, decided to embed journalists in combat units across Iraq and on six warships in the area. Given that the US military had blamed the media for losing public support for the Vietnam War, that the 1983 invasion of Grenada and the 1989 war in Panama saw heavy control of the press, and that the First Gulf War had been largely limited to CNN's coverage, it came as a surprise that the US military would allow hundreds of journalists, photographers, and camera crews to cover the war in 2003. Embedding news crews affects the tone and nature of the overall coverage. From the boot camp to the front lines, embeds quickly took on an air of camaraderie. They had to follow military guidelines and use military transportation. Overall the tone and slant of the stories and film footage shown in the US media were biased to the United States, and, to a lesser extent, those in the British media to the British. An empirical study of the coverage by embeds "revealed that embedded coverage of 'Iraqi Freedom' was more favorable in overall tone toward the military and in depiction of individual troops."[17] The authors conclude with a warning concerning the craft of objective journalism when they state:

> However, for the journalism establishment, embedding embodies a "professionally treacherous" reef. Journalists get to cover combat operations close up, giving them the access to combat operations that they want. But, in the process, they lose perspective and, thus, sacrifice the idealized standard of reporter objectivity.[18]

The bias of the embeds was not unforeseen by the Pentagon, or they would not have allowed it. Many independent or unilateral journalists, who are likely to be more critical of the war effort and the lack of evidence of weapons of mass destruction, were kept out of Iraq by the US military and were forced to watch the war, likely on CNN, from neighboring Kuwait.

Finally, CNN was treated like any other network and had several embeds along with all the competing networks. CNN no longer had the virtual monopoly coverage it had enjoyed in the First Gulf War. In addition, the use of the Internet by reporters as well as soldiers also managed to outrun or to scoop the traditional media. (The phenomenon of blogging and tweeting is covered in Chapter 6.)

The BBC

The BBC is significant for two major reasons. The first is that it operates a global television service in direct competition with CNN and a host of other regional networks. Second, as the early public service, non-commercial British radio network, the BBC was exported around the world as a media model to a vast number of British colonies. As a direct result, non-commercial, government-controlled broadcasting in the public interest was what millions listened to and then watched with the introduction of television. The commercial model with advertising did not come to many nations outside the United States until after World War II. And even then it was introduced slowly and frequently with oppressive regulations, many favoring the public broadcasters.

Radio

The BBC was founded in 1922; it went on the air in 1923 as a private radio corporation but quickly floundered. By early 1927, it had become a public corporation as the British government moved in to save the new medium. Since then, BBC Radio has never sought advertising revenue, depending instead on two external sources of income. The first came directly from the British government in the form of an annual grant, the second from license fees associated with all radio receivers. This licensing fee procedure was replicated with the introduction of television in the United Kingdom and is still in effect today.[19]

From its earliest days, the BBC was committed to public service broadcasting. Sir John Reith, an early general manager of the BBC, describes its mission this way:

> Broadcasting must be conducted, in the future, as it has in the past, as a Public Service with definite standards. The Service must not be used for entertainment purposes alone … To exploit so great and universal an agent in the pursuit of entertainment alone would have been not only an abdication of responsibility and a prostitution of power, but also an insult to the intelligence of the public it serves.[20]

This focus on quality programming became a central tenet of the BBC. Soon the BBC became a model for other nations as radio began to expand around the world. Many of these nations were part of the former extensive network of colonies known as the British Commonwealth. The British not only exported their civil service, the English language, and their monarchy, but they also exported the public service broadcasting ethic and model of the BBC. As early as 1927, the BBC began experimenting with short-wave radio in order to broadcast to United Kingdom's far-flung and numerous colonies around the globe. By 1932 the BBC started a regular Empire Service by means of short wave. On Christmas Day that year, King George V became the first ruling monarch to broadcast live on radio his greeting to his subjects throughout the world. His speech writer was the world famous Rudyard Kipling, author of *The Jungle Book*.

The BBC got a major international boost and acquired an extensive audience through its high-quality reporting during World War II. It became the international voice of World War II and had no global rival. It also amassed substantial political power and influence; for years after World War II, it was able to severely limit the growth of commercial broadcasting and competition in the United Kingdom.

Television

The BBC started the world's first public television service on November 2, 1936. It was transmitted from Alexandra Palace to fewer than 400 television sets. Before World War II, television did not catch on quickly, mainly due to the lack of programs, the limited range of transmission, and the high cost of television receivers. Because television receivers were expensive, as was the license fee, only wealthy people could afford them. Therefore, programming was aimed at an elite, wealthier audience.

On September 1, 1939 television transmission was shut off when World War II began. Without television, the BBC concentrated on radio and quality reporting of war activities. It also started airing a nightly war report after the regular evening news. By the end of World War II, the BBC had gained a great global reputation as a high-quality and objective news broadcaster. And on June 8, 1946 BBC television transmission started again to cover the Victory parade.

From 1936 to 1955, there was only one television channel, BBC TV, later known as BBC One. But on September 22, 1955, for the first time the BBC faced some competition with the introduction of the Independent Television, or ITV. ITV ended the BBC monopoly and introduced a new and completely different style of television. ITV also gave viewers, for the first time, a choice.

One major difference between ITV and BBC TV was that ITV was funded and sponsored by outside advertisers. Also, unlike BBC TV, which used cinema newsreels and still pictures to broadcast the news, ITV used a less formal style of reporting imported from US evening television newscasts. ITV quickly developed a substantial following.

Further choice in television channels opened up with the arrival of BBC Two in 1964. This allowed the BBC to air popular programs on BBC One, and more specialized, in-depth programs on BBC Two. Another technical move that helped promote BBC Two was the fact that in 1967 it was the first channel to start a color service. Because color televisions were expensive, many British people could not afford them. Also, the first color programs were few and far between. Other early disadvantages of color televisions were that they were bulky, unreliable, and had poor color quality. However after a few years, most of the problems were worked out, and on May 16, 1969 BBC One and ITV were given permission to begin working on their own color services. By the mid-1970s, color televisions were smaller, cheaper, and more reliable, and color programming became the norm.

In the early 1980s the Conservative prime minister Margaret Thatcher established a committee to investigate the possibility of seeking advertising revenue for the BBC. However, this did not materialize, and the BBC's commitment to high-quality, non-commercial programming remained intact.

Thanks to the threat during the Thatcher years of being partially privatized or driven by commercial interests, in the 1990s the BBC began to investigate other possible avenues of income. As a result, a new digital broadcasting service was established to compete with Rupert Murdoch's BSkyB. The BBC also began to market a foreign service that is now available on cable in North America and elsewhere. The BBC's online homepage is one of the most frequently accessed websites in the United Kingdom. Currently the United Kingdom also has the BBC equivalent of CNN, shaped in part by the Gulf War when CNN covered the war and the BBC and other European media were forced to play catch-up. The BBC's 24-hour all-news channel – News 24 – has been a success to date.

In November 1991 the BBC launched a world service television, otherwise known as BBC World. It is a public service channel funded by the British Foreign Office using satellite technology to reach an extensive foreign audience. BBC World is an international news and information television channel broadcast in English 24 hours a day for a global audience. It provides news, business, and weather, as well as the best of the BBC's current affairs, documentary, and lifestyle programming. The companion BBC World Service Radio has an estimated global audience of over 30 million listeners and is broadcast in 43 languages.

In the late 1990s the BBC started a second international channel, BBC Prime. This global entertainment channel covers a broad range of programming. BBC Prime is available in most core, semiperipheral, and peripheral regions. Programs dealing with classics, cult comedy, and music do particularly well.

BBC broadcasting has been honed and refined over the years and is now the envy of many of the world's major broadcasters. It has set the world standard by which others are judged. BBC World Service operations are not easily duplicated, because its quality standards are unique. But with the advance of competition, particularly CNN, as well as other satellite and Internet services, some are questioning the role and expense of BBC's World Service.

The BBC is currently facing a problem related to economics and future government funding. Because it now attracts under 50 percent of the domestic audience, there is growing concern that the traditional support for the license fee-funding concept may decline. Although the BBC has a loyal core of supporters, others strongly support the notion that commercial stations, advertising, market share, and ratings should determine the future of broadcasting. Critics claim that the traditions of public support, public service, and subsidizing media are vestiges of a bygone era. Many now want the future of the BBC and other broadcast services to be determined by open market forces rather than by officials behind closed government doors.

Royal Charter, 2006–2016

Like all major broadcasters, the BBC is facing a changing landscape. But since 1927 a unique aspect of the BBC is that it operates under the authority of a British Royal Charter. The charter spells out in detail its public service mandate. There are various UK parliamentary hearings and studies looking at the future of the BBC, including its global media services, its presence on the Internet, and the contentious commercial activities run by BBC Enterprises. A significant part of the BBC Enterprises' services includes BBC America and the selling of Teletubbies paraphernalia. The balance between resource allocations to national versus international services will also come under close scrutiny.

The BBC is facing the reality, as are other broadcasters, that digital communication has brought convergence and more channels. Today the BBC confronts more commercial competition, both domestic and foreign, the evolution of the Internet, and new satellite channels. This will all be open to public discussion and debate, since the BBC is a government corporation.

The Royal Charter and Agreement outlines the terms and scope of funding, as well as the operational areas in which the BBC provides service, on either a non-commercial or a commercial basis. Currently there are three major sources of revenue of the BBC: the license fee, somewhat controversial commercial activities which are growing, and government grants. All this is for a network that captures about half the total British radio audience and less than a third of the television audience.

Critics of the BBC have two major complaints about its operations. The first is that the mandated funding through the license fee is being used as a cross-subsidy for other multimedia activities. These include the children's channels CBBC and CBeebies, which both Viacom and Disney objected to; various BBC Internet sites; and the very successful BBC Enterprises' commercial activities. Two radical solutions have been offered. The first is to do away with the license fee altogether and to make all services commercial. The second is to stick to only non-commercial activities and to sell off the profitable commercial ventures.

The second major complaint is about standards and quality. In 2004 the Hutton Report strongly criticized the news and public affairs divisions for lack of proper oversight in relation to a controversial story about Iraq. The chairman and chief executive of the BBC resigned over the matter. Others condemn the BBC for debasing its shows by chasing high audience ratings as it mimics US networks by broadcasting mindless reality shows. These critics want higher-quality shows that reflect world-class production standards, scripts, and on-air talent.

In the midst of the broad range of issues that will inform the public debate and debate in the British House of Commons is another matter potentially involving all public broadcasters, namely the desire of the World Trade Organization (WTO) to include cultural industries under its tariffs. One example illustrates the possible significance of WTO's plans to the BBC. The current financing of the BBC involves an annual license fee on all radio and television receivers, which provides a huge subsidy to the BBC. The WTO does not allow subsidies in its rules, since they distort the commercial, market-based playing field. Thus the BBC could find itself facing a financial crisis if the WTO pushes the matter. (See Chapter 5 for more detailed discussion of the WTO.)

BBC Scandal

Once considered the gold standard of objectivity and honesty, the venerable BBC faced its worst nightmare in over a half century over pulling a news magazine piece before the broadcast date. It came to light in 2012, when long-time popular BBC television host Jimmy Savile was accused of sexually abusing hundreds of boys and girls during his years with the national public television network. A BBC news show, *Newsnight*, had a crew working on the story during the fall of 2011, which was cancelled without explanation by Peter Rippon, the head of the news magazine show. But in October 2012 a competing commercial channel exposed the larger story and soon even the British Parliament, the police, and the vast BBC audience was demanding answers and accountability. Caught up in the growing scandal was the former BBC director-general Mark Thompson who is now CEO of the *New York Times*. Thompson let tribute shows for Savile air around Christmas 2011 despite the internal turmoil at the BBC over the earlier cancellation by Rippon and others. Some of the abuse was alleged to have taken place at BBC studios, and in hospitals and schools. Savile died before all this came to light but other former BBC staff are being questioned.

The new BBC director-general, George Entwistle, lasted 54 days before resigning after additional problems in the news division occurred on his watch. A much broader issue is now in play. Essentially news acceptance by an audience is based on trust in the network as well as the information itself. Since its beginning as a public broadcaster, the BBC has championed accuracy, honesty, and objectivity. This earned the trust of the British public which was paying for the BBC with their license fee, first on radios and then on television sets. The current license fee is $231 per annum per household. Given the new broadcasting reality of several news channels and sources, some of the British public, as well as in Parliament, are questioning the cost and direction of the shaken BBC.

This tarnished media outlet is now the second one to shake the trust and faith of the British public. The other was the lengthy phone-hacking scandal and parliamentary inquiry involving News Corp (see Chapter 7).

Deutsche Welle

Deutsche Welle is the German online and worldwide radio and television broadcaster. Information is provided 24 hours a day, including up-to-date information on German and European domestic and foreign issues, as well as economic and financial trends focusing on the Frankfurt stock exchange and the euro. Deutsche Welle TV offers 24-hour, commercial-free service, which includes news, sports, and cultural affairs programming. It provides programming in German, Arabic, English, and Spanish.

Deutsche Welle began with short-wave radio transmissions in May 1953, and it is financed mainly with German government funds. In April 1992 Deutsche Welle TV began transmission and was then on air 14 hours a day. Deutsche Welle TV is now carried by cable systems throughout Europe and is rebroadcast in many parts of the world. Deutsche Welle has also set up Internet services in order to compete in the public affairs arena with the BBC, CNN, and Voice of America. Since its inception, Deutsche Welle has received substantial German government support. But with the end of the Cold War and the reunification of Germany, political support and federal government funding became problematic. In the 1990s it had a staff of 2,200, which has now been reduced to 1,200. Almost all public broadcasters across Europe have been subject to public funding cuts.

Finally, Deutsche Welle is offering an innovative master's degree in media studies, which focuses on training staff from peripheral regions with a hands-on and intercultural approaches.

Euronews

In 1993 the European Union established its own transnational news network known as Euronews. It is headquartered in France and broadcasts television news in eight languages, which include Russian and Arabic. The impetus to create this trans-European television news network was almost a direct result of CNN's coverage of the First Gulf War. The European networks were either nowhere to be found in Baghdad at the beginning of the war, or as the war progressed found themselves increasingly relying on CNN's coverage to follow the action. The US military kept foreign networks away from the battles. In response, 18 European public broadcasters, including France, Italy, Germany, Spain, Belgium, and

Greece, put up substantial funding to establish Euronews. In addition to government subsidies, Euronews accepts commercial advertising. Spain pulled out in 2008 in order to support the Spanish international network. Another notably absent member of Euronews is the United Kingdom. Like CNN, the BBC is in direct competition for the Euronews audience (for more on Euronews, see Chapter 9).

Channel NewsAsia

A new Asian-based news channel, Channel NewsAsia (CNA), began service in 2000. Like Euronews, which is attempting to bring a European perspective to European and global events, CNA is seeking to bring an Asian perspective on global news events to the Asian region. It is based in Singapore and has close government ties. CNA is seeking to compete with the major global news services such as CNN International, the BBC, and CNBC Asia. With an all-Asian staff, it has 10 bureaus and about 150 journalists across Asia, more than the three English-language all-news networks combined. Like the BBC, CNA is attempting to serve a market of about 16 million households, whereas CNN International is the clear regional leader, with about 30 million subscribers. CNA is trying to appeal to the Asian demographic in hopes of attracting viewers from across the most populated region in the world by focusing on news by Asians and from an Asian editorial perspective. Some journalists and media critics are concerned about the undetermined role of the Singapore government on the status of CNA independence.

US Department of State and Broadcasting Board of Governors

The US federal government created the United States Information Agency (USIA) during World War I. Its initial purpose was to coordinate federal international information and to counter negative foreign propaganda. USIA became an independent agency in 1953 and expanded its activities to include a broad range of international information, education initiatives, cultural exchanges, and media relations. In 1998, under the Foreign Affairs Reform and Restructuring Act, USIA was essentially divided into two sections. Much of the public diplomacy and foreign exchange activities were relocated in the State Department. The International Broadcasting Bureau (IBB) became a freestanding, separate agency at the same time to oversee all US, non-military, international broadcasting services. In 1999 the USIA was disbanded altogether.

The activities transferred to the State Department currently include long-standing programs that have an impact on media systems and journalists in other nations. For example, the College and University Affiliations Program (CUAP) seek to establish relations between US universities and their foreign counterparts. Examples of programs include a Palestinian media center, a grant to a Jordanian university to develop distance learning, and a grant to the University of Chile to establish an environmental science research agenda. The US State Department also funded the Aegean Young Journalists program, which brings together Greek and Turkish journalists. Many of the programs and partnerships funded have similar activities such as workshops, study tours, internships, and a US-based study tour. Another initiative is the Citizen Exchange Program (CEP), which brings both journalism professors and journalists from semiperipheral and peripheral nations to the

Table 11.1 The Broadcasting Board of Governors' activities, 2013

1	Voice of America
2	Radio Free Europe, Radio Liberty, Radio Free Asia
3	Worldnet Television and Film Service
4	Radio and TV Martí
5	Middle East Broadcasting Networks: Radio Sawa; Al-Hurra TV

United States for workshops and information exchanges. A goal of this program is to instill in delegates free-press values so that, as their media systems are privatized or created, they will reflect the journalist values and practices of an open and democratic society.

Through the Broadcasting Board of Governors (BBG), the US federal government has substantial involvement in international broadcasting. It is responsible for all US non-military international broadcasting services funded by the federal government. The BBG oversees four major broadcasting outlets, shown in Table 11.1. All of these services receive annual grants from the US federal government and policy guidance from the US secretary of state.

The end of the Cold War era has seen a noticeable shift in and questioning of the role of these federally funded global broadcasting services. In their initial years, these services were designed as US propaganda voices through which to present, in local languages around the world, the US foreign policy position, the ideology of fighting communism, and US political and free-market economic values. Now there is a greater emphasis on promoting US commercial and export interests abroad instead of the hard-line political rhetoric of the Cold War era. There is also a movement to focus on public diplomacy issues as outlined in Chapter 4.

Voice of America

The Voice of America (VOA) was founded in 1942 and was heavily funded by Congress during the Cold War. In the first three decades it focused on fighting communism and combating the global spread of Marxism. Following the end of the Cold War, the VOA is attempting to reposition itself. It is an international radio and television service and has a weekly global audience of about 100 million people. It broadcasts on short wave and medium wave, and through satellite transmissions, in English and 43 other languages. There are over 1,000 hours of programs a week and it uses its own correspondents at 23 news bureaus around the world, as well as freelance reporters. VOA provides news, information, and cultural programming around the globe. Some of the programs promote the benefits of democracy, the free press and free markets, human rights, and the American way of life, politics, and business. All programming originates from its Washington headquarters, but under the 1948 Smith–Mundt Act, VOA is prohibited from broadcasting within the United States.

In the fall of 1994 VOA began television programming. Shortly thereafter it experienced a 20 percent budget cut and began accepting corporate underwriting to improve its budget. VOA TV simulcasts in six foreign languages, including Spanish and Chinese.

A notable distinction between the VOA and the BBC is that the former emphasizes a US orientation and a White House viewpoint, whereas the latter focuses on world news and global trends, without the kind of bias of VOA. Internationally, the VOA is viewed as a propaganda arm of the US government, whereas the BBC is perceived to be independent, objective, and more credible.

Radio Free Europe, Radio Liberty, and Radio Free Asia

Radio Free Europe (RFE), Radio Liberty (RL), and Radio Free Asia (RFA) are private, non-profit corporations funded by the BBG. RFE and RL reach 20 nations across Europe and central Asia. They have 19 bureaus and broadcast in 28 languages. Their programming is pro-American and promotes free enterprise economies. To some extent they are still caught up in the old Cold War mentality and duplicate VOA's mission and programming. RFA seeks to provide American news and views to Asian nations lacking a free press. It broadcasts in 10 languages, mostly Chinese-related. It also has a website for those with Internet access in the region.

Worldnet Television and Film Service

Worldnet was launched in 1983 and is transmitted by satellite from television studios in Washington, DC. The programming is directed at US embassies and other broadcasters around the world. It programs 24 hours a day in English, but other programs are available in a number of languages such as Arabic, Russian, French, Spanish, and Chinese. Worldnet programs range from public affairs forums to science discussion, to international call-in programs. Worldnet also transmits some public broadcasting programs, such as PBS's *NewsHour*.

Radio and TV Martí

In 1983 the US Congress approved the establishment of Radio Martí under the provision that it would adhere to the Voice of America's regulations In addition, the Reagan administration and the Cuban American National Foundation agreed that the station would be based in Washington, DC, to make clear that this was the official voice of the US government, and not an outlet of Cuban exile organizations. Given these provisions, Radio Martí went on the air in May 1985. TV Martí first broadcast in March 1990. In 1998, under legislation passed by Congress, Radio and TV Martí headquarters and operations moved from Washington, DC to Miami, Florida. Since that time Cuban exile extremists have dominated the staffing of both the radio and television studios. The only constant since the move has been a high staffing turnover. The tone, professionalism, and vitriolic anti-Castro rants are all likely to change with President Obama's more conciliatory approach toward Cuba.

Under the VOA, Radio Martí's programs are to be produced in accordance with the following VOA regulations (US Public Law 94.30):

The long-range interests of the United States are served by communicating directly with the people of the world by radio. To be effective, the Voice of America (the broadcasting Service of the United States Information Agency) must win the attention and respect of listeners. These principles will therefore Govern Voice of America (VOA) Broadcasts.
   Following are the three policies stated:

1   VOA will service as a consistently reliable and authoritative source of news. VOA news will be accurate, objective and comprehensive.
2   VOA will represent America, not any single segment of American society, and will therefore present a balanced and comprehensive projection of significant American thought and institutions.

3   VOA will present the policies of the United States clearly and effectively, and will also present responsible discussion and opinion on those policies.[21]

These provisions are designed to insure accuracy, objectivity, and balance in content.

Radio Martí broadcasts seven days a week, 24 hours a day, on medium wave and short wave. Its broadcasts includes news, music, and a variety of feature and news analysis programs. With a staff of over 100 employees, Radio Martí provides news, talk radio, and information programs. News and news-related programming make up half of its daily schedule. Radio Martí's goal is to fill the information gap caused by more than three decades of Cuban government censorship, There is a one-hour noon newscast which includes a live interview/discussion segment with experts or individuals in Cuba and correspondents around the world. In addition, there is a half-hour newscast at 4 p.m., as well as live coverage of special events in the United States and around the world that stress the importance of Cuba. Topics with relevance to Cuba that are covered include congressional hearings and speeches by Latin American heads of state at major regional and hemispheric events. Despite complaints from the Cuban media, Radio Martí's programs offer listeners a Cuban American perspective on current events. In addition, the broadcasts offer feature and special programs with a wide range of information and entertainment. Some of the programs include round-table discussions; commentaries by experts on political, economic, social, religious, and human rights issues; and testimonies from former political prisoners and from human rights and labor sectors.

Despite efforts by Cuban president Castro to jam the transmission of Radio Martí, Cubans tune in to it in significant numbers. It was for this reason that TV Martí was established: to provide Cuban viewers with programming available in other countries and in the western hemisphere. In addition, TV Martí provides in Spanish news features on life in the United States and other nations, entertainment, and sports. It also provides commentary and other information on events in Cuba and elsewhere in order to promote the cause of freedom in and for Cuba. TV Martí is on the air only for about five hours a day.

Its technical operations are mounted aboard a balloon tethered 10,000 feet above Cudjoe Key, Florida. The signal is then relayed to a transmitter and a highly directional antenna mounted aboard an aerostat for broadcast to Cuba. TV Martí's transmission system delivers a clear television signal to the Havana area. Although jamming efforts by the Cuban government make it difficult to receive the signal in the city center of Havana, mobile monitoring indicates that international reception is possible in some outlying areas of the city and other more remote parts of Havana province.

There is a downside to the unique manner in which TV Martí is transmitted. As mentioned, TV Martí's signals are transmitted from a balloon tethered above the Florida Keys. Also on board is radar to track drug flights and high-speed boats from Latin America. When TV Martí goes on, the radar goes off. Some critics argue that drug smugglers base their activities around the transmitting schedule, which gives them the best time to avoid detection.

Radio and TV Martí have experienced internal management problems. Ultra-conservative Cuban exiles dominate management, and the staff consists of fanatical Cuban exiles living in the Miami area. Several journalists have complained and ultimately left because of editorial interference with their stories and assignments. Some claim that they have declining audiences in Cuba and that both propaganda-driven networks are relics of a bygone era and should be closed altogether.

Middle East Broadcasting Networks

This unit operates two main networks, Al-Hurra (The Free One) TV and Radio Sawa (Together), on a budget of over $100 million from the BBG. They both broadcast in Arabic across 22 countries in the Middle East. Radio Sawa began in 2003 and television in 2004. The radio provides a mix of Western and Arabic popular music and has large audiences among teenagers and people in their twenties. The television audience has not been as great, especially compared to its competitor Al Jazeera. It does not help that its news division is located outside the region, in Springfield, Virginia which is not exactly a hotbed of Arabic life or news stories. The Arab media has heaped scorn on the efforts of the BBG, claiming that these are propaganda tools and avoid reporting on civilian casualties caused by American or NATO bombings.

Conclusions

The first decades of the twentieth-first century are witnessing significant and long-term changes in global communication. The first was the rise of CNN, which began as a small ultra-high frequency (UHF) station in Atlanta, Georgia, and rose to become the predominant global network for breaking news. CNN's effectiveness and expansion were aided substantially by the introduction of small satellite earth stations capable of linking CNN's corporate broadcasting center with journalists in any part of the world almost instantaneously. Whether the breaking news was occurring in a major urban center such as Paris or Beijing, or in a remote desert or isolated rural area in Asia, Iraq, or Kosovo, CNN was able, with a technician and a single reporter, to broadcast live.

CNN's success also created a problem. As its role, model, influence, and ability to broadcast major events grew, other nations became concerned that their own governments' policies, including foreign policy, were being ignored or marginalized while CNN broadcast a primarily US perspective on international events. As a result, some nations started to develop alternatives to CNN. One of the most notable is the BBC. Although it is currently limited in terms of its reach, over time the BBC could become a major global broadcaster in the international television news arena as it once dominated the global radio networks. Euronews is a good example of a network created to present a pan-European perspective on European and world news for Europeans. That was also the expectation of the French when they launched France 24.

Other interesting changes are the substantial growth of Arabic services by major stakeholders. These services have been developed for radio, television, and the Internet. Along with this, the focus of, and funds from, former communist countries is shifting to semiperipheral regions.

Initially many radio services, particularly those off-shore, were based on short-wave radio technology, which, thanks in particular to the Internet, is becoming obsolete. A more pressing issue is that of continuing financial support for these primarily government-funded global media services. With the end of the Cold War and the decline in the fear of a nuclear attack, there has been a corresponding reduction in governments' desire to fund global radio networks. All short-wave global networks are feeling the stress of decreasing support, both politically and financially. For example, the Canadian Broadcasting Corporation's excellent foreign short-wave service, Radio Canada International (RCI), was closed down during the 1990s as a result of budget cuts. Part of RCI's budget was redirected to promote Canadian exports abroad. Other services have not fared as badly, but all are experiencing declining rather than expanding budgets. Some of these services, particularly the BBC and the Voice of America, are shifting attention to the possibility of using the Internet as a way of extending their audience reach and justifying government funding. Many are also soliciting external corporate advertising or corporate underwriting for selected programs.

A final point is that the major global news networks are based in core nations – CNN in the United States, the BBC in the United Kingdom, Deutsche Welle in Germany, and France 24 in France. These core-based global television news systems are designed for major export markets around the world because the majority of the services are commercially based and seek to extend their commercial viability by attracting larger audiences with the appropriate demographics for their advertisers. So these global systems have two basic audiences, one within the nations where the corporations are based and the other scattered around the world. Some of these systems are in remote villages and others are in major urban centers with potential audiences in the millions. With the expansion of cable systems and satellite technology, the potential for niche, particularly news or expat, networks was recognized early by major innovators and is now being mimicked by broadcasters on a global scale. But all global news networks present a core-nation perspective on the news they cover, and they all cover news in peripheral regions only rarely and usually only when it is about a coup, civil war, an assassination, or a major disaster.

With the end of the Cold War, media relics such as Radio Free Europe and Radio Liberty should be taken down like the Berlin Wall. Also, the Pentagon has begun a "deceptive" practice of creating foreign-language websites which present only favorable "news" about what the United States is doing and leaving out statistics on civilian casualties. Manufactured stories and this kind of military public relations benefit neither American journalism nor foreign audiences.[22]

On a positive note, the US State Department is establishing a new counter-propaganda unit to create FM stations, expand mobile phone services, and train local journalists across Pakistan and Afghanistan. The unit seeks to counter the Taliban militants' ability to win the war of words and images. Winning the war of capturing the hearts and minds is as important as winning the war on the ground. As the *New York Times* reported: "'Concurrent with the insurgency is an information war,' said Richard C. Holbrooke, the special representative for Afghanistan and Pakistan, who will direct the effort. 'We are losing that war.'"[23]

Why it took the Pentagon so long to recognize this problem illustrates the outdated thinking of US military leaders. The same *New York Times* piece points out that in the Taliban regions of Pakistan there are only four legal FM stations, while the militants run over 150 illegal stations. Making this new counter-propaganda unit at the State Department a success will require not only substantial funds but also that the CIA, Pentagon, and the military on the ground do not undercut or challenge this new media effort.

Notes

1. Although the focus of this book is on global media, MSNBC and Fox News are relevant models for potential global expansion. They also provide considerable international coverage of leading stories, many connected with the global war on terrorism.

   MSNBC, launched in July 1996, combines three technologies – broadcast, cable, and the Internet – to provide 24-hour news from around the world. It was jointly owned by Microsoft and General Electric's NBCUniversal, and primarily combined the national and international news resources of the NBC system along with the financial, business, and technology resources of Microsoft. Rupert Murdoch's News Corporation, on the other hand, owns Fox News Channel. It went on air in October 1996 and provides 24-hour all-news global coverage, in direct competition with both MSNBC as well as Time Warner's CNN.

   An interesting phenomenon emerged during the NATO bombing of Yugoslavia in 1999. These three all-news networks clearly have an insatiable appetite for news coverage 24 hours a day, which also includes extensive commentary on global events themselves, in addition to broad coverage of news conferences, videos of bombing attacks, interviews with refugees, and so on. A new phenomenon during the Kosovo air strikes by NATO involved the significant new dimension of retired military personnel appearing again and again on all three networks to comment, mostly negatively, about NATO's actions and strategies. As a result, not only did President Clinton have to contend with political opposition to his military strategy in Washington, but he had a new wave of critics –an endless cadre of retired generals who were, from time to time, reaching substantial audiences through the all-news networks. This translated, in terms of public opinion, into a larger and more skeptical US public concerning the United States' role in NATO, as well as its military interests in Yugoslavia.

In general, CNN has been able to attract more domestic viewers than either of its competitors, but there is one notable exception. In June 1999 MSNBC opted to pay the BBC for three hours of live coverage of the British royal wedding of Prince Edward and Sophie Rhys-Jones. For the first time in its brief broadcasting history, MSNBC beat CNN in total households that single day by featuring live a British royal wedding

2. Michael Wolff, "Can a New CEO Save CNN? Cable Network Stuck In the Past," *USA Today* (October 15, 2012), B1.

3. Quoted in Hank Whittemore, *CNN: The Inside Story*, Toronto: Little, Brown, 1990, pp. 295–6.

4. Philip Taylor, *War and the Media: Propaganda and Persuasion in the Gulf War*, Manchester: Manchester University Press, 1998, p. 7.

5. Don M. Flournoy and Robert K. Stewart, *CNN: Making News in the Global Market*, Luton, UK: John Libbey Media, 1997, p. ix.

6. Quoted in Flournoy and Stewart, *CNN*, p. 34.

7. Flournoy and Stewart, *CNN*, pp. 208–9. Additional details about CNN may be found in Piers Robinson, *The CNN Effect: The Myth of News Media, Foreign Policy and Intervention*, London: Routledge, 2002; Royce Ammon, *Global Television and the Shaping of World Politics*, Jefferson, NC: McFarland, 2001; and S. Kull, C. Ramsay, and E. Lewis, "Misperceptions, the Media, and the Iraq War," *Political Science Quarterly* 118(4) (December 2003), 569–98.

8. John Cook, "CNN's Free Fall," *Brill's Content* (April 2001), 68.

9. Cook, "CNN's Free Fall," 122.

10. Piers Robinson, *The CNN Effect: The Myth of News Media, Foreign Policy and Intervention*, London: Routledge: 2002.

11. V. Hawkins, "The Other Side of the CNN Factor: The Media and Conflict," *Journalism Studies* 3(2) (May 2002), 225–40.

12. Margaret Belknap, *"The CNN Effect: Strategic Enabler or Operational Risk?" US WC Strategy Research Project*, US Army War College, Carlisle Barracks, PA, 2001.

13. W. C. Soderlund, E. D. Briggs, T. P. Najem, and B. C. Roberts, *Africa's Deadliest Conflict: Media Coverage of the Humanitarian Disaster in the Congo*, Waterloo, Canada: Wilfrid Laurier University Press, 2012, p. 162.

14. W. C. Soderlund, E. D. Briggs, K. Hildebrandt, and A. S. Sidahmed, *Humanitarian Crisis and Intervention: Reassessing the Impact of the Mass Media*, Sterling, VA: Kumarian, 2008, pp. 287–80 (emphasis original).

15. Scott Collins, *Crazy Like a Fox: The Inside Story of How Fox News Beat CNN*, New York: Portfolio, 2004.

16. Jason Zengerle, "Fiddling with the Reception," *New York Times Magazine* (August 17, 2003), at http://www.nytimes.com/2003/08/17/magazine/fiddling-with-the-reception.html?pagewanted=all&src=pm, accessed August 28, 2013.

17. Michael Pfau et al., "Embedding Journalists in Military Combat Units: Impact on Newspaper Story Frames and Tone," *Journalism and Mass Communication Quarterly* 81(1) (Spring 2004), 83.

18. Pfau et al., "Embedding Journalists in Military Combat Units," 84.

19. Asa Briggs, *The BBC: The First Fifty Years*, New York: Oxford University Press, 1985.

20. R. H. Coase, *British Broadcasting*, London: Longmans, Green, 1950, p. 46.

21. http://www.bbg.gov/broadcasters/standards-principles/, accessed August 28, 2013.

22. Peter Eisler, "Pentagon Starts Foreign News Sites: Journalism Groups Call Sites Deceptive Effort to Control Message Abroad," *United States Today* (May 1, 2008), 6A.

23. Quoted in Thom Shanker, "US Turns to Radio Stations and Cellphones to Counter Taliban's Propaganda," *New York Times* (August 16, 2009), 6.

12

The Role of Global
News Agencies

Introduction

This chapter covers global wire services, which are major components of the global communication system. These wire services bring to international communication different sets of stakeholders, yet each service has a significant role in the daily activities of multinational media enterprises. They are also under industry pressure to expand globally, to achieve broader scale and scope. As the global economy unfolds the wire services follow. Since World War II, the debate surrounding international communication has in large part focused on international wire services. During the 1960s the global wire services became the first and frequent targets of peripheral nations and other critics. During the NWICO debates of the 1970s, most of the issues involved some aspect of wire-service behavior, location (they are all based in core nations), or corporate structure.[1]

Two general problems arose in discussions about core-nation-based global wire services. First, the wire services focused on covering news that was mainly relevant to colonial powers or dealt with regions where core-headquartered corporations had branch plants. The three major global services, Thomson Reuters, Associated Press, and Agence France Presse, are based in London, New York, and Paris respectively. The second major problem was that coverage of peripheral nations focused on negative news such as civil strife, natural disasters, or sensational and bizarre events. The wire services reported little if any good news about the poorest regions in Africa, Latin America, or Asia. For most people their view of the rest of the world is mediated by what the media covers or does not cover. The world is defined in large part by what and how these wire services cover breaking news abroad.

Two general groups of researchers attempted to document the wire services' one-way news flow and the imbalance in both East–West and North–South coverage. One group sought funding and a voice from UNESCO, and by the late 1970s its rhetoric and demands had become shrill. The other group consisted of various pockets of scholars in the United States,

Global Communication: Theories, Stakeholders, and Trends, Fourth Edition. Thomas L. McPhail.
© 2014 John Wiley & Sons, Inc. Published 2014 by John Wiley & Sons, Inc.

Table 12.1 Global news agencies, 2013

Thomson Reuters
Associated Press (AP)
Agence France Presse (AFP)
Bloomberg
Dow Jones & Company
Xinhua News Agency
Inter Press Services (IPS)

Europe, the Nordic countries, Latin America, and elsewhere who conducted independent research, frequently using content analysis of a specific medium, usually print. In the final analysis, almost all of the research was critical of the wire services. Researchers frequently studied the print press to document what were perceived as structural problems in the core-based and controlled wire services. With the end of the Cold War, East–West tensions have evaporated for the most part, but certain structural criticisms remain concerning North–South news coverage.

The major global news agencies (see Table 12.1) are detailed in this chapter. Reuters and the Associated Press are not only the giants but they also control vast television news reporting and Internet interests around the globe, in addition to their historical interest in print-based journalism.

Thomson Reuters

The earliest wire service was Reuters, which dates back to October 1851, when Paul Julius Reuter, a German immigrant, opened an office in London. Reuters transmitted stock market quotations between London and Paris and in its early era focused on business news. The agency soon became known as a news source and started covering wars and elections because they impacted the business environment. Eventually it extended its services to the entire British press, as well as the press in the British colonies and other European countries. Reuters expanded its services and began transmitting general and economic news from all around the world. Reuters' successful news service was booming. In 1865 it was the first wire-service company in Europe to transmit the news of President Lincoln's assassination in the United States.

Through technological advances such as the telegraph and undersea cable facilities, Reuters news services expanded beyond Europe to include the Far East by 1872 and South America by 1874. In 1883 Reuters began to use a "column printer" to transmit messages electronically to London newspapers. This format allowed editors to simply cut and paste stories from the Reuters feed. The use of radio further expanded the wire service in the 1920s, allowing Reuters to transmit news internationally. In 1927 Reuters introduced the teleprinter to distribute news to London newspapers. In 1939 the company moved its corporate headquarters to 85 Fleet Street, London[2], and then in 2003 to Canary Wharf.

Reuters' continued success and modernizing of services continued into the latter half of the twentieth century. It expanded in 1964 with the Stockmaster service, which transmitted financial data internationally. In 1973 the company launched Reuters Monitor, which transmitted news and foreign exchange prices. Following a dramatic increase in profitability, Reuters was floated as a public company in 1984 on the London Stock Exchange and on National Association of Securities Dealers Automated Quotations (NASDAQ) in the United States.

In 1960 Reuters began to buy shares in Visnews, a global television news film agency. It continued buying shares of Visnews until 1992, when it bought out Visnews completely and renamed the company Reuters Television (RTV). RTV is the world's leading supplier of international news material for television, reaching 1.5 billion people daily and delivering material directly to media customers by satellite or terrestrial land-based systems. Customers include broadcasters and newspapers around the world, but the news is tailored especially to financial markets. Broadcasters are supplied with fast, reliable news video ranging from major events to human interest stories, from sports to business. RTV service is the oldest comprehensive real-time news and information service that covers breaking news around the globe. It is ideal for those who want to know what is happening around the world because it often includes secondary stories not widely reported in the United States; these stories are broadcast extensively in other nations, however. Reuters' only major competition in supplying news to broadcasters started in 1994 with the Associated Press Television News (APTN), which was established when the Associated Press bought out World Television News.

Reuters' corporate position as an international market leader is based on its four strengths:

- a worldwide information and news-reporting network known for speed, accuracy, integrity, and impartiality;
- a constantly developing communications network and a product line distinguishable by its breadth and quality;
- comprehensive financial databases for both real-time and historical information; and
- a proven reputation for reliability and continuous technological innovation.

Reuters offers its clients financial, media, and professional products and services. The financial products include data feeds to financial markets and the software tools to analyze data. Under the financial umbrella are transaction products, which enable traders to deal in the foreign exchange, futures, options, and securities markets. The media division delivers news in multimedia, including television images, still pictures, sound, and graphics. Reuters' professional product division packages the news in the form of electronic briefings for corporate executives in insurance, advertising, transportation, health care, and other corporate and professional sectors.

In 2008 Reuters was purchased by Thomson Corporation, a communication conglomerate with strong financial data services based in Toronto, Canada. The new combined company was restructured into two divisions: professional and markets. The professional division consists of the news and information unit that was Reuters. The markets division focuses on law, tax, and health care. Some concerns were raised about the history of Thomson and its historical focus on financial and business news rather than general news or public interest stories. The new owners agreed to follow the Reuters Trust Principles which were established in 1941, at the height of World War II, when Reuters reaffirmed its commitment to objective journalism practices along with integrity and freedom from bias or intimidation. The Reuters Trust Principles are:

1   that Thomson Reuters shall at no time pass into the hands of any one interest, group or faction;
2   that the integrity, independence and freedom from bias of Thomson Reuters shall at all times be fully preserved;

3   that Thomson Reuters shall supply unbiased and reliable news services to newspapers, news agencies, broadcasters and other media subscribers and to businesses, governments, institutions, individuals and others with whom Thomson Reuters has or may have contracts;

4   that Thomson Reuters shall pay due regard to the many interests which it serves in addition to those of the media; and

5   that no effort shall be spared to expand, develop and adapt the news and other services and products of Thomson Reuters so as to maintain its leading position in the international news and information business.[3]

Today, Thomson Reuters supplies the global financial markets and the news media with the widest range of information and news products including real-time financial data; collective investment data; numerical, textual, historical, and graphical databases; and news, graphics, news video, and news pictures. Approximately half a million users located in close to 60,000 organizations access Reuters information and news worldwide. In 2011 the company restructured itself into one company to deliver content, technology, and services to end users. In 2012 Thomson Reuters had 60,000 employees in over 100 countries.

The Thomson Reuters editorial reference service unit from London and the daily news diary unit from Washington were relocated to India to save money. Senior journalists are concerned that outsourcing will move up the "food chain" over time and that the quality of editing as well as reporting on businesses will decline. Several Thomson Reuters journalists are concerned about the future impact of the outsourcing practice as well as the dominance of financial news. In 2013 a deputy editor of Thomson Reuters was charged with assisting the hacking collective Anonymous in altering the website of the *Los Angeles Times*.

Summary

Reuters established the first international wire-service business. It had the major advantage of following the growth and spread of the British Empire around the world. It has continued to be the pre-eminent financial- and business-oriented global wire service, but when new markets emerge, Reuters also covers general or breaking news stories around the world thanks to its enormous staff. Today it is a global media and financial conglomerate. Reuters was one of the first media firms to recognize the significance of the Internet and to develop a broad range of Internet services and sites. Finally, RTV is one of the two major global television news feeds, serving almost all major networks in Europe, North America, and elsewhere. Along with the Associated Press, Thomson Reuters is the dominant global wire and video provider for almost all broadcasters and publishers.

Associated Press

The Associated Press is another wire service with roots that date back to the mid-1800s. In May 1848 officials representing six New York City newspapers sat around a table at the *New York Sun*'s office discussing the high cost of collecting news, particularly from Europe, by telegraph. The newly invented telegraph made the transmission of news by wire possible, but costs were so high that they strained the resources of any single paper. These newspapermen worried about the high cost of covering the Mexican–American War. David Hale of the *Journal of Commerce* argued that only a joint effort between New York's papers could make the telegraph affordable and effectively prevent telegraph companies from constraining newsgathering. The six highly competitive newspapers, although reluctant at first, agreed to a historic plan of cooperation, and AP was born.[4] AP was from the start a news cooperative and its unique ownership structure continues today. Over 1,700 member newspapers now own and control the not-for-profit cooperative. They elect an 18-member board which sets policies and rates; strategic planning. Over 5,000 radio and television stations are clients of AP services.

A year after AP was established, Boston newspapers joined the New York founders of AP Regional. Newspaper groups soon followed – Western Associated Press, Southern Associated Press, Philadelphia Press, and several others. Washington and foreign news were staples from the start. In 1849 Daniel Craig established the Associated Press's foreign bureau in Halifax, Nova Scotia, the first North American port of call for Cunard's ocean liners. Headline news arrived from Europe with each incoming vessel and was telegraphed to New York. This was the practice until the establishment of the transatlantic cable in 1856 which made the Halifax port outmoded for news.

Today, AP's World Service distributes news and photos to 8,500 international subscribers and translates the report into several languages. It offers news directly in only five languages: English, French, Spanish, German, and Dutch. For a newsgathering agency it is surprising that it does not offer coverage in Arabic or Chinese. It has clients in 121 countries and a full-time news and photo staff of about 1,100 domestically and 500 abroad. The journalists abroad work out of 240 bureaus. AP has won 28 Pulitzer Prizes for photography, the most of any news company. With the demise of its competitor, United Press International, in 1993, AP became a major US wire service, alongside Reuters.

To meet the growing demand for sports coverage, in 1946 AP established the first news agency wire service dedicated entirely to sports. AP also published and circulated an annual AP sports almanac. Today, the sports wire and all other AP wires transmit 9,600 words a minute.

In 1941 radio had become one of the most important means of communication in the United States, and AP was the broadcast pioneer. Between 1933 and 1941, AP's broadcast division had supplied news to radio stations owned by newspaper members only when the news was of major importance. But AP changed that by launching a separate radio broadcast wire called Circuit 7760, the first news organization to operate a broadcast news circuit 24 hours a day, seven days a week. Just one year after Circuit 7760 was launched, AP's broadcast wire was serving more than 200 stations in 120 cities. AP continued to gain broadcast members, and in the 1940s the AP Radio network was launched. It provided hourly newscasts, sportscasts, and business programs to member radio stations and eventually became the first radio network in the world to be delivered by way of satellite. By 1979 the first news wire designed specifically for television stations was introduced.

AP's global video news was called APTN. It is currently Reuters' only major competitor. APTN has full-time video newsgathering facilities in 70 bureaus and more than 300 clients, including ABC, NBC, CNN, CBS, Fox News channels, and Univision. APTN's primary service provides top international news stories as well as regional coverage in North America, Latin America, Asia, and Europe. By the mid-1990s, APTN provided video footage of the day's top news stories by satellite to broadcast organizations worldwide. APTN emphasizes enterprise journalism and the practice of telling the entire story in narrative form at critical moments in different international time zones.

Also by 1994, AP had launched AP All News Radio (ANR), a 24-hour radio newscast. ANR makes it possible for stations in all market sizes to carry the popular and profitable all-news format. Today, more than 50 radio stations are ANR affiliates, and they can easily insert local news and advertising into the ANR format. And finally APTN joined with Trans World International (TWI) in 1996 to launch SNTV, a sports news video agency. The partnership has claimed market leadership, drawing on the strengths of the world's largest newsgathering organization and the world's largest independent supplier of sports programming. SNTV currently serves over 300 broadcasters worldwide.

Because of the ever changing newspaper and broadcast industry, AP remains a leader because of its new businesses and technological developments. Several new initiatives have enabled AP to support and enhance its worldwide newsgathering. For example, the agency sells packaged news to non-members such as governments and corporations. AP's Information Services Department sells AP Online – a group of subject-specific news wires tailored to each client's industry, public policy, or news needs – to these clients. AP also sells photos to non-members through AP Images. AP Telecommunication is another subsidiary, which provides members and non-members with data and network communication technologies. AP's AdSend group speeds advertisements from agencies and retailers to newspapers as needed. In response to the widespread use of the Internet, AP formed the Multimedia Services Department for AP members to use on their home pages. In 1991 AP developed the AP Leaf Picture Desk so that nearly every newspaper in the United States could receive photos into a personal computer for editing and production. Also in 1991 AP's Graphics Bank became the first online graphics archive for television, using standard telephone lines. In 1994 AP introduced the first digital camera for photojournalists, called the AP News Camera 200. The Associated Press's news business developments are proving successful, and so is the agency's application of technological advances.

DataStream is AP's premier news service, which delivers a full report of world, national, state, and sports news. Limited DataStream is tailored for mid-sized dailies that desire a complete news report but may have fewer resources for copy and wire desks. Limited DataStream with expanded sports provides enhanced sports content. AP Basic is tailored for smaller newspapers that emphasize local coverage but still need a high-speed wire with AP's depth and breadth of world, national, and state news. Dial-In Report is for very small newspapers that need a minimum of copy. Latin coverage, or the LatAm wire, provides coverage in Spanish of Mexico and other Latin American countries. AP's western regional service, or West Wire, has a staff in 13 western states that focuses on stories of high interest in the West.

AP's broadcast services include radio news programming. The programs feature the week's biggest news stories through interviews with newsmakers and foreign correspondents. ENPS (Essential News Production System) is an electronic, multi-platform news production system, which will soon be the largest broadcast newsroom computer system in the world, linking radio and television journalists, production areas, and archives in more than 226 locations. ENPS is designed for audio/visual, web, mobile, and social media.

AP has been involved with two major controversies. The first is over copyright issues involving unauthorized use of AP products. This is primarily an Internet phenomenon. Google, bloggers, websites, and assorted news aggregators are using AP copy without attribution or payment in most instances. AP is seeking syndication fees from violators but it is a daunting challenge because the problem is so widespread.

The second issue is more serious and could threaten the viability of the company in the long run. This issue deals with the various fees member companies need to pay for the AP product lines. Almost every newspaper is losing money and circulation so they want AP to reduce their fees. Some are threatening to quit AP altogether. AP in response is offering discounts and adjustments to keep subscribers. But as a result AP's revenues will continue to fall at a rate of about 10 percent per year. Lay-offs and less news are a likely result; and with less news more papers and broadcasters will demand lower syndication fees thus precipitating another round of lay-offs, and so on. With declining newspaper sales, AP may end up as collateral damage. In over a half a century very few viable daily newspaper have been started.

Synopsis

AP has integrated several major technical innovations into its various services, along with a broad array of wire-service-based news, photos, audio, and video feeds, including Internet online services to clients around the globe. It is estimated that more than a billion people each day read, hear, see, or watch AP news or photos. AP has become North America's premier wire-service corporation. Its rise was accentuated by the financial problems faced by its one-time competitor, United Press International. AP's main global rival is Reuters, which offers competing services for almost every AP line from news to the Internet. An issue of importance for the future of AP is that some of the 1,550 US member newspaper owners are facing competition from other external media outlets, which are now purchasing some of AP's Internet products. This strain on the cooperative may lead to changes over time. Other problems are copyright issues and rebellion about fees from print and electronic media.

United Press International

The history of United Press International (UPI) goes back over 90 years. E. W. Scripps founded the United Press in 1907 to cover news from around the world. In 1935 United Press became the first major US news service to supply news to radio stations. In 1958 United Press merged with William Randolph Hearst's International News Service to become United Press International. At that time, UPI was an aggressive and prestigious news service competing directly with AP. During the 1960s UPI had over 6,000 employees and more than 5,000 news subscribers. It began the first global wire-service radio network, providing radio stations with voice reports from correspondents around the globe. Several years later, in the 1980s, the news service was the first in the industry to let subscribers choose to receive copy by topic and subtopic, rather than by a broad category only. At one point, UPI had over 1,200 radio clients. By 1995 the company had completed a system for global satellite transmission that virtually eliminated the need to send news over telephone landlines. But management, ownership, and client problems forced UPI to cut back services. UPI's domestic news bureaus closed offices across the United States. In 1999 UPI sold its broadcast news business to its one-time rival, AP, which picked up all US-based UPI radio and television clients.

UPI was privately owned by a group of Saudi Arabian investors, but in 2000 it was sold to News World Communications (NWC), which is operated by the ultra-conservative Unification Church, which was founded and is still run by the Rev. Sun Myung Moon. Rev. Moon specializes in sensational journalism with an extremely conservative slant. He is a wildly grandiose figure who for several decades has publicly proclaimed that he is the second coming of the Christian messiah. He also enjoys conducting mass marriages of his followers. NWC publishes 20 newspapers worldwide, including the *Washington Times*. The sale prompted Helen Thomas to resign from UPI after 57 years. UPI is history.

Agence France Presse

AFP is the world's third largest wire service, after Reuters and AP. AFP is the world's oldest news agency, dating from 1835, and one of the world's largest wire services providing full-text articles to its clients around the world. AFP covers politics; economic affairs; diplomacy; culture; science; and international, national, business, and sports news written by journalists and correspondents in Europe, the Middle East, North America, South America, and Africa.[5] Many of the bureaus are still based in former colonies of France or in major cities where Reuters and AP have competing bureaus.

AFP has bureaus in 110 countries and operates in 165, employing 1,200 staff journalists and photographers, along with 2,000 stringers, reporting out of almost every country in the world. Of these correspondents, 102 are stationed in peripheral nations (22 in Latin America and Mexico and 80 in Africa and Asia). AFP's coverage is not a lucrative proposition, but the agency's operations are subsidized by the income from the many official French government and embassy subscriptions. The English-language service is distributed worldwide and includes reports, round-ups, analyses, and news. Subscribers to AFP include 7,000 newspapers and 2,500 radio and television stations. Their largest single customer is the French government.

Starting in January 1997, the AFP news feed was integrated into Bloomberg's multi-panel information screen, produced in London on the European Canal Satellite. The Canal Satellite is an all-digital French direct broadcast channel on several different cable services. The agency also distributes selected news stories from AP. AFP runs the farthest-reaching network of any other news service, providing unmatched depth and breadth of coverage from regions where the other services are weak or absent. AFP is recognized as the premier supplier of information from Asia, Africa, and the Arab-speaking nations.

Over the years, AFP has proved itself a leader in journalistic enterprise. For example, it was the first to announce the deaths of Stalin, Pope John Paul I, and Indira Gandhi. AFP has earned many compliments and awards for its continued coverage of some of the world's biggest stories, including the 1999 war in the former Yugoslavia and the conflict in Chechnya. Prior to the Second Gulf War, AFP was openly skeptical of the Bush administration's claims about Iraq possessing weapons of mass destruction. Unlike the American press, particularly the all-news channels, which were all too willing to become part of the war propaganda machine, AFP stood its ground in its objective analysis of the build-up to the invasion of Iraq. As a result, it was shunned by the White House and excluded from some press briefings. Over time its professionalism and coverage were vindicated.

Today, the agency continues to expand worldwide, reaching thousands of subscribers (radio, television, newspapers, companies) from its main headquarters in Paris and regional centers in Washington, DC, Hong Kong, Nicosia, and Montevideo. All share the same goal – to guarantee a top-quality international service tailored to the specific needs of clients in each region. It also does more reporting from peripheral nations than any other global service.

Bloomberg

Bloomberg was established in New York in October 1981 by Michael Bloomberg when he formed Innovative Market Systems, which in 1986 became known as Bloomberg L.P.[6] After 15 years with the investment firm Salomon Brothers, Bloomberg identified the need for a business press suited to around-the-clock global financial information. He started from New York, but was opening world offices, first in London by 1987, then in Australia by 1989, and the business has continued to grow worldwide since then. Bloomberg news is available in five languages, English, French, Spanish, German, and Japanese, and provides services to over 260,000 users in over 125 countries. The focus of its coverage is in economics, business, financial markets, technology, and global stock markets and trends. Its main source of income is leasing Bloomberg terminals to business clients.

The first Bloomberg television product, launched in 1994, was called Bloomberg Business News, followed by Bloomberg Information TV, and finally European Bloomberg Information TV. Bloomberg Television is a 24-hour financial news channel that reports the economic and political news that affects markets. Its unique TV Data Screen provides financial data and breaking news headlines at all times, even during commercials. It draws on the vast resources of the global Bloomberg organization, including more than 1,600 reporters and editors in 94 bureaus around the world. Bloomberg Television reaches over 100 million TV-watching households through national cable distribution, the US Network, DirecTV, and the Bloomberg service, and it airs three half-hour television shows: Bloomberg Business News, Bloomberg Personal, and Bloomberg Small Business. Bloomberg Television offers the top 50 major news stories every half-hour 24 hours a day.

As mentioned earlier, since 1997 Bloomberg has integrated a major news feed from AFP into its multi-panel information screen. The news feed is produced in London and aired on Canal Satellite, the all-digital French direct broadcast system. CEO Bloomberg, who is also the former mayor of New York City, owns 72 percent of the firm; Merrill Lynch owns 20 percent; and Bloomberg employees hold 8 percent.

Bloomberg is a latecomer to the global wire and video service business. Yet it came into the business at a fortuitous time and has an entrepreneurial leader in Michael Bloomberg. With the expansion of cable channels, particularly all-news channels, and the Internet, Bloomberg has found a ready market and a viable niche. The company's various services, which have a clear economic focus, are available to clients who reside nearly exclusively in core and semiperipheral nations. As peripheral nations become economically viable and interact with greater frequency with core-based enterprises, subscribing to Bloomberg will make sense, particularly for government and business leaders.

Dow Jones & Company

Founded in 1882, Dow Jones & Company (DJC) has been publishing the major global newspaper of business, the *Wall Street Journal*, since 1889. Since 2007 it has become part of News Corp. In 1976 Dow Jones began the *Asian Wall Street Journal* and in 1983 *Wall Street Journal Europe*. DJC also publishes major financial magazines such as *Barron's*, since 1921, and the *Far Eastern Economic Review*, since 1946. In the 1990s DJC started a joint venture in Russia, where it publishes *Hedomosti*. DJC also controls the Ottaway newspaper chain with 19 dailies and 15 weekly newspapers in the United States. With its financial orientation, Dow Jones competes directly with Bloomberg and Thomson Reuters for corporate and government clientele. On the electronic side, the Dow Jones news wires have over a million subscribers globally. Dow Jones also owns half of CNBC Europe and CNBC Asia. In 1999 DJC joined with Reuters to establish a new interactive electronic global service to provide business information for corporate and professional clients.

In late 2004 DJC won a fierce bidding war to acquire MarketWatch, Inc., a highly profitable online financial news and information provider, for $519 million. MarketWatch's two sites are the popular CBS MarketWatch and BigCharts.com, which together attract eight million unique visitors a month.

Finally, DJC is known for its Dow Jones Industrial Average (DJIA), which was established in 1896 and consists of a pool of 30 blue-chip US stocks. The DJIA appears globally in newspapers and magazines, and on radio and television business programs. Also in 1999 the DJIA made one of its biggest changes in its 103-year history. Originally, only New York Stock Exchange stocks were included in the 30 stocks that make up the DJIA barometer. Now the Chicago-based NASDAQ Stock Market has some companies on the DJIA. Also added were Home Depot and SBC. The four stocks dropped to make room for the newcomers were Chevron, Sears, Union Carbide, and Goodyear. All four had been in the DJIA since at least 1930. Even Woolworth Company was dropped in 1997 to make room for Wal-Mart Stores. In 1991 Walt Disney joined the index as US Steel was dropped. General Electric joined the index in 1928. News Corp, Viacom, Google, and Time Warner are not on the index, nor is any advertising agency.

Currently, the 2009 DJIA consists of the following major US blue-chip stocks: 3 M, Alcoa, American Express, AT&T, Bank of America, Boeing, Caterpillar, Chevron Corporation, Cisco Systems, Coca-Cola, Disney, DuPont, Exxon Mobil, General Electric (parent of NBCUniversal), Hewlett-Packard, Home Depot, IBM, Intel, J. P. Morgan Chase, Johnson & Johnson, Kraft Foods, McDonald's, Merck, Microsoft, Pfizer, Procter & Gamble, United Technologies, Verizon, Wal-Mart, and Walt Disney. The DJIA reflects the evolution in the US economy from industrial society to an information, media, and high-technology society. All 30 firms have significant global activities and all are major stakeholders in the global economy. Each new round of changes will likely see additional information-based corporations, such as Google, being added.

Xinhua News Agency

This is China's leading integrated news company. It is striving for a global role by delivering media services to the regions of China through print and the Internet, as well as online advertising and web solutions throughout Asia. Xinhua was established in 1931 and is the state news agency of the People's Republic of China. It is headquartered in Beijing and operates a large number of bureaus in China. Globally Xinhua employs more than 7,000 journalists who report on Chinese and world affairs. It publishes several periodicals, has a public relations group, and runs a journalism school. Xinhua is tightly controlled and watched by senior Chinese government officials, particularly in the wake of the violent suppression of protesters in Tiananmen Square. Xinhua is known for its long, dull articles that avoid any criticism of Chinese government officials or actions, and "all foreign news made available to Chinese publications and broadcasters is first processed by Xinhua translators and editors."[7] In addition to its print products, Xinhua is moving into Internet activities, but its content is still dull and heavily censored.

Inter Press Services

IPS was started in 1964 by Roberto Savio in Rome. IPS has become a major news agency and has developed into an innovative system for intercultural communication. The agency operates in a manner different from other global news services by promoting a horizontal flow of news on a cooperative basis among developing countries. It also distributes information about developing-nation clients to industrialized countries. IPS is a worldwide, non-profit association of journalists and others in the field of journalism that aims to promote a global communication strategy. That strategy is to bring together civil societies, policymakers, and national and international media.[8]

IPS operations consist of IPS News, IPS Telecommunications, and IPS Projects. The IPS News service is an independent global news wire. IPS Telecommunications offers technical expertise for the upgrading of developing nations' communication and information infrastructures. IPS Projects was established to design, manage, and report on projects in the fields of training, information and exchange, and increasing public and media awareness of the importance of global issues.

IPS also has connections with non-governmental organizations (NGOs). For the most part, NGOs have gained widespread recognition for their work with the poor and the oppressed. NGOs have developed as important and increasingly major actors within certain societies, which are mainly in peripheral nations. IPS and NGOs have developed a strategy for cooperation in the twenty-first century. The strategy consists of five major objectives:

- *providing news and content*: producing stories and analyses, which explain how events and global processes affect individuals and communities, especially the marginalised and voiceless;
- *capacity-building*: empowering journalists, media organisations and civil society to be better able to communicate effectively by leveraging IPS' unique character as a Southern-focused news agency, offering a different kind of training and follow-up;
- *dissemination and networking*: building an information bridge linking civil society, international institutions, policy makers, donors and individual readers, to promote an ongoing dialogue about communication and development for a better world.[9]

A network of journalists in more than 100 countries backs IPS, with satellite communication links to 1,000 outlets. In addition, IPS has regional editorial centers that operate in Africa, Asia, the Caribbean, Europe, Latin America, and North America. More than 250 journalists cover over 100 countries and provide news and information services for more than 1,000 clients. To date, IPS has two-thirds of its correspondents in peripheral nations who are natives of the countries in which they work. IPS focuses its news coverage on events and the global processes affecting the economic, social, and political development of peoples and nations. IPS reports more than news that is considered "emergency" or negative news; its stories concentrate on issues such as the gap between rich and poor, international trade negotiations, human rights, refugees and international migration patterns, conflict and peacekeeping, environmental protection and sustainable development, population issues, and international debt crises. The IPS World Service news report is delivered via satellite to subscribers. These services are available through online computer facilities, electronic databases, and printed bulletins. An Asian television station also uses IPS feature stories as pegs for documentaries.

IPS products include printed publications, bulletins, columns, and telecommunications. It operates five newspapers under its printed publications division. *Terra Viva Conference Daily* is an independent tabloid newspaper published during major UN conferences such as the 1996 World Food Summit in Rome. *Terra Viva Europe Daily Journal* is produced at the United Nations in New York. Contents include a daily faxed selection of highlights from the IPS wire aimed at policymakers and decision-makers. The *G-77 Journal* is published for the 77 developing countries within the UN system. *IPS Features* is a package of 10 IPS features, special reports, and columns mailed to media clients in the Pacific Rim region. *Rural Development* is a monthly bulletin produced by IPS Africa and the weekly *Africa Bulletin*. News and information in the bulletins include developments, drugs, human rights, religious affairs, environment, investment, energy, population, arts and entertainment, technology, and Latin American integration. The IPS Columnist Service provides a series of exclusive columns written by statesmen and stateswomen, officials, opposition leaders, opinion-makers, leading cultural figures, and experts offering insights on major issues. The last product offered by IPS is a telecommunications carrier service, an international information carrier for a variety of organizations.

In conclusion, IPS represents a model of development journalism. It seeks out positive development news from and among peripheral nations. IPS has found an ally in NGOs, and they work together to assist the causes and activities of peripheral nations. IPS is seldom used by major newspapers or broadcasters from core nations.

Conclusions

The major global news agencies operate in a highly competitive environment. The Associated Press competes on a daily basis with Thomson Reuters and, to a lesser extent, with Bloomberg, Dow Jones, and Agence France-Presse. Both AP and Thomson Reuters have added television news services to their product lines. They also are active in Internet services. New services with a financial focus, such as Bloomberg and Dow Jones, appear to be thriving, while historically broad service companies such as UPI, and now even AP, appear to be suffering organizational and fiscal crises.

The major services are all based in the industrialized core nations, with an extensive bureau network in other core nations and nearly all semiperipheral nations. The United States is now home to both leaders, AP and Thomson Reuters. The peripheral regions lack bureaus, have only stringers, or are inundated with core-news crews when a major coup, earthquake, or bizarre event occurs that affects core nations' interests or catches the attention of an editor.

The wire services will in all likelihood continue to thrive and even grow in influence as the cost of placing foreign correspondents abroad escalates rapidly. Many managing editors are now willing to accept wire-service copy or news footage from outside organizations such as Reuters TV or APTN rather than have to bear the expense of placing correspondents abroad on a permanent basis. With modern airline transportation, digital equipment, and satellite feeds, major news outlets dispatch reporters abroad on a crisis-by-crisis basis instead of having a large number of foreign bureaus. This practice of sending a plane loaded with media types is frequently referred to as "parachute journalism." Finally, networks and others let CNN set the international agenda, so when CNN covers a foreign news story, the other networks and services simply match the coverage. But if CNN does not cover a foreign event, for example some of the civil wars and famines across Africa, the event most likely will go unreported by the other major media outlets.

Electronic colonialism permeates the wire services, which both directly and indirectly promote a core-based focus and emphasis in reporting values. Their journalists, editors, and management are almost all products of elite universities, have a superb command of the English language, and enjoy decent, and in some cases substantial, salaries. This group is not about to promote a revolution or seriously question the economic structure of the global economy that is providing them, their families, and their firms with a sound financial future. They are part of the ruling elite. This in part accounts for the emphasis on financial news and information, rather than on general interest news, detailed pieces on major social problems, or development issues. Although the wire services were major players in the early days of the NWICO debate, they now completely ignore the debate and concerns raised by either peripheral nations or academic critics from core nations. Their philosophy and outlook is straightforward: basically, they do what they do because it works and is profitable. They are promoting their own lifestyle and outlook in other nations, particularly those in semiperipheral and peripheral regions, so that these areas can become future customers for their expanding range of services, which are quickly morphing into Internet e-journalism product lines. By default they are leaving to the emerging blogging world on the Internet the coverage of many stories which the wire services now consider too trivial or controversial. (For more on the blogging phenomenon see Chapter 6.)

Notes

1. Oliver Boyd-Barnett, *The International News Agencies*, London: Constable, 1980; William Hachten and James Scotton, *The World News Prism*, Ames: Iowa State University Press, 2002; Peter Golding and Phil Harris (eds.), *Beyond Cultural Imperialism: Globalization, Communication and the New International Order*, London: Sage, 1997; "How News is Shaped," *Journalism and Mass Communication Quarterly* 77(2) (Summer 2000), 223–72.

2. Donald Read, *The Power of News: The History of Reuters*, Oxford: Oxford University Press, 1992.

3. http://thomsonreuters.com/about-us/trust-principles/, accessed August 25, 2013.

4. Oliver Gramling, *AP: The Story of News*, New York: Farrar & Rinehart, 1940; Peter Arnet, Vincent Alabiso, Chuck Zoeller, and Kelly Smith-Tunney (eds.), *Flash! Associated Press Covers the World*, New York: Abrams, 1998.

5. Jean Huteau, *AFP: Une histoire de l'Agence France-Presse: 1944–1990*, Paris: R. Laffont, 1992.

6. Michael Bloomberg and Matthew Winkler, *Bloomberg by Bloomberg*, New York: Wiley, 1998.

7. Jon Swan, "I Was a 'Polisher' in a Chinese News Factory," *Columbia Journalism Review* (March/April 1996), 34.

8. Much of IPS's coverage focuses on major United Nations conferences dealing with global topics. An examination of amount and kind of coverage provided by IPS, AP, and Reuters is found in C. Anthony Giffard, "The Beijing Conference on Women as Seen by Three International News Agencies," *Gazette* 61 (July 1999), 327–41. American newspapers do not use IPS stories.

9. http://www.ipsnews.net/about-us/, accessed August 29, 2013.

13

Arab Media and the
Al Jazeera Effect

Lawrence Pintak

Introduction

There could have been no Arab Spring without the Arab media revolution. The long-simmering resentments that drove citizens into the streets in Tunisia, Egypt, Libya, and elsewhere might have ultimately forced change, but the rapidity with which the uprisings spread was the result of a digital one-two punch that took the seeds planted in social media and spread them at lightning speed through satellite television.

Call it the Al Jazeera effect. The launch of the region's first all-news satellite channel in 1996 shook the very foundations of Arab journalism. Since the 1950s, Arab media had largely served as a mouthpiece for the region's regimes. All broadcasting outlets and most newspapers were owned by Arab governments, tame political parties, or regime friends. The term "television journalism" was an oxymoron. Investigative journalism was unknown.

Then the young emir of Qatar, who had recently deposed his father in a bloodless coup, decided to invest $140 million in a new channel with a mandate to freely report the news. The launch of Al Jazeera changed everything. Suddenly, television shows were discussing issues that ordinary people had only talked about behind closed doors. Political dissidents, militant activists, and, most shocking in a region where Israel's name was an epithet, even Israeli officials were being interviewed on television.

It was an inspiration to journalists laboring under the old model of media as government mouthpiece. Within a decade, independent or semi-independent newspapers, magazines, and television channels could be found from Morocco to Yemen – and everywhere Arab journalists were pushing the envelope of censorship and control. With the Arab Spring, that envelope began to burst.

Global Communication: Theories, Stakeholders, and Trends, Fourth Edition. Thomas L. McPhail.
© 2014 John Wiley & Sons, Inc. Published 2014 by John Wiley & Sons, Inc.

History of Arab Media

The Arab media was born out of the chaos following the defeat of the Central Powers in World War I and the collapse of the Ottoman Empire. This nascent Arab media fostered a shared sense of "Arabness" in the face of the now defeated Ottoman Turks and helped drive the rising political concept of Arab nationalism. Such politicization would remain the hallmark of Arab journalism. In his benchmark study, William Rugh classified the Arab media according to a series of typologies based on the prevailing journalistic ethos in each group of countries.[1] There were clear divisions between these numerous styles of media, but each reflected a level of politicization that, to varying degrees, remains today.

Lebanon was always the Tower of Babel of the Arab world's media. With the outbreak of civil war in the early 1970s, Beirut's streets became the battleground of the Middle East. A shifting array of militias acted as surrogates for the region's rival governments: pro-Iraqi militias fought pro-Syrian militias; Saudi-backed militias battled Libyan-funded militias; Nasserites fought Baathists; Christians clashed with Muslims; Sunnis struggled against Shiites. That chaos was reflected in the media. A cacophony of newspapers and radio stations represented the spectrum of the country's – and the region's – political ideologies. But even in the relative freedom of Beirut, there were limits. Control came not in the form of government sanctions, but in a bullet or remote-controlled bomb. One of the leading papers, Saudi-backed *Al Hayat*, was eventually forced to abandon Lebanon for London. The British capital would emerge as the Arab world's de facto media headquarter as *Al Hayat* was joined by another Saudi-funded paper, *Asharq Al-Awsat*, the Palestinian paper *Al Quds al Arabi*, and a variety of others. These would come to be known as the "pan-Arab media," produced outside the region but distributed across the Arab world.

While the shift of the pan-Arab press to London brought a modicum of freedom to these largely Saudi-controlled publications, television news remained firmly in the grip of Arab regimes. All television stations and, with only a few exceptions, all radio stations were owned by governments. Inevitably, newscasts opened with the head of state and consisted largely of "protocol news," a mind-numbing series (almost exclusively) of men shaking hands, cutting ribbons, and drinking tea. For the most part, real news was nowhere to be found. For international coverage – even events in the country next door – these government channels relied largely on Western video news agencies based in the United Kingdom or the United States.

The seeds of modern Arab television news were planted during the 1990–1 Gulf War. If you happened to live in Saudi Arabia in the days after Saddam Hussein ordered Iraqi forces to invade Kuwait, it is likely that you were blissfully ignorant of the fact that war had broken out on your doorstep. For more than 48 hours after the invasion, the Saudi media remained silent on the conflict as the panicked House of Saud scrambled to decide how to respond. It was the equivalent of the French being unaware that Spain had invaded Italy. But not every Saudi was oblivious. Satellite dishes, though still illegal in most Arab countries, had already begun sprouting on rooftops across the region. And while there were no Arab satellite channels, there were plenty being beamed in from the West – among them CNN and the BBC, both broadcasting news in English 24 hours a day. For those with dishes, all eyes turned to these Western broadcasters.

Arab governments quickly realized that they were losing their stranglehold on information. Egypt immediately began broadcasting the output of its state-run TV channel via satellite; but it was just the same old turgid government newscast, devoid of any reporting from the war zone, received via satellite dish instead of an antenna. No one was fooled. Once the conflict was over and Saddam Hussein had been neutralized, the House of Saud set about dealing with this other threat to their rule – the loss of their monopoly on information. In London they set up the Middle East Broadcasting Centre (MBC), a pan-Arab satellite channel that combined entertainment with newscasts that more closely resembled those produced in the West. MBC was owned by members of the royal family rather than the government itself, so its reporters were freer than their colleagues at other Arab media outlets, but it still operated under clear strictures. MBC would eventually evolve into the MBC Group, the largest broadcast organization in the region, with a constellation of entertainment, music, sports and news channels based in Dubai. But that would come later, after the launch of Al Jazeera, the channel that changed the way Arabs saw the world and their own region.

Al Jazeera

Long before Al Jazeera became the channel the Bush administration loved to hate, it had earned the wrath of Arab officials from Morocco to Yemen. Appearing on Al Jazeera were political dissidents, Islamic militants, and all the other voices Arab regimes thought they had silenced. As a result, Al Jazeera's reporters were banned at various times from 17 of the 22 member countries of the Arab League.

The Saudis were particularly incensed by this upstart channel. Al Jazeera not only impinged on their near-monopoly of pan-Arab media, but the station also had the temerity to give voice to those who would question the House of Saud. As one Saudi newspaper wrote:

> The poisonous ideas that are conveyed via the Western satellite channels are easy to handle because the viewer knows the thought they are trying to convey in advance. However, when this poisonous thought is conveyed via an Arab satellite channel, it becomes all the more dangerous because it is concealing itself behind our culture.[2]

Ironically, given later accusations of bias and unprofessionalism, Al Jazeera's original news team were almost all veterans of the BBC's Arabic television service, which had withdrawn from an ill-fated joint venture with Saudi-owned Orbit TV when it became clear that the BBC and the Saudi royal family – not surprisingly – had different ideas about what constituted journalism. The channel's staff saw themselves as agents of democratic change in a region trapped in the grip of autocracies.

"Using the Western style, we have broken many taboos," Ibrahim M. Helal, then Al Jazeera's chief editor, told *New York Times*, "of course, we upset most other Arab countries."[3] The staff of Al Jazeera, and many outside the newsroom, saw that as a very good thing. One official in the Clinton White House called the channel a "beacon of light,"[4] and Israeli cabinet minister Gideon Ezra told the *Jerusalem Post*: "I wish all Arab media were like Al Jazeera."[5]

Then came 9/11 and Al Jazeera shifted its focus from the oppression of Arab regimes to the so-called "war on terror" and the US invasions of Afghanistan and Iraq. Just days after the attacks of September 11, Al Jazeera aired the first of many videotaped pronouncements from Osama bin Laden. Without Al Jazeera, the al-Qaeda leader might never have achieved the mythic status he would come to enjoy. As the fireside radio chat was President Franklin Delano Roosevelt's "bully pulpit" – the means through which he reached the American people – during World War II, so too did the Qatar-based satellite channel serve as bin Laden's pipeline to the Arab and Muslim people as he launched his military and propaganda assault on the United States.

Al Jazeera's top editors argued that any Western news organization with exclusive access to a major news figure would have done exactly the same thing; and, in fact, the four major American networks all ran the early bin Laden tapes until the White House appealed to their patriotism and the practice was halted. But it wasn't just the channel's relationship with bin Laden that rankled the Bush administration. Its reporters were inside Kabul showing the impact on civilians of the American bombardment of the Afghan capital; they were in Baghdad broadcasting live from the receiving end of the American "shock and awe" assault; and, later, they were inside Fallujah during the US siege of that Iraqi rebel stronghold. Al Jazeera's audience saw a grim and bloody side of these conflicts that was largely absent from American television screens, and the images were presented by reporters whose commentary reflected the general Arab sense of outrage.

"Arabic TV does not do our country justice," President Bush complained in early 2006, "they put out some kind – sometimes put out propaganda that just is – just isn't right, it isn't fair, and it doesn't give people the impression of what we're about."[6] What, to many Western eyes, was biased and sensational coverage was, to many Arab journalists, the natural response to events playing out in their front yard, not dissimilar from the flag-waving of the American media after 9/11.

"We belong to this Arab nation and we are there to cover from our own perspective," said Al Jazeera's chief editor, Ahmed Sheikh, "sometimes it may prove to be very difficult to be impartial. You find yourself carried away with your sentiments."[7] It was precisely that sensibility which so resonated with Arab viewers after decades of seeing their own region through the prism of a Western TV camera lens. "The genius of Arab Satellite TV is that it [has] captured a deep-seated common existential pain called Arab sensibility and turned it into a picture narrative that speaks to something very deep in the Arab psyche," according to Abderrahim Foukara, Al Jazeera's Washington, DC bureau chief.

Media Wars

The emir of Qatar did not launch Al Jazeera to salve the Arab psyche or because he wanted a membership card at the local press club. He did it for the same reason that he invited the US military to move its Gulf Central Command to Qatar – to make himself a player in the region. Though one of the world's richest countries, thanks to oil and natural gas, Qatar was a tiny peninsula – hence Al Jazeera's name, which translates as "The Peninsula" – jutting out from Saudi Arabia. Geographically and politically it was hidden in the shadow of its much more powerful neighbor. Until Al Jazeera, pan-Arab media had been dominated by the Saudis. Al Jazeera gave the emir the power to drive public opinion in directions the Saudis did not necessarily like. That is why, early on, Saudi Arabia banned Al Jazeera journalists from operating within its borders and unofficially barred its advertising agencies, which dominated the Gulf, from buying commercials on Al Jazeera. Then, on the eve of the US invasion of Iraq, the Saudis launched their own all-news satellite channel, Al Arabiya. Those two channels have, ever since, been at the heart of the media wars that occasionally wrack the region.

The 2008–9 Israeli assault on Gaza was one example. The Arab world split into two camps, with Qatar, Syria, and several Gulf states firmly backing Hamas, while Saudi Arabia and Egypt sought to limit the militant group's political gains at the expense of the more secular Palestinian president Mahmoud Abbas. Al Jazeera's coverage was vivid and emotional, focusing on close-ups of dead and wounded children. Al Arabiya took a somewhat more cautious approach, eschewing the most gruesome footage and refusing to label the Palestinian dead as "martyrs." "Our coverage was closer to the people," Al Jazeera's Ahmed Sheikh told this writer as a ceasefire was put in place. Nabil Khatib, chief editor at Al Arabiya, shot back: Al Jazeera, he said, was "satisfying the mob" and leading "a campaign for Hamas."

The degree to which the two channels reflected the politics of their respective patrons underlined the fact that the end of overt government ownership of television in the region did not usher in a period of unbridled media independence. Far from it. The rise of non-government media in the Arab world has been accompanied by the rise of a corporate feudalism, in which members of royal families, would-be politicos, and cronies of national leaders have come to dominate the media landscape. The Dubai-based MBC Group was emblematic of this trend. Controlled by a son-in-law of the late King Fahd of Saudi Arabia, it owned the top-rated satellite entertainment channels and Al Arabiya, along with a major stake in another regional giant, the Lebanon-based LBC channel, as well as the region's largest advertising agency and television ratings agency. Pan-Arab channels based in Egypt were largely in the hands of business interests close to Hosni Mubarak; Muammar Gaddafi's son had the monopoly on TV in Libya; and so the pattern continued across the region.

"I'm competing against countries, not companies!" Mohammed Alayyan, publisher and chairman of the independent newspaper *Alghad* and CEO of ATV in Jordan, complained.[8] It was all a natural extension of a similar system of control in the pan-Arab print media. "*Al Hayat* is not a commercial project," the paper's then number two, Abdulwahab Badrakhan, explained in 2005, "it is in the first place a political project, like *Asharq Al Awsat*. *Asharq Al Awsat* and *Al Hayat* never [make] money, and you can understand that because you can consider us as public relations."

Another manifestation of that competition–control model could be found in the so-called "media cities" that dotted the region. The first, and most successful, was created in Dubai, a city-state in the United Arab Emirates. Essentially a media duty-free zone, it promised both economic incentives and a hands-off political approach. That mix attracted regional channels like the MBC Group and its Al Arabiya channel, Western news organizations, such as Reuters, and broadcasters from various developing world countries where domestic strictures were constraining. Up the road, Abu Dhabi set up twofour54, a media city named for its geographic coordinates, which attracted, among others, a major regional CNN center. Egypt created a similar project where many of its home-grown satellite channels were based; and copy-cat centers sprouted up even in places like Syria, where media was tightly controlled. But the promise of freedom soon proved hollow.

Two private Pakistani channels based in Dubai Media City, GEO TV and Ary One, discovered the hollowness when Pakistan declared martial law in 2007; after the channels refused a demand from the Musharraf government to sign a new media "code of conduct," Emirati authorities gave them two hours to stop broadcasting. Officials left little doubt that the principles of press freedom on which Media City was supposedly based had taken a back seat to Emirati foreign policy. "As an entity within the UAE, Dubai Media City would also observe the broadcast principals of the country's foreign policy and prevent the telecast of news and material that would undermine those principles," said Amina Al Rustamani, executive director of Dubai Media City.[9]

Media and Change in the Arab World

Media remained a tool of power, whether political, economic, or religious. That was readily apparent as the ideological – and psychological – battles of the Arab uprising played out both on the streets and on the airwaves. These were as much media wars as physical battles. Through media, governments – and the families behind them – were seeking to control and manipulate the pace of change. The contrasting coverage of the Syrian and Bahraini uprisings epitomized that. Coverage of the Syrian revolt on Qatari-owned Al Jazeera and Saudi-owned Al Arabiya was aggressively anti-regime, no surprise given that both governments were arming and financing the forces seeking to oust President Bashar Assad. But when the Shiite majority revolted against the Sunni Muslim monarchy in the Gulf state of Bahrain, a stone's throw from Qatar and Saudi Arabia, those same channels took a kid-glove approach, even as their governments sent in troops to put down the uprising.

Al Jazeera may have set the tone for an aggressive new style of journalism in the Arab world, but at the end of the day it was still owned by a government. Its "red lines" – the limits beyond which reporters venture at their peril – included stories that might negatively impact on Qatari foreign policy. Across the region, "media freedom" remained a relative term. Every news organization worked within "red lines" dictated by a variety of factors including the country in which the news organization was located, ownership, and the politics of the outlet. "As long as you don't write about the king, the military, religion or sex you can cover anything you want," a Jordanian journalist said of reporting in that kingdom.[10]

But guessing exactly what was off limits was often the biggest challenge. "Even sunny weather can be censored if it is a bad news for agriculture. Taboo topics are updated by the government on a daily basis," explained Sihem Bensedrine, the editor of the online magazine *Kalima*, a frequent target of Tunisian government repression. "I do not think the political system is developed enough to encompass the truth," said another reporter.[11]

Local Journalism

The newscasts of the pan-Arab satellite news channels were dominated by the big stories of the day: Iraq, Palestine, Lebanon, and the simmering confrontation between the Sunni Muslim Arab states and Shiite Iran. This was not unexpected. This was big power politics playing out on the Arab stage. What was missing was the street-level view of individual countries, cities, and villages. In the obsession with the dramatic issues of life and death on a grand scale, the questions of who was fixing the roads or the state of the schools were lost.

"There is a huge amount of information that is missing because the local stations will not provide it to the viewer and we do not provide it to the viewer because it is local," Nabil Khatib, news chief at pan-Arab Al Arabiya explained, "things that would make the Arabs better citizens by knowing more about their own realities they are not getting it from anywhere. So there is a huge portion of important data that is missing from their consciousness and this is negatively affecting any democratization process."

Nor were they getting that from the state-run broadcasters. "On the local level we ignore the local aspects of interest to the people, such as raising children and educating them and leave these national issues for larger issues such as Iraq and Palestine," Abd el-Latif el-Menawy, then head of news at Egypt TV, confirmed. "This is one way that some of the state-owned channels use to escape, because of their inability to tackle local topics. Most of [my] colleagues working in the local media lack the concept of local news."

The reason those channels wanted to "escape" such stories was that these were the areas that caused trouble. For the most part, Arab governments were happy to have their broadcasters fulminating about Israel or focusing on American military actions in Iraq, but they quickly became uncomfortable if the "red lines" around local politics, human rights, or even the domestic economy were crossed. And while the pan-Arab broadcasters occasionally touched on these stories, it was usually only when they became of major regional interest, as in the case of labor unrest in Egypt or pre-election clashes in Bahrain. Otherwise, they were, by definition, *local* stories of little interest to the satellite channels' broad regional audiences. In the West, the national networks, like CBS in the United States or the BBC in Britain, focus on the national and international stories while their local affiliates in places like Binghamton or Birmingham report on the potholes and school board meetings. In the Arab world, there was no equivalent.

That would begin to change with the Arab Spring. During Egypt's 18-day revolution, Cairo-based satellite channels ignored previous restrictions that had prevented them from producing news and 24/7 coverage of the uprising. Once Mubarak was overthrown and the focus of the regional satellite channels shifted to other revolts, the local stations became a critical source of information about the gritty day-to-day developments for Egyptians trying to understand this new political landscape.

Change Agents

That Arab journalists helped drive the Arab revolts was inevitable. In the decade after the launch of Al Jazeera, the very ethos of Arab journalism was transformed. Even among editors on government-controlled newspapers, there was now a desire to push the envelope. A survey of journalists in 13 Arab countries found that 75 percent of them said the prime mission of Arab journalism was to drive political and social change.[12] The same survey found that, despite accusations of anti-American bias, 62 percent of Arab journalists had a positive view of the American people, though, not surprisingly, their attitude toward the Bush administration's Middle East policy was almost unanimously negative. Half the journalists surveyed described their political philosophy as "democrat," and about one-third said reform must be "radical," and a majority of the journalists saw their own governments as posing as great a threat to the region as US policy.

In the face of such sentiments in the newsroom, governments continued to fight a rearguard action against these journalistic insurgents. Those efforts came in the form of laws and regulations, such as the much criticized 2008 Arab League Satellite Media Charter, a retrogressive Big Brotheresque document that reaffirmed the right of governments to pull the plug on satellite broadcasters for a host of vague reasons that included perceived insults to Arab leaders. More chillingly, the backlash against the media also included widespread intimidation, assaults, and jailing of journalists across the region, and, in some cases, their murder. Arab countries regularly landed at the bottom of the Freedom House list of countries where media is free,[13] and their leaders were just as regularly among those named "predators of press freedom" by Reporters Sans Frontières.[14] As Salaheddine El Hafez, secretary general of the Arab Journalists' Association, told a press freedom conference in late 2006. "The margins of freedom for the Arab press are severely limited and we have evidence of that in our daily lives."[15]

Arab governments kept talking about media liberalization but in most parts of the region so-called press "reform" laws failed to strip away regulations under which journalists could be jailed for the slightest perceived transgression – and often *increased* the level of control. Truth was no defense. Many journalists found themselves jailed for libel as the result of stories that were factually correct.

In Egypt, where media regulations adopted in 1995 were referred to by journalists as the "Press Assassination Law," the 2005 election brought a slight loosening of the reins on media, but once the last vote was tallied scores of journalists – including women – were attacked, beaten, threatened, or jailed. "Egyptian journalism," said Osama al-Ghazli Harb, chief editor of *Al Siyasah Al Dawliyah*, "is developing on a tortured journey owing to political manipulation." In Iraq, the deadliest place in the world for reporters and home to scores of newly created media outlets, journalists were being killed if they were perceived as being too close to the government, too close to the resistance, or too close to particular political parties. "Sometimes they target journalists just to scare journalists in general," according to Al Arabiya executive editor Nabil Khatib. Militant groups ran their own pseudo news agencies and one motive for the attacks was to make it impossible for other news organizations to operate. "They are supplying the media [with information and footage] and they pressure you in a way to impose their agenda on you," Khatib explained. "Of course we refuse, because we do not want to be used by any party whoever it is – so we pay the price." The tactics were effective. By the spring of 2007, Al Arabiya had lost 11 staffers to violence in Iraq, several in targeted assassinations, and was left relying largely on local freelancers. "You feel that you are covering the war as if through glass," Khatib lamented.

Even in Al Jazeera's home country of Qatar, while the emir took steps like creating a center to defend media freedom around the globe, his advisory council was demanding harsh penalties for journalists who criticized the government. One top Egyptian cleric demanded that journalists who insulted the government be lashed with a whip. Others, often shadowy figures working for governments or extremist groups, went even further. One Tunisian journalist had his fingers cut off before being murdered; female journalists in Egypt were sexually assaulted by police agents and warned there was more to come if they did not avoid certain stories; in countries from Yemen to North Africa other women journalists found themselves the targets of government-sponsored sexual smear campaigns; and in Lebanon, journalists were afraid to turn the ignition key of their cars after a string of bombings left two of the country's best-known journalists dead and a talk show host maimed.

It wasn't only governments that journalists feared. Religious groups sought to frog-march journalists according to their own agendas, whether militant jihadists in places like Iraq, Yemen, and Algeria, or more traditional religious institutions. In Saudi Arabia, a religious court ordered journalist Mansour Nogaidan of the daily *Alriyadh*, to receive 75 lashes for calling for freedom of speech and criticizing Wahabism, Saudi Arabia's strict interpretation of Islam.

"I am not exaggerating when I say the Arab press is witnessing one of the worst periods of its life," Salaheddine El Hafez, vice editor-in-chief of Egypt's *Al Ahram* newspaper and secretary general of the Arab Journalists Association, told a press freedom conference in late 2006. "The margins of freedom for the Arab press are severely limited and we have evidence of that in our daily lives."[16]

Bloggers, Citizen Journalism, and New Media Activism

The lack of media freedom in many Arab countries meant that bloggers took on an importance that rivaled that of their colleagues in the West. By one count in 2009, there were close to 40,000 active Arab blogs. The vast majority of those were personal diaries, but a sizable proportion provided politically driven reportage on local events within their own countries. Egyptian bloggers, who constituted about one-third of the Arab blogosphere, have been at the forefront of this Arab form of "citizen journalism." They broke numerous stories that were off limits to the mainstream Egyptian media, most famously by posting online videos of Egyptian police torturing ordinary citizens. Their influence stemmed not from the number of people who viewed their blogs, in part because Internet penetration remained low in Egypt and many parts of the Arab world, but in the ripple effect produced when mainstream reporters picked up and republished their stories. Bloggers represented the cross-section of Arab politics. But they were only one manifestation of new media in the Arab world. "Facebook Girl," a young Egyptian political activist, rose to prominence when she started a group on the social networking site aimed at supporting striking workers at a time when Egypt was also suffering from a shortage of bread. The group became the focal point for a national strike and inspired other groups around the region.

While the leaders of the Facebook group were overt activists, the line between bloggers and journalists was much more blurred. Some of the bloggers were journalists seeking an outlet for stories they could not publish in mainstream media. A small but influential group of Egyptian bloggers who gained notoriety from around the time of the 2005 Egyptian presidential elections represented a hybrid of frustrated young activists who sometimes acted as journalists – breaking stories of official torture, sexual harassment, and other controversial events – but also writing highly opinionated, sometimes libelous, and often obscene essays, insisting all along that they were not journalists. "Yes, I'm biased and I like it this way," blogger Mahmoud Saber told one interviewer.[17] It was these young web-savvy activists who later provided the digital spark that ignited the 2011 uprisings.

Despite fears among US policymakers that online activists were driving anti-American opinion, an exhaustive study by Harvard's Berkman Center for Internet and Society found that "bloggers are far more concerned with domestic political issues than with the United States or its wars in the region. Criticism of domestic political leaders is the most frequent political topic … followed by criticism of terrorism."[18]

The debate over the difference between a blogger and a journalist intersected discussions of the political nature of Arab journalism. The assassinations of journalists in Lebanon, widely assumed to have been the work of operatives controlled by the government of Syria, underscored the overlap between politics and journalism in the Arab world. One of the victims, *An Nahar* publisher Gibran Tueni, was a leader of the anti-Syrian political bloc in the Lebanese parliament, and the other two were outspoken opponents of Syria's military presence in Lebanon.

Many Arab journalists saw no contradiction between political engagement and their role as journalists; they sought to balance their obligations as Arab citizens and their responsibilities as Arab journalists. "You have a very big responsibility [as a journalist]," said Ibrahim Hamidi, a Syrian who was *Al Hayat's* Damascus bureau chief, "but this responsibility has two faces. I do not run after scoops because I know a lot of scoops that may harm the country. I might be not objective, but it is the country that you live in that really matters more than your job. The priority is the safety of your country."

Yet corruption was the norm in many newsrooms. An "envelope culture" prevailed, in which it was accepted practice for cash to change hands for stories. It was a product of the abysmal salaries at all but the top satellite channels. New reporters at Egypt's government-owned newspapers were paid in the $80- to $90-a-month range and the situation was only slightly better at the private papers, while the monthly salary for a newly hired journalist at state-run Egypt television and radio was just $35. The official salary for top editors was often measured in the hundreds, rather than thousands, of dollars. Even in Saudi Arabia, with its high cost of living, the average starting salary for a reporter was about $920 a month. Journalists there jokingly call it "the beggar's job." "You come up short either way," said *Arab*

News executive editor Somayya Jabarti, "low pay and trouble getting serious stories published." One poll found that 40 percent of Arabic-language journalists said they would reprint a press release in return for a gift. "It's the whole structure of the job," Jabarti explained; "if they are well paid and well-trained, they won't need the gifts or envelopes."

Individuals were not alone in being tempted by bribes. According to Abdel Bari Atwan, editor-in-chief of the pan-Arab Palestinian daily *Al Quds Al Arabi*, his paper was regularly offered "subsidies" by governments ranging from conservative monarchies to radical nationalists.

In the survey mentioned above, Arab journalists chose the lack of "professionalism" and "ethics" as the greatest challenges to their industry. "There is no comparison, to be honest, between the press in the West and the press in the Arab world," according to Osman Mirghani, deputy editor-in-chief at the Saudi-owned pan-Arab newspaper *Asharq Al Awsat*. He saw Western journalists as far more professional than his Arab colleagues, adding: "Having said that, the press in the Arab region is developing, is evolving and I think is moving forward."

The predominance of opinion in the Arab media was another issue. Al Jazeera's Code of Ethics stated that its reporters must "distinguish between news material, opinion and analysis to avoid the pitfalls of speculation and propaganda."[19] Yet its airwaves, and the pages of most Arab newspapers, were thick with opinion masquerading as reportage. Such an intermingling was rooted in the history of Arab journalism. Constrained from reporting facts, newspapers served as the mouthpiece of governments, so readers turned to them as reflections of governmental thinking. Former *Al Ahram* editor Mohamed Hassainein Heikel is revered as one of the greatest Arab journalists, even though he doubled as adviser and confidante to the late Egyptian president Gamal Abdul Nasser.

No incident better illustrated the differences between Western and Arab journalism than the controversy over the publication of cartoons regarded by Muslims as insulting to the Prophet Muhammad. Originally published in a Danish newspaper, the cartoons eventually sparked outrage across the Arab world, with riots in Beirut and Damascus, where the Danish embassies were attacked and burned. Many Western journalists immediately defended the paper's right to publish the cartoons on the basis of freedom of speech. But Arab journalists responded that media freedom must be tempered with respect and responsibility. "When I insult your religion or your feelings it is crossing the limits of freedom of expression," Salama Ahmed Salama, Egypt's most respected columnist, said during the crisis. "For many Europeans, such things are not so important, but here religion is a daily food and we cannot just accept this." Elements within the Danish Muslim community, and their counterparts in the Arab world, exploited the crisis for their own political ends, but that did not change the fact that it highlighted the sensitivity Arab journalists brought to such issues. "Freedom of expression is only half of the truth," Rashid Khashana, Tunis correspondent for the pan-Arab daily *Al Hayat*, observed at the height of the debate; "the second part is that we must respect things sacred for Christians, Muslims and Jews."

Restrictions on criticism of figures in power were a constant barrier to Arab journalists, but at the same time, many genuinely subscribed to the view first laid out by pioneering Lebanese publisher Boutros al-Boustani in the late nineteenth century. "In order for newspapers to be beneficial to society," al-Boustani wrote, they must avoid publishing stories that violated "the right principles."[20] To be sure, not everyone agreed. But in the above-mentioned study, 80 percent of Arab journalists surveyed partly or completely agreed with the statement "Journalists must balance the need to inform the public with the responsibility to show respect."[21]

Emerging Models

One example of that "balanced" approach to journalistic responsibility could be found in Abu Dhabi, where some 200 veterans of major US and European newspapers filled the newsroom of the *National*, a flashily designed paper modeled on Singapore's *Straits Times*. Founded by Martin Newland, the former top editor at Britain's *Daily Telegraph*, who later handed over the reins to Hassan Fattah, a former *New York Times* Middle East correspondent, the paper was ultimately owned by the government of Abu Dhabi via the country's $850 billion investment fund.

"We are part of a broader reform initiative," said Fattah, defending the paper's relatively toothless approach to covering the country, "by definition, we will push boundaries and try to make change, but in the Arab world change does come slowly." The truth of that statement was underscored by a new UAE media law implemented not long after the paper was launched, which included heavy fines for carrying "misleading news" that harmed the economy or for insulting members of the government or royal family.

The fact that Arab journalists themselves held a nuanced view of their role emphasizes the danger of generalizing about the state of Arab journalism. On some levels, the situation was dire; the reports from press freedom groups like Reporters Sans Frontières and the Committee to Protect Journalists made for grim reading. Yet barely a month went by without the announcement of another satellite channel being formed or newspaper license being issued. Indeed, at a time when the news industry in the United States and Europe seemed on the brink of collapse, prospects for Arab journalists were bright. While the graduates of Western journalism schools faced the very real prospect of unemployment, Arab news organizations were besieging the few journalism schools in the region with offers to hire their graduates.

In some ways, the balance of power in international media was shifting from the West to the Arab world, with its vast wealth and newly emergent media. A decade after launching Al Jazeera, Qatar created an English-language sister channel, Al Jazeera English, in the hopes of gaining the same kind of influence in the global South that the Arabic channel had given it in the Arab world. It soon emerged as a major player on the global media scene, winning praise from US secretary of state Hillary Clinton and other world leaders for its coverage of the Arab Spring. That success gave birth to an entire family of news channels in places like Turkey, the Balkans, and Indonesia. But penetration of the United States remained elusive as the channel fought the perception that Al Jazeera was a "terrorist" network. Finally, in early 2013 Qatar's deep pockets allowed it to buy a piece of the US market. Its $500 million purchase of Current TV, founded by former vice president Al Gore, cleared the way for the launch of Al Jazeera America, a new US-based channel that competed with the American networks on their own turf.

Conclusion

"Journalism is a part of change," Prince Bandar bin Khaled al Faisal, the owner of Saudi Arabia's *Al Watan* newspaper and grandson of the late King Faisal, said on the sidelines of a 2005 international media conference he had helped fund, "and this conference is an effort to say, 'OK, maybe we should expedite the process a little bit because we really do have a lot to lose.'"

Just how much they had to lose became evident with the 2011 media-driven uprising. In its wake, governments continued to struggle with how to cope with this new media landscape and, for those still in power, how to avoid losing ultimate control. For some, that meant tightening the noose on journalists; for others, bolstering their own "tame" media owned directly or via proxies; for many governments, it was a combination of both. None were just throwing open their doors. Even Qatar, home of Al Jazeera, tightly controlled its own domestic media, and post-Mubarak Egypt was marked by efforts to impose draconian new press restrictions.

Such contradictions were common; government responses often reflected a lack of understanding of the new rules of the game. That was evident at the height of the Egyptian uprising, when the government-owned Egypt TV broadcast images of a peaceful Cairo even as bloody clashes occurred on the street in front of television headquarters.

Beyond satellite television and newspapers, social media were helping change the rules of the game. The information dam had become a leaking sieve. The "democratization of media" meant even the poorest peasant was likely to have a mobile phone, giving him or her access to a new world of communications. The Syrian uprising offered a case study, as media-savvy opposition activists fed the world a steady stream of footage documenting the carnage, even when "mainstream" reporters were unable to penetrate the country.

For Arab journalists, before and after cascading revolts, it was one step forward, one step back, a half-step forward. They were inspired by the change they were helping to achieve, but daily they were also forced to cope with the realities of reporting in societies built on secrecy and, after the revolts began, fighting a rearguard action.

Ultimately, Arab governments would never be able to completely control the flow of information across their borders. But that didn't mean they would not continue to try, just as Arab journalists would cling to the conviction that, as Yemeni editor Hamzi Bokari put it, "Journalism is a weapon of mass destruction for oppressive governments."

Notes

1. William A. Rugh, *The Arab Press: News Media and Political Process in the Arab World*, Syracuse, NY: Syracuse University Press, 1979.
2. Quoted in Mohammed El-Nawawy and Adel Iskandar, *Al-Jazeera: How the Free Arab News Network Scooped the World and Changed the Middle East*, Cambridge, MA: Westview Press, 2002, p. 116
3. John Kifner, "At Arab All-News Channel, Western Values Prevail," *New York Times* (October 12, 2001), B7.
4. Quoted in "The World through Their Eyes," *Economist* (February 24, 2005), at http://www.economist.com/node/3690442, accessed August 26, 2013.
5. Dan Williams, "A Real News Maker," *Jerusalem Post* (July 13, 2001), 2B.
6. George W. Bush, "President's Remarks at U.S. University Presidents Summit on International Education," at http://georgewbush-whitehouse.archives.gov/news/releases/2006/01/20060105-1.html, accessed September 2, 2013.
7. Unless otherwise indicated, all quotations are from interviews conducted by the author.
8. Lisa Schnellinger and Mohannad Khatib, *Fighting Words: How Arab and American Journalists Can Break Through to Better Coverage*, Washington, DC: International Center for Journalists, 2006, p. 15.
9. "National Media Council clarifies closure of GEO, ARY TV Stations," *WAM: Emirates News Agency*, November 17, 2007, at http://www.wam.org.ae/servlet/Satellite?c=WamLocEnews&cid=1193028279857&pagename=WAM%2FWamLocEnews%2FW-T-LEN-FullNews, accessed August 26, 2013.
10. Quoted in John Smock, "Final Report, Knight International Press Fellow," unpublished report submitted to International Center for Journalists, Washington, DC, summer 2006, p. 57.
11. Quoted in Smock, "Final Report, Knight International Press Fellow," pp. 57–8, 61.
12. Lawrence Pintak and Jeremy Ginges, "The Mission of Arab Journalism: Creating Change in a Time of Turmoil," *International Journal of Press/Politics* 13(3) (2008), 193–227.
13. *Freedom of the Press 2008: A Global Survey of Media Independence*, Washington, DC: Freedom House, 2008.
14. *Predators of Press Freedom*, Paris: Reporters Sans Frontières, 2007.

15. "Media Forum Examines Widespread Press Freedom Abuses," *World Association of Newspapers* (December 11, 2006), at http://www.ifex.org/north_africa/2006/12/12/media_forum_examines_widespread/, accessed September 2, 2013.

16. "Media Forum Examines Widespread Press Freedom Abuses."

17. "Culture 101: Beyond the Blog," *Egypt Today* (March 2009).

18. Bruce Etling, John Kelly, Robert Faris, and John Palfrey, "Mapping the Arabic Blogosphere: Politics, Culture, and Dissent". Berman Center Research Publication No. 2009–06, at http://cyber.law.harvard.edu/sites/cyber.law.harvard.edu/files/Mapping_the_Arabic_Blogosphere_0.pdf, accessed September 2, 2013.

19. http://www.aljazeera.com/aboutus/2006/11/2008525185733692771.html, accessed September 2, 2013.

20. Quoted in Ayalon, "*Sihafa*: The Arab Experiment in Journalism," *Journal of Middle East Studies* 28(2) (1992), 258–80, at 268.

21. Lawrence Pintak, *The New Arab Journalist: Mission and Identity in a Time of Turmoil*, London: I. B. Tauris, 2011, p. 196.

14

Toward Globalization

The Approaches and Accomplishments of the Four Media Giants in Asia

Junhao Hong

In the last two decades or so, media in Asia, especially in the media giant countries such as China, Japan, India, and South Korea, have become more and more globalized as a result of various motivations and strategic approaches.

China: A Newly Emerged Major Player in the Global Media Arena

For nearly three decades from 1949, when communist China was established, to the mid-1970s when the country was still under the control of Mao Zedong, the late chairman of the Chinese Communist Party, and his followers, Chinese media were completely closed to the outside world. The media were used purely as a party machine by the Chinese Communist Party for political and ideological ends.

Mao's death in 1976 and China's new leaders' "open door" policy, which started in the late 1970s and early 1980s, have since drastically changed the country's course, including the mass media system, which is one of the most enormous and complex media systems in the world. Over the past three decades, Chinese media, ranging from newspapers, magazines, books, radio and television broadcasting, to film production, have all experienced tremendous changes. After 30 years of reform, they are no longer purely a propaganda machine of the communist authorities, but are a multi-function service. While their fundamental role remains little changed as the mouthpiece of the Communist Party and the government, they are now also considered as a provider of information and entertainment to the people and as a public service. Moreover, the media have become an

Global Communication: Theories, Stakeholders, and Trends, Fourth Edition. Thomas L. McPhail.
© 2014 John Wiley & Sons, Inc. Published 2014 by John Wiley & Sons, Inc.

important part of the economy. The government long ago terminated subsidies to media organizations, though all media organizations are still considered as government institutions. They must now survive through market competition for advertising revenues, and the media have become a crucial part of the overall economy by making financial contributions to the government. In the decades since the 1970s, market orientation and commercialization (at least in name) have become the Chinese media's lifeline which support the everyday existence and operation of the "communist" media system.

Since the 1980s, all the sectors of China's media industry have experienced unprecedented growth. The number of newspapers published rose from 186 in 1978 to 1,939 in 2010, and their advertising revenue from RMB 0.96 billion in 1978 (about $0.12 billion at the time) to RMB 48.7 billion in 2011 (about $8.7 billion at the time). The number of magazines increased from 930 in 1978 to 9,884 in 2010. Television programming grew from 38,100 hours in 1985 to 97,750 million hours in 2010. Television penetration was 97.82 percent in 2011, whereas it had only been 57.3 percent in 1982. Digital cable television, especially, has seen astonishing growth since the turn of the twenty-first century. The number of digital cable TV subscribers increased from a total of 276,000 in 2003 to more than 100 million in 2011, growing more than 362-fold in just eight years. Despite the fact that radio broadcasting has been affected by TV's development as well as by the emergence of Internet-based new media, the advertising revenue from radio broadcasting still grew several hundredfold from RMB 18 million in 1986 (about $2.2 million at the time) to RMB 5.4 billion in 2011 (about $0.86 billion at the time). As for book publishing, the total number of books published in 1978 was only 15,000, but in 2010 328,387 books were published. The most eye-catching change is probably the growth of the number of Internet users. The Internet did not emerge in China until 1997. In 1998 there were just 2.1 million Internet users in a country of 1.2 billion people, far behind most developed nations. But by June 30, 2012, China's Internet users had increased to 538 million, surpassing the total number of Internet users (245 million) in the United States, thus making China the country with the most Internet users in the world (*2009 China Statistics Yearbook*, 2009; China Internet Network Information Center, 2012; *Collections of China Journalism and Publishing Statistics, 1978–2008*, 2009; Cui & Hou, 2012; Deng, 2012; He, Zhang, & Wang, 2012; Hu, Li, & Huang, 2012; Miao, Yue, & Lu, 2012; Yin & Cheng, 2012).

In 2011, the total revenue from China's media industry reached RMB 638 billion (about $101 billion at the time). This amount reflects a 9.2 percent increase over the total media revenue in 2010, a 27.8 percent increase over the total media revenue in 2009, a 51.5 percent increase over the total media revenue in 2008, a 70.1 percent increase over the total media revenue in 2007, and a 90 percent increase over the total media revenue in 2006 (Cui & Hou, 2012). In other words, China's media industry doubled its scale in just five years, moving toward becoming an increasingly sizable and noticeable player in the global media arena.

For a long time, China Radio International (CRI) was the third largest external broadcasting service in the world, following Voice of America (VOA) as the largest and Radio Moscow as the second largest one. In the last two decades or so, CRI has seen rapid expansion. Not only has it now replaced Radio Moscow (now renamed Voice of Russia) to become the world's second largest external broadcasting service, but in many aspects it has even surpassed VOA in terms of expansion speed and broadcasting languages. Particularly since the beginning of the 2000s the Chinese Communist Party and government have launched a series of campaign to push Chinese media organizations to internationalize as part of China's new strategy to boost its soft power. With both policy support and financial subsidies from the government, in 2011 CRI established 13 new FM broadcasting stations abroad. By the end of 2011, it had launched a total of five overseas regional stations and 18 overseas production and broadcasting centers, increasing the number of CRI's FM broadcasting stations outside China to 70. The daily broadcasting hours of CRI reached 3,000 (Hu, Li & Huang, 2012; *2009 Report on Development of China's Radio, Film and Television*, 2009). The government claimed these developments and expansions represented important progress in the history of Chinese media.

Meanwhile, the seven channels of China Central Television (CCTV) oriented to a foreign audience, which broadcast in six foreign languages, have also been expanding their overseas market. The seven channels are now reaching audiences in 171 countries all over the world. Their total number of worldwide subscribers has reached 249 million. CCTV's offices in the United States and Europe both expanded substantially. Moreover, CCTV has established a joint venture with the United States' Satellite TV to transmit its *Great Wall* programs directly to American audiences through Satellite TV. In only a few years the subscribers of *Great Wall* programs have reached 100,000, and the *Great Wall* program is becoming well known. At the same time, the "open door" policy has also substantially internationalized and globalized China's media market as well. In recent years, on average more than 100 foreign TV dramas, that is, more than 1,000 episodes, have been imported into the country, compared to a nominal number 30 years ago. Now, more than 70 countries regularly trade television programming with China. Moreover, eight foreign TV channels, including those belonging to the media tycoon Rupert Murdoch, are now permitted to broadcast in certain areas, and a total of 34 foreign TV channels are allowed to be seen in thousands of hotels across China (Hong, Lu, & Zou, 2008; Hong, 2009).

During the last decade or so, China's only privately owned – or the only non-governmentally owned – satellite TV organization, Phoenix TV, has moved quickly to target its broadcasting services at an international audience rather than just at an audience within China. This Hong Kong-based television broadcaster was launched in 2000, with the unacknowledged support of the Chinese government, in an attempt to broadcast the "voice of China" to people of Chinese origin across the world. It has already become a multifaceted world media conglomerate, owning electronic media such as Phoenix Chinese Channel, Phoenix Movie Channel, Phoenix News Channel, Phoenix Europe Channel, and Phoenix America Channel, print media such as Phoenix Weekly, and online media such as Phoenix Online Service. Phoenix's audiences and readers are found all over the world (Hong, Lu, & Zou, 2008).

China has become one of the world's main film production nations. In 1978 China produced only 46 feature films (excluding those that were produced in Hong Kong and Taiwan; subsequent figures also exclude Hong Kong and Taiwan). Ten years later, in 1997, the number increased to 88. But after entering the twenty-first century, China's film production has proliferated. In 2002 a total of 100 feature films were produced, and the number jumped to 140 in 2003, 212 in 2004, 260 in 2005, 330 in 2006, and 402 in 2007. In 2011 558 feature movies were produced in China, making the country the third largest film producer in the world (*2009 China Statistics Yearbook*, 2009; Liu & Lu, 2009; Yin & Cheng, 2012).

The box office revenue of China's movies has increased dramatically as well. In 2004 box office revenue reached a historical high, RMB 3.7 billion (about $450 million at the time). By 2011, it had become RMB 13.1 billion (about $2.08 billion at the time), demonstrating a 254 percent growth over 2004 and a 28.93 percent growth over 2010. Moreover, 53.61 percent of the box office in 2011 was from movies produced in China, surpassing the box office from imported movies. Furthermore, Chinese movies have been shown in theaters in many countries and have often become a focal topic of social occasions. In 2011 52

Chinese-produced movies were imported by 22 countries. Of the RMB 13.1 billion revenue from films in 2011, RMB 2.02 billion (about $321 million) came from overseas. Despite the fact that in the last few years the global film market has been shrinking, China's film industry has been growing healthily. Its overseas box office revenue was RMB 0.6 billion in 2003 (about $72 million), RMB 1.1 billion in 2004 (about $132 million), RMB 1.7 billion in 2005 (about $210 million), RMB 1.9 billion in 2006 (about $232 million), and RMB 2 billion in 2007 (about $286 million) (Liu & Lu, 2009; Yin, 2009; Yin & Cheng, 2012). These steady increases demonstrate the growth of the export of Chinese movies and the increasing popularity of Chinese-produced movies among both audiences across the world and international film-makers. For example, in the year 2011 alone, 49 Chinese-produced movies won a total of 74 awards at 17 international film festivals (Yin & Cheng, 2012). In addition, in the past few years China has co-produced several dozen movies with other countries or areas, including Hong Kong, Korea, Singapore, Malaysia, the United Kingdom, The Netherlands, France, the United States, and Canada. Each year, almost all the top 20 grossing movies domestically were co-produced by China and other countries (Liu & Lu, 2009; Yin, 2009).

Since the beginning of the twenty-first century, China International Television Corporation, which belongs to the Ministry of Radio, Film, and Television, has been coordinating a number of China's leading central and regional TV stations and television production companies to attend the Cannes Film Festival (MipTV and Mipcom) to promote Chinese TV programs. The China Film Overseas Promotion Corporation has been helping both state movie studios and independent film production companies to exhibit movies at this and other international film festivals. Since 2007, the China Film Forum has become a regular part of the Cannes Film Festival, and it has received growing attention and interest from renowned film-makers from all over the world (Xu, 2007).

At the same time, China has also hosted international TV festivals to promote sales of Chinese television programs to foreign TV companies. Among others, the Shanghai International TV Festival, the Chengdu International TV Festival, the Hangzhou International Animation Festival, the Beijing International TV Week, the Guangzhou International Documentary Convention, the China International Film and TV Fair, the China Radio Development Forum, China-ASEAN (Association of Southeast Asian Nations) Radio & TV Summit, have become internationally recognized important events. More and more foreign companies regularly attend these events and the sales of Chinese TV programs and movies at these festivals and fairs have increased steadily (Hong, 2009).

As part of the Chinese government's Going Abroad Project, which encourages and helps TV stations and production companies broadcast more Chinese voices and images to the world, many Chinese TV stations and production companies now have branches or joint venture businesses in various countries across the world. Chinese-produced television programs are now available in the United States, the United Kingdom, France, Spain, Portugal, Japan, Korea, Singapore, Australia, New Zealand, Russia, Mongolia, Vietnam, Thailand, Laos, Cambodia, and Burma (Hong, Lu, & Zou, 2008).

Animation production was one of the most successful aspects of the Going Abroad Project. In 2008 a CCTV-produced 52-episode animation series, *Xiao Li Yu Li Xian Ji* (The Little Carp's Adventures), was imported by 51 countries. Its budget was RMB 30 million. This program alone made RMB 11.86 million (about $1.7 million) from the overseas market, setting a new record. *The Story of Three Kingdoms*, China's first high-definition animation program that was co-produced with Japan, was sold to more than 40 foreign TV companies in 20 countries (Lu, 2009). From 2007 to 2011, China's animation production grew dramatically year by year. In 2007 the total amount of animation produced was

101,900 minutes, but it increased by 19.2 percent in 2008 to reach 131,042 minutes, by 28.6 percent in 2009 to 171,816 minutes, by 31.1 percent in 2010 to 220,530 minutes, and by 18.5 percent in 2011 to 261,224 minutes (Deng, 2012).

The advertising industry in China has grown remarkably in the last few years. In 2011 advertising revenues from radio and television reached RMB 82.62 billion (about $13.11 billion), a 15.89 percent increase over the figure in 2010. The advertising revenue of other media industries has kept growing in the last few years as well. For example, the online advertising revenues in 2011 reached RMB 51.2 billion, a 59.4 percent of growth over 2010. In 2011 the advertising revenues of online gaming industry alone reached RMB 41.4 billion, a 26.4 percent increase over 2010. Even a traditional media industry such as film saw its advertising revenue in 2011 reached RMB 17.84, a 13.5 percent increase over 2010 (Cui & Zhou, 2009; Cui & Hou, 2012).

The "open door" policy has not only allowed China to open its market to foreign companies, including foreign and transnational media companies, but the government has also vigorously encouraged Chinese media organizations to export media and cultural products to other countries. Despite the fact that many scholars think the government's push for Chinese media to enter the global media arena is more of a political than an economic move, after years of effort the Chinese media have become active new players in the global media arena and are much more noticeable than a couple of decades ago.

The globalization of the Chinese media follows a bifurcated strategy. Media organizations are no longer interested only in the domestic market; they are also aiming at the much bigger and more profitable international market, especially the markets of Western nations. With the restructuring of China's political system and economic approach since the late 1980s, the Communist Party and government are more eager to use the export of Chinese media and cultural products to expand China's soft power in the world. In other words, while the Chinese media practitioners are eager to use globalization as an opportunity to gain a share of the global media market, the Chinese authorities are more eager to have China's voice heard in the world's political, economic, and cultural forums, and thus exert more soft power in the global arena.

Especially during the past few years, China has accelerated the pace of internationalization and globalization of its media. Among a number of new actions, three strategic ones are particularly worth noting. The first was the establishment of China Satellite News Gathering Alliance (CSNG) in December 2008. CSNG consists of China's 50 leading television broadcasters, with CCTV as the leader of this alliance. The purpose of this action was to change China's television broadcasting from many scattered individual "trees" to a mustered "forest" so that it can compete with CNN and the BBC in the world television arena. The second action was Xinhua News Agency's launch of a visual news service, thus bringing it up to the same level as the leading global news agencies such as Associated Press (AP) and Reuters, which are effective and competitive in the world media market by transmitting both print and visual news items to their subscribers (Lu & Gao, 2009). The third action was a billion-dollar decision on the internationalization of China's media. Earlier in 2009 the Chinese Communist Party and the central government decided to allocate RMB 45 billion (about $7 billion) to an unprecedented "media project." The project is to build up China's media "aircraft carrier" in an attempt to give them more power to compete with the world media giants, such as Time Warner, AOL, Disney, News Corp, Viacom, and Bertelsmann, in the global arena. However, the most important and ultimate purpose of all these actions for the internationalization and globalization of China's media is still a simple and political one: to give China a greater say in world affairs, to let its voice be heard across the world, and to help balance the currently still seriously unbalanced world information and communication order. As soon as this unprecedented strategic media project was revealed by the Western media, it immediately attracted great worldwide attention. Despite the Chinese government's official denial of the project, many Chinese media organizations have already started to work vigorously toward its fulfillment.

Japan: A Worldwide Conqueror through Animation

Japan is a major player in some aspects of the media and entertainment industry. In particular, it is strong in the global trading of animation and horror films. Japanese animé (animation) and horror movies represent a level of expertise that is not seen in any other country. In the last few decades, Japan's film and animation industries have been remarkably successful both in their home and in the overseas markets. One of the reasons why Japanese films and animations have made their mark worldwide is their themes.

Japanese film exports are highly concentrated on animations and horror movies. Figures 14.1 and 14.2 depict the market share of Japanese animation films and their box office revenues. Animation films accounted for the majority of Japanese exports to the United States. For example, between 2000 and 2008, 91 percent of the Japanese titles released in the US market were animations whereas other genres of films accounted only for 8 percent. The figure was 60 percent for Italy, and 27 percent for South Korea. Horror films comprised 44 percent of Japan's film exports to South Korea. In general, Japanese animation makes up more than 60 percent of the world animation market.

The big-hit films in Japan's domestic market or the films that win awards at international film festivals are widely distributed abroad. For example, *Howl's Moving Castle*, which was nominated for an Oscar in 2006 and won another eight awards in 2005–6, broke several records at the Japanese box office and was shown in many foreign countries such as Korea, France, Taiwan, Hong Kong, and the United States (WebJapan, 2005). According to statistics published by Japan's Ministry of Economy, Trade and Industry in November 2004, the film's

Figure 14.1 Japanese animation's market share, 1992–2003
Source: Based on data from JETRO, 2005a.

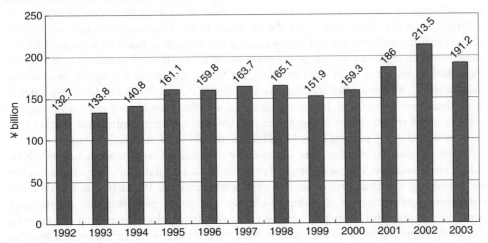

Figure 14.2 Box office revenues for feature-length animations in Japan, 1997–2003
Source: Based on data from JETRO, 2005a.

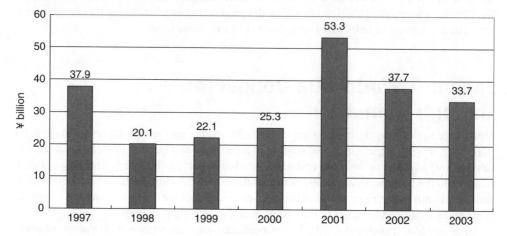

success raised the total animated film ticket sales to 16 times more than in the same month of the previous year.

In order to expand its global reach, Japanese film production companies started joint productions with their American or other Asian counterparts. For example, Disney is now buying Japanese animé, together with games and other products, for distribution in other regions. It is also considering joint film and animé productions in Japan. Disney has established an entertainment content purchasing division within its Japanese subsidiary. Like Disney, many foreign television stations and distribution companies are now investing in animation and film productions in Japan or in joint productions with Japanese companies.

An animé production company, IG, whose productions *Ghost in the Shell* and other titles won numerous overseas fans, established a US subsidiary that retains lawyers and accountants familiar with American business practices and legal affairs to help their sales negotiations and joint productions with American distributors. Another major production company, Toei Animation, also established a US subsidiary in 2004.

Using new communication technology, Japanese producers and distributors are testing a new global joint venture. Toei Animation is now distributing animation titles via the Internet, and its consumers can directly download and watch their programs from its archives. Since the direct sales from the producer to the consumer through the Internet allows consumers all over the world to access the content without distributors or exhibitors, consumers can enjoy the programs at a more reasonable price and in relative comfort. Hal Film Maker set up a joint venture with a Chinese company for animé production, programming, and character merchandising (Japan External Trade Organization, 2005a). With these new approaches, Japanese animation and films are aiming to expand business across various regions in the world. In the past few years, Japanese animation market sales have increased by 5.1 percent from $1.48 billion in 2006 to $1.88 billion in 2011.

Many Japanese productions are increasingly outsourcing to subcontractors in China, Korea, and elsewhere. They send original prints and other digital data to the subcontractors for animating, coloring, and other less complex operations. While Japanese production companies concentrate on planning, financing, and other processes that require high expertise, the subcontractors perform the more mundane tasks of animating and coloring the work. Some market experts estimate that over 90 percent of the Japanese animation

Table 14.1 Japanese films remade by major Hollywood studios

Remake title	Japanese title	Genre	Year	Total gross ($million)	No. of theaters
Last Man Standing	Yojimbo	Action	1996	18	2,579
Godzilla	Godzilla series	Action	1998	136	3,310
The Ring	Ringu	Horror	2002	129	2,927
The Grudge	Juon: The Grudge	Horror	2004	110	3,348
Shall We Dance?	Shall We Dance?	Drama	2004	58	2,542
The Ring Two	Ringu	Horror	2005	76	3,341
Dark Water	Honogurai mizu no soko kara	Horror	2005	25	2,657
Eight Below	Antarctica	Adventure	2006	82	3,122
The Grudge 2	Juon: The Grudge 2	Horror	2006	39	3,214
Pulse	Kairo	Horror	2006	18	2,323

Source: Based on data from JETRO, 2005b, 2009.

industry is outsourced. Most market experts agreed that Japanese animation production's outsourcing stands at 60 percent. There is no doubt that very few animation titles are produced solely in Japan now. For example, Studio Ghibli, a Japanese animation company headed by the world-renowned directors Hayao Miyazaki and Isao Takahata, subcontracted part of the work on *Spirited Away* to Korean companies. Some animation productions now even have their own production studios in other countries. For example, Toei Animation has more than 130 employees at its production house in the Philippines (Bynum, 2008).

The remaking of Japanese films has recently been very popular in Hollywood. After the remake of a Japanese horror film, *The Ring*, turned out to be a big hit in the US market in 2002, many American film producers have bought the rights from Japanese films (mainly horror films) and animations,. As shown in Table 14.1, recently remade Japanese films include *The Grudge, Dark Water, Pulse, The Ring, The Ring Two,* and *Shall We Dance? The Ring* and *The Grudge* were the most profitable in the US market. Remade by DreamWorks, it garnered more than $129 million in the US box office and $230 million worldwide, almost six times the remake cost. DreamWorks bought the remake from the director Nakata Hideo for only $1.2 million and spent another $40 million to remake the film (Xu, 2008). Between 1996 and 2008, 10 Japanese films were remade by the major Hollywood studios. Table 14.1 shows the titles, genres, and release years of these films.

The remakes in recent years have received much more attention than previous remakes of Japanese films because of their scale and profitability. Previous remakes were isolated and random events, but in recent years marketing strategies have changed. For example, the Americanized *Ring*'s success was followed by other sales of Japanese horror films such as *Ring Two* (purchased by DreamWorks), *Dark Water* (purchased by Disney), and *Jouon* (purchased by Columbia Pictures) (Bynum, 2008; Xu, 2008).

Table 14.2 Domestic spending in Japan's film entertainment industry, 2005 ($ million)

Box office spending	1,799
Home video spending	5,902
Total spending	7,701

Source: Based on data from PwC, 2006.

Horror films account for the majority of remakes that have been produced or are being planned. For example, of the 10 major sales of remake rights, eight were horror films, while only two were dramas. This is mainly because Japanese horror movies seem to appeal to a wide range of audiences around the world. As Taplin (2007) explains, the appeal of Japanese horror films derives from solid and well-crafted storytelling, whereas Hollywood movies rely heavily on special effects and pyrotechnics. In addition, the demand of audiences for exotic cultures and action are fueling the current trend of remakes.

A modernized system of production and distribution, and the home market effect, are some of the main factors for the wide acceptance of Japanese films and animations. Given the second largest entertainment market in the world, Japan has a good home market to support the growth of cultural products. This market size for entertainment and cultural products has helped Japanese films and animations to expand their business abroad. Japan has the largest film market in Asia, at $7.7 billion, as shown in Table 14.2, which accounts 47 percent of the total media spending. Domestic films do well at the box office, increasing their ratio of the market to more than 40 percent, but overall box office spending has fallen in large part because of the low demand for American films. The weakness of US films at the Japanese box office has seriously impacted domestic spending in the film market.

In 2004 62.5 percent of Japan's box office revenue was from imported films and 37.5 percent from domestic films, which is relatively high compared to Western nations other than the United States. The ratio of domestic to imported films in terms of box office revenue and of film releases has increased by 17.8 percent and 8.01 percent, respectively. According to JETRO (2005a), animation films have boosted the market since the mid-1990s. *Spirited Away* set a record of 23.5 million movie-goers. In addition, some other big animation hits such as Studio Ghibli's *Howl's Moving Castle* and *Sekai no Chuushin de Ai wo Sakebu* also helped to boost the domestic share. While domestic films are expanding their market share, imported films are slowly but steadily losing their dominant position in Japan. For example, the success of *Howl's Moving Castle* in 2004 helped the domestic films' market share rise to 37.5 percent. This suggests that domestic films have a competitive advantage over foreign films and are creating a positive home market effect. In terms of the number of releases, a total of 165 first-run domestic films were released in 2003, showing a big growth from the previous years. The number of domestic film releases has steadily increased during the last few years by 8 percent annually. The ratio of domestic films in the market has increased from 44.6 percent in 2001 to 47.8 percent in 2004 (JETRO, 2005a).

While Japanese animations are widely accepted all over the world, Japanese TV programs are less accepted by other nations, particularly other Asian countries, for political reasons. Korean and Chinese memories of Japanese occupation led to these countries banning Japanese television programs. However, as Taiwan lifted its ban on Japanese programs in 1993 and South Korea relaxed its ban in the late 1990s, exports of Japanese TV dramas to Taiwan and South Korea have rapidly increased. According to an annual report of Japan's Ministry of Internal Affairs and Communications (2012), the total export of Japanese TV

Figure 14.3 Exports of Japanese TV programs by region, 2010
Source: Based on data from Ministry of Internal Affairs and Communications, 2012.

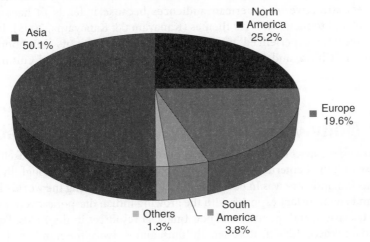

Figure 14.4 Exports of Japanese TV programs by genre, 2010
Source: Based on data from Ministry of Internal Affairs and Communications, 2012.

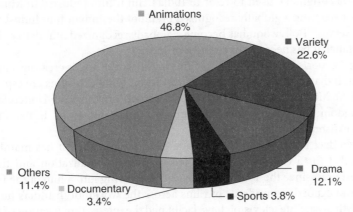

programs in 2010 was worth approximately ¥6.25 billion. Recently, Japanese TV dramas have also been shown to many foreign audiences with widespread acceptance, including in other Asian countries.

As Figure 14.3 shows, Asia is now the most important target market of Japanese television programs, at 50.1 percent, followed by North America (25.2%), Europe (19.6%), South America (3.8%), and others (1.3%). Between 2011 and 2012 the Asian market grew from 43.2 to 50.1 percent, while the European and North American markets declined from 25.5 percent to 25.2 percent, and from 27.6 percent to 19.6 percent, respectively. In terms of genre, as shown in Figure 14.4, animation (46.8%) was the most widely accepted by the global audience, followed by variety programs (22.6%), drama (12.1%), sports (3.8%), and documentary (3.4%). Animation and drama are the two most accepted genres for import by other countries.

The boom of Japanese TV program exports started in the early 1990s when STAR TV began to carry Japanese dramas to neighboring countries. For example, a Japanese drama, *Oshin*, was aired in 28 countries. Even in Iran, which has low cultural proximity to Japan, the drama's ratings hit a historic high of 70 percent nationwide. However, there are still some obstacles to Japanese TV dramas breaking into the US market. Japanese drama is less attractive to American audiences because it tends to have slow story development and to focus on local themes (Kanayama & Kanayama, 2005). In addition, Japan has recently experienced increased competition from its neighboring media giants, Taiwan, China, and South Korea, in the regional media and cultural product market.

India: Bollywood as Hollywood in the East

With the growing impact on the global film industry, India is transforming itself into a new powerhouse of filmed entertainment in the global media market. Although by the end of the 1980s its film industry was in bad shape, India is now becoming the world's largest film producer and an important exporter with the growing Indian diasporas overseas, the entry of satellite television, and the inflow of new financial resources in the 1990s. For example, in 2009 India released 1,200 feature-length films, almost twice the number of films (694) released by the United States in that year (UNESCO, 2011).

India's film industry is now affectionately nicknamed Bollywood, from "Hollywood" and "Bombay," the former name for Mumbai, the center of India's film production. Bollywood was originally used to refer to India's Hindi film industry in Mumbai, but the term is now becoming a globally recognized brand of the Indian film industry. As Mishra (2006: 3) observes, "Bollywood has become a globally recognized brand; like Darjeeling tea or the Taj Mahal, it has become an emblem of India."

Bollywood exports a massive scale of films to the world, and is creating a major cultural force both in India and overseas (Lorenzen & Taeube, 2009). Its films are especially widely accepted in the Middle East, Asia, Africa, East Europe, and now the United States and the United Kingdom too, where there are many immigrants from India, Pakistan, and Bangladesh (Mishra, 2006).

Despite the fact that India's film industry has a long history, it has mainly served the national market for a century. However, led by media liberalization and the growth of overseas diasporas, since the 1990s India has been evolving into a hub of the film industry, producing and exporting hundreds of films across the world. Both India's huge diasporas and the growth of satellite television have facilitated the internationalization of Indian films, helping Bollywood become a powerhouse that produces more than 800 films annually in 15 languages including Hindi, Tamil, and Telugu. Bollywood is now producing and exporting its films with a 60 percent growth rate in the last four years, and is integrating into the global media economy (Lorenzen & Taeube, 2009).

The Indian film entertainment industry obtains around $200 million to $360 million in revenue from overseas annually (KPMG and CII, 2005; Lorenzen & Taeube, 2009). In addition, Zee TV, India's biggest Hindi TV channel, has about four million subscribers abroad, earning 40 percent of its revenue from exports, and Comcast, the leading cable provider in the United States, is now offering its video-on-demand services for Bollywood films to its subscribers (Lorenzen, 2009).

According to 1998 data (see Figure 14.5), the main importers of Indian films in recent years were the Middle East with 35.4 percent of India's total film exports, the former Soviet Union nations with 14 percent, and Indonesia with 14 percent. More recently, Indian films have been consumed in large part by Indian diasporas or the same language groups in the countries. For example, countries like Bangladesh with a 136 million Bengali-speaking

Figure 14.5 Main importers of Indian films in the late 1990s
Source: Based on data from Lorenzen, 2009.

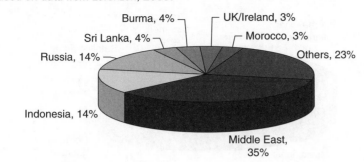

population, Sri Lanka with 3.5 million Tamils, and Malaysia with 1.5 million Tamil speakers are all good potential markets for Indian films (KPMG & CII, 2005; Lorenzen, 2009).

Since the late 1990s, the Indian film industry has seen a huge growth in exports to the Indian diasporas in North America, the United Kingdom, and a range of Arabic countries, and they have recently started entering other Asian countries as well. In the past, the distribution of Indian films abroad was difficult due to geographical and technological problems. For example, the British and North American markets were geographically dispersed and therefore difficult to cover with a small number of screens for Indian films. However, more efficient distribution methods like DVDs and home videos are guaranteeing better dispersal for Indian productions, which has enabled the growth of film exports at 30 to 50 percent annually (Lorenzen & Taeube, 2009). According to KPMG and the Confederation of Indian Industry (2005), two major Indian film distributors report that the US and UK markets account for more than half their export revenues. India has accounted for the largest proportion of foreign films screened in the US market recently, and some Indian films are big hits, earning more than $1 million in their first week. In 2005 Bollywood films in the United States were estimated to have earned $100 million (Woodman-Maynard, 2006). As shown in Figure 14.6, the proportion of revenue from international distribution is the same as that from domestic theaters.

The new Indian diasporas have played a significant role in making the Indian film industry more stable and profitable. These diasporas have a much higher purchasing power than the Indian home market or the old diasporas. Consumers in the new diaspora markets may have a greater willingness to pay for filmed entertainment and therefore the media market is more potentially profitable. Therefore, the box office revenues in these new diasporas are higher per capita than in the domestic market. In 2005 the average ticket price in the United States, the United Kingdom, and Australia ranged from $8 to $15, whereas in India the average ticket price was only 35 cents. Thus, the booming exports to these new markets have increased Bollywood's exports earnings by a 30 to 50 percent annual growth rate in the last five years (KPMG, 2005). As shown in Table 14.3, the average overseas earnings of the top 20 Indian films amounted to $192.9 million. *Three Idiots* is the highest grossing film, with $23.9 million in overseas markets, followed by *My Name is Khan* ($22.15 million), *Don 2* ($11.7 million), and *Kabhi Alvida Naa Kehna* ($10.77 million).

Kabhi Alvida Naa Kehna is probably the best example of a Bollywood film's success in the world market, and *Veer-Zaara* was the top-grossing Bollywood film in 2006 both at home and internationally, earning over Rs 445 million (about $11 million) (Box Office India, 2009). The main importers of Indian films are the United Kingdom and the United States. *Veer-Zaara* opened strongly in the United Kingdom and the United States in 2006

Figure 14.6 Sources of Bollywood film revenue, 2005
Source: Based on data from Rao, 2005.

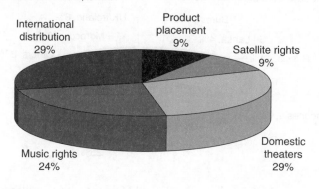

Table 14.3 Overseas earnings of top-grossing Indian films

Rank	Title	Overseas revenue ($ million)
1	Three Idiots	$23.90
2	My Name is Khan	$22.15
3	Don 2	$11.70
4	Kabhi Alvida Naa Kehna	$10.77
5	Om Shanti Om	$10.08
6	Ra One	$9.20
7	Dhoom 2	$8.57
8	Rab Ne Bana Di Jodi	$8.43
9	Veer-Zaara	$8.20
10	Bodyguard	$8.15
11	Kabhi Khushi Kabhie Gham	$8.00
12	Jodha Akbar	$7.55
13	Don	$7.46
14	Black	$7.40
15	Singh is King	$7.27
16	Zindagi Na Milegi Dobara	$7.25
17	Ghajini	$7.06
18	Fanaa	$6.86
19	Devdas	$6.65
20	Kuch Kuch Hota Hai	$6.25

Source: Phelps, 2012.

with the first weekend grosses of $1.3 million (Rs 62.4 million) in the United States and $1.4 million (Rs 62.8 million) in the United Kingdom, making it one of the most successful debuts of a Bollywood film. The success of this film did not wane significantly, as it has earned $3.6 million (Rs 175 million) so far in the United States, $3.1 million (Rs 150 million) in the United Kingdom, and $2.5 million (Rs 120 million) in the rest of the world.

Since Bollywood has been fastest in tapping into global business opportunities, many players in the industry are turning their eyes to the overseas markets and are developing new business strategies. For example, in order to capitalize on the growing global market, Bollywood producers like Yash Chopra and Subhash Ghai have set up distribution offices in the United Kingdom and the United States (Pendakur, 2003). Over the last decade, Yash Raj Films, the top distribution house in India and twenty-seventh in the world, has performed well, particularly in exports. Through Yash Raj Films' own offices in the United Kingdom, the United States, the United Arab Emirates, and India, YRF Studios has also widened its horizons by marketing and distributing DVDs and VCDs of classic Indian films (Yash Raj Films, 2009).

Another significant movement toward internationalization can be seen in the India China Film Cooperation Commission. India and China joined forces to create the commission to "strengthen cooperation and promote bilateral exchanges between India and China in the entertainment sector" (Jayaram, 2005). The commission is considering raising film quotas for each country's films (PwC, 2006). Indian film-makers expect that co-production with China would help to break into the highly restricted market in China. China has a screen quota policy that limits the number of foreign films shown. Therefore, co-productions with China may help Indian films circumvent the restriction. Besides China, India also has many co-production treaties with other countries, such as the United Kingdom, Brazil, France, Germany, Italy, New Zealand, Poland, and Spain (Mahanty, 2012). In the view of Rao (2007), these business strategies can help what Shukla (2003) calls "interpenetrating globalism," whereby nationalities come together and yet remain highly discrete overseas.

The home market effect, overseas diasporas, and the change in government regulation are major factors for Bollywood's continued export growth (Kohli-Khandekar, 2006). As Lorenzen and Taeube (2009) note, the home market boom has served to facilitate Bollywood's recent growth in revenues as well as exports. With a high annual growth rate of 25 percent, Bollywood is the fastest growing of the film-making industries. In terms of output, it is the most prolific in the world, with the commercial film cluster turning out more than 800 films a year (Rao, 2005).

Despite the world's sluggish economy recently, both India's box office and home video revenues have quickly recovered from negative growth. Box office revenue fell sharply from $1,770 million in 2008 to $1,524 million in 2009. However, it rose 9.8 percent in 2010 to $1,673 million. The growth of the domestic film market was fueled by both higher ticket prices and the increase in the number of movie-goers. In 2010 the number of movie-goers was 2,650 million, a 6 percent increase from 2,500 million in 2009. In the meantime, the average ticket price went up to $0.63 in 2010 from $0.61. In addition, the introduction of 3D screens also contributed to the profitability of the film industry in India. In 2008 there were only 112 3D screens in India, but the number doubled to 279 in 2009. Domestic spending on home video sales and rentals has also recovered since 2009. Between 2008 and 2009, home video revenue declined sharply by 20.99 percent. However, it has been growing again since 2009. The growth rate was 5.47 percent in 2009 and 10.37 percent in 2010.

As shown in Table 14.4, the total domestic film market in India rose 12.07 percent in 2007 and 10.48 percent in 2008, but dropped 12.59 percent in 2009. Nevertheless, it recovered by 9.83 percent in 2010. India is projected to have the fastest growing film entertainment industry in the next few years, with a two-digit compound annual increase in the total home video market.

Wildman and Siwek (1988) state that generally producers with a large home market have a clear advantage in international competition because the large markets provide them with

Table 14.4 Domestic spending growth in the Indian film entertainment industry (%)

	2007	2008	2009	2010
Box office spending	11.70	13.75	−13.90	9.78
Home video spending	15.71	−20.99	5.47	10.37
Total spending	12.07	10.48	−12.59	9.83

Source: KOCCA, 2011.

greater incentive to make large investment in their productions. They suggest that the larger investment enables the producers to put more elements that are appealing in the films, and therefore the films can overcome the handicap caused by the cultural differences between home and export markets. As India's GDP is rising rapidly and the middle class grows, Bollywood has also taken advantage of the growth in national demand. Aided by the growing home market, Bollywood is doing well in financing, producing, and marketing over 800 films annually. From a Hollywood perspective, most Bollywood firms are small and independent films because their budget is smaller than Hollywood's blockbusters, and the producers rarely have vertical ties with distributors. The average Indian film budget is $3 million, in contrast to the average budget of $45 million for a Hollywood movie (Rao, 2005). However, these relatively small-budget films are able to compete in mainstream box offices with high returns on investment, proving the diversity and dynamism of Bollywood.

The Indian film industry has ethno-geographical advantages because of the large and widely dispersed Indian diasporas. India has the second largest overseas population in the world after China. There is a potential audience of more than 20 million Indians overseas (see Table 14.5) who are familiar with Indian culture and films (Ministry of Overseas Indian Affairs, 2012). By selling Bollywood films to an audience who is already familiar with Indian culture and values, the industry can garner additional revenue from them as well as make larger investment in their productions in the expectation of future returns from the audience. Therefore, in one sense, the diasporas are potentially another home market for Bollywood films. These wealthy diasporas function as the most powerful asset for the industry.

The Indian government provides Bollywood with neither state subsidies nor any special tax exemption. However, several recent changes in government regulations have positively affected the performance and exportability of Bollywood films. For example, the Indian government now allows foreign direct investment (FDI) in film financing, production, distribution, marketing, and associated activities related to the film industry. Before 1992, the government prohibited foreign investors from directly supporting the domestic film industry. However, after 1992 the government has begun to open up the market to foreign investors. In 2005 the government decided to fully open the industry up to foreign investors, thus allowing Bollywood to attract more finance from oversea diasporas (Lorenzen & Taeube, 2009). Thanks to the inflow of capital to Bollywood, producers can make blockbuster films that may appeal even more to audiences, which enhances the exportability of their films.

Also, since 2001 the Indian government has classified the film industry as an industry that is able to receive finance from the banking industry. The new policy framework has enabled film productions or distributors to get investment from private banks, insurance companies, and other financial institutions. The new framework has enhanced transparency

Table 14.5 Indian diasporas, 2011

Diaspora	Population (000s)	Diaspora	Population (000s)
United States	2,245	Trinidad & Tobago	552
Malaysia	2,050	Qatar	500
Saudi Arabia	1,789	Australia	448
United Arab Emirates	1,750	Myanmar	357
Sri Lanka	1,602	Bahrain	350
United Kingdom	1,500	Guyana	320
South Africa	1,218	Fiji	314
Canada	1,000	France (Reunion Island)	275
Mauritius	882	Netherlands	215
Oman	719	Thailand	150
Singapore	670	France (Guadeloupe, St Martinique)	145
Nepal	600	Suriname	140
Kuwait	579	Others	1,540
TOTAL	21,910		

Source: Ministry of Overseas Indian Affairs, 2012.

and fair competition in the film industry. Currently, many financial institutions are investing in Bollywood films. After the reclassification of the film industry by the government, the Industrial Development Bank has provided 55 films with finance. The Bank of Baroda has invested Rs 500 million in *Taj Mahal*, and the Bank of India has invested Rs 600 million in several film projects (Bist, 2004).The changes in government regulations have modernized the production system of the Indian film industry, which has greatly contributed to the internationalization of the film industry.

There are different opinions on Bollywood. As Bollywood becomes more profitable and expands its business globally, some scholars have raised concerns over the globalization of the Indian film industry. Mishra (2006) argues that current Bollywood films fail to reflect India's authentic culture and values. He asserts that the influence of overseas diasporas as a source of finance is so significant that Bollywood films are conveying only the "feel good" version of Indian culture (Mishra, 2006). Currently, foreign market earnings are responsible for around 30 percent of film budgets, equal to or exceeding domestic earnings. In this situation, producers cannot but consider the taste of foreign audiences in planning their films and eliminating the elements that may not translate culturally to an overseas audience. Thus, most Bollywood films targeting foreign audiences focus on entertainment rather than reality. From this perspective, globalization means Westernization or Hollywoodization.

In addition, advertising and the sales of secondary products are increasingly important in film production. Product placement and the sales of music rights account for 9 percent and 24 percent, respectively, of Bollywood revenue. This situation is making producers focus more on the tastes of middle-class and upper-class audiences. As Rao (2007) indicates, film producers in Bollywood are increasingly focusing on urban audiences who can pay more and buy more and whose tastes need to be catered for. The most popular recent Bollywood films, such as *Kabhi Kaho Na Pyar Hai* (2000), *Kushi Kabhi Gum* (2001), *Kal Ho Naa Ho* (2003), *Hum Tum* (2004), and *Dus* (2005), featured Westernized themes and MTV-style musical numbers (Mishra, 2006; Rao, 2007). Furthermore, advertising, music rights, and secondary products have been growing. Product placement in films is estimated at around Rs 1,000 crores, equivalent to $181 million, in 2010 (PwC, 2011). The increasing revenues from advertising and secondary products often make film producers focus more on the taste of those who has purchasing power. Thus, as Mishra (2006) observes, Bollywood is becoming a dream world with materially successful Indians who want to see only the "feel good" version of Indian culture.

Korea: The Continuing Global Sweeping of "K-Pop"

Over the past few years, Korean popular culture, including soap operas, music, and films, has gained a popularity in East Asia that is now spreading to other regions with low cultural and geographical proximity, such as North America, the Middle East, and Europe. According to the Korean Ministry of Culture, Sports, and Tourism (2012), in 2011 exports of Korean cultural products, including books, computer games, animation, cartoons, television programs, recorded musical tapes, and "tie-in" products, accounted for $4.6 billion. Despite the global economic recession, exports of Korean cultural products have continued to increase. Journalists have dubbed the increased circulation of Korean popular culture around the world as the "Korean wave" (*Hallyu*) (Faiola, 2006).

According to some scholars, the "Korean wave" started from the big hit of a Korean television drama in China, *What is Love All About?* The drama aired on the national CCTV in 1997, turning out to be an unexpected hit. When the television station re-broadcast the drama the following year in a prime-time slot, it received the second highest rating in China's television history (Heo, 2002; Shim, 2009).

Since then, in response to popular demand, several television stations in Hong Kong, Taiwan, and Singapore have begun to broadcast imported Korean TV dramas and these have gained a huge audience. For example, in 1999 another Korean drama serial, *Star in My Heart*, became a big hit in Taiwan and China, which led to other Korean television programs being broadcast in the region. With the sudden popularity of such Korean dramas, many television stations in Taiwan, such as FTV, CTV, and Power TV, began importing and broadcasting Korean TV programs instead of Japanese programs (H. M. Kim, 2005). In 2000 the high demand for Korean programs led a cable channel in Taiwan to specialize in airing Korean TV dramas. For historical and political reasons, Taiwan had been especially receptive to Japanese and Korean TV dramas. But the Korean drama *Jewel in the Palace* was watched by half the population in Taiwan, creating a *han-liu* (Taiwanese for "Korean wave") that dominated young consumers' tastes in entertainment, fashion, and commercial goods. In addition to the huge success in Taiwan, Korean TV shows also became the most watched television dramas in the region (Chan, 2009).

Korean TV dramas have spread to neighboring countries such as Japan and Hong Kong rapidly, as well as to other East and Southeast Asian countries (Faiola, 2006; Maliangkay, 2006; Shim, 2009). In the past few years, Korean television stations have regarded Korean TV dramas as a substitute for expensive Japanese TV dramas because they were much cheaper than Japanese dramas as well as being commercially profitable. For instance, in

2002 Korean TV dramas were only about a quarter of the price of Japanese ones, and a tenth of the price of Hong Kong ones (Shim, 2009). Therefore, in the economic recession, many Asian buyers preferred to buy the cheaper Korean TV programming than other, more expensive Asian TV programming. As Chua (2006) claims, the Korean wave is the result of a conscious strategy of television stations to establish their presence among local, national, and international audiences. Thus, as the demands for Korean TV dramas and other television programs have continuously increased, Korean television programs, along with other Korean cultural products, have attracted a fan base in the overseas markets. The total exports of Korean television programs were approximately $229 million in 2010, an increase of 23.9 percent from $184 million in 2009.

The Korean wave in the music industry began in China in the late 1990s. A satellite television channel based in Hong Kong, Channel V, regularly aired Korean pop music videos from 1998, which contributed to the huge fan base of Korean pop stars in Asia (Shim, 2009). Channel V has helped these pop stars expand their fan base in Singapore, Malaysia, Taiwan, and China. For example, in 1998 a Korean boy band, H.O.T., reached the top of the pop charts in China and Taiwan. In 2000 their concert tickets were sold out in Beijing, attracting more than 12,000 youth for each concert. The Korean pop sensation can be found even in Japan, which has the second biggest music industry in the world. In 2002 a Korean female pop singer, Boa, released her debut Japanese album, *Listen to My Heart*, which reached the top of the Oricon Weekly Chart, Japan's equivalent of the Billboard Charts, and became an RIAJ-certified million-seller album, making it the first album by a Korean artist to reach the top. Following her success, many Korean pop singers have promoted their albums in Japan, and some of them, including Boa, are now expanding into the global market. SM Entertainment, the largest Korean-based agency, producer, and publisher of pop music, increased its presence by opening subsidiaries in the United States, Japan, Hong Kong, and China.

In fact, Korea was not a traditional powerhouse of pop music in the world. Just a decade ago, Korean popular culture rarely received much attention from the industry or the academy. As Kawakami and Fisher (1994) comment, Korean popular music did not have anything to match the remarkable contemporary sounds of Indonesia, Okinawa, or Japan. However, the Korean pop music, commonly referred to as K-Pop, is now entering in to the mainstream of world's music industry and is gaining a global audience. For instance, a Korean singer, Psy, was a global hit with his song "Oppan Gangnam Style," earning approximately $8.1 million in 2012 (Y. Lee & Nakashima, 2012). The total export of Korean music products in 2010 reached $8.3 million, an increase of 166.3 percent from the previous year (Ministry of Culture, Sports, and Tourism, 2012).

The Korean wave was seen in film entertainment too. In 1999 a Korean blockbuster, *Shiri*, was released in Japan, Hong Kong, Taiwan, and Singapore, attracting critical acclaim as well as large audiences (S. Kim, 2004). It became the most popular Korean movie, seen by over six million people in Korea and over 1.2 million in Japan. In the view of Joo (2005), *Shiri* heralded a departure from the past by tapping the hitherto ignored commercial viability of Korean films. After *Shiri* and other pioneers, many Korean films have become regular fixtures in cinemas across Asia. For example, *Joint Security Area*, which was released in 2000, became one of the biggest hit films in Japan and was shown on as many as 280 screens (S. Kim, 2004).

Korean films are now spreading to North American and Europe with more blockbusters (Frater, 2003a; Shim, 2009). In response to the growing demand for Korean film, major US distribution companies such as Fox and Columbia have added Korean films to their global distribution runs (Frater, 2003b; Shim, 2009). Recently, some Hollywood studios have

Table 14.6 Exports of Korea's cultural products, 2007–2010

Cultural products	Sales ($000)/annual growth (%)				Market share (%)
	2007	2008	2009	2010	
Film	24	21/−13.8	14/−32.9	14/−3.8	0.4
Publishing	213	260/22.1	250/−3.8	357/42.8	11.1
Cartoons	4	4/3.7	4/1.8	8/93.7	0.3
Animation	73	81/10.74	90/11.25	97/8.00	3.0
Advertising	94	14/−84.86	93/555.45	76/−18.89	2.3
Music	14	16/18.60	31/89.88	83/166.28	2.6
Games	781	1094/40.06	1241/13.44	1606/29.44	49.8
Character	203	228/12.50	237/3.62	276/16.83	8.6
Television programs	151	171/13.51	185/7.72	229/23.87	7.1
Intellectual property	275	340/23.57	346/1.69	363/5.09	11.3
Content solutions	113	108/−4.38	113/5.26	116/2.71	2.7
Total	1945	2338/20.21	2603/11.37	3225/23.88	100

Source: Ministry of Culture, Sports, and Tourism, 2012.

bought the rights to remake Korean films. By the end of 2008, more than 25 Korean films' remake rights had been sold at prices ranging from $300,000 to $1 million (K. Kim, 2008). In 2009 DreamWorks remade a Korean horror film, *A Tale of Two Sisters*, after buying the rights at $2 million (Clark, 2009). The total export of Korean feature-length movies grew by 16.5 percent to $8.6 million in 2011. The main buyers of Korean films are Asian countries, particularly Japan and China, which together account for 56.9 percent of sales (Ministry of Culture, Sports, and Tourism, 2012).

With the growing presence of the Korean wave in regional and international markets, the export of Korean cultural products has grown fast. Korea's export of cultural products increased from $2.6 billion in 2009 to $3.2 billion in 2010, with a growth rate of 23.9 percent (Ministry of Culture, Sports, and Tourism, 2012). Total cultural product exports rose to a compounded annual growth rate of 21.9 percent in the past four years. As shown in Table 14.6, video games (49.8%) and publishing (11.1%) were the first and second largest exports. However, the significant increase in the growth rate was made possible largely by cartoons (42.3%), games (31.1%) and music (90.8%).

Many popular TV dramas are produced by Korea's independent production companies and content providers. However, in most cases terrestrial broadcasters, such as KBS1, KBS2, MBC, SBS, and EBS, provide the productions with financial support and buy both television programs and the right to redistribute the programs. They account for more than 60 percent of the overseas sales of TV programs.

As shown in Table 14.7, Korea's neighbors, such as Japan, China, and the Southeast Asian nations, are the top importers of Korean cultural products. In 2010 sales to these countries accounted for 72.7 percent of Korea's total cultural product exports. Japan was still the

Table 14.7 Importers of Korean cultural products, 2010 ($ thousand)

	China	Japan	Southeast Asia	North America	Europe	Others	Total
Film	966	2,258	3,488	1,421	4,518	932	13,583
Animation	1,577	18,810	1,151	52,463	19,527	3,299	96,827
Music	3,627	67,267	11,321	432	396	219	83,262
Games	595,864	435,254	242,521	147,761	138,125	46,577	1,606,102
"Tie-in" sales	49,368	16,457	27,226	85,327	59,668	38,282	276,328
Cartoons	568	1,527	2,004	1,723	2,258	73	8,153
Publishing	23,790	30,204	149,984	88,009	20,976	44,918	357,881
TV programs	20,955	49,713	49,555	2,815	2,318	1,702	127,058
Intellectual property	33,621	141,322	168,063	8,611	3,398	8,267	363,282
Content solutions	17,331	37,426	16,593	15,376	16,497	13,264	116,487
Total	747,667	800,238	671,906	403,938	267,681	157,533	3,048,963
Percentage	24.5	26.2	22.0	13.2	8.8	5.2	100.0

Source: Ministry of Culture, Sports, and Tourism, 2012.

Figure 14.7 Exports of Korean audiovisual products by region, 2010
Source: Based on data from KOCCA, 2011.

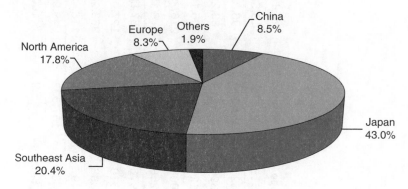

largest buyer of Korean cultural products, which accounted for 26.2 percent of the total exports. Games and intellectual properties were the main products that Japanese buyers imported from Korea, which accounted for 54.4 percent and 17.7 percent, respectively, of Korea's total exports to Japan. China was the second largest market of Korean cultural products. China held 24.5 percent of the total exports of Korean cultural products. In particular, China was the main target market for Korean games, accounting for one-third of that industry's sales. Southeast Asia imported 36.1 percent of games, 22.3 percent of books, and 25.0 percent of intellectual properties from Korea. North America and Europe mainly imported games, sales of "tie-ins," and publishing products from Korea.

For the audiovisual product categories such as film, animation, music, and television programs, as shown in Figure 14.7, the major importers were Japan (43%), Southeast Asia (20%) and North America (18%). Together with the East and South Asian countries, Asia as a whole imported 71% of Korea's cultural products exported, which means that Asia is the main target market of Korean audiovisual products. It implies that Korean audiovisual products are mainly consumed among the consumers who are in the cultural and geographical proximity of Korea.

The number of exported Korea films has steadily increased, reflecting the success of the Korean wave in the international film market. This is a particularly interesting trend, given the dominance of Hollywood films and the overlooked Korean films in the international film market until a few years ago. Sales of the remake rights of Korean films has increased since 2001 when Miramax bought the remake right of a Korean comedy film, *My Wife is a Gangster*. A list of films recently remade or in the process of being remade includes *Il Mare*, *My Sassy Girl*, *My Wife is a Gangster*, *A Tale of Two Sisters*, *Seven Days*, and *Ryung*. The most prominent one in this list is the Korean horror film *A Tale of Two Sisters*. DreamWorks purchased the rights at $2 million. The deal topped $1 million paid for the right to remake the Japanese film *The Ring*, which was the most successful and profitable remake in the US market (S. Lee, Kim, & Sung, 2009). The list of Korean films being purchased by Hollywood certainly marks a new trend.

The Korean wave is a product of newly liberalized media market. According to S. W. Lee and Waterman (2006), countries that have relatively high domestic consumer spending on a given media product tend to have relatively high exports of that product to other nations. In addition, the deregulation of the film and television markets has expanded the growth of domestic markets and contributed to the exportability of Korean cultural products.

Table 14.8 Domestic spending in Korea's film entertainment industry, 2004–2010

Box office	2004	2005	2006	2007	2008	2009	2010
Spending ($ million)	850	898	926	992	979	1,094	1,151
Annual growth (%)	18.5	5.7	3.1	7.1	−1.3	11.7	5.7
No. of movie-goers (million)	135	146	153	159	151	157	147

Source: Based on PwC, 2011.

As a result of media deregulation and liberalization in the late 1990s, Korea has seen the rapid growth of its cultural industries. For example, as shown in Table 14.8, the domestic film market has been expanding continuously since the late 1990s, earning $1.15 billion in 2010. Between 2004 and 2010, the compound annual growth rate of box office revenues was 5.2 percent. With the release of popular domestic films in the early 2000s, South Korea has become the second largest film market in the region (PwC, 2006). With the increase in the number of movie-goers, there has been an increase in the production of domestic films. The market share of domestic films reached a record high in 2006 of 63.8 percent of the total market share. These changes have contributed to a dramatic transformation of the Korean film market from a rigid, strictly regulated one to a dynamic one.

Some scholars believe that the Korean wave is partly a result of the government's proactive role in invigorating its cultural industry. The Korean government played an important role in guiding and facilitating the development of cultural industry (Zhu & Berry, 2009). One of the former Korean presidents called himself the "President of Culture," and in 1999 established the Base Law for the Cultural Industry Promotion by allocating $148.5 million to promote cultural production (Zhu & Berry, 2009). In this favorable environment, a number of international film festivals have been held in Korea, like the Seoul International Film Festival and the Pusan International Film Festival. These activities were designed to attract foreign buyers of Korean films. During the administration of the above-mentioned president, the budget for the cultural sector increased to around $1.3 billion, mainly for promoting the film industry, which accounted for 1.15 percent of the total government budget in 2002 (Shim, 2009). Recently, the government introduced various programs to support local films. In early 2006 the Ministry of Culture and Tourism introduced a $400 million film development fund to support local films and to provide tax relief for investment in the film industry (PwC, 2006). Additionally, the Korean Film Council (KOFIC), with the backing of the Ministry of Culture, Sports, and Tourism, strongly supports the production and export of Korean films. Since 2007, KOFIC has managed $430 million in the Film Development Fund to support the Korean film industry. The fund is mainly financed from government funds and is partly supported by ticket sales.

In addition to both direct and indirect financial support from the government, the more lenient censorship and media liberalization have also contributed to the growth of Korean popular culture. Several scholars claim that the Korean wave is indebted to media liberalization in Asia from the late 1990s (Dator & Seo, 2004; Shim, 2009). They indicate that deregulation and democratization in Korea in the late 1990s have played a significant role in improving the quality of Korean popular culture. As Dator and Seo (2004) note, full freedom of expression is now guaranteed, and previously taboo subjects, such as ideological struggles, have been allowed without fear of censorship. The more lenient censorship policy in Korean films has allowed the new generation to deal with such sensitive subjects as political issues and homosexuality. For example, *Shiri*, a Korean blockbuster dealing with North–South relations, was released in 1999, and attracted 6.5 million movie-goers. Two years later, another blockbuster entitled *Joint Security Area* beat the box office record, and was seen by 2.5 million in Seoul alone. Similarly, a gangland saga, *Friend*, broke the box office record, attracting more than 8.2 million attendances nationwide (Dator and Seo, 2004).

Many researchers have viewed the Korean wave as a result of revitalized interest in Asian values among Asian people who share a similar process of modernization (Chan, 2009; Chua, 2006; Iwabuchi, 2008; H. M. Kim, 2005; Shim, 2009). Cultural proximity refers to an audience's tendency to have a strong preference for film content originating from their own or a similar cultural background, which includes language and the nationality of actors (S. Lee, Kim, & Sung, 2009). Therefore, some scholars view the success of Korean products as being due to the blend of good looks and the lack of profanity and sex, in line with a Confucian tradition, which would also appeal to other East and Southeast Asian countries. With the benefit of cultural proximity, Korean dramas and films are outperforming their upscale Hollywood or Japanese ones in other Asian countries. Korean dramas and films tend to emphasize Confucian values, such as family orientation, respect for the elderly, and a preference for sons, which is only too familiar to Chinese, Vietnamese, and Japanese audiences.

As H. M. Kim (2005) explains, the values reflected in Korean dramas and films are very familiar to audiences in other Asian countries. This is especially true in the four most popular Korean dramas in Asian countries: *Fireworks, All about Eve, Autumn in My Heart*, and *Winter Sonata*. Popular Korean programs commonly focus on the five values of harmony, tension, compromise, participation, and agreement, which are most appealing to Asian people who have a similar culture frame (M. Kim, 2004). Therefore, cultural proximity is a very important factor in explaining the surge of Korean cultural products, particularly in East Asia (K. Yin & Liew, 2005). For example, Singaporean audiences have reinforced local identities in addition to the apparent familiarities of Koreans. Shim (2009) emphasizes how Korean pop culture skillfully blends Asian and Western values to create its own mix.

In fact, Korean popular culture is a mix of the earlier established Japanese, Chinese, and Western pop cultures. While some scholars support the sense of regionalism or cosmopolitanism the Korean wave is creating (Dator & Seo, 2004; Shim, 2009), others feel that it is just another foreign culture clearly differentiated from the local culture (K. Yin & Liew, 2005). For example, some scholars criticize Korean cultural products for being based on modern Western ideas, for example, Hollywood-style blockbusters or American-style pop music. The development of the Korean media industries and their advance into regional markets are clearly a sign of the resilience of the subaltern – and of the "contamination of the imperial," considering the context of decades-long American domination of global cultural industries (Shim, 2009).

Also, due to the huge fandom for Korean culture, Korean celebrities have a big impact on consumer culture. It is easy to find Asian youth dressing up in the style of Korean celebrities in Vietnam or Taiwan (Shim, 2009). Given their infatuation with Korean culture, regional fans are eager to imitate Koreans, and this phenomenon has provoked a backlash (Maliangkay, 2006). The huge popularity of Korean cultural products raises concerns about cultural sovereignty. As Korean cultural products have spreading across various Asian countries, some have called for a ban on their import. From the perspective of cultural imperialism, they define the Korean wave as a cultural invasion and urge their governments to protect their domestic cultural industries from it. Several governments have indeed introduced protection programs. Among them, China's State Administration of Radio, Film and Television decided to cut its imports of Korean drama by half in 2006. Also in 2006 the Taiwanese government imposed a ban on the scheduling of foreign programs in prime-time slots and cut almost 80 percent of imports from Korea. In Japan, many blogs began to express antipathy to the Korean wave's cultural imperialism and are urging people to fight the invasion (Maliangkay, 2006). But some scholars feel that, while Korean pop culture may erode the audience's local identity, the argument against cultural imperialism often overlooks the fact that Korean cultural products are contributing to an increase in the diversity of the Asian cultural industries and are protecting it from the invasion of Western cultural imperialism.

At any rate, the Korean wave is now expanding beyond cultural products to drive a substantial increase in the sales of other Korean product categories from cars to tourism to electronics (Yoon et al., 2008). As Chua (2006) states, the fan base for Korean dramas has gone beyond the television screen, spawning behavioral changes in consumers. S. Lee (2003) sees Korean dramas as stimulating tourism, raising the number of tourists from China, Taiwan, Hong Kong, Singapore, Malaysia, and Thailand who come to Korea visit the sites where the dramas were shot. Led by the upsurge of popular cultures in Asia, Korea's media have evolved into some of the most dynamic markets, producing a wide range of cultural products from recorded music to film to computer games.

Media globalization in Asia is an ongoing process. However, there are several things to note. First, not only is Asia a vast region, with the world's largest population, but the countries in Asia also have different political, economic, and media systems, and very different cultural heritages. As a result, the pace, scale, scope, and focus of media globalization in Asian countries varies from one to another. Therefore, the above discussion of individual countries cannot necessarily be generalized to the whole of Asia. Second, the motivations in different countries for pushing media globalization also vary widely, ranging from the political and economic, to the cultural and ideological. Thus, more in-depth studies are needed to fully investigate the overt or covert rationale for media globalization. Third, like many other new trends, media globalization is also a double-edged sword. In different social settings and at different times, media globalization may have either positive or negative current or potential consequences or both kinds of consequences together.

References

2009 Report on Development of China's Radio, Film and Television (2009) Beijing: Xinhua Publishing House.

Bist, R. (2004, May 29) Indian Film Financing Comes of Age. *Online Asia Times*. At http://www.atimes.com/atimes/South_Asia/FE29Df05.html, accessed August 26, 2013.

Box Office India (2009) Overseas Earnings. At http://www.boxofficeindia.com/cpages.php?pageName=overseas_earners, accessed August 26, 2013.

Chan, J. (2009) *Toward Television Regionalization in Greater China and Beyond*. Paper presented at the International Conference on K-Pop, Seoul, South Korea.

China Internet Network Information Center (CNNIC) (2012) *CNNIC 30th Survey Report*. Beijing: China Internet Network Information Center.

Chua, B.-H. (2006) *East Asian Pop Culture: Consumer Communities and Politics of the National*. Paper presented at the International Conference on Cultural Space and the Public Sphere, Seoul, South Korea.

Clark, P. (2009, July 1) The Uninvited: A Horror/Suspense Movie Review. *Examiner*. At http://www.examiner.com/x-14390-Hartford-Movie-Reviews-Examiner~y2009m7d1-The-Uninvited-A-horrorsuspense-movie-review, accessed August 26, 2013.

Collections of China Journalism and Publishing Statistics, 1978–2008 (2009) Beijing: State Journalism and Publishing Bureau.

Cui, B., & Hou, Y. (2012) Convergence and Transition: China's Media Market 2011. In B. Cui (ed.), *2012 Report on Development of China's Media Industry*. Beijing: Social Sciences Academic Press, pp. 1–13.

Cui, B., & Zhou, K. (2009) Seeking Opportunities in Crisis: China's Media in 2009. In B. Cui (ed.), *2009 Report on Development of China's Media Industry*. Beijing: Social Sciences Academic Press, pp. 3–35.

Dator, J., & Seo, Y. (2004) Korea as the Wave of a Future: The Emerging Dream Society of Icons and Aesthetic Experience. Journal of Futures Studies 9(1), 31–44.

Deng, L. (2012) Review of China's Animation and Gaming Industry 2011. In B. Cui (ed.), *2012 Report on Development of China's Media Industry*. Beijing: Social Sciences Academic Press, pp. 195–207.

Faiola, A. (2006, August 31) Japanese Women Catch the "Korean Wave." *Washington Post*. At http://www.washingtonpost.com/wp-dyn/content/article/2006/08/30/AR2006083002985.html, accessed August 26, 2013.

Frater, P. (2003a, May) Italy's Eagle Swoops on Its First Korean Title. Screen Daily 12(5), 7–8.

Frater, P. (2003b, February) Korea's Jail Breakers Given New Dimension. Screen Daily 12(2), 4–5.

He, D., Zhang, S., & Wang, W. (2012) Developing Situation of China's Media Industry 2011. In B. Cui (ed.), *2012 Report on Development of China's Media Industry*. Beijing: Social Sciences Academic Press, pp. 22–9.

Heo, J. (2002) The "Hanryu" Phenomenon and the Acceptability of Korean TV Dramas in China. Korean Journal of Broadcasting 16(1), 496–529.

Hong, J. (2009) Television. In *Berkshire Encyclopedia of China*. Great Barrington, MA: Berkshire, pp. 2212–16.

Hong, J., Lu, Y., & Zou, W. (2008) CCTV in the Reform Years: Setting Up a New Model for China's Television? In Y. Zhu & C. Berry (eds.), *TV China*. Bloomington: Indiana University Press, pp. 40–55.

Hu, Z., Li, J., & Huang, W. (2012) Development Report of China's Television Industry 2011. In B. Cui (ed.), *2012 Report on Development of China's Media Industry*. Beijing: Social Sciences Academic Press, pp. 140–8.

Iwabuchi, K. (2008) Cultures of Empire: Transnational Media Flows and Cultural Disconnections in East Asia. In P. Chakravartty & Y. Zhao (eds.), *Global Communications: Toward a Transcultural Political Economy*, pp. 143–61. Lanham, MD: Rowman & Littlefield.

Japan External Trade Organization (JETRO) (2005a) Industrial Report: Japan Animation Industry Trends. Japan Economic Monthly (June), 36–9.

Japan External Trade Organization (JETRO) (2005b) Japanese Film Industry. *Japan Economic Monthly* (July), 22–6.

Japan External Trade Organization (JETRO) (2009) Japanese Film Industry. *Japan Economic Monthly* (August), 18–23.

Jayaram, P. (2005, April 22) Chinese premier in India: India, China to end border dispute, launch strategic partnership. *News India Times*. At http://www.newsindia-times.com/nit/2005/04/22/tow14-top.html, accessed October 11, 2010.

Joo, J. (2005) From Periphery to Center: The Rise of the Korean Film Industry Since the Late 1990s. Paper presented at the New York Conference on Asian Studies. At http://www.google.com/url?sa=t&source=web&ct=res&cd=1&url=http%3A%2F%2Fwww.newpaltz.edu%2Fasianstudies%2Fnycas%2F2005%2520GRAD%2520Ryan%2520Prize%2520Jeongsuk%2520Joo.pdf&ei=RN5WSvmqMMOGtgfHycHdCg&usg=AFQjCNEVwQ7wtF4wrXdYAJU5cCp1jE-IPg&sig2=Eozs1unUnzYDAJL-eZ5b1g, accessed August 26, 2013.

Kanayama, T., & Kanayama, T. (2005) Japan. In A. Cooper-Chen (ed.), *Global Entertainment Media: Content, Audiences, Issues*. Mahwah, NJ: Lawrence Erlbaum, pp. 145–60.

Kawakami, H., & Fisher, P. (1994) Eastern Barbarians: The Ancient Sounds of Korea. In S. Broughton & M. Ellingham (eds.), *World Music: The Rough Guide*. London: Rough Guides, pp. 468–72.

Kim, H. M. (2005) Korean TV Dramas in Taiwan: With an Emphasis on the Localization Process. *Korea Journal* 5(12), 183–205.

Kim, K. (2008, October 18) Korean Film's Remake Rights Sold to Hollywood. *MaxMovie* 8(3), 11–14.

Kim, M. (2004) Cultural Proximity and the Type of Korean Television Programs in Asian Market. Paper presented at the 6th World Media Economics Conference. At http://www.cem.ulaval.ca/pdf/kim.pdf, accessed August 26, 2013.

Kim, S. (2004) "Renaissance of Korean National Cinema" as a Terrain of Negotiation and Contention between the Global and the Local: Analyzing Two Korean Blockbusters, *Shiri* (1999) and *JSA* (2000). *Essex Grad Journal* 3(5), 18–20.

KOCCA (2011) *Surveys of Overseas Content Industries: India*. Seoul: Korea Creative Contents Agency.

Kohli-Khandekar, V. (2006) *The Indian Media Business*, 2nd edn. New Delhi: Response Books.

KPMG & Confederation of Indian Industry (CII) (2005) *Indian Entertainment Industry Focus 2010: Dreams to Reality*. New Delhi: Confederation of Indian Industry.

Lee, S. (2003, April 8) Seoul Survivor. *Straits Times* (Singapore) (April 8), 16.

Lee, S., Kim, E., & Sung, H. (2009) On the Exportability of Korean Movies. *Review of Development Economics* 13(1), 28–38.

Lee, S. W., & Waterman, D. (2006) Theatrical Feature Film Trade in the United States, Europe, and Japan since the 1950s: An Empirical Study of the Home Market Effect. Paper presented at the TPRC Conference on Communication, Information, and Internet Policy, Arlington, VA.

Lee, Y., & Nakashima, R. (2012) PSY's Riches from "Gangnam Style" Not Made at Home. Washington Times http://www.washingtontimes.com/news/2012/dec/5/psys-riches-from-gangnam-style-not-made-at-home/?page=all, accessed September 9, 2013.

Liu, L., & Lu, J. (2009) Overview of the Development of China's Movie Industry. In In B. Cui (ed.), *2009 Report on Development of China's Media Industry*. Beijing: Social Sciences Academic Press, pp. 247–53.

Lorenzen, M. (2009) *Go West: The Growth of Bollywood*. Handelshøjskolen, Denmark: Copenhagen Business School.

Lorenzen, M., & Taeube, F. A. (2009) *Breakout from Bollywood? Internationalization of Indian Film Industry*. Handelshøjskolen, Denmark: Danish Research Unit for Industrial Dynamics.

Lu, B. (2009) China's Animation Products Begin to Enter the International Market. In B. Cui (ed.), *2009 Report on Development of China's Media Industry*. Beijing: Social Sciences Academic Press, pp. 298–302.

Lu, D., & Gao, F. (2009) Surrounding, Breaking Out, or Entering. In B. Cui (ed.), *2009 Report on Development of China's Media Industry*. Beijing: Social Sciences Academic Press, pp. 228–34.

Mahanty, S. (2012, November 25) India and China Negotiate Film Co-Production Deal. *New York Daily News*. At http://india.nydailynews.com/business/10c3905f7dbe1dcfdc51d3fab821a10c/india-and-china-negotiate-film-coproduction-deal, accessed August 26, 2013.

Maliangkay, R. (2006) When the Korean Wave Ripples. *IIAS Newsletter* 33(2), 15.

Miao, W., Yue, X., & Lu, S. (2012) Analysis on China's Media Industry Segments of the Market 2011. In B. Cui (ed.), *2012 Report on Development of China's Media Industry*. Beijing: Social Sciences Academic Press, pp. 30–8.

Ministry of Culture, Sports, and Tourism (2012) *Annual White Paper of Content Industy in 2011*. Seoul: Ministry of Culture, Sports, and Tourism.

Ministry of Internal Affairs and Communications (2012) *Annual Report*. Tokyo: Ministry of Internal Affairs and Communications.

Ministry of Overseas Indian Affairs (2012) *Population of Non-Resident Indians: Country Wise*. New Delhi: Ministry of Overseas Indian Affairs.

Mishra, V. (2006) *Bollywood Cinema: A Critical Genealogy*. Wellington, NZ: Asian Studies Institute.

Pendakur, M. (2003) *Indian Popular Cinema: Industry, Ideology, and Consciousness*. New York: Hampton Press.

Phelps, E. (2012) Understanding Electoral Turnout Among British Young People: A Review of the Literature. *Parliamentary Affairs* 65(1), 281–99.

PwC (2006) *Global Entertainment and Media Outlook 2006–2010*. New York: PricewaterhouseCoopers.

PwC (2011) *Indian Entertainment and Media Outlook 2010*. NewYork: PricewaterhouseCoopers.

Rao, S. (2005) India. In A. Cooper-Chen (ed.), *Global Entertainment Media: Content, Audiences, Issues*. New York: Routledge.

Rao, S. (2007) The Globalization of Bollywood: An Ethnography of Non-Elite Audiences in India. *Communication Review* 10(1), 57–76.

Shim, D. (2009) Hybridigy and the Rise of Korean Popular Culture in Asia. *Media, Culture & Society* 28(1), 25–44.

Shukla, S. (2003) *India Abroad: Diasporic Cultures of Postwar America and England*. Princeton, NJ: Princeton University Press.

Taplin, J. (2007) "Crouching Tigers": Emerging Challenges to U.S. Entertainment Supremacy in the Movie Business. *Observatorio Journal* 2, 167–190.

UNESCO (2011) New Release of Cinema Data. At http://www.uis.unesco.org/culture/Pages/cinema-data-release-2011.aspx, accessed August 26, 2013.

WebJapan (2005) Howl's Moving Castle. *Trends in Japan*. At http://web-japan.org/trends/arts/art050314.html, accessed August 26, 2013.

Wildman, S. S., & Siwek, S. E. (1988) *International Trade in Films and Television Programs*. Cambridge, MA: Ballinger.

Woodman-Maynard, K. (2006) Bollywood and the Indian Film Industry. *Indian Business*. At http://www.indianbusiness.com/article/bollywood-the-indian-film-industry, accessed July 18, 2010.

Xu, G. (2008) Remaking East Asia, Outsourcing Hollywood. In L. Hunt & L. Wing-Fai (eds.), *East Asian Cinemas: Exploring Transnational Connections on Film*. New York: I. B. Tauris, pp. 192–202.

Xu, M. (2007) New Plan of China Film Overseas Promotion Corporation. *Variety China* (May 14), 9.

Yash Raj Films (2009) Company Info. At http://www.yashrajfilms.com/AboutUs/CompanyInfo.aspx?SectionCode=PRO001, accessed August 26, 2013.

Yin, H. (2009) Memo on 2008 China's Film Industry. In B. Cui (ed.), *2009 Report on Development of China's Media Industry*. Beijing: Social Sciences Academic Press, pp. 254–74.

Yin, H., & Cheng, W. (2012) Memo of China's Film Industry 2011. In B. Cui (ed.), *2012 Report on Development of China's Media Industry*. Beijing: Social Sciences Academic Press, pp. 170–94.

Yin, K., & Liew, K. (2005) Hallyu in Singapore: Korean Cosmopolitanism or the Consumption of Chineseness? *Korea Journal* 5(7), 161–6.

Yoon, J. S. et al. (2008) *A Research for Promoting a Continuous Development of Korean Wave*. Seoul: Korea Foundation for International Culture Exchange.

Zhu, Y., & Berry, C. (2009) *TV China*. Bloomington: Indiana University Press.

15

The Role of Global Advertising

Introduction

Commercial advertising thrives in a free enterprise environment. Market-driven economies require advertising in order to succeed in merchandising goods and services both domestically and globally. Today, cultural industries, like others, seek marketing and advertising campaigns in order to create consumer awareness and increase sales. They do this nationally and, increasingly, internationally. As major multimedia corporations became more global, so their need for global advertising grows. And as the global economy expands, so does the need for global products, global brands, and global services such as advertising. Marketing and advertising globally has cost and brand image advantages. British Airways, Coca-Cola, Ford, General Motors, British Petroleum, General Electric, Microsoft, Disney, McDonald's, and Procter & Gamble have created persuasive global strategies involving a global corporate vision with a single voice or theme. For example, in 1994 "IBM announced the appointment of one advertising agency with the prime responsibility for executing IBM's strategic voice singularly around the world."[1] Now many multinational corporations seek out a single ad agency with a global reach to provide a broad range of advertising-related services. The biggest unresolved issue in global advertising is still focused around a historical debate concerning standardization of all advertising versus adaptation of copy as well as strategies to local markets and tastes.[2] In the future the scales will likely tilt toward the standardization approach as multinational firms seek greater economies of scale, and with the huge advertising budgets company headquarters will demand a greater role in the decision-making process.

The expansion of major multinational advertising agencies has become a key component in international communication for five major reasons:

1 Corporations themselves are going increasingly global and taking their core-based advertising agencies with them. This includes communication corporations as well as

Global Communication: Theories, Stakeholders, and Trends, Fourth Edition. Thomas L. McPhail.
© 2014 John Wiley & Sons, Inc. Published 2014 by John Wiley & Sons, Inc.

other sectors such as transportation, food and beverage, natural resources, credit cards, and so on. As the global economy expands, so does advertising.

2   As multimedia outlets – from privatized radio and television networks in Europe to new media and print outlets in Latin America – expand, they require successful advertising campaigns in order to generate the revenue and to attract the new customers necessary to succeed as viable commercial enterprises.

3   The growth of satellite-delivered broadcasting channels, along with a rapid expansion of cable systems and networks, have in turn generated demand for increased use of advertising agencies in order to develop a sufficient customer base for either the new services themselves or the products they advertise.

4   Their competition is doing it, so they have to either merge or be left behind.

5   The industry is changing as global ad spending is migrating to digital and automated trading of ad space. This is creating competition from Google, Facebook, and other new high-tech companies.

The following sections highlight the major global advertising agencies that now rank among the biggest firms in the world (Table 15.1). They are not the advertising agencies of an earlier era which offered a limited menu of services to a few corporations within a single nation. Today, these advertising agencies are truly global in scope. Many are working with global products and offering a vast array of services far beyond print,[3] graphics, and placement advice, services that include everything from accounting practices, to training, to total quality management (TQM) practices, to data collection and analysis, all to assist with the development of corporate strategy plans and web-based activities.[4] The modern advertising agency is a major partner with its clients, working together so that both become successful commercial undertakings. It is difficult to conceive of international communications in the current and future global environment without global advertising agencies as a key component.

Collectively these companies spend billions annually on competitive advertising globally. This is the main reason why every major global ad agency has to have a significant corporate presence in the United States. Also, every one of the 10 largest advertisers has major global markets outside the United States, and therefore their ad agencies have to go global in order to keep and properly service these lucrative and prestigious accounts.

These agencies are based in core nations and they carry with them to all semiperipheral and some peripheral nations the values, attitudes, and business practices of their home nations. For example, these agencies employ the latest in research[5] including surveys, focus

Table 15.1 Top advertising companies, 2013

1	Omnicom Group (United States) and Publicis Group (France)
2	WPP Group (United Kingdom)
3	Interpublic Group (United States)
4	Dentsu Inc. (Japan)
5	Havas Advertising (France)
6	Hakuhodo DY Holdings (Japan)
7	Acxiom (United States)
8	MDC Partners (United States and Canada)
9	Asatsu-DK (Japan)

Table 15.2 Top 10 global advertisers by expenditure, 2013, according to Nielsen

1	Procter & Gamble
2	Unilever
3	L'Oréal
4	Ford Motor Company
5	Toyota Motor Corporation
6	General Motors
7	Volkswagen Group
8	AT&T
9	McDonald's
10	Nestlé

groups, knowledge management,[6] and demographic analysis, so that foreign customers look to these agencies rather than to local, frequently small, firms, which do not have the arsenal of services, staff resources, or highly educated professionals with MBA or PhD credentials, that they would need in order to compete effectively. Finally, the issue of advertising is not restricted to narrow concerns such as the availability of services from major multinational advertising agencies; rather, there is a larger, more conceptual concern of market economies functioning in a free enterprise and democratic environment. Advertising does not fare well or serve any substantial purpose, for example, in totalitarian countries. In such countries, there are usually only a few products of substantial value to purchase, and even when such products are available only the ruling elite would have the funds to purchase them. Advertising is a necessary part of the expanding market-based global economy, in which nation-states, whether in the peripheral or semiperipheral regions, not only have to contend with foreign media, but also with foreign advertising agencies. With deregulation, privatization, and expanding economies, the strategic goal of more and more nations has to take into account as a high priority the consequences of advertising for consumers as well as for their cultures as a whole. Thus, the impact of global advertising has become an important ingredient in an examination of international communication. A good example of the growing role of advertising is the deregulation sweeping western Europe that is resulting in a substantial increase in the number of commercial radio, television, and cable services. This broadly based philosophic and economic movement has consequences for other nations as well, particularly those in eastern Europe:

> Thus, the different East European regimes were confronted not only with the dangers inherent in the importation of programs. They also had to face the more serious dangers inherent in the importation of a mode of organization of the audiovisual sphere inspired by the logic of private enterprise, and of a matrix governed by values in total contradiction with those which they continued to defend.[7]

Today, few defend or call for a return to government-owned and controlled media, or media with no advertising. More media, more choice, along with plenty of advertising, is the accepted environment being promoted by multinational conglomerates, clients, and ad agencies alike.

The hallmark of global advertising is the trend embracing mergers and acquisitions. For many years the British firm WPP Group held the number one spot. In 2004 WPP purchased Grey Global Group of New York for nearly $1.5 billion. In October 2008 WPP purchased Taylor Nelson Sofres for £1.6 billon in order to stay on top, only to be toppled by the merger of Omnicom and Publicis in 2013.

The question is why there are so many mergers in this industry. The answer is fourfold. First, it is hoped that some positive synergy will come about as a result of the expansion. Second, in some cases, the firms want to acquire creative talent that is not available in-house. Third, firms may seek to acquire a strategic niche to complement their current strengths. And fourth, some firms realize that they have to be aggressive and expand before a competitor attempts a take-over either of them or of a rival they are looking at. Havas of France may be in this position since it failed to win the bidding war with WPP for Grey Global. It is very difficult for mid-sized advertising firms like Havas to survive in the highly competitive global arena.

Finally, all ad agencies have creative talent, but to have one's commercial stand out from the rest is a daunting task. Since there are thousands of commercials seeking our attention, it takes imagination and creativity to get one's message to stand out. Frequently this means being on the cutting edge or pushing the ad or marketing envelope. If an ad goes too far, controversy often results. Two companies known globally for pushing the envelope are Benetton and Nike. For example, Nike ran racy ads during the 2000 Olympics and some media pulled them. Also in 2004 Nike had a large media campaign in China featuring Le Bron James of basketball fame. In the commercial he slays a dragon, a symbol of Chinese culture and historic pride. Nike finally pulled that ad. On the other hand, Benetton uses provocative ads to promote social issues. One of their global ads had an oil-drenched duck in a pool of oil – no clothes or other products were shown in the picture.

Omnicom Group and Publicis Group

Omnicom and Publicis are the world's largest advertising organization. The two giants merged in 2013 and have two head offices. Omnicom is headquartered in the United States and Publicis in France. Omnicom was formed in 1986 and is a strategic holding company. Its 2008 revenue exceeded $13 billion. Like other global advertising firms, it had been experiencing slower growth since 9/11, but it appears to be moving forward with many of the top industry talent. Omnicom employs 71,000 people and has grown recently with the addition of new affiliates. High-profile clients include PepsiCo, McDonald's, General Electric, Intel, Dell, Visa, and AT&T. Omnicom provides marketing and consulting services through its Diversified Agency Services unit, which includes Fleishman-Hillard, one of the world's largest public relations firms.

The Omnicom Group operates three global agency networks (BBDO Worldwide, DDB Worldwide, and TBWA Worldwide), plus a range of independent agencies including Cline, Davis & Mann (CDM); Goodby, Silverstein & Partners; and GSD&M. The three global agency networks all rank in the top 10 global advertising agencies.

BBDO Worldwide, headquartered in New York City, operates nearly 300 offices in 77 countries. From 1994 through 1998, BBDO received 200 broadcast advertising awards in the five major global competitions, substantially more than any other agency. In 2001 it was chosen as the leading global agency of the year by several trade publications. Major global business comes from PepsiCo, Ikea, FedEx, and General Electric. DDB Worldwide, headquartered in New York City, operates over 200 offices in 90 countries. At the 45th

International Advertising Festival in Cannes, DDB agencies won a total of 34 Lions (the Oscars of the advertising world), more than any other advertising agency network, for the third year in a row. Major global accounts are the Sheraton Hotels and FTD. TBWA Worldwide, the last of the three networks of Omnicom, is also headquartered in New York City. It operates 258 offices in 77 countries. In the United States *Creativity* magazine named TBWA Worldwide Creative Agency of the Year for four years in a row. Major companies with TBWA Worldwide global accounts are Adidas, Apple, Infiniti, McDonald's, Sony PlayStation, and Visa.

Ketchum PR Agency: Ethics Issue

The Omnicom Group owns the public relations firm Ketchum. (It also owns another major public relations firm Fleishman Hillard, which also got into billing troubles in California.) In 2005 Ketchum received much unwanted media attention for laundering a large federal government contract with the Department of Education. It turns out that Ketchum hired a prominent conservative commentator, Armstrong Williams, to covertly hype an education program without disclosing that he was on the pay-roll of Ketchum. Nor did he or Ketchum say openly which federal department was paying for Omnicom's PR agency. Another of the commentator's clients for his newspaper columns was the Tribune Company, which immediately fired him for his ethical lapse. Williams did a number of shows on radio and television, as well as print pieces, without divulging that he was being well paid for propaganda pieces for the federal government. The public relations professional association, the Public Relations Society of America, and many others deplored this ethical mess which Ketchum had facilitated. After weeks of negative media attention, Ketchum finally admitted its ethical lapse. It will be interesting to see, if over time, other clients, such as Cingular, Home Depot, Eastman Kodak, and PepsiCo, decide to leave this ethically challenged agency – or what the parent conglomerate, Omnicom Group, does about the image nightmare Ketchum has created for it.

Publicis is the largest ad agency in Europe and was founded in 1926. Following its merger with Omnicom, it now has the largest global footprint, with over 56,000 employees in 104 nations. Since 1998 one of its main subsidiaries has been San Francisco-based Publicis & Hal Riney, which provides Publicis with a strategic foothold in the lucrative North American market. Its major clients include Sprint and Hewlett-Packard but in 2002 it lost the $300 million Saturn account.

In 2000 Publicis Group purchased Saatchi & Saatchi for $1.9 billion as part of its global expansion. In 1999 it bought 49 percent of Chicago-based Burrell Communications. Burrell is a large ad agency specializing in African American markets. It has several major clients including Coca-Cola, McDonald's, Procter & Gamble, and Sears.

Through a series of major strategic acquisitions, including buying out major rival Saatchi & Saatchi in 2000, Publicis is seeking to become a European and global agency offering a broad range of services. It is trying to move into emerging multinational markets by responding to industry pressure to add foreign subsidiaries.

The Saatchi brothers co-founded Saatchi & Saatchi in 1970. The company used to be part of the advertising giant Cordiant, which in 1997 split into two firms, Cordiant Communications and Saatchi & Saatchi. Since the split of the giant company, business has been good for both parties, which have a large European focus. The international holding company Saatchi & Saatchi currently has operations in advertising, marketing, and communications and employs 6,000 workers. Its namesake advertising agency, which generates more than 80 percent of the company's sales, has about 150 offices in more than 90 countries and serves global clients such as Procter & Gamble, Toyota, and General Mills.

The Saatchi brothers made some individuals wealthy when they overpaid for venerable agencies in their misguided strategy to buy their way to the number one spot. For example, when Charles and Maurice Saatchi purchased Bates, then the third largest US ad agency, for $400 million down in 1986 and another $50 million in 1998, it was the highest price paid for an advertising agency. The brothers also paid a premium for two other US agencies that year, Dancer Fitzgerald Sample and Backer & Spielvogel. A year later, they attempted to buy J. Walter Thompson, the United States' oldest advertising agency.

The ongoing global acquisition frenzy in the ad industry can be traced back to the Saatchi brothers. In 1994 Maurice Saatchi was dismissed as chairman of the holding company, and Charles Saatchi left a short time later. The company continued without them and managed to acquire major accounts such as Toyota and Procter & Gamble. More than half of its worldwide billings come from North America. Saatchi & Saatchi is key in assisting Publicis become a more dominant global agency.

In 2002 Publicis purchased US-based Bcom3 for $3 billion. Bcom3 was the result of a merger in 2000 between BDM, the Leo Group, and the MacManus Group. Bcom3 was 20 percent owned by Dentsu. The merged firms provide a broad range of communication services such as advertising, public relations, marketing, research, and media buying and planning. One of the partners, Leo Group, has a proud history. Leo Burnett, the founder, has been responsible for creating some of the most successful marketing icons in the United States, including such campaigns as Tony the Tiger, the Marlboro Man, the Pillsbury Doughboy, and the Jolly Green Giant. Founded in 1935, the company provides a full range of advertising, marketing, and communication services to clients such as Coca-Cola, Nintendo, Walt Disney, General Motors, Kellogg's, and Procter & Gamble. Burnett has a 49 percent stake in UK-based Bartle Bogle Hegarty. Burnett's international billings alone were close to $7 billion, and several of its blue-chip clients have been with the firm for decades. Over $4 billion in billings come from non-US-based offices, reflecting Burnett's effective global strategy. Yet the merged firm was still only mid-sized in a land of ad giants and thus to survive it was sold to Publicis. In turn Publicis, which has acquired several key firms, now provides its international clients with seamless and multifaceted ad and marketing advice. For example, it has acquired two of the world's top digital agencies, Digitas and Razorfish. This makes considerable strategic sense since Internet-based advertising is increasing while at the same time print and television advertising are declining. Publicis recently invested in a mobile polling start-up which focuses on emerging markets around the globe.

WPP Group

WPP is the second largest advertising and communication services group in the world. It consists of over 326 companies with over 3,000 global offices operating in 110 nations. WPP employs more than 165,000 people. The company is largely the creation of English businessman Martin Sorrell, who made his name as financial director of advertising at Saatchi & Saatchi, which he joined in 1977 and where he played a key role in its growth through acquisitions.[8] However, in 1986 Sorrell set out to create his own advertising firm, the WPP Group. In the first half of 1987 WPP turned its attention to the United States market and acquired several US companies.

WPP is the world's second largest communication group, providing services to local, multinational, and global clients, including more than 300 of Fortune's Global 500. WPP is engaged in advertising, media planning and buying, market research, consulting, public relations, and specialist communications. More than 50 percent of WPP's sales come from advertising, and it derives more than 88 percent of its sales from outside the United Kingdom. This full-service agency specializes in the planning, production, and placing of advertising for clients in all categories, from radio commercials, to posters and print, to interactive television commercials, to Internet and business. Although advertising makes up half its sales, WPP also offers clients media planning and buying, market research and consulting, public relations, and specialty communications. Some of WPP's global clients are IBM, Kraft Foods, GlaxoSmithKline, Procter & Gamble, Johnson & Johnson, Nestlé, and Unilever. WPP's most important single territory is the United States, which in 2008 accounted for around 35 percent of its income; the United Kingdom accounted for about 13 percent. The 2008 revenues were over £7.4 billion (about $12.3 billion). This is a significant increase from the early 1990s, when WPP was forced to suspend all dividend payments and refinance its considerable debt.

Some of WPP Group's major subsidiaries are Young & Rubicam (Y&R), JWT, Ogilvy & Mather Worldwide, Schematic, Mindshare, Hill & Knowlton, Kantar Group, and Research International. Through WPP's subsidiaries, the group is moving into new areas such as the Internet, data mining, behavior modeling, and customer retention work. WPP purchased Y&R in 2000 in a $4.7 billion acquisition to form the world's largest advertising and services group. In 2008 Y&R was the fourth largest US ad agency, with 16,000 employees in 186 offices all over the world. It offers a broad range of ad, media, and communication services as well as the controlled public relations giant Burson-Marsteller. Y&R was an employee-owned private company until 1998 when it went public to raise funds for further global expansion. It utilized a number of globally based video-conferencing sites for both management and clients. Through these sites, Y&R attempts to focus its creative resources, regardless of location, to meet clients' needs. It has a major global marketing subsidiary called Wunderman, which uses a technology focus to assist clients with e-commerce and Internet-based marketing needs and solutions. Wunderman has over 6,000 employees working in over 50 nations. Overall WPP's clients constitute over 340 of the Fortune Global 500 companies.

Interpublic Group

The world's number three advertising group, the Interpublic Group of Companies (IPC), is headquartered in New York and employs over 45,000 people. It serves a total of more than 4,000 multinational, regional, and local clients. The company's roots trace back to 1930 when two firms merged to create McCann Erickson. IPC has five global operating divisions: Constituency Management Group, FCB Group, Independent Agencies, McCann Erickson Worldwide, and the Partnership. The various divisions serve the advertising, marketing, and other strategic needs of clients including global companies such as Axe, Coca-Cola, Johnson & Johnson, Unilever, and General Motors. IPC's revenue in 2012 was over $7 billion. Over the last 20 years, IPC's revenue has increased by more than 1,100 percent and its net income has risen 1,800 percent.

IPC has offices in more than 100 countries. Its international public relations unit is one of the largest PR firms in the world. Interpublic is the parent organization of a growing number of leading advertising agencies and marketing communications companies. As the holding company, IPC creates ads through its global networks: McCann Erickson, Lowe Worldwide, Gotham Inc., Jack Morton Worldwide, MRM Worldwide, Octagon Worldwide and Draftfcb. The McCann Erickson Worldgroup was formed as a worldwide communications firm; it is dedicated to providing a full spectrum of high-quality marketing, research, and communication services. It is one of the most powerful networks of ad agencies in the world and has a rapidly expanding portfolio of marketing communications companies that operate in parallel with the ad agencies. It has also recognized the increasing significance of social media. For example, Kandace Hudspeth, global director of social media at McCann Erickson highlights the shift to digital media: "The social media phenomenon is far more than one of the 'bright shiny objects' that tend to catch the attention of Madison Avenue, Ms. Hudspeth said, because the intensifying interest among consumers in social media means 'there's a real need from a marketplace perspective to have an offering in the space' that would 'help the brands we work with be set up for success.'"[8]

Dentsu Inc.

Dentsu is the fourth largest global ad agency and the top agency in Japan. The roots of Dentsu date back to 1901 when Hoshiro Mitsunaga founded the Japan Advertising Ltd and the Telegraphic Service Company. By 1946, Dentsu had become a commercial broadcasting, public relations, and advertising entity that modernized through extensive market research. In 1951 Dentsu incorporated its radio and television divisions and produced Japan's first television broadcast. By 1959, it had expanded to the United States by opening an office in New York. Two years later, in 1961, Dentsu joined with Young & Rubicam, the US-based agency, to become a joint venture firm for several major accounts. Dentsu agency continued to expand globally with offices in Chicago, Los Angeles, Honolulu, Paris, Melbourne, and Taiwan. By the mid-1970s, Dentsu was ranked the number one global advertising agency. By the 1980s, it was broadening its efforts with its Total Communication Service and the opening of additional offices in Europe and the Middle East.

The company has over 31,000 employees and is headquartered in Tokyo. It maintains and operates 32 offices in Japan and has subsidiaries and affiliates in 27 countries around the globe. Dentsu is particularly strong in the United States, Asia, and the Middle East. It dominates by collecting half of Japan's prime-time billings. Dentsu has over 6,000 clients and some of its major global clients are Canon, Sony, Hitachi, Bell Atlantic, and Toyota. It also has a division that specializes in sports marketing.

The Dentsu corporate philosophy was revised in 1986. Originally developed to define Dentsu's "role as a full-service communications company, the corporate philosophy is now composed of corporate objectives, employee qualifications, 10 work guidelines, and the slogan that reflects the company's commitment: 'Communications Excellence.'"[9] The managers of Dentsu offer total communication services that include account services, market research and strategic planning, creative development, media services, sales promotion, corporate communications, sports marketing, event promotion, new media and digital advertising, and advertising support systems. Dentsu is committed to making sure each client's message reaches its designated target through its Total Communication Service.

Dentsu has a strategic partnership with Young & Rubicam (acquired by WPP in 2000). In 2012 it purchased the British-based Aegis Group which alone has 16,000 employees and operates in over 80 nations globally.

Havas Media

Havas Media is a leading pan-European agency based in France, like Publicis. It operates in over 88 countries in addition to Europe, and employs around 15,000 people worldwide. Europe represents 59 percent of its revenue, with France the major player, and North America providing 30 percent of its revenue. Since 75 percent of all global advertising is by US firms, global advertising agencies that are not US-based require an effective network of subsidiaries in the United States to succeed as global firms. In Latin America, Havas Advertising operates in Mexico, Brazil, and Argentina. It also has a major sports planning and marketing subsidiary. Major clients include Walmart, Kraft, and British Petroleum.

Havas had been aiming to become one of the top global advertising agencies in the next decade, but in 2005 it missed buying US-based Grey Global to the British ad conglomerate WPP. As an international agency, Havas should increase its multicultural activities through a global strategy of meeting the needs of clients and their products through a larger network of global brand managers. Havas also needs to increase its Internet and web activities. Havas's global ad agency is known as Euro RSCG Worldwide. The merger of the French ad firm Publicis with the American Omnicom has put considerable pressure on Havas to partner with another firm or face a dim future.

Hakuhodo DY Holdings

Hakuhodo is the second largest advertising conglomerate in Japan and the sixth largest in the world. It is headquartered in Tokyo. The holding company was established in October of 2003. It has over 10,000 employees and two main branches: its advertising and marketing companies and its integrated media companies. The advertising companies include Hakuhodo, Daiko, and Yomiko. Hakuhodo dates back to 1895 and in addition to its 22 offices in Japan, it has 68 offices across 18 countries worldwide. Clients include such brands as Sony, Panasonic, Lycra, DuPont, and Toshiba. Daiko was founded in 1945 and focuses on the Japanese and Asian markets. In 2005 alone, it brought in $1.5 billion. Its clients include Nintendo, Panasonic, and Nike Japan. Yomiko was founded in 1929, and like Daiko, it concentrates on the domestic market with some activity in China. These three advertising companies joined together in 2003 primarily to compete better with their rival, Dentsu.

Acxiom Corporation

With only 6,000 employees Acxiom is a little-known firm but works on every continent. It specializes in providing marketing technology and services and works through three divisions: marketing and data services, IT infrastructure management, and other services. The company has amassed the largest global database on customers, with over 50 trillion data transactions per year. This is why, in part, they have acquired major clients like FedEx, IBM, Microsoft, and AT&T.

MDC Partners

MDC Partners, previously known as Maxxcom, is based in Toronto and New York City. Founded in 1986, it is Canada's largest advertising group. However, MDC is best known for its American holdings in Crispin Porter & Bogusky and Kirshenbaum Bond. It has interests in three additional marketing companies. It has over 6,000 employees and works in two divisions: strategic marketing services and performance marketing services. Almost one-fifth of MDC's income is from Sprint alone. Other clients include American Express, Under Armour, Chrysler, Serta, and Vanguard.

Asatsu-DK

Founded in 1999 with the merger of Asatsu and Dai Ichi Kikaku, Asatsu-DK (ADK) is Japan's third largest advertising firm after Dentsu and Hakuhodo. ADK has 38 offices in 15 countries around the globe and enjoys a good working relationship with one of its main shareholders, the WPP Group, which owns 20 percent of ADK stock. ADK also has a 5 percent interest in the WPP Group. While ADK is heavily involved in advertising, over half its income is generated by its media and television division. ADK's client list includes Toyota, Fuji, Nissan, Honda, Mercedes, and Ford among others.

Conclusions

The premier global advertising, marketing, and communication service agencies are in a highly competitive market for creative as well as web-savvy talent and additional customers who have a global footprint. The global agencies, all based in core nations, are located in North America, Japan, and Europe. The European and Japanese agencies need to have a major presence in North American markets because that is where the bulk of the corporations that engage in substantial international advertising are located. All major advertising firms have an extensive network of subsidiaries and offices in core, semiperipheral, and a few peripheral nations. Many of the offices are located in former colonies, particularly those of the United Kingdom, Spain, or France. During the past decades, a substantial amount of consolidation has taken place in the industry. The large firms are becoming larger in order to offer a broader range of services to current and prospective clients. Given the continuing global privatization of media outlets, as well as the increase in channel capacity as a result of technological innovations such as digital and mobile systems, there will be growing demand in both industrialized and emerging nations for commercially effective media advertising in the future. The merger mania continues and is putting pressure on many ad firms to seek partners. The ad world is shifting dramatically with growing activity in digital, mobile, and web-based advertising, and with new stakeholders such as Google and other Silicon Valley firms.

Finally, critics of cultural imperialism blame US ad agencies for their global reach on behalf of multinational clients. Yet the actual picture is quite different. The second largest ad agency in the world – WPP Group – is British. In fact, most of the top global ad agencies are not US-owned or US-controlled, with the exception of the Omnicom Group, the Interpublic Group, Acxiom, and MDC Partners. In reality, a set of core nations – the United States, France, the United Kingdom and Japan – are collectively spreading the advertising mantra and customer research services around the globe for a growing number of multinational firms. These giant ad firms and their clients have a strong vested corporate interest in expanding the global economy.

The role and impact of global advertising is a key component which helps define and substantiate both world system and electronic colonialism theories. The following list outlines the key links between global advertising agencies and world system and electronic colonialism theories.

- The major global ad agencies are all based in core nations. They act as savvy electronic imperialists on behalf of their global clients.
- All major agencies have to be based in or have major subsidiaries in the United States. US multinational firms purchase the bulk of global ads.
- All major agencies have offices in the major cities of other core nations.
- All major agencies have offices in semiperipheral nations, and this is the richest segment for future growth. Emerging markets are the new ad frontier.
- Due to the saturation and maturity of core markets, ad agency expansion is now available primarily through two routes: corporate expansion to additional major cities in the semiperipheral zones, particularly in Latin America or Asia; and acquisition of medium and small ad agencies, or related businesses in core nations. The big will get bigger in this industry.[10] Interpublic's bid to take over True North, WPP's buying of Grey Group, and Publicis' purchase of Bcom3 are excellent examples of this trend.
- Mid-sized ad firms, such as Havas, are poorly positioned or equipped to succeed in an industry of global giants.
- Major ad agencies employ extremely creative personnel plus cutting-edge research techniques to produce effective marketing and media commercials for their clients. As a result, they are major players in the electronic colonialism of the global marketplace. The firm NeuroFocus is focusing on the next generation of research techniques for the advertising industry to find out what is in the minds of consumers.
- There are no major agencies headquartered in peripheral nations. Nations in this least affluent zone consider themselves fortunate to host a branch office of some core-based major agency. The major agencies offer such a plethora of sophisticated services that indigenous ad firms in other zones find it virtually impossible to compete effectively for large international accounts.
- There is a fundamental shift occurring in the advertising business. Basically, traditional print media are reducing their advertising expenditures annually by about 10 percent. By contrast, the amount of advertising on the Internet and on mobile devices is increasing by about 10 percent annually. This movement from old media, particularly print (including such icons as the *Reader's Digest*), to new digital media will continue to benefit Internet-based companies.

Finally, the major agencies have branched out to offer full-service, seamless packages ranging from accounting to management training, to assessment, to strategic planning, to web and mobile media so that clients in semiperipheral and peripheral zones become ensnared in electronic colonialism practices without fully contemplating the long-run behavior, impact, and attitude shifts required.

In these latter zones, the countries with market-driven economies and expanding media outlets will experience more competition from core-based agencies seeking new accounts, including the strong possibility that core-based agencies will invest in local ad agencies as fully or partially owned or controlled subsidiaries. From the perspective of electronic colonialism, advertising has a greater role and impact on minds, lives, values, and ultimately purchasing behaviors than the audio or video programming or print copy that accompany or surround these ads. The goal of ad agencies is to influence attitudes, behaviors, and ultimately lifestyles. Their aim is to replace traditional buying habits with new behaviors leading to the consumption of core nations' goods and services. To some extent, global ad agencies are the foot-soldiers of electronic colonialism theory. They are promoting Western core nations' values and products to an ever increasing number of individuals and nations across the globe on a daily basis.

In the future, with the expansion of the global economy and markets, along with more media technologies, new commercial opportunities will appear for aggressive global ad agencies. This will clearly extend beyond cable, wireless, and satellite channels to include tablets and mobile devices. Major agencies are experiencing industry pressure to achieve a broader scale and scope by expanding their services and acquiring subsidiaries as they themselves confront global competition. More than half of the gross revenue of all major agencies now comes from global billing. Domestic billings, even in the United States, are no longer sufficient to sustain a major player among the global agencies. All stakeholders need a plethora of clients in an expanding range of countries, primarily the emerging regions since the core nations, in general, have mature or saturated markets. Advertising is an industry in which the chief stakeholders need to continue to grow and to acquire other firms before they find themselves being acquired by some other aggressive firm based in Europe, Japan, or the United States.

Notes

1. Wayne McCullough, "Global Advertising which Acts Locally: The IBM Subtitles Campaign," *Journal of Advertising Research* 36 (May–June 1996), 12.

2. M. Agrawal, "Review of a 40-year Debate in International Advertising Practitioner and Academician Perspectives to the Standardization/Adaptation Issue," *International Marketing Review* 12 (March 1995), 26–48.

3. "Press: Still the Largest Medium," *International Journal of Advertising* 18 (August 1999), 405–11.

4. Wossen Kassaye, "Global Advertising and the World Wide Web," *Business Horizons* 40 (May–June 1997), 33–42; Kuen-Hee Ju-Pak, "Content Dimensions of Web Advertising: A Cross-National Comparison," *International Journal of Advertising* 18 (May 1999), 207–232; and David Schumann and Esther Thorson, *Advertising and the World Wide Web*, Mahwah, NJ: Lawrence Erlbaum, 1999.

5. Demetrios Vakratsas and Tim Ambler, "How Advertising Works: What Do We Really Know?" *Journal of Marketing* 63 (January 1999), 26–43; Marieke Derlooij, *Global Marketing and Advertising*, London: Sage, 1997.

6. Michael Ewing and Doug West, "Advertising Knowledge Management: Strategies and Implications," *International Journal of Advertising* 19 (May 2000), 225–44.

7. Tristan Mattelart, "Transboundary Flows of Western Entertainment across the Iron Curtain," *Journal of International Communication* 6(2) (December 1999), 118.

8. Quoted in "A Top Agency Expands Its Footprint," *New York Times* (March 26, 2013), at http://www.nytimes.com/2013/03/27/business/media/mccann-always-on-renames-and-expands-agencys-social-media-unit.html?_r=0, accessed August 27, 2013.

9. http://www.dentsu.com/about/summary/history/p1978.html, accessed September 5, 2013.

10. Andreas Grein and Robert Ducoffe, "Strategic Responses to Market Globalization among Advertising Agencies," *International Journal of Advertising* 17 (August 1998), 301–20.

16

Summary and Conclusions

Introduction

This chapter reviews major aspects of the theories and landscape of global communication. Although there is currently relatively little concern about NWICO and the role of specialized United Nations agencies such as the International Telecommunication Union (ITU) and UNESCO, there is still concern about the cultural, social, and economic impacts of global communication trends. An unexpected exception is the ITU's role in the World Summit on the Information Society (WSIS). With widespread utilization of the Internet, transnational corporate acquisitions and mergers between media, telecommunications, and advertising corporations, and the expanding economic role of cultural industries, the issue of global communications has moved to a higher plane.

The impact of communications corporations is no longer a trivial or marginal matter for policymakers, researchers, and investors. All core nations rely for their economic health and viability on the success in foreign countries of their communications corporations. In previous decades, other leading corporations, such as those in the agriculture, automotive, natural resources, or aerospace industries, made major contributions to the creation of new jobs and new wealth, but that is no longer the case. Particularly with the end of the Cold War, the aerospace industry, which includes military aircraft, has seen a substantial reduction in employment, impact, and influence. As a result, the success of cultural industries, domestically and in foreign markets, has become a vital component of successful international trade. Those nations that enjoy the services of successful global communication corporations such as Disney, Time Warner, Viacom, Sony, News Corporation, Bertelsmann, and NBCUniversal, clearly count on these firms continuing to be successful in order to keep domestic employment high, as well as keep to their trade ledgers favorably balanced.

Cultural industries are a concern of national and international policymakers as well as of major corporations in North America, Europe, and Asia. With the drive to increase

Global Communication: Theories, Stakeholders, and Trends, Fourth Edition. Thomas L. McPhail.
© 2014 John Wiley & Sons, Inc. Published 2014 by John Wiley & Sons, Inc.

market share, coupled with more sophisticated technology and advertising, many new markets are being inundated with media fare created and owned by large foreign stakeholders. Now even more and larger foreign communication stakeholders are competing aggressively with each other in nations and markets on other continents – frequently several time zones and cultures away. This is particularly true in semiperipheral nations, which are the next frontier for multinational communication corporations. Core-based firms are aggressively developing and promoting new media opportunities in semiperipheral nations in order to increase their market share. Whether these firms are building new modern multiplex movie theaters or expanding access to the Internet, the semiperipheral nations have become the commercial battlefield for core communication stakeholders. Also, sponsored media seminars and workshops dealing with the values and practices of Western free press traditions are increasingly offered in semiperipheral nations. In this collective process, some indigenous cultures and languages are at significant risk.

Finally, the proliferation of global music, movies, advertising, and websites for pre-teens and teenagers has led to a new generation and a culture gap. These groups now have common experiences of audio and visual materials, activities, language, topics, and in many cases clothing and values that cut across this key demographic segment in North America, Asia, and Europe. These audio and video materials give them similar expressions and worldviews that are increasingly remote or different from those of their parents or even their older siblings. The attitudes, dress, language, and behavior of the adolescents (who are particularly heavy media consumers) in this growing global segment, including MTV groupies, Britney Spears lookalikes, rap music and Bart Simpson wannabes, are increasingly at odds with those of their parents' or their teachers' generation. Between them and their grandparents, particularly those who have migrated from another nation and whose first language is not English, this phenomenon has created an even greater cultural and behavioral divide.

As a result of the impact of global communication, many teenagers around the world have more in common with each other, thanks to MTV and social websites, than they do with other normative groups with whom they interact, including parents, grandparents, relatives, and teachers. The long-run implications of this relatively recent global media phenomenon have yet to be determined, researched, or fully understood.

One attempt to understand the role of media in society and its impact on culture is to view it through the concept of mediatization as well as of electronic colonialism theory (ECT), which look at mass media as having profound interrelated effects on institutions, individuals, and their culture and society. In "The Mediatization of Society" Stig Hjarvard stated:

> Mediatization is to be considered a double-sided process of high modernity in which the media on the one hand emerge as an independent institution with logic of its own that other social institutions have to accommodate to. On the other hand, media simultaneously become an integrated part of other institutions like politics, work, family, and religion as more and more of these institutional activities are performed through both interactive and mass media. The logic of the media refers to the institutional and technological modus operandi of the media, including the ways in which media distribute material and symbolic resources and make use of formal and informal rules.[1]

Mediatization takes a broader look at the significance of the mass media, much like ECT. In his article on "Science and the Media," Peter Weingart notes the key role the media play in terms of forming public opinion as well as the perception of self.[2]

Global Economy

For the major multimedia conglomerates, all located in Western core nations, the evolving reality is that their domestic markets are pretty well saturated. To create new customers at home is challenging and expensive in terms of advertising, marketing, and promotion. But a new revenue stream is being explored elsewhere. The semiperipheral and peripheral developing nations represent a new and vast frontier. Here is why.

In 2000 the global gross domestic product of non-core nations was 20 percent. By 2012 it had risen to 38 percent, and it is predicted to approach 50 percent by 2020. Two nations alone – China and Brazil – will drive much of the growth. For example, in Brazil four of the top five all-time feature films box office hits are American: *Titanic*, *Jaws*, *The Towering Inferno*, and *E.T.* Only one Latin American film, produced by Embrafilme, makes the top five list. This is why Hollywood is looking for international hits for future growth. A good example is the five installments of *The Twilight Saga*, which has earned close to $3 billion worldwide, most of it coming from sales outside North America. The same can be said of Disney's expansion strategy and its continuing growth in Asia, or the fact that all of the world's largest advertising agencies have offices in over 100 nations. The dynamic global economy is driving decision-making across the media spectrum, and its role and force will only increase over time.

This book has covered the major stakeholders across the communication, media, and advertising sectors. The information has been updated in every chapter. But that is only part of the scene. The other part consists of the almost daily mergers, acquisitions, and inventions, with the inventions frequently leading to new companies, such as Amazon, eBay, or Google. Down the road there may be a shift from personal computers to mobile devices and tablets. What impact that may have on traditional networks has yet to be determined. Basically the broadcasters have sold eyeballs and ears – called audiences – to advertisers. With the audience now able to access content from various mobile sources, and skip the advertisements, a new model will emerge to tap the revenue stream, or else the business may fail in the long run.

Two examples are the proposed spin-offs by Time Warner and News Corp. Time Warner is in the process of dividing product lines into two separate companies: one will focus on television and film production units and the other, to be named Time Inc., on print publications. Some of its iconic brands are *People*, *Time*, *Sports Illustrated*, and *In Style*. Time Warner hopes the move will bring strategic clarity to both companies. Yet across the print spectrum the clear trend is falling sales as well as revenues. News Corp is similarly splitting its assets for basically the same reasons. Rupert Murdoch will be chairman of both companies. The splitting of print from video may set a strong precedent across the entire industry, as print entities look more and more like dinosaurs. Michael Wolff, media analyst for *US Today*, sums up the situation:

> Print, at the nadir of its 600 year history, is about to be tested further … Print is a technological embarrassment … Arguably, too, big media threw print over the side of the boat to digital, letting it become a loss leader. Certainly it has defended video with vastly more wiles and aggression.[3]

As outlined in the early chapters, international communication theory is going through a transformation. Earlier attempts at theorizing have failed to develop models or research agendas that match the reality of the contemporary role of global communication. Theories of modernization, dependency, and cultural imperialism have failed to satisfactorily explain global communication. The old theories only explain part of the global picture.

The theoretical failings are partly a function of three related factors. The first is the end of the Cold War and the corresponding decline in influence of socialist media critics, whose ideas and rhetoric are no longer relevant. The second is related to numerous technical advances such as the new major global communication phenomenon, convergence, digital environments, smartphones and tablets, the Internet, and the reach of the latest satellites. The third is the emergence of several major global communications stakeholders, many of which are owned and controlled by companies outside the United States. European countries, Japan, Canada, Mexico, and others have major stakeholders in this important expanding sector. Collectively, these factors have led to the need to reanalyze and reformulate the theoretical underpinnings of the discipline of international communication. That is what this book is all about. It proposes a new theoretical perspective that unites world system theory (WST) with ECT. This combination places the discipline on a contemporary theoretical foundation for the purpose of explaining the global communication landscape. Various activities continue to increase the need for understanding the various components that collectively influence international communication. The preceding chapters cover the salient features as well as the expanding globalization of the corporate giants in this field. Even though some of the stakeholders shift, through mergers and so on, the underlying core analysis (WST and ECT) as laid out in this book remains viable and credible.

Before reviewing these components, remember that the impact on international communication of the end of the Cold War should not be underestimated. First, much of the research undertaken in the 1970s and 1980s focused on issues or media content that had a distinct ideological focus and slant which emphasized the dichotomy between capitalist and socialist worldviews. This outmoded dichotomy renders many of the studies and their conclusions marginal or suspect in the new post-Cold War environment. Second, the volume of international news was higher during the Cold War because many publishers, editors, and journalists set their priorities according to the Cold War dichotomy and resulting international tensions. It was a great deal simpler for editors when the thrust of US foreign policy could be summed up in two words: "stop communism." Third, with that old dichotomy almost invisible, the interest and attention paid to international news has shifted because of terrorism and 9/11. After the terrorist attacks of September 11, 2001 international news came back on the media's radar big-time. The global war on terrorism, the war in Afghanistan, and the war in Iraq – the trifecta of agenda-setting – reclaimed the front pages and face-time of television news around the globe. Fourth, as the global economy continues to expand through a series of mergers and acquisitions in the communications and other sectors, we would expect global business news coverage to increase in order to monitor the expanding global economy. Finally, the United States is looking for a new role within UNESCO; for a number of years it has also played a precarious role within the United Nations, including withholding its substantial financial dues for a considerable period in the 1990s.

Rather than promoting global organizations and encouraging greater multilateral cooperation through the United Nations and specialized UN agencies and organizations, the United States has never appeared as either a team player or a major leader in multilateral organizations. This US attitude is anomalous considering that the vast majority of global corporations are headquartered in the United States. US corporations have the greatest vested interest in global peace and stability, as well as in economic and monetary systems that are functional and stable. Yet with the end of the ideological confrontation and a reduction in serious international threats, the US government seeks only a peripheral role, if any, in almost all global agencies that influence, examine, monitor, or set rules affecting international communication. In some cases, isolationists in Washington have adopted a fortress mentality, or only support global communication policies that clearly benefit the United States, frequently at the expense of other nations. (See below for further discussion of this.)

New World Information and Communications Order

The New World Information and Communications Order (NWICO) dominated international communication debates for several decades. A combination of newly independent nations, many of which were former colonies of core nations, as well as the ideological interests of communist republics, propelled the issue of news flow and the role of the mass media into a contentious position. Industrialized core countries view the press as independent and non-governmental – that is, as broadcasting and communication corporations owned by public shareholders, as well as delivery systems. Although the shrill ideological rhetoric of the supporters of NWICO has faded, the current process is clearly not a balanced one, when the underlying issue of what determines international news flow is examined more closely.

Global mass media do not work in a vacuum; they work in an environment in which certain factors dominate the decision-making process, which virtually guarantees that certain news will be covered extensively whereas other news will be virtually ignored. For example, two broad roles have emerged from global media studies that account for a great deal of what does or does not get covered: gatekeeper roles and logistical roles.[4] Examples of gatekeeper impacts include wire service decision-making, negative news such as a tsunami, or the coups-and-earthquakes syndrome. The logistical impacts include economic interconnectedness, cultural affinity, such as being a former colony, speaking the English language, or regionalism. From a straight economic perspective, much of what happens in peripheral nations is of little monetary consequence to core nations. The major exceptions are significant deviances from the norm, such as when there are major earthquakes, coups, tidal waves, or civil war, particularly if the event is covered by CNN. News from peripheral, developing, nations reaches the front pages or television sets in industrialized core nations only when the news is bad. Otherwise, the vast number of nations in the peripheral zone receive no media attention at all year after year.

Electronic Colonialism Theory

Electronic colonialism theory[5] posits that cultural products produced, created, or manufactured in another country have the ability to influence, or possibly displace, indigenous cultural productions, artifacts, and media to the detriment of the receiving nations. On one level, ECT examines economic transactions through which a number of large multinational communication corporations engage in the selling of culturally embedded goods and services abroad. These corporations view the transactions as revenue-producing activities that increase market share and maximize profits for them and their shareholders. All of this is accomplished in unison with other firms, particularly advertisers, and multilateral agencies such as the World Trade Organization (WTO), ITU, UNESCO, or the Organisation for Economic Co-operation and Development (OECD). ECT also looks at the social and cultural impacts of these economic activities. Their effects include attitude formation, particularly among young

Table 16.1 The most important communication companies in the world, 2013

1	Disney
2	Viacom
3	Time Warner
4	British Broadcasting Corporation
5	Sony
6	News Corporation
7	Bertelsmann
8	Omnicom/Publicis
9	Associated Press/Reuters
10	Comcast's NBCUniversal

consumers who seek out foreign cultural products, ranging from comic books to music, videos, and mobile phones, which represent distant cultures and dreams – products that have been designed in a totally different environment and culture.

ECT provides the theoretical backdrop for examining the long-run global consequences of core nations' multimedia offerings in semiperipheral and peripheral nations. It provides a means for examining and understanding some of the broader issues, particularly in emerging nations, concerning the plethora of cultural products, messages, and industries from a global perspective. The major communication industries tend to be located in a few wealthy core nations, whereas their customers are dispersed around the globe and come from different linguistic, social, economic, religious, and political environments. ECT speculates that these differences will over time shrink in favor of the producing nations, which frequently work in English. This movement toward English as the language of the "global village" even applies to the European Union. The only language that most Europeans speak, other than their native tongue, is English. Most meetings, including academic conferences, across Europe are increasingly being conducted in English. Many European MBA programs are taught in English with textbooks in English.

As it attempts to find a new transnational identity, Europe still has no major global players in the Internet domain. Intel, Microsoft, IBM, Apple, Google, Yahoo!, YouTube, MySpace, Twitter, Ask.com, and Lycos are all American companies with a global footprint. The European Union has established a number of programs to correct this situation, none of which has managed to get enough traction to be considered a threat to the above firms.

Three important factors are evident in Table 16.1. First, all these companies are located in a single zone – the core region; not even one is from the semiperipheral zone. Second, the language of the global media is English and over time this will continue to be even more so. Third, except for the BBC, all have and need to have a strong presence in the crucial US market.

Over time, most of the corporations described in the preceding chapters will have more customers and make more revenue outside the nations in which their head offices are located. They are truly global and not national entities.

Let us look at two examples to illustrate this point. First, more corporations are moving toward a single, global strategy in their advertising. Firms such as the Ford Motor Company are seeking to consolidate their advertising and marketing expenditures within a single advertising agency with a global reach and workforce. The Ford advertising budget is over

$1 billion a year. This requires a vast number of employees from Ford's advertising agency – the WPP Group of the United Kingdom[6] – to carry out an effective global marketing and advertising campaign. Only a few years ago, large corporations such as Ford would have utilized perhaps half a dozen agencies in various parts of the world to carry out their corporate advertising. Now they view this fragmentation as both too expensive and counterproductive.

The second example is Coca-Cola.[7] This is a $2 billion account for Interpublic Group of New York. Coca-Cola's off-shore sales exceed the domestic distribution of its global brand. Previously, Coca-Cola had over 30 advertising agencies handling its products around the world. Now it is attempting to focus on a global strategy and a global message in order to increase foreign sales substantially.

The purpose of providing these two examples is to make the point that the purpose of global activities on behalf of major corporations is to maximize sales and thus profits in more and more nations around the world. These nations and customers are concentrated in other core as well as semiperipheral regions.

Basically, ECT explains the phenomenon of a dominant Anglo-Saxon paradigm which, through the English language, has been spread globally through two primary means. The first, the British Empire, provided the base for what would lead to the current domination of media industries by primarily American firms. The empire took British literature and culture, the model of the BBC, Reuters, and the English language and spread them around the world. The second force is the contemporary global media scene, which is dominated by Hollywood movies, American and British music and textbooks, CNN, Associated Press, Western syndicated television series and popular culture, major Internet host sites such as Google, and the English language. The rapidly growing video streaming sector is dominated by Windows Media Player, Apple, RealPlayer, and Adobe Flash. That is why non-English speaking nations are at a loss as to what to do about the long-term implication of ECT, or how they can create a global winner in the media and technology arenas.

World System Theory

World system theory[8] is a means of viewing global activities in the international communication field from a theoretical perspective. WST basically divides the world into three major sectors: core, semiperipheral, and peripheral. Core nations, which are relatively few in number, exercise vast economic influence and dominate relationships and transactions with the other two zones. The United States, the European Union, and Japan are some of the dominant stakeholders in the core group. This group has the power to define the rules, timing, and content of transactions with nations or regions in the other two zones. Some current core nations, such as Australia, Norway, Canada, and New Zealand, are becoming increasingly concerned that they may slip into the semiperipheral zone if they are not able to attract, finance, and keep their information industries, entrepreneurs, and educated workers. The impact of News Corp shifting from Australia to the United States is an example of how central the leading core nation, the United States, is to the global economy. Barnett and Salisbury examined WST with reference to communication and information studies. Looking at data from the international telecommunication network, they conclude: "The results indicate that the network is composed of a single group with the United States and the other Western economic powers at the center and the lesser developed countries at the periphery. A nation's centrality in the network is significantly correlated with its GDP per capita."[9]

There are a substantial number of semiperipheral nations. They interact with core nations but currently lack the power and economic institutions to join the elite core group.

China, Mexico, Brazil, India, and some of the Middle East nations are trying to reposition themselves as core nations. Some other semiperipheral nations are attempting to fast-track their entry into the core region by requesting membership in the European Union. That is why the current EU community is likely to grow to 30 or so nations over time.

Finally, the peripheral zone is made up of developing nations. These nations and regions have relatively little, if any, power, and their economic dealings with the semiperipheral and core nations benefit these two last zones. Many African, Latin American, and most Asian nations belong to the periphery. They are basically exploited by the other zones; they have few media exports, little connectivity to the Internet, little education, little technology, poor health, poor literacy rates, and much poverty.

World system theory's characterization of the global nations provides a theoretical framework for addressing the question of why communication industries located in core nations have the market and economic advantage in dealing with the other two zones. To some extent, WST is an extension of the one-way flow argument developed decades ago, but when we look at the traffic patterns – whether in music, movies, television series, the Internet, or any other cultural product – clearly the core zone dominates, the semiperipheral is next, and the peripheral is at the very bottom of the hierarchy. All major communication corporations, whether in advertising, print, wire services, movies, electronics, video, or Internet, have their world headquarters in core nations; they have extensive dealings with semiperipheral nations, including purchasing subsidiaries, to insure market penetration, but relatively little corporate presence in the periphery.

The theories of electronic colonialism and world systems together form a continuum which describes and explains the underlying essential elements in international communications. ECT focuses primarily on the impact on or attitudes of individuals and groups. It deals with what happens to individuals when they are repeatedly exposed to foreign-produced communications that have cultural cachet. The messages they receive convey foreign personalities, foreign dress, foreign history, foreign norms, foreign values, and foreign tastes. Frequently these values are at variance with indigenous cultures and lifestyles, particularly in peripheral nations. These individuals and groups are viewed as customers and, combined or aggregated, they are seen in terms of market share. To a large and growing extent, the goal of global communication corporations is to make electronic colonies of large segments of the population around the globe in order to increase market share and maximize profits. ECT utilizes a cultural lens.

WST moves the analysis into the economic territory that underpins the global trading system within which communication industries operate. WST focuses on the substantial activities and power within communication industries located in core nations, and how they utilize this power for systematic advantage in their economic relationships with semiperipheral nations and peripheral nations. WST focuses more on the macroeconomic and policy dimensions of the corporate decision-making process, whereas ECT focuses more on the impact of foreign products, ideologies, and software on individuals, and their minds.

Electronic Colonialism Theory Plus World System Theory

Combining the two theories provides the most powerful explanation of the contemporary phenomenon of global communication that is available to students, policy analysts, corporate planners, and researchers alike. The failures of modernization, development, and cultural imperialism theories, as well as other scattered attempts to explain certain narrow, micro segments of the international communication field, have not moved the discipline much beyond either anecdotal impressions or ideologically laced charges. These charges and lack of data to support them are particularly transparent and obvious in NWICO activities. As the role of international communications continues to expand, these two combined theories represent an opportunity for greater insight and understanding of this most significant global phenomenon.

McPhail's Paradox: The United States, Modernity, and Future Actions

There is no doubt that the United States has the greatest vested interest in the global economy. As a nation-state it has the largest number of multinational companies, many in the communication sector, which depend on global commerce and transactions as a major source of jobs and income. The United States needs global order and rules to keep its industries functioning and growing. They are the prime beneficiaries of global rules and the global economy. They need the United Nations and its specialized agencies, like UNESCO, WTO, and ITU, to function effectively. But there is within the United States a clear cultural chasm or disconnect between those who are progressive, concerned, and educated and those who feel threatened by change, immigrants, international agencies, and new ideas. But the United States needs the global economy and the global economy needs the United States.

Yet the US population in general, and the federal government in particular, are among the harshest critics of international agencies. They stand against modernity. They feel threatened by transnational agreements and frequently are in violation of them. The loss of faith in the United Nations is a by-product of the United States' frequent circumventing of it. It was out of UNESCO for years and withheld funds to the United Nations for years thanks to Senator Jesse Helms. The United States is one of the most frequent violators of WTO's rules promoting free trade. The US imposition of steel tariffs is a case in point. In other sectors the United States simply refuses to participate, ratify, sign, or support global measures even though it is a major stakeholder.[10] The Kyoto Protocol, the Law of the Sea, the Mine Ban Treaty, the Convention on the Rights of the Child, the Convention on the Elimination of Discrimination against Women, the International Criminal Court, and other international initiatives designed to produce an orderly, safer, and better world lack a US signature or support.

Rather than promoting international tolerance and cooperation, and furthering global social justice, the United States promotes a narrow, ethnocentric goal of "America first." The United States projects an image of not wanting to be a global team player. It does not get the bigger picture. Although the most powerful nation on earth, it avoids global leadership roles in the UN system and multilateral organization elsewhere. It is as if it fears the consequences or desires to shun modernity. Yet it currently is, and is clearly going to continue to be, the nation that should be leading and supporting all global rules, laws, practices, and organizations. All the US-based multinational communication conglomerates need all of the preceding global rules to work.[11]

In contrast, Australia, Canada, the Nordic nations, and many others promote social justice through multilateral organizations. Not the United States. Canada as the United States' largest trading partner is a symbolic case study. Canada is in endless trade fights with the United States. The latter is quick to initiate bilateral trade fights across a number of sectors – fish, lumber, steel, beef, and cultural industries. The smaller nation of Canada does not look for special consideration from the United States, but even compromise is outside the rhetoric of the US State Department for its largest trading partner. The United States seeks to crush its Canadian trading partner. It plays hardball at every turn. Even though Canada is a relatively minor actor on the world stage, the United States' policy strategy is to treat it as an enemy. Never mind that Canada allowed hundreds of US commercial airlines to land in Canada after 9/11, or that Canadian hydroelectric companies routinely assist US states hit by natural catastrophes, or that over 130 Canadian soldiers have been killed in Afghanistan. US foreign policy continues to protect and maximize American interests. It is ethnocentric: no compromise, no concessions.

In the new environment of the post-Cold War era, the US business empire rules. It is no longer the hegemony of the British Empire that rules the seas, but the US empire that rules the global airwaves and most international media. An example is the United States' complaint to the WTO against Canada over the issue of mainstream culture. Canada, where over 80 percent of magazine sales are US magazines, had sought a modest relief position. The United States objected since it considers any attempt to protect an indigenous cultural industry as unacceptable. The issue was a "split run" of US-imported magazines where token Canadian advertising and content were required by Canadian regulations but were strongly protested by US publishers. When is 80 percent of a foreign market not enough? When it has to satisfy an American media conglomerate in cooperation with the US federal government. The WTO rules in the United States' favor and the United States now enjoys more than 85 percent of Canadian domestic magazine sales.

The global economy is the life-blood of a vast number of American multinational firms; just consider Apple, IBM, Microsoft, Time Warner, Disney, News Corp, and Viacom. Yet who is the first to criticize the United Nations or UNESCO or other international agencies and agreements? And US media like the *Wall Street Journal*, Fox, Sinclair Broadcasting, the *National Review*, and the *New York Post* champion this paradoxical stand. It is not as if they are discussing small nations like Greenland or New Zealand, which would be relatively unscathed if the global trading system collapsed; the United States would be devastated. But they and many in the media, like Sarah Palin, Anne Coulter, Rush Limbaugh, Brit Hume, Glenn Beck, Sean Hannity, and Bill O'Reilly, are the biggest complainers across a broad range of issues when it comes to the United Nations, social programs, bilingualism, outsourcing, immigration, global trade, or international agreements. It is clearly a paradox seemingly better understood by foreigners than Americans themselves at all levels of work, government, and the media.

As many core nations move beyond modernity to postmodernity, the position of the United States on the world stage is in stark contrast in terms of its overall response to the possibilities of being a global communication leader.[12] It is more likely to be perceived globally as a rather narrow-minded, somewhat vindictive, disliked nation in international forums. In the future, how the United States handles the delicate issues of culture, media, diversity, and participates in multilateral agencies and forums will likely determine the outcome of this paradox. US history is not on its side.

Conclusions

It is difficult to formulate conclusions when dealing with international communications. The field is in a state of flux, and global changes affect it on a daily basis. The three major engines driving the change are innovations in communication technologies, the global war on terrorism, and the global economy. The world is a different and better place because of international communications. Many citizens are better informed, major corporations have experienced success, and employment opportunities have expanded because of the possibilities and potential provided by innovations in international communications. But beyond broad generalizations, there are still a few more specific conclusions that can be drawn from an understanding of the various stakeholders, nations, and global communication corporations. The following four conclusions focus on sovereignty, continued globalization, and the Internet. Clearly, other conclusions may be drawn, but given the rapid pace of change in this sector, the following are the most likely predictions.

First, the audio and video history of international communications has been and will continue to be dominated by US music, television, feature films, and Internet portals. From the likes of Disney cartoons and animation movies, *I Love Lucy, Melrose Place, Dynasty, Dallas, Baywatch, Cheers, Star Trek, Cosby, The Simpsons,* to *Wheel of Fortune, The Muppet Show, Friends, Sopranos, Sex and the City,* and *House,* American television shows have dominated television sets and now mobile devices around the world. The same is true for CDs, DVDs, and movie screens as well. In fact DVD sales now represent a major tertiary (following the primary screening on television or in theaters, then syndication rights) source of windfall profits for rights holders. Some of the leading DVD sales that are once again contributing to the financial health of the studios are *The Lord of the Rings, Shrek, Star Wars, Harry Potter, Spider-Man, Seinfeld,* and *The Simpsons.* Networks and studios are scrambling to put out additional digitized releases of old stock at a rapid rate as most US and other core-nation homes acquire DVD players or streaming video devices.

The important fact about all this is that no one is forced to watch these shows or listen to the music. There is no gun to anyone's head to watch American television and movie productions, or to listen to American music. They do it because the scripts, production values and sets, acting or singing talent, animation, and budgets create world-class programs. Also, foreign buyers from commercial and non-commercial television networks from around the world flock to New York, Hollywood, and Las Vegas trade shows to bid for the syndication rights to US television network or cable shows and series.

This demand by off-shore buyers has been increased by the proliferation of new television stations and movie multiplexes, cable systems, satellite channels, DVDs, tablets, and iPod players. More individuals in core and semiperipheral countries have more leisure time and disposable income, and are able to understand English, particularly teenagers, and thus contribute to the escalating global demand. Coupled with the Internet, which is American-centric, mainly in English, and carries more and more audiovisual content, this tends to insure the continuing influence of American multimedia conglomerates. This influence is also cultural in nature. Since core nations are highly competitive and already have mature markets at home, the greatest impact of these phenomena is likely to be most prevalent in developing nations. Over the next decade it will be the semiperipheral nations that are the battleground for the stakeholders discussed in this book. Finally, the marketing and advertising budgets of the global media conglomerates are huge. Their sophisticated tactics to attract customers around the world leave little to chance.

As a collective result of the above, the electronic colonization of vast numbers of people continues. Just as the British ruled the world by controlling the seas, so now the United States and a few other core nations rule the airwaves, television and movies screens, mobile media, and the emerging digital universe. The minds of the many, without regard to time or space, are clearly influenced by the flow and content of a vast range of core-nation media products and options. As a result, ECT is becoming more powerful as a theory for understanding and organizing the impact of global communication over time.

Second, the plethora of transborder activities among major media, advertising, telecommunications, and Internet firms is rendering historic national boundaries, and in some cases policies, obsolete. The ability of US communication firms to transmit information or products globally, as well as for foreign firms to sell their cultural products in the lucrative US market, is making national communication policies and political boundaries an issue of the past rather than the future. For example, CNN, Fox News, MSNBC, the BBC, Associated Press, Reuters, Euronews, and others go wherever there is news. Time Warner, Disney, Sony, Bertelsmann, Viacom, NBCUniversal, and even the BBC seek foreign markets or audiences where there is a viable consumer base and a potential for profitability. The Internet goes wherever there is a modem, a computer, or any Internet access, which may be hard-wired or wireless. Thus, as global communication companies, along with their advertising agencies, expand their markets and merge with more and more foreign firms, the concept of a single head office, or of a single nation controlling, taxing, or regulating global communication firms, is less likely. This change in sovereignty received an unexpected boost with the collapse of the Berlin Wall and the eventual lessening of international tension that was prevalent during the Cold War. There were no longer two dominant superpowers, each with enormous arsenals of propaganda and weapons to protect their nation-states as well as those of their allies. During the 1990s a vacuum emerged as only a single global power remained – the United States. Into this vacuum moved the major stakeholders in the global economy. Multinational corporations simply usurped economic power and some political power in order to promote their interests across national boundaries. For example, today several multinational corporations are more powerful and have greater reach and greater influence than any nation in the periphery. Google is a prime example. We now live in a world where a single individual, for example Bill Gates of Microsoft or other Internet entrepreneurs, are wealthier than the entire group of nation-states in the periphery. It appears that although the concept of the nation-state has lasted about 600 years, technological innovations are now defying it. This phenomenon will push multinational organizations and transnational regional agreements into ever more important roles, because domestic and national control are now clearly pre-Internet phenomena. Institutions such as the United Nations, UNESCO, ITU, WTO, World Intellectual Property Organization (WIPO), OECD, and the European Union are willingly adopting entirely new regulations, currency, and ways of doing things in the post-sovereignty era. This is the post-sovereignty reality. Yet at the same time, many of these same firms and phenomena, such as the Internet and mobile devices, are fueling a resurgence of nationalism and localism, and some hope that they are a means of protecting and reinforcing indigenous cultures, groups, and languages.

Third, a fundamental aspect of the global economy will dominate the current and future global landscape of international communications. Specifically, the economies of scale are driving substantial corporate mergers and acquisitions.[13] This is true of every aspect of the cultural industries phenomenon, starting with advertising agencies and moving on to global media, wire services, and Internet corporations. Old media in particular, for which print products are the predominant revenue generators, will have to either acquire new media themselves, be bought out by some aggressive new media entrepreneur, or fail. There will be no standing still in the global communication sector. Stakeholders will either move aggressively to expand market share through innovation, mergers, and acquisitions, or they themselves will become targets for either friendly or hostile take-overs. The global economy is not user-friendly or cost-effective to small players in the communication sector.

The transfer of concepts, philosophies, and practices of liberalization, deregulation, and privatization across all core and semiperipheral nations has meant that the communication sector, which tended to be focused mainly within nation-states, has now taken on global dimensions. This is true across all elements of the industry – advertising, media, both audio and video, as well as in technology, particularly the Internet and mobile media. The leading nation in the globalization phenomenon is the United States, but the European Union and Japan have also been extremely active in the globalization process. This is particularly true in two ways:

1   The activities and strategic plans of Japan's Sony, Germany's Bertelsmann, France's Publicis, and the United Kingdom's BBC and WPP are informing and influencing others as to how to compete in the global economy.
2   All major European communication firms recognize that they must have some presence in the United States in order to be an effective global stakeholder.

All major communication industries, regardless of national origin, have identified the North American market as essential for major stakeholder status in the globalization process. Finally, another aspect of globalization is the combination of old and new media. The merger of AOL and Time Warner, despite its missteps, defines the phenomenon, but it also reinforces and expands the globalized role that all communication industries need to identify, deal with, and ultimately take on.

The globalization of the communication industry has several consequences. First, the original thrust of cultural imperialism was too loudly critical of the Hollywood feature film industry. This is now an uninformed perspective, because Hollywood is no longer totally owned by US interests. Instead, foreign communication conglomerates such as Sony of Japan and Bertelsmann of Germany have substantial global media holdings. The global communication industry is not a monolithic empire, but rather a phenomenon that is now widely dispersed among core nations, with a few semiperipheral nations desperately trying to obtain core-like status through their own expansion via select mergers and acquisitions, particularly in the film industry. Within the communications sector, strategic planning is about global planning, not domestic or national planning.

Fourth, the role of the Internet is still evolving. Just a few decades ago the Internet was a relatively isolated technical phenomenon for which scientists and other experts were still developing key components and applications for scientific or primarily industrial applications. Two decades later, the Internet has become a major phenomenon affecting global communication and commerce in unheard-of ways. The volume of usage, the depth and breadth of users worldwide, and the dramatic impact on mobile devices, e-commerce, e-learning, and e-public policy are astonishing. Yet, in spite of its significant role across core nations in particular, the Internet is still in its infancy. The development of the Internet today is similar to the invention of the printing press, the early days of the assembly line, or the early applications of the computer chip. We are in the early phase of what will become a mature industry, which will likely eventually be replaced by some other technological invention or by a mix of technologies and other factors.

One other significant aspect of the Internet is that it has empowered the individual to make different choices in different ways. Individuals may obtain news directly from the Internet without the filtering of publishers, editors, or journalists. Or they can create their own blogs or vblogs and seek an audience for their musings. Individuals anywhere on the planet can purchase cultural products or view them on their devices without leaving their home, school, car, or place of business. This phenomenon is not just available to individuals in a single or a few nation-states; it is a globally dispersed phenomenon in which geography becomes irrelevant, particularly as wireless Internet connections pop up around the globe.

The prevalence of the Internet is related to the issue of sovereignty because the information on the Internet is as portable as the technology itself. Industrial era concepts such as space, location, control, bricks and mortar, and monopoly are marginalized in the age of the Internet.

Finally, as evidenced by mergers across the stakeholders, the communication industry recognizes that multinational conglomerates will become the model and new benchmark for successful global communication stakeholders. This will involve a blurring of traditional boundaries of all communication sectors, as the global economy forces the application of the Internet into every segment of the international communication market. The digital output and world of core nations will speed the Internet into homes and villages around the globe in record time. Over time, more semiperipheral nations will mature into core nations, and then the issue will become how and which peripheral nations will move into the semiperipheral zone. The cutting edge of technological innovations influencing the Internet, however, will continue to appear first and quickest across core nations.

As people flock to mobile media capable of video streaming and as cable networks continue to create award-winning shows, the fragmentation of the audience that was once the territory of networks will cause some major rethinking in order to even survive in the new era. One network, Disney's ABC, is attempting to get ahead of the curve and competition. In 2013 they announced:

> The Walt Disney Company has an app in the works that may render Hulu passé for some people. The app will live stream ABC programming to the phones and tablets of cable and satellite subscribers, allowing those subscribers to watch "Good Morning America" on a tablet while standing in line at Starbucks, for instance, or watch "Nashville" on a smartphone while riding a bus home from work. With the app, ABC, a subsidiary of Disney, will become the first of the American broadcasters to provide a live Internet stream of national and local programming.[14]

Connection between Public Diplomacy and ECT

The chapter on public diplomacy marks a new beginning in terms of the potential role of the media on a global scale. The goals and means are fairly clear. The goals are to influence the hearts and minds of others by non-military interventions on all scales, but the means are scarce when it comes to the proper funding of initiatives. The lack of funding reveals a blind spot concerning the potential of public diplomacy. The US defense budget for 2013 is over $600 billion. The US public diplomacy budget, no matter how you calculate it, is less than 1 percent of the military budget. Yet military force alone cannot win the war against terrorism. Body counts and prisoners are not indexes of success in terms of hearts and minds.

The 9/11 Commission Report stated that "We have come together with a unity of purpose because our nation demands it. September 11, 2001 was a day of unprecedented shock and suffering in the history of the United States. The nation was unprepared."[15] Today the United States is still unprepared; in fact, it may have more enemies out there than it did on 9/11. The wars in Afghanistan and Iraq have been a breeding ground for extremist causes and recruitment in the Middle East and elsewhere. The *9/11 Commission Report* continues: "Across the government, there were failures of imagination, policy, capabilities, and management … The most important failure was imagination."[16] The emergence of a new stateless terrorist enemy was missed by both the US military as well as its Cold War response and rhetoric. This is a sad commentary on the evolution and outcome of what President Eisenhower, a decorated general, warned against some five decades ago. In his farewell address after eight years as president, Eisenhower warned against the mighty and adverse influence of the military-industrial complex.[17]

There is no public diplomacy complex. It is a loose group of NGOs, foundations, and frail government projects which are collectively drowned out by the lobbyists and warrior hawks that Eisenhower warned about. The New York writer Frank Rich put it this way:

> You might wonder whether networks could someday cut out the middlemen – anchors – and just put covert lobbyists and publicists on the air to deliver the news. Actually, that has already happened. The most notorious example was the flock of retired military officers who served as television "news analysts" during the Iraq war while clandestinely lobbying for defense contractors eager to sell their costly wares to the Pentagon.[18]

The US amply funds several military colleges but not a single peace or public diplomacy college. If only 10 percent of the military budget were to be redirected to public diplomacy and winning the hearts and minds of those labeled the enemy or terrorists then some progress may be made. But the imagination of the top US officials has been paralyzed by the post-9/11 environment where military contractors moved swiftly and effectively into the policy vacuum.[19]

What is the Relationship of All This to ECT?

In general, communication media carry two sets of values; the one is the impact of the hardware itself,[20] the other is the software or content. It is the spread and impact of core-manufactured content of all genres that electronic colonialism is concerned with. Technology itself is not neutral.[21] For example, the use of computers is guided by essential codes which must be followed and which alter how users obtain information. But setting aside the hardware and looking at the software leads to this observation: core-based, mostly American, media carry cultural and linguistic (mostly English) values. These values cut across a number of different attitudes and behaviors, depending on the receiver, for example young children become Disney or Sponge Bob fanatics, or teenagers switch from their own local music to the latest imported hits on MTV.

But there is a deeper meaning conveyed by this entire new media, particularly in peripheral and poorer regions of the world. Over time and with increasing consumption of media fare, they want to become like us. They want our clothes and lifestyle, and they seek the good life that they can see us enjoy. I realize that there is no study confirming this, but there are traces of this phenomenon in some of the empirical studies.[22] We know that, with the reunification of Germany, the democratic West did not want to become like the communist East; rather the East wanted to become like the West. They wanted freedom, choice, better lives, and access to even more media and popular culture. This package also comes with democracy and free enterprise businesses. The East Germans learned all this by watching and listening to British and American shows, movies of all sorts, and music from jazz to the Beatles. The television series *Dallas* and *Dynasty* did more to undermine communism than all of the US propaganda campaigns. The same overall picture is also true of the other former communist countries which stampeded to become members of the open and democratic European Union after the end of the Soviet Union. Here is the essential point and connection with ECT. Spreading democracy around the world at the end of a gun simply does not work. Declaring people enemy combatants, using drones, and putting them in jails like Abu Ghraib or Guantanamo not only does not work but actually increases recruitment of more radical enemies of the US and other core nations. What appears to work is spreading mass media to other nations through a broad range of public diplomacy initiatives. The more foreign nations consume modern communication, the more they will want to be like us. That is why some foreign nations and some religions ban or shun Western media. They understand that Western media bring with them Western values and show people enjoying freedom. The Internet is China's, Iran's, and other authoritarian and military regimes' worst nightmare.

In closing, I realize that those in the cultural imperialist camp and cultural purists from around the world will lament any increase in American-style media and culture around the world, but mass media do work to spread the message and mechanisms of choice. They promote the image of a better life. But as long as the military-industrial complex that Eisenhower warned us of continues to hijack both dollars and policy concerning global matters, then making the world safer is one of the last things the current post-9/11 approach will achieve.

Notes

1. Stig Hjarvard, "The Mediatization of Society: A Theory of the Media as Agents of Social and Cultural Change," *Nordicom Review* 29(2) (2008), 105.
2. Peter Weingart, "Science and the Media," *Research Policy* 27(8) (1998), 869–79.
3. Michael Wolff, "Will Cast-Off Print Get Its Groove Back?" *US Today* (March 18, 2013), 1B–2B.
4. Haoming Denis Wu, "Investigating the Determinance of International News Flow: A Meta-Analysis," *Gazette* 60 (December 1998), 493–512.
5. Thomas L. McPhail, *Electronic Colonialism*, Newbury, CA: Sage, 1986.
6. "WPP Leads Way in Global Ties to Clients," *Wall Street Journal* (December 1, 2000), B6.
7. "Coke Gives Nod to Interpublic for Ad Contract," *Wall Street Journal* (December 4, 2000), B12.
8. Thomas R. Shannon, *An Introduction to the World System Perspective*, Boulder, CO: Westview Press, 1996. James Mittelman looks at the variables underlying globalization in *The Globalization Syndrome: Transformation and Resistance*, Princeton, NJ: Princeton University Press, 2000. It is informative concerning the resistance to cultural hegemony.
9. George Barnett and Joseph Salisbury, "Communication and Globalization: A Longitudinal Analysis of the International Telecommunication Network," *Journal of World Systems Research* 2(16) (1996), 20.
10. The issue of US isolationism is not new. For example, the United States never ratified the 1919 Treaty of Versailles, which formally ended World War I. The treaty included the formation of a League of Nations, which was heavily promoted by US president Woodrow Wilson. Despite extensive efforts by Wilson, including a cross-country speaking tour to get support from radio, magazines, and newspapers, the ethnocentric isolationists in Washington prevailed. Other nations that signed the treaty were France, Germany, England, Italy, and Japan. Noted US aviation hero, Charles Lindbergh and other fascist sympathizers campaigned aggressively against US entry into World War II, which began in 1939. Their support of Hitler prevailed until the bombing of Pearl Harbor in December 1941. That turned out to be that generation's 9/11. The George W. Bush administration also ignored or flouted international laws and agreements against torture, openly ignoring the Geneva Convention, which seeks to limit the atrocities of war.
11. Noted media scholar William Hachten has a similar take on the situation: "the fact remains that international society is marked by the absence of collective procedures, by competition rather than cooperation, and by the lack of a commitment to a common goal – in other words, a situation that approaches anarchy" (*The World News Prism*, Ames: Iowa State University Press, 2002, p. 12).
12. For a discussion of the failure of the United States to do the empire walk well, see Deepak Lal, "An Imperial Denial," *Yale Global Online* (January 6, 2005), at http://yaleglobal.yale.edu/content/imperial-denial, accessed August 29, 2013.

13. "Cross-Border Mergers Soared Last Year," *Wall Street Journal* (July 19, 2000), A18. This article traces merger activities, and it notes a 50 percent increase in 2000 over the 1998 rate. This rate continues today following a lull after 9/11. The United States, United Kingdom, Sweden, Germany, France, and Canada dominate the global buying. One sector, advertising, is particularly active.

14. Brian Stelter, "ABC works on an app for live streaming shows to mobile devices," *New York Times* (March 18, 2013), at http://www.nytimes.com/2013/03/19/business/media/abc-works-on-an-app-for-streaming-shows-to-mobile-devices.html?_r=0, accessed August 29, 2013.

15. "Executive Summary," *The 9/11 Commission Report*, Washington: Replica Book, 2004, p. 1.

16. "Executive Summary," *The 9/11 Commission Report*, p. 9.

17. "President Eisenhower's Farewell Address to the Nation, January 17, 1961," at www.youtube.com/watch?v=8y06N SBBRtY, accessed August 29, 2013.

18. This type of imaginative experiment in public diplomacy is not limited to what the United States should do differently and creatively; other core nations have a vested interest in reducing terrorism and extremism as well. And the money is there, but it is being misapplied. Consider that the North Atlantic Treaty Organization (NATO) was created in 1949, to provide a common defense strategy against the threat of the then powerful Soviet Union and to counter the global spread of communism. The old Soviet Union imploded in 1989, with the fall of the Berlin Wall. Did NATO's rationale and purpose imploded as well? Not quite. The military-industrial complex is alive and too well. NATO has just ordered 180 huge military aircraft at a cost of over $25 billion. Imagine the number of schools, libraries, and hospitals that could cover the needs and change the hearts and minds of children in many peripheral nations. NATO's armaments budget is now actually larger than during the Cold War. It and the Pentagon continue to ignore the fact that the Internet ultimately supports the emergence of civil society and promotes a drive toward choice and democratic institutions.

19. You will recall that in Chapter 1 we referred to four epochs of colonization: military, Christian, mercantile, and electronic. Most of the theory developed in the book was the last and current phase of electronic colonialism. But the second phase, the brutal Christian Crusades against Muslims and other religions, has reappeared in two instances. The first was President Bush's remarks soon after September 11, 2001 to a "crusade" against terrorism, which were followed by the attack on the mostly Muslim population in Iraq. The second instance is still playing itself out and is directly connected to a military contractor Blackwater. This firm acted as a private army in Iraq and is run by a fundamentalist Christian conservative, Erik Prince. Prince recruits retired military and former CIA agents to go on what he reportedly claims is a religious crusade against Muslims in Iraq. The use of deadly force is under investigation by both the US Congress and the Department of State. These two recent examples of the concept of the crusades returning has been picked up by the media, particularly the Fox networks and the *Wall Street Journal*, who have defended Blackwater and Erik Prince on their twenty-first-century crusade across Iraq.

   A related story details how the CIA in 2004 secretly hired Blackwater to assassinate select al-Qaeda leaders without notifying the US Congress as required by law (J. Risen and M. Mazzeti, "CIA Said to Use Outsiders to Put Bombs on Drones," *New York Times* (August 20, 2009)). Finally, by 2010 the US Department of Defense had more than 100,000 military contractors, such as Blackwater and Halliburton, in Afghanistan on various deadly missions, basically acting as private armies, at a time when there were about 65,000 US soldiers on the ground.

20. Marshall McLuhan, *Understanding Media: The Extensions of Man*, New York: McGraw-Hill, 1964.

21. Jacques Ellul, *The Technological Society*, New York: Knopf, 1964; Martin Heidegger, *The Question Concerning Technology and Other Essays*, New York: Harper & Row, 1977.

22. Pippa Norris and Ronald Inglehart, *Cosmopolitan Communications: Cultural Diversity in a Globalized World*, New York: Cambridge University Press, 2010. Yet not everyone agrees with Norris and Inglehart. Angus Deaton, an expert on foreign aid and poverty thinks the aid does more harm than good. A reviewer of his 2013 book, *The Great Escape*, Princeton University Press states "It corrupts governments and rarely reaches the poor, he argues, and it is high time for the paternalistic West to step away and allow the developing world to solve its own problems." "A Surprising Case Against Foreign Aid," *New York Times* (October 13, 2013), B4.

Select Bibliography

2009 China Statistics Yearbook. Beijing: State Statistics Bureau, 2009.

2009 Report on Development of China's Radio, Film and Television. Beijing: Xinhua, 2009.

The 9/11 Commission Report: Final Report of the National Commission on Terrorist Attacks upon the United States. Washington: Replica Books, 2004.

Albarran, Alan B., and Chan-Olmsted, Sylvia M. *Global Media Economics: Commercialization, Concentration and Integration of World Media Markets*. Ames: Iowa State University Press, 1998.

Alexander, Alison, Owers, James, and Carveth, Rod (eds.). *Media Economics: Theory and Practice*. Mahwah, NJ: Lawrence Erlbaum, 1998.

Aouragh, Miriyam. "Social Media, Mediation and the Arab Revolutions." *TripleC (Cognition, Communication, Co-Operation): Open Access Journal for a Global Sustainable Information Society* 10(2) (2012), 518–36.

Artz, B., and Kamalipour, Y. (eds.). *The Globalization of Corporate Media Hegemony*. Albany: State University of New York Press, 2003.

Auletta, Ken. *Media Man*. New York: W. W. Norton, 2004.

Axford, Barrie, and Higgins, Richard. "The European Information Society: A New Public Sphere?" In Chris Rumford (ed.), *Cosmopolitanism and Europe*. Liverpool: Liverpool University Press, 2007.

Bagdikian, Ben. *The Media Monopoly*. Boston: Beacon, 2000.

Banks, Jack. "MTV and the Globalization of Popular Culture." *Gazette* 59(1) (1997), 43–60.

Banks, Jack. "Music Video Cartel: A Survey of Anti-Competitive Practices by MTV and Major Record Companies." *Popular Music and Society* 20(2) (1996), 173–97.

Barber, Benjamin R. "Democracy at Risk: American Culture in a Global Culture." *World Policy Journal* 15(2) (1998), 29–42.

Barnett, G. A., and Salisbury, J. G. "Communication and Globalization: A Longitudinal Analysis of the International Telecommunication Network." *Journal of World Systems Research* 2(16) (1996), 1–20.

Barnett, George A., Salisbury, Joseph G. T., Kim, Chul Woo, and Langhorne, Anna. "Globalisation and International Communication: An Examination of Monetary, Telecommunications and Trade Networks." *Journal of International Communication* 6(2) (1999), 7–49.

Barnett, Robert. *The Global Jukebox: The International Music Industry*. New York: Routledge, 1996.

Beltran, Luis. "Alien Premises, Objects and Methods in Latin American Communication Research." *Communication Research* 3 (1976), 107–34.

Bloomberg, Michael, and Winkler, Matthew. *Bloomberg by Bloomberg*. New York: Wiley, 1998.

Bob, Clifford. *The Marketing of Rebellion: Insurgents, Media, and International Activism*. New York: Cambridge University Press, 2005.

Boyd-Barrett, Oliver. "National and International News Agencies." *Gazette* 62(1) (2000), 5–18.

Brevini, Benedetta, Hintz, Arne, and McCurdy, Patrick. *Beyond WikiLeaks: Implications for the Future of Communications, Journalism and Society*. Basingstoke: Palgrave Macmillan, 2013.

Brüggemann, Michael. "How the EU Constructs the European Public Sphere." *Javnost: The Public* 12(2) (2005), 57–74.

Byun, H. *Analysis and Projection for Korean Industry in 2009*. Seoul: Korea Film Council, 2009.

Campbell, Robert. *The Golden Years of Broadcasting: A Celebration of the First Fifty Years of Radio and TV on NBC*. New York: Scribner's, 1976.

Carveth, Rod. "The Reconstruction of the Global Media Marketplace." *Communication Research* 19(6) (1992), 705–24.

Cave, Martin, and Collins, Richard. "Regulating the BBC." *Telecommunications Policy* 28(3–4) (2004), 249–72.

Chalaby, Jean K. *Transnational Television in Europe: Reconfiguring Global Communications Networks.* London: I. B. Taurus, 2009.

Chalaby, Jean K. *Transnational Television Worldwide: Towards a New Media Order.* London: I. B. Tauris, 2005.

Chang, T. K., and Lee, J. W. "Factors Affecting Gatekeepers' Selection of Foreign News: A National Survey of Newspaper Editors." *Journalism Quarterly* 69 (1992), 559–61.

Chin, Tony. *CBS: The First 50 Years.* New York: General Publishing, 1999.

Chua, B. H. "East Asian Pop Culture: Consumer Communities and Politics of the National." Paper presented at the Cultural Space and the Public Sphere: An International Conference, 2006.

CNNIC 30th Survey Report. Beijing: China Internet Network Information Center, 2012.

Coase, R. H. *British Broadcasting.* London: Longmans, Green, 1950.

Cohen, Y. "Foreign Press Corps as an Indicator of International News Interest." *Gazette* 56 (1995), 89–100.

Collections of China Journalism and Publishing Statistics, 1978–2008. Beijing: State Journalism and Publishing Bureau, 2009.

Coombs, Tim. "The Internet as Potential Equalizer." *Public Relations Review* 24 (1998), 289–303.

Corner, John, Schlesinger, Philip, and Silverstone, Roger. *International Media Research: A Critical Survey.* London: Routledge, 1997.

Cottle, Simon, "Taking Global Crises in the News Seriously: Notes from the Dark Side of Globalization." *Global Media and Communication* 7 (2011), 77–95.

Cowen, Tyler. "French Kiss-Off: How Protectionism Has Hurt French Films." *Reason* 30(3) (1998), 40–8.

Crystal, David. *English as a Global Language.* Cambridge: Cambridge University Press, 1997.

Cui, B., and Hou, Y. "Convergence and Transition: China's Media Market 2011." In B. Cui (ed.), *2012 Report on Development of China's Media Industry,* pp. 1–13. Beijing: Social Sciences Academic Press, 2012.

Cui, B., and Zhou, K. "Seeking Opportunities in Crisis: China's Media in 2009." In B. Cui (ed.), *2009 Report on Development of China's Media Industry,* pp. 3–35. Beijing: Social Sciences Academic Press, 2009.

Cullity, Jocelyn. "The Global Desi: Cultural Nationalism on MTV India." *Journal of Communication Inquiry* 26(4) (2002), 408–25.

"Culture 101: Beyond the Blog." *Egypt Today* (March 2009).

Dahlgren, Peter. *Television and the Public Sphere: Citizenship, Democracy and the Media.* London: Sage, 1995.

Danaher, K. *10 Reasons to Abolish the IMF and World Bank.* New York: Seven Stories Press, 2001.

Dator, J., and Seo, Y. "Korea as the Wave of a Future: The Emerging Dream Society of Icons and Aesthetic Experience." *Journal of Futures Studies* 9(1) (2004), 31–44.

De Beer, Arnold, and Merrill, John. *Global Journalism.* Boston: Allyn & Bacon, 2004.

Defleur, Melvin, and Ball-Rokeach, Sandra. *Theories of Mass Communication.* New York: Longman, 1975.

Dieckmann, O. "Cultural Determinants of Economic Growth: Theory and Evidence." *Journal of Cultural Economics* 20(4) (1996), 297–320.

Elasmar, Michael G. "Opportunities and Challenges of Using Meta-Analysis in the Field of International Communication." *Critical Studies in Mass Communication* 16(3) (1999), 379–89.

Ellul, Jacques. *The Technological Society.* New York: Knopf, 1964.

El-Nawawy, Mohammed, and Iskandar, Adel. *Al-Jazeera: How the Free Arab News Network Scooped the World and Changed the Middle East.* Cambridge, MA: Westview Press, 2002.

European Commission. "The Commission's Contribution to the Period of Reflection and Beyond: Plan D for Democracy, Dialogue and Debate." COM 494 final. At http://europa.eu/legislation_summaries/institutional_affairs/decisionmaking_process/a30000_en.htm, accessed September 4, 2013.

European Commission. "White Paper on a European Communication Policy." COM 35 final, 2006. At http://europa.eu/documents/comm/white_papers/pdf/com2006_35_en.pdf, accessed August 7, 2013.

Featherstone, Michael (ed.). *Global Culture: Nationalism, Globalization and Modernity.* London: Sage, 1990.

Fernández-Quijada, David. "Strategies of Transnational Media Corporations in the Spanish Television Industry." *Observatorio Journal* 3(2) (2009), 85–112.

Fiske, John, and Hartley, John. *Reading Television.* London: Methuen, 1978/2003.

Flournoy, Don M., and Stewart, Robert K. *CNN: Making News in the Global Market.* Luton: John Libbey Media, 1977.

Fox, Elizabeth. *Latin American Broadcasting.* Luton: University of Luton Press, 1997.

Frater, P. "Italy's Eagle Swoops on Its First Korean Title." *Screen Daily* (May 2003). At http://www.screendaily.com/italys-eagle-swoops-on-its-first-korean-title/4013555.article, accessed August 7, 2013.

Frater, P. "Korea's Jail Breakers Given New Dimension." *Screen Daily* (February 2003). At http://www.screendaily.com/koreas-jail-breakers-given-new-dimension/4012334.article, accessed August 7, 2013.

Freedom of the Press 2013: A Global Survey of Media Independence. Washington, DC: Freedom House, 2013.

Frydén Bonnier, Minna. "Europeanization in European News Broadcasts? A Comparative Study of Euronews and Rapport." Master's thesis, Department of Political Science, Stockholm University, 2007.

Gershon, Richard A. *The Transnational Media Corporation: Global Messages and Free Market Competition*. Mahwah, NJ: Lawrence Erlbaum, 1997.

Giddens, Anthony. *Modernity and Self-Identity*. Stanford, CA: Stanford University Press, 1991.

Giffard, C. Anthony, and Rivenburgh, Nancy K. "News Agencies, National Images, and Global Media Events." *Journalism and Mass Communication Quarterly* 77(1) (2000), 8–21.

Gilboa, Eytan. "The CNN Effect: The Search for a Communication Theory of International Relations." *Political Communication* 22 (2005), 27–44.

Golding, Peter, and Harris, Phil (eds.). *Beyond Cultural Imperialism: Globalization, Communication, and the New International Order*. London: Sage, 1997.

Grant, Peter, and Wood, Chris. *Blockbusters and Trade Wars*. Toronto: Douglas & McInytre, 2004.

Grein, Andreas, and Ducoffe, Robert. "Strategic Responses to Market Globalization among Advertising Agencies." *International Journal of Advertising* 17(3) (1998), 301–20.

Gripsrud, Jostein. "Television and the European Public Sphere." *European Journal of Communication* 22(4) (2007), 479–92.

Habermas, Jürgen. *The Structural Transformation of the Public Sphere*. Cambridge: Polity, 1962/1989.

Hachten, William, and Scotton, James. *The World News Prism: Global Media in an Era of Terrorism*. Ames: Iowa State Press, 2002.

Hall, Thomas D. "The World-System Perspective: A Small Sample from a Large Universe." *Sociological Inquiry* 66(4) (1996), 440–54.

Hallin, Daniel C., and Mancini, Paolo. *Comparing Media Systems Beyond the Western World*. Cambridge: Cambridge University Press, 2011.

Hallin, Daniel C., and Mancini, Paolo. *Comparing Media Systems: Three Models of Media and Politics*. Cambridge: Cambridge University Press, 2004.

Hanink, D. M. *The International Economy: A Geographic Perspective*. New York: Wiley, 1994.

Hedley, Alan. "Technological Diffusion or Cultural Imperialism? Measuring the Information Revolution." *International Journal of Comparative Sociology* 39(2) (1998), 198–223.

Heidegger, Martin. *The Question Concerning Technology and Other Essays*. New York: Harper & Row, 1977.

Heo, J. (2002) "The 'Hanryu' Phenomenon and the Acceptability of Korean TV Dramas in China." *Korean Journal of Broadcasting* 16(1), 496–529.

Hersh, Seymour. *Chain of Command: The Road from 9/11 to Abu Ghraib*. New York: HarperCollins, 2004.

Hills, Jill. *The Struggle for Control of Global Communication*. Urbana, IL: University of Illinois Press, 2002.

Hjarvard, Stig. "The Mediatization of Society: A Theory of the Media as Agents of Social and Cultural Change." *Nordicom Review* 29(2) (2008), 105–34.

Hoggart, Richard. *An Idea and Its Servants: UNESCO from Within*. London: Chatto & Windus, 1978.

Hojman, David. "Economic Policy and Latin American Culture: Is a Virtuous Circle Possible?" *Journal of Latin American Studies* 31 (February 1999), 167–90.

Hong, J. "Television." In Linsun Cheng (gen. ed.), *Berkshire Encyclopedia of China*. Great Barrington, MA: Berkshire, 2009.

Hong, J., Lu, Y., and Zou, W. "CCTV in the Reform Years: Setting Up a New Model for China's Television?" In Y. Zhu and C. Berry (eds.), *TV China*, pp. 40–55. Bloomington: Indiana University Press, 2008.

Hopkins, Mark. "A Babel of Broadcasts." *Columbia Journalism Review* 38(2) (1999), 447.

Hoskins, Colin, McFadyen, Stuart, and Finn, Adam. *Global Television and Film: An Introduction to the Economics of the Business*. Oxford: Clarendon, 1997.

Hudson, Heather. *Global Connections: International Telecommunications Infrastructure and Policy*. New York: Van Nostrand Reinhold, 1997.

Hughes, Sallie, and Lawson, Chappell. "The Barriers to Media Opening in Latin America." *Political Communication* 22 (2005), 9–25.

Huteau, Jean. *AFP: Une histoire de l'Agence France-Presse, 1944–1990*. Paris: R. Laffont, 1992.

Iwabuchi, K. "Cultures of Empire: Transnational Media Flows and Cultural Disconnections in East Asia." In P. Chakravartty and Y. Zhao (eds.), *Global Communications: Toward a Transcultural Political Economy*, pp. 143–61. Lanham, MD: Rowman & Littlefield, 2008.

Janus, N. "Transnational Advertising: Some Considerations of the Impact on Peripheral Societies." In R. Atwood and E. McAnany (eds.), *Communication and Latin American Society: Trends in Critical Research, 1960–1985*. Madison: University of Wisconsin Press, 1986.

JETRO. "Japanese Film Industry." *Japan Economic Monthly* (May 2005). At http://www.jetro.go.jp/en/reports/market/pdf/2005_33_r.pdf, accessed August 7, 2013.

Joshi, Lalit, and Malcolm, Derek (eds.). *Bollywood: Popular Indian Cinema*. London: Dakini Books, 2002.

Kakuchi, S. "Japan's Indie Film Industry Reeling." *Asia Times.* At http://www.atimes.com/atimes/Japan/EI18Dh03.html, accessed August 7, 2013.

Kanayama, T., and Kanayama, T. "Japan." In A. Cooper-Chen (ed.), *Global Entertainment Media: Content, Audiences, Issues.* London: Routledge, 2005.

Kawakami, H., and Fisher, P. "Eastern Barbarians: The Ancient Sounds of Korea." In S. Broughton and M. Ellingham (eds.), *World Music: The Rough Guide*, pp. 468–72. London: Rough Guides, 1994.

Keyton, Jeffrey. *Not Teflon: MTV Design.* New York: Universe, 2004.

Kennedy, Paul. *The Rise and Fall of the Great Powers.* New York: Vintage, 1989.

Khiabany, G. "Arab Revolutions and the Iranian Uprising: Similarities and Differences." *Middle East Journal of Culture and Communication* 5(1) (2012), 58–65.

Kim, H. M. "Korean TV Dramas in Taiwan: With an Emphasis on the Localization Process." *Korea Journal* (Winter 2005), 183–205.

Kim, Kyungmo, and Barnett, George. "The Determinants of International News Flow: A Network Analysis." *Communication Research* 23(3) (June 1996), 323–52.

Kim, S. K. "'Renaissance of Korean National Cinema' as a Terrain of Negotiation and Contention between the Global and the Local: Analysing Two Korean Blockbusters: Shiri (1999) and JSA (2000)." *Essex Grad Journal* 5 (2004). At http://europa.eu/legislation_summaries/institutional_affairs/decisionmaking_process/a30000_en.htm, accessed September 4, 2013.

Kim, Y. D. *A Comparative Study of Production System for Television Dramas between Korean and Japan.* Seoul: Korean Broadcasting Institution, 2009.

Kleinsteuber, Hans J. "Habermas and the Public Sphere: From a German to a European Perspective." *Javnost: The Public* 8(1) (2001), 95–108.

Knightley, Phillip. *The First Casualty.* New York: Harcourt Brace Jovanovich, 1975.

Kohli-Khandekar, V. *The Indian Media Business* (2nd edn). New Delhi: Response Books, 2006.

KPMG and Confederation of Indian Industry. *Indian Entertainment Industry Focus 2010: Dreams to Reality.* New Delhi: Confederation of Indian Industry, 2005.

Kraidy, Marwan. "The Global, the Local, and the Hybrid: A Native Ethnography of Globalization." *Critical Studies in Mass Communication* 16 (1999), 456–76.

Kunelius, Risto, and Sparks, Colin. "Problems with a European Public Sphere: An Introduction." *Javnost: The Public* 8(1) (2001), 5–20.

Kwasi, Ansu-Kyeremeh (ed.). "Indigenous Communication in Africa: Concept, Applications, and Prospects." *Perspective on Indigenous Communication in Africa.* Legon, Ghana: School of Communication Studies Printing Press, 1998.

Lee, Raymond L. M. "Globalization and Mass Society Theory." *International Review of Sociology/Revue Internationale de Sociologie* 12(1) (March 2002), 45–60.

Lee, S. "Seoul Survivor." *Straits Times* (Korea) (April 8, 2003), 16.

Lee, S. W., and Waterman, D. "Theatrical Feature Film Trade in the United States, Europe, and Japan since the 1950s: An Empirical Study of the Home Market Effect." Paper presented at the TPRC Conference on Communication, Information, and Internet Policy, 2006.

Lee, S., Kim, E., and Sung, H. "On the Exportability of Korean Movies." *Review of Development Economics* 13(1) (2009), 28–38.

Lewis, S. C., Zamith, R., and Hermida, A. "Content Analysis in an Era of Big Data: A Hybrid Approach to Computational and Manual Methods." *Journal of Broadcasting & Electronic Media* 57(1) (2013), 34–52.

Lewis, Seth, and Reese, Stephen. "What is the War on Terror? Framing through the Eyes of Journalists." *Journalism and Mass Communication Quarterly* 86 (Spring 2009), 85–118.

Lilleker, Darren G. *Key Concepts in Political Communication.* London: Sage, 2006.

Lim, Yon Soo, Barnett, George, and Kim, Jang Hyun. "The Structure of International Aid Flows and Global News Media." *Journal of International Communication* 14(2) (2008), 117–42.

Linden, Ank. "Overt Intentions and Covert Agendas." *Gazette* 61(2) (1999), 153–75.

Lingenberg, S. "The Audience's Role in Constituting the European Public Sphere: A Theoretical Approach Based on the Pragmatic Concept of John Dewey." In N. Carpentier et al. (eds.), *Researching Media, Democracy and Participation.* Tartu, Estonia: Tartu University Press, 2006.

Liu, L., and Lu, J. "Overview of the Development of China's Movie Industry." In B. Cui (ed.), *2009 Report on Development of China's Media Industry*, pp. 247–53. Beijing: Social Sciences Academic Press, 2009.

Lorenzen, M. *Go West: The Growth of Bollywood.* Handelshøjskolen, Denmark: Copenhagen Business School, 2009.

Lorenzen, M., and Taeube, F. A. "Breakout from Bollywood? Internationalization of Indian Film Industry." *Journal of International Management* 14 (2008), 286–99.

Lu, B. "China's Animation Products Begin to Enter the International Market." In B. Cui (ed.), *2009 Report on Development of China's Media Industry*, pp. 298–302. Beijing: Social Sciences Academic Press, 2009.

Lu, D., and Gao, F. "Competition Analyses of China's Television Industry." In B. Cui (ed.), *2009 Report on Development of China's Media Industry*, pp. 228–34. Beijing: Social Sciences Academic Press, 2009.

MacBride, Sean. *Many Voices, One World*. New York: Unipub, 1980.

Machill, Marcel. "Euronews: The First European News Channel as a Case Study for Industry Development in Europe and for Spectra of Transnational Journalism Research." *Media, Culture & Society* 20(3) (1998), 427–50.

Machill, Marcel, Beiler, Markus, and Fischer, Corinna. "Europe-Topics in Europe's Media." *European Journal of Communication* 2(1) (2006), 57–88.

Madden, Normandy. "Cable, Satellite Media Lure Influential Viewers." *Advertising Age International* (October 1999), 36.

Malek, Abbas. "Introduction: News Media and Foreign Policy: A Field Ripe for Research." *Journal of International Communication* 4(1) (1997), 1–10.

Martinez, Arnando. "The New World Order and What We Make of It." *World Policy Journal* 16(3) (1999), 692.

Mattelart, Tristan. "Transboundary Flows of Western Entertainment across the Iron Curtain." *Journal of International Communication* 6(2) (1999), 106–21.

McChesney, Robert W. "The Internet and US Communication Policy-Making in Historical and Critical Perspective." *Journal of Communication* 46(1) (1996), 98–124.

McCullough, Wayne. "Global Advertising which Acts Locally: The IBM Subtitles Campaign." *Journal of Advertising Research* 36 (May–June 1996), 11–15.

McDonald, Ian R., and Lawrence, Regina G. "Filling the 24×7 News Hole: Television News Coverage Following September 11." *American Behavioral Scientist* 48(3) (2004), 327–40.

McKee, Kathy Brittain. "Why I [Still] Want My MTV: Music Video and Aesthetic Communication" (book review). *Journalism and Mass Communication Quarterly* 81(3) (2004), 718–20.

McLuhan, Marshall. *The Gutenberg Galaxy*. Toronto: University of Toronto Press, 1962.

McLuhan, Marshall. *Understanding Media: The Extensions of Man*. New York: McGraw-Hill, 1964.

McLuhan, Marshall, and Fiore, Quentin. *Understanding Media: The Extension of Man*. New York: McGraw-Hill, 1964.

McLuhan, Marshall, and Fiore, Quentin. *The Medium Is the Message*. New York: Bantam Books, 1967.

McNair, Brian. *Journalism and Democracy: An Evaluation of the Political Public Sphere*. London: Routledge, 2000.

McPhail, Thomas. "Canadianisation of European Broadcasting: Is an Electronic Berlin Wall the Answer?" In *Broadcasting and Research: Experiences and Strategies*, pp. 15–30. Amsterdam: ESOMAR, 1988.

McPhail, Thomas. "The Communication Economy Sweepstakes: Few Winners, Many Losers: A Canadian Case Study." *Informatologia Yugoslavia* 17(1–2) (1985), 97–105.

McPhail, Thomas. *Development Communication: Reframing the Role of the Media*. Oxford: Wiley-Blackwell, 2009.

McPhail, Thomas. *Electronic Colonialism: The Future of International Broadcasting and Communication*, rev. 2nd edn. Newbury, CA: Sage, 1986.

McPhail, Thomas. *The Future of the Daily Newspaper: Public Policy Issues*. Montreal: Institute for Research on Public Policy, 1980.

McPhail, Thomas. "Inquiry in International Communication." In M. Asante and B. Gudykunst (eds.), *Handbook of International and Intercultural Communication*, pp. 47–66. Newbury, CA: Sage, 1989.

McPhail, Thomas, and Barnett, George. "An Examination of the Relationship of United States Television and Canadian Identity." *International Journal of Intercultural Relations* 4 (1980), 219–32.

McPhail, Thomas, and McPhail, Brenda. *Communication: The Canadian Experience*. Toronto: Copp Clark Pitman, 1990.

McPhail, Thomas, and McPhail, Brenda. "Television and Development Communication: A Canadian Case Study." In Andrew Moemeka (ed.), *Communicating for Development: A Pan-Disciplinary Perspective*, pp. 191–218. Albany: State University of New York Press, 1994.

McPhail, Thomas, with Judge, S. "Direct Broadcast Satellites: The Demise of Public and Commercial Policy Objectives." In Indu Singh (ed.), *Telecommunications in the Year 2000: National and International Perspectives*, pp. 72–9. Norwood, NJ: Ablex, 1983.

McPhail, Thomas, with McPhail, Brenda. "The International Politics of Telecommunications. Resolving the North–South Dilemma." *International Journal* 42 (1987), 289–319.

Melkote, Srinivas, Shields, Peter, and Agrawel, Binod (eds.). *International Satellite Broadcasting in South Asia*. Lanham, MD: University Press of America, 1998.

Menge, Peter. "1998 ICA Presidential Address: Communication Structures and Processes in Globalization." *Journal of Communication* 48(44) (1999), 142–53.

Merrill, John, Berenger, Ralph, and Merrill, Charles. *Media Musings: Interviews with Great Thinkers*. Spokane, WA: Marquette Books, 2004.

Mishra, Vijay. *Bollywood Cinema*. New York: Routledge, 2001.

Mishra, Vijay. *Bollywood Cinema: A Critical Genealogy*. Wellington, New Zealand: Asian Studies Institute, 2006.

Mitchell, Tony. "Treaty Now! Indigenous Music and Music Television in Australia." *Media, Culture & Society* 15(2) (1993), 299–308.

Mittelman, James H. *The Globalization Syndrome: Transformation and Resistance*. Princeton: Princeton University Press, 2000.

Moemeka, Andrew. "Development Communication: A Historical and Conceptual Overview." In Andrew Moemeka (ed.), *Communicating for Development*. Albany: State University of New York Press, 1994.

Mohammadi, Ali (ed.). *International Communication and Globalization*. London: Sage, 1997.

Morris, Merrill, and Ogan, Christine. "The Internet as Mass Medium." *Journal of Communication* 46(1) (1996), 39–50.

Müller, Milton. *Ruling the Root: Internet Governance and the Taming of Cyberspace*. Cambridge, MA: MIT Press, 2002.

Murdock, Graham. "Television and Citizenship: In Defence of Public Broadcasting." In A. Tomlinson (ed.), *Consumption, Identity and Style: Marketing, Meanings and the Packaging of Pleasure*, pp. 77–101. London: Routledge, 1990.

Norris, Pippa, and Inglehart, Ronald. *Cosmopolitan Communications: Cultural Diversity in a Globalized World*. New York: Cambridge University Press, 2010.

Nostbakken, David, and Morrow, Charles (eds.). *Cultural Expression in the Global Village*. Ottawa: Southbound, 1993.

Paek, Hye-Jin, and Pan, Zhongdang. "Spreading Global Consumerism: Effects of Mass Media and Advertising on Consumerist Values in China." *Mass Communication and Society* 7(4) (2004), 491–515.

Papathanassopoulos, Stylianos. "Europe: An Exemplary Landscape for Comprehending Globalization." *Global Media and Communication* 1 (2005), 46–50.

Parameswaran, R. "The Other Side of Globalization: Communication, Culture, and Postcolonial Critique." *Communication, Culture & Critique* 1(2008), 116–25.

Park, Hong-Wan. "A Gramscian Approach to Interpreting International Communication." *Journal of Communication* 48(4) (1998), 79–99.

Paterson, Chris A. "International Television News Agency Coverage of Conflict." *Journal of International Communication* 4(1) (1997), 50–66.

Pauwels, Caroline, and Lisen, Jan. "The WTO and the Audiovisual Sector." *European Journal of Communication* 18 (2003), 291–314.

Pintak, Lawrence, and Ginges, Jeremy. "The Mission of Arab Journalism: Creating Change in a Time of Turmoil." *International Journal of Press/Politics* 13(3) (2008), 193–227.

Predators of Press Freedom. Paris: Reporters Sans Frontières, 2007.

Price, Monroe E. *Television, the Public Sphere and National Identity*. Oxford: Oxford University Press, 1995.

Pringle, Hamish, and Marshall, Jim. *Spending Advertising Money in the Digital Age: How to Navigate the Media Flow*. London: Kogan Page, 2011.

PwC. *Global Entertainment and Media Outlook 2006–2010*. New York: PricewaterhouseCoopers, 2006.

Ramaprasad, J. "Content, Geography Concentration and Consonance in Foreign News Coverage of ABC, NBC, and CBS." *International Communication Bulletin* 28 (1993), 10–14.

Rao, S. "The Globalization of Bollywood: An Ethnography of Non-Elite Audiences in India." *Communication Review* 10(1) (2007), 57–76.

Rao, S. "India." In A. Cooper-Chen (ed.), *Global Entertainment Media: Content, Audiences, Issues*. London: Routledge, 2005.

Read, Donald. *The Power of News: The History of Reuters*. Oxford: Oxford University Press, 1992.

Ries, Al, and Trout, Jack. *Positioning: The Battle for Your Mind*. New York: McGraw-Hill, 2001.

Riffe, D. "Linking International News to US Interest: A Content Analysis." *International Communication Bulletin* 31 (1996), 14–18.

Riley, Patricia, and Menge, Peter. "Introduction." *Communication Research* 25(4) (1998), 355–8.

Robertson, Alexa. *Cosmopolitan Narratives: The World of Television News*. Cambridge: Polity, 2010.

Rogers, Everett. "Communication and Development: The Passing of the Dominant Paradigm." *Communication Research* 3(2) (1976), 213–40.

Rogers, Everett. *Modernization among Peasants: The Impact of Communication*. New York: Holt, Rinehart and Winston, 1969.

Rooke, Richard. *European Media in the Digital Age: Analysis and Approaches*. Harlow, UK: Longman, 2009.

Rosenblum, Morton. *Coups and Earthquakes*. New York: Harper & Row, 1979.

Rostow, Walter. *The Stages of Economic Growth*. New York: Cambridge University Press, 1960.

Rothkopf, David. "In Praise of Cultural Imperialism." *Foreign Policy* 107 (1997), 38–53.

Rugh, William A. *The Arab Press: News Media and Political Process in the Arab World*. Syracuse, NY: Syracuse University Press, 1979.

Sambrook, Richard. "The Poliak Lecture: Holding on to Objectivity." Speech given at Columbia University, October 27, 2004.

Schafer, D. Paul. "The Millennium Challenge: Making the Transition from an 'Economic Age' to a 'Cultural Age.'" *World Futures* 51 (1998), 287–320.

Schiller, Herbert. *Communication and Cultural Domination*. White Plains, NY: International Arts and Sciences Press, 1976.

Schlesinger, Philip. "The Babel of Europe? An Essay on Network and Communicative Spaces." In Dario Castiglione and Chris Longman (eds.), *The Language Question in Europe and Diverse Societies: Political, Legal and Social Perspectives*. Oxford: Hart, 2007.

Schlesinger, Philip. "A Cosmopolitan Temptation?" *European Journal of Communication* 22(4) (2007), 413–26.

Schlesinger, Philip. "Wishful Thinking: Cultural Politics, Media, and Collective Identities in Europe." *Journal of Communication* 43(2) (1993), 6–17.

Seaver, Brenda. "The Public Dimension of Foreign Policy." *Harvard International Journal of Press/Politics* 3(1) (1998), 65–91.

Semetko, Holli, de Vreese, Claes H., and Peter, Jochen. "Europeanised Politics – Europeanised Media? European Integration and Political Communication." *West European Politics* 23(4) (2000), 121–41.

Sengupta, Subir. "Analysis of Television Commercials from India and the United States." *Gazette* 57 (1996), 1–16.

Shah, Hermant. "Modernization, Marginalization, and Emancipation: Toward a Normative Model of Journalism and National Development." *Communication Theory* 6(2) (1998), 143–67.

Shannon, Thomas R. *An Introduction to the World System Perspective*. Boulder, CO: Westview Press, 1996.

Shen, P. "'It Came from the East.' Japanese Horror Cinema in the Age of Globalization." *gnovis* 2(9) (Spring 2009). At http://gnovisjournal.org/2009/05/13/it-came-east-japanese-horror-cinema-age-globalization/, accessed August 7, 2013.

Shim, D. "Hybridigy and the Rise of Korean Popular Culture in Asia." *Media, Culture & Society* 28(1) (2009), 25–44.

Shoemaker, P., and Reese, S. *Mediating the Message: Theories of Influence on Mass Media Content*. New York: Longman, 1991.

Shukla, S. *India Abroad: Diasporic Cultures of Postwar America and England*. Princeton, NJ: Princeton University Press, 2003.

Spark, Alasdair. "Wrestling with America: Media, National Images, and the Global Village." *Journal of Popular Culture* 29 (1996), 83–97.

Splichal, Slavko. "In Search of a Strong European Public Sphere: Some Critical Observations on Conceptualizations of Publicness and the (European) Public Sphere." *Media, Culture & Society* 28(5) (2006), 695–714.

Starr, Paul. *The Creation of the Media: Political Origins of Modern Communication*. New York: Basic Books, 2004.

Statham, P. "Making European News: How Journalists View Their Role and Media Performance." *Journalism* 9(4) (2008), 398–422.

Stevenson, Robert. *Global Communication in the Twenty-First Century*. New York: Longman, 1994.

Stewart, J. *Disneywar: The Battle for the Magic Kingdom*, New York: Simon & Schuster, 2004.

Swan, Jon. "I Was a 'Polisher' in a Chinese News Factory." *Columbia Journalism Review* 27 (March–April 1996), 33–6.

Taplin, J. "'Crouching Tigers': Emerging Challenges to US Entertainment Supremacy in the Movie Business." *Observatorio* 2 (2007), 167–90.

Taylor, Philip. *Global Communications, International Affairs and the Media since 1945*. London: Routledge, 1997.

Taylor, Philip. *War and the Media: Propaganda and Persuasion in the Gulf War*. Manchester, UK: Manchester University Press, 1988.

Tehranian, Majid. "Foreword." In Y. Kamalipour (ed.), *Images of the US Around the World: A Multicultural Perspective*. Albany: State University of New York Press, 1999.

Thomas, Bob. *Building a Company: Roy O. Disney and the Creation of an Entertainment Empire*. Boston: Hyperion, 1999.

Thompson, J. B. *The Media and Modernity: A Social Theory of the Media*. Stanford, CA: Stanford University Press, 1995.

Thussa, D. *International Communication: Continuity and Change*. London: Arnold, 2000.

"Top Advertisers and Product Categories in Markets Worldwide." *International Journal of Advertising* 18(1) (1999), 123–8.

Trenz, Hans-Jörg. "Media Coverage on European Governance." *European Journal of Communication* 19(3) (2004), 291–319.

Tunstall, J. *The Media Are American*. New York: Columbia University Press, 1977.

UNESCO. "Convention on the Protection and Promotion of the Diversity of Cultural Expressions 2005." At http://portal.unesco.org/en/ev.php-URL_ID=31038&URL_DO=DO_TOPIC&URL_SECTION=201.html, accessed August 7, 2013.

UNESCO. "The Power of Culture." At http://portal.unesco.org/culture/en/ev.php-URL_ID=18717&URL_

DO=DO_TOPIC&URL_SECTION=201.html, accessed August 29, 2013.

UNESCO. *World Report on Cultural Diversity*. At http://www.unesco.org/new/en/culture/resources/report/the-unesco-world-report-on-cultural-diversity/, accessed August 7, 2013.

Van de Steeg, Marianne. "Rethinking the Conditions for a Public Sphere in the European Union." *European Journal of Social Theory* 5(4) (2002), 499–519.

Van Rossem, R. "The World System Paradigm as General Theory of Development: A Cross-National Test." *American Sociological Review* 61 (1996), 508–27.

Volkmer, Ingrid. *News in the Global Sphere: A Study of CNN and Its Impact on Global Communication*. Luton, UK: University of Luton Press, 1999.

Wagnleitner, Reinhold. "The Empire of the Fun, or Talkin' Soviet Union Blues: The Sound of Freedom and US Cultural Hegemony in Europe." *Diplomatic History* 23(3) (1999), 499–524.

Wallerstein, I. "After Developmentalism and Globalization, What?" *Social Forces* 83(3) (2005), 1263–78.

Wallerstein, I. *The Modern World System*. New York: Academic Press, 1976.

Wanta, Wayne, Golan, Guy, and Lee, Cheolhan. "Agenda Setting and International News: Media Influence on Public Perceptions of Foreign Nations." *Journalism and Mass Communication Quarterly* 81(2) (2004), 364–77.

Ward, David. "The Democratic Deficit and European Union Communication Policy. An Evaluation of the Commission's Approach to Broadcasting." *Javnost: The Public* 8(1) (2001), 75–94.

Ward, David. *European Union Democratic Deficit and the Public Sphere: An Evaluation of EU Media Policy*. Amsterdam: IOS Press, 2002.

Ware, William, and Dupagne, Michel. "Effects of US Television Programs on Foreign Audiences: A Meta-Analysis." *Journalism Quarterly* 71(4) (1994), 947–59.

Watts, Steven. *The Magic Kingdom: Walt Disney and the American Way of Life*. Boston: Houghton Mifflin, 1998.

Westerstahl, J., and Johansson, F. "Foreign News: News Values and Ideologies." *European Journal of Communication* 9 (1994), 71–89.

Wheeler, Mark. "Supranational Regulation: Television and the European Union." *European Journal of Communication* 19(3) (2004), 349–69.

Whittemore, Hank. *CNN: The Inside Story*. Toronto, Canada: Little, Brown, 1990.

Widholm, Andreas. "From Television Flows to Generic Structures: Reflections on Form and Content of Euronews and BBC World News." Unpublished conference paper, Department of Journalism, Media and Communication, Stockholm University, 2009.

Wildman, S. S., and Siwek, S. E. *International Trade in Films and Television Programs*. Cambridge, MA: Ballinger, 1988.

Woodman-Maynard, K. "Bollywood and the Indian Film Industry." *Indian Business* (2006).

Wu, Haoming Denis. "Investigating the Determinants of International News Flow: A Meta-Analysis." *Gazette* 60(6) (1998), 493–512.

Xu, G. "Remaking East Asia, Outsourcing Hollywood." In L. Hunt and L. Wing-Fai (eds.), *East Asian Cinemas: Exploring Transnational Connections on Film*, pp. 192–202. New York: I. B. Tauris, 2008.

Xu, M. "New Plan of China Film Overseas Promotion Corporation." *Variety China* (May 14, 2007), 9.

Yin, K., and Liew, K. "Hallyu in Singapore: Korean Cosmopolitanism or the Consumption of Chineseness?" *Korea Journal* 45(4) (2005), 206–232.

Yoon, J. S., Kang, M., Yoon, H., Choi, S., Kim, Y. D., et al. *A Research for Promoting a Continous Development of Korean Wave*. Seoul: Korea Foundation for International Culture Exchange, 2008.

Zhu, Y., and Berry, C. *TV China*. Bloomington: Indiana University Press, 2009.

Index